Understanding Economic Development

To my much loved wife Sandra, who knows this work as well as I do, but who had the patience to listen.

Understanding Economic Development

A Global Transition from Poverty to Prosperity?

Colin White

Former Professor of Economics, Graduate School of Management, La Trobe University, Melbourne, Australia

Edward Elgar

Cheltenham, UK • Northampton, MA, USA

Published by
Edward Elgar Publishing Limited
The Lypiatts
15 Lansdown Road
Cheltenham
Glos GL50 2JA
UK

Edward Elgar Publishing, Inc.
William Pratt House
9 Dewey Court
Northampton
Massachusetts 01060
USA

Paperback edition 2011

This book has been printed on demand to keep the title in print.

A catalogue record for this book
is available from the British Library

Library of Congress Control Number: 2009933390

ISBN 978 1 84720 781 4 (cased)
ISBN 978 0 85793 386 7 (paperback)

Typeset by Servis Filmsetting Ltd, Stockport, Cheshire

Printed and bound in Great Britain by
Marston Book Services Limited, Didcot

Contents

Preface

I became an economist because I sought the answer to a simple question, how do you accelerate the rate of economic growth in different countries and reduce the worldwide problem of poverty? It is clear that in order to understand how to do this you need to understand the determination of economic growth in the past. This book is an attempt to meet the challenge of reconciling a long-term with a short-term perspective and to bring together the general and the particular in a persuasive explanation of the inception of modern economic development. Despite an explosion in relevant publications on economic growth, there is still no good explanation of why modern economic development has occurred where and when it has. It is disappointing that that there is such a marked disproportion between the effort expended and its return. There are still no agreed policies on how governments can promote modern economic development. If there were, economic development would no longer be exceptional and the absence of significant economic development so common.

This book is the culmination of an academic career which has followed a sinuous course through the disciplines of economics, economic history and the area of management studies. The evolution of these discipline areas is disappointing from an intellectual perspective. There are themes which I have pursued throughout this career, notably concern with the analysis of economic performance both of nation states and of enterprises, focusing on why some units achieve good performance and others not. Country performance is the result of the performance of a large number of enterprises. I began my career studying history and economics at Cambridge University. During the 1960s there was a pessimism about the prospects for economic development ever becoming anything more than a European phenomenon and at Cambridge, a major debate about how to conceptualize the process of economic growth. There were serious criticisms of the basic neoclassical approach to economics. I still remember James Meade beginning a course on economic principles by saying that he would begin with 24 assumptions about the economic world he was analysing and relax them one by one – still to my mind an extremely odd way of getting to the real world. In that period I began research on an aspect of Soviet planning – an experience which told me what policies you should not adopt, and moved on to the study of long-term comparative economic history, reflecting a feeling that there are persistent tendencies in history much stronger than often thought, that the Russian Revolution of 1917 has changed much less than usually assumed. This interest was reinforced when I migrated to Australia and extended my knowledge to its history and that of other areas of new settlement, and later to the Asian economic miracle.

The debate on economic growth petered out for nearly 20 years. The focus turned away from economic growth until the late 1980s when the new growth theory became the focus of attention, initiating another critique of key aspects of neoclassical growth theory, including a failure to properly account for technical change and increasing returns. There is a sense of déjà vu about the development of the new economic growth theory in the 1990s. Old issues were reopened, old weaknesses of neoclassical economics re-explored. Yet once more the new theory was reabsorbed into the neoclassical model, as had Keynesianism and neo-Keynesianism been before. There were some improvements. There has been a much more systematic attempt to test the theory against the real world and a more open-minded approach to exploring the theory by a few individuals. During this renaissance of interest in economic development, I was engaged in administration heading, successively, departments of economic history, economics and management. The fragmentation in method and approach of what should be linked disciplines is alarming. My research interest became focused for a period on strategy, at both the corporate and government levels, and the influence of risk and uncertainly on foreign direct investment decisions. In the latter work I was surprised to find in financial theory a total dominance of neoclassical economics and a failure to see the divorce between textbook models and reality. The end of the Cold War and the dissolution of the Soviet Union, with the simultaneous transition of planned to market systems, has left economics dominated by one theoretical paradigm. Throughout this period I have continued to read economic history and to note the application of rigorous theory and quantitative techniques even within this area, following the cliometric revolution. The total dominance of neoclassical economics has puzzled and troubled me, given its obvious and much discussed weaknesses. As a consequence, I set about a systematic reading of the rather large literature on economic growth theory which now exists, in an attempt to understand how economic theorists working within the neoclassical paradigm understand the economic growth process and what can be taken out of the theory helpful to understanding the process of economic development. Neoclassical theory is too entrenched to disappear. Sometimes theorists, when undisturbed by rival approaches, become trapped by their own theory, not even attempting to show the implications of that theory for understanding real world processes. There is a tendency to take for granted a particular paradigm without justifying its main assumptions and the world view on which it rests. Neoclassical economists are poor publicists for their own theory and they do not even notice the horror with which it is greeted by many in other disciplines, a horror arising from the failure to relate the theory to real world problems. There is a desperate need for better understanding of the process of economic development and of what neoclassical theory can contribute to that understanding.

PART I

Introduction: theory and history

> History and theory are complementary rather than competitive, because history has a comparative advantage in longrun dynamic analysis and economics in shortrun static analysis. The challenge in the future will be for the supporters of each approach to work together to create a new synthesis in economics, which will be concerned with the longrun as well as the shortrun, and with economic processes as well as economic outcomes. (Snooks 1993: 3)

Over the last two hundred or so years modern economic development has had a revolutionary impact on human life. This book is concerned, not with the nature of that impact, rather with its causes. There is no good explanation of modern economic development, despite the many attempts to provide one. The continuing mystery of modern economic development poses a number of questions – why it came so suddenly to dominate the world; why it did not occur earlier; and why it occurred where it did.[1] After thousands of years of very slow economic growth, why has the world economy suddenly experienced an enormous explosion of change, in a dramatic fashion lifting the standard of living of the ordinary person in the developed world and massively increasing the consumption of energy and the impact of human beings on their environment? Can we do more than develop, in Swan's words, 'a device for sorting out our ideas' (Swan 1970: 203, quoted in Wilkinson 1973: 1)?

The book advocates a particular approach to identifying the determinants of such development, arguing that it is a failure of approach which undermines most attempts at explanation. In science in general, but in the social sciences in particular, there is a tension between the need to both generalise and to take account of the unique nature of any experience (Frayn 2006). There is often a natural preference for a narrative of the relevant events and a resistance to the use of abstract models. Yet understanding economic development and communicating that understanding requires a good grasp of both theory and narrative. There is a considerable literature focusing on each. Yet few people attempt to combine the two approaches, assuming a mutual exclusiveness, with a consequently limited persuasiveness of relevant explanation and an apparent lack of progress in our understanding. The aim of this book is to explore ways to reconcile the two approaches.

Part I of the book consists of four chapters. These four chapters set up the approach to the problem of explaining modern economic development. The first chapter analyses modern economic development and explores the issues raised by that development, notably the different ways in which researchers have approached its causation. The second chapter considers how economists have dealt with this problem, in particular the growth theory of neoclassical economics. The third chapter focuses on an important concept in economic growth theory, the notion of convergence, the possibility that all the world is becoming like the leading economies, rich and developed, so that the past experience of the developed is the future experience of the undeveloped. It analyses the different definitions of and weighs the empirical evidence for any kind of convergence. The final chapter reviews the weaknesses of the economist's approach and considers how they might be countered. It explores the approach of those who stress the uniqueness of each experience, which is the domain of the historical narrative.

1. The role of theory and history in explaining modern economic development

> The road to development is extremely complex, and the ultimate guide to that path must therefore be more complex than an arrow pointing confidently in one direction. (Lindauer and Pritchett 2002: 28)

It is important to get the approach to the inception of modern economic development right. Eric Jones (2006: 37) has argued that, whereas by the principle of Ockham's razor we should in any explanation avoid redundancy[1], economic development is a complex phenomenon and this complexity cannot be ignored. Since the process is a complex one, any explanation is itself likely to be complex. This book is an exploration of that complexity. Experience shows that narrow explanations of modern economic development, in particular mono-causal explanations, are inadequate in identifying the determinants of that development. The first section of this chapter explores what is meant by modern economic development. In the second section there is a discussion of the various ways in which the challenge of explaining economic development has been met. The third section considers the three inputs required for a successful approach – narratives, theory and data, and introduces the comparative approach. The final section presents the problem as a 'mystery', rather than a 'puzzle'. It indicates the nature of the questions to be addressed. The chapter concludes with a review of the content of the book.

THE CHALLENGE

The most important problems confronting the world today are a significant lack of economic development and the poverty associated with that lack. In comparison with such problems, the difficulties of global warming and control of the level of carbon emissions are minor irritants, adjustment problems easily solved with a sufficient degree of international cooperation. Such assertions beg the question of what exactly is meant by the term economic development, or what constitutes poverty. Economic development is a process having as its core element a persistent and significant increase in a measure of aggregate output per head of population, and of the linked income.[2] Modern economic development is a process by which economic development becomes self-sustained: there are powerful forces making for its continuation.[3] It is possible, in the style of Galor (2004: 43), to talk of a modern growth regime, in which there are powerful positive feedback effects reinforcing economic development, which more than offset any negative feedback effects reversing that development. For example, a rise in income increases investment in physical or human capital, which in turn further increases income. Such a regime is the focus of neoclassical economic theory and is often contrasted with a Malthusian regime, alleged to be the condition of most human beings before the modern period (Clark 2007). In this regime, negative feedback effects have a greater impact than positive ones. For example, there is a potent negative feedback from a rise in income per head to an increase in fertility, and therefore in population, which reverses the initial increase in income per capita. During this regime, income per head seldom moves above a subsistence level (see Chapter 11).

For any developed economy there is a transition from the Malthusian to the modern growth regime, a transition whose duration and nature is the focus of considerable interest, as Findlay and O'Rourke describe it, a transition from the Malthusian to the modern growth regime of Solow (Findlay and O'Rourke 2007: 317). The degree of discontinuity in this transition, and its speed, is a matter of considerable debate. An increasing number of commentators see two turning points – there is an initial acceleration in economic development, comprising both '. . . the emergence of sustained and rapid (by historical standards) extensive growth, and . . . the emergence of sustained and rapid (by historical standards) intensive growth' (Lipsey, Carlaw and Bekar 2005: 296). In this first phase, there is still much more extensive than intensive growth; in the second, the appearance of a truly sustained growth regime, during which intensive growth becomes predominant as the rate of population growth falls below that of aggregate output (Galor 2004), usually as a consequence of a significant decline in fertility. In the industrial core of Western and Central Europe, the former occurs as early as the late eighteenth and early nineteenth centuries and the latter towards the end of the nineteenth century. The latter reinforces the former turning point.[4] There are two key changes of regime – population change ceases to have an inverse relationship with income per head and technical change becomes continuous, rather than episodic.

Because of the importance of political boundaries to economic policy making and to collection of statistics, the relevant geographic unit for study is usually the state, the typical political unit today. States differ enormously in the size of territory which they control. Some states, notably those with federal structures, are like groupings of separate countries. Yingyi Qian (Rodrik 2003: 299) makes the point that, if today each of China's provinces were counted as a distinct economy, and most of them are the size of states elsewhere in the world, during the past two decades about 20 out of the top 30 growth regions in the world would be provinces in China. Furthermore if the aggregate level of output or income were the relevant variable, then such states as California in the USA would make the top ten. However, there is plenty of evidence that, while initially economic development is uneven – and this might apply within China, one of the consequences of modern economic development is a regional convergence of output or income per head within the relevant developed economies (Barro and Sala-i-Martin 2004: chapter 11). Since, initially at least, there may be marked differences in the level of economic development within countries, a country is not always the most useful reference unit; regional analysis may be more appropriate.

The process of economic development, pursued over a sufficiently long period of time, has as an important consequence a marked lifting of the average standard of living well above the historic norm. Even apparently low rates of growth lead to significant increases in periods of time which from a historical perspective are short. This is the result of compounding. A 1 per cent growth rate leads to a doubling of output in 70 years, less than today's average span of life. An apparently small acceleration in the rate of economic growth is likely to have dramatic effects on welfare, political standing and military strength, justifying the use of the term revolutionary to describe the relevant consequences. Modern economic development is more than simply an increase in income or output, whether considered per capita or in absolute terms. The process of economic development has as its core characteristic the ability of the relevant society to generate and/ or absorb a rapid rate of innovation, mostly technical in nature but also organizational. Such an acceleration in the rate of innovation leads to a continuing improvement in the efficiency with which the conventional factor inputs of land, labour and capital are used and a more rapid growth of productivity. Modern economies routinely invest in the activities which improve their capacity to generate innovation – this is another positive feedback effect. They also develop the capacity to learn, from their own economic activities and those of others, and to exploit the knowledge they develop. Even the extensive destruction of physical capital by war does not stop the process of economic development since the relevant knowledge is held by the survivors.[5]

The measure of development usually selected is gross domestic product per head. There are weaknesses with the concept, including imputation, index number and income distribution problems, and one authority has criticised the assumption that it measures welfare, since there are among populations no fixed preferences (Guha 1981: 122–6). Some argue for a wider definition, so that GDP is supplemented by a life expectancy and/or an education index. The dramatic increase in longevity during the modern era means that the growth of GDP per head underestimates the improvement in welfare of all populations in the world. However, there is a sense in which movement in both indices of health and education could be seen either as cause or consequence rather than characteristic of the process of economic development. Reducing mortality, which is linked with reducing morbidity and decreasing fertility, and increasing literacy assist in promoting economic development by creating more human capital (see Chapter 7), which is an important input into economic growth. Sustained economic development gives a society an improved capacity to reduce mortality and to spread education. In their turn, given the right circumstances, both promote further economic development. There are potent positive feedback effects in this area, as in many others. Unfortunately, it is also possible to reduce mortality rates without giving the relevant country the capacity to generate self-sustained economic growth; the resulting acceleration in the rate of growth of population may heighten the development problem by absorbing investment in capital widening rather than deepening. Nor does having the ability to educate the population guarantee sustained economic development, since it is unclear that the resulting human capital is appropriate to modern economic development. Since there is a direct, if loose, relationship between GDP and indices of this kind, any analysis does not gain much by making more complicated the measuring rod. Moreover, there is good evidence that the usual measures underestimate the improvement in welfare which has occurred in the modern world because of dramatic improvements in the quality of goods consumed. Price fails to reflect these quality improvements. The classic paper is on lighting, where it is argued that the quality-adjusted price of a lumen of light has fallen by a factor of 4000 since the year 1800 (Nordhaus 1998), and that a similar underestimate may hold for other sectors of the economy which together amount to as much as two-fifths of the typical economy.

The process of modern economic development is accompanied by a restructuring of the economy. The old term, industrial revolution, once used to describe the inception of modern economic development, puts the emphasis on a shift in economic activity away from the primary sector, mainly agriculture, to the secondary sector, manufacturing. More recently, the shift has been to the tertiary sector, services. In terms of the structure of the economy, whether defined by contribution to GDP or by employment share, modern economic development is a two-phase process

of structural change, progressive movement from agriculture to manufacturing and then from manufacturing to services. The second phase is
relatively neglected, partly because it is so recent. It offends our prejudices,
since we often see services as in some sense parasitical.[6]

Such a restructuring, if it occurs quickly, makes ambiguous any measure
of the rate of economic growth, or indeed of efficiency increase (Clark
2007: 249–56), since the weighting of different products or services by price
and the existence of different price weights relating to the different output
compositions at the start and finishing dates of the period under study
implie different growth rates.[7] This problem is central to debates about the
speed of change, notably the growth rate, during the Industrial Revolution
in Britain (Crafts and Harley 1992: appendix one illustrates the problem
and the implications of differing weighting of cotton) and to disagreements about the growth rates during the first two five-year plans in the
USSR (Bergson 1964, discussed by Allen 2003). The concept of economic
growth is an ambiguous one, with the ambiguity increasing with the degree
and speed of restructuring. It is possible to represent the same process of
inception of modern economic development as occurring rapidly or much
more sedately, according to your perspective.

Over the long term, there has been much change, mostly in the direction
of slowly making societies, polities and economies more complex, more
capable of producing a surplus above the subsistence level. The level of
world population gradually increased, organisational change and population growth interacting in a complex manner. Sometimes innovation
appears faster, as with the neolithic transition from hunter gathering to
agriculture, although this process was long drawn out. Technical change
has always characterised human societies. Lipsey, Carlaw and Bekar
(2005: 132) refer to 24 general purpose technologies, starting with the
domestication of plants and animals, but extending through the 10000
years of history since the Neolithic Revolution. Some economic historians talk in terms of the universality of economic growth. Snooks (1993)
argues that typically there are periods of significant growth of about 300
years, which are ended by either external or internal shocks which cause
a collapse of the impulse to growth. While individual civilisations do not
raise their level of well-being permanently, moving through cycles of rise
and fall, human society at large is on an ascending curve. This argument
is supported by data which show in the case of England at least three long
upturns, with growth rates impressive even by standards of the so-called
Industrial Revolution. Other work supports in general terms the view of
Snooks, although his statistics almost certainly exaggerate the degree of
the upturns. Cameron (1997) focuses on these growth 'logistics' as central
to his economic history of the world. At no time in history has the level

of output or income been stable. The levels tend to fluctuate, and not with any regularity, although there is much controversy about the cyclical nature of economic activity, particularly in the modern era. In the pre-modern era, there were many periods of notable increase in GDP, even per head of population, but these increases were reversed at some point of time. There were also 'dark ages'. Such fluctuations conceal the slow and steady expansion in the world economy.

The leading economies, a group of countries whose output per head is bunched at a high level, define what it means to be developed. On any rea-sonable definition, only about 20 countries located in the Triad of North America, the European Union and Japan are today economically devel-oped, together accounting for about 20 per cent of the population of the world, a proportion which is declining because of falling birth rates in the developed world, despite migration from the undeveloped world and the ascent of some Asian developing countries into the group of privileged countries. There is enormous scope for an improvement in the income levels of the other 80 per cent of the world's population. Economies which have a low and stagnant level of output are best described as undeveloped economies, ignoring the frequent use of euphemisms which conceal their true state. Most countries have levels of output per head which are very low by the standards of the most developed, with differences of magnitude over 100 not unusual. There is an obvious gap between the two groups, one being breached by a small number of fast-growing economies. The contemporary distribution of output per head is in Quah's (1996) terms bi-modal or twin-peaked. This has two implications – both a marked dif-ference in mean income in the two groups and a weak tendency for coun-tries to move from one group to the other, reflecting the obvious difficulty of initiating modern economic development. Economies which have a persistent momentum of increase are developing countries, although they may still have levels of output per head which are relatively low, some-times very low, compared with the developed economies. At some point of time, the increase in GDP per head in a country which has been developing over a long period of time takes the economy above an arbitrary threshold level indicating a developed economy.

It is interesting to note how common is the phenomenon of growth, growth recurring, as E.L. Jones (1988) has labelled it. An increasing number of instances of what Goldstone (2002) has rather graphically called 'efflorescences' have been identified, limited periods of time during which an economy manages to generate a significant increase in output per head, or manages to maintain existing levels of output per head but with a large increase in population. This has prompted Goldstone to write: 'World civilisation has had many periods of efflorescence that led nowhere: the

Egyptian New Kingdom, classical Greece, the "Industrial Revolution" of the early Sung in China, the caliphate of Baghdad, even the "Golden Age" of Holland: all seemed to put their societies in a path to world leadership, only to be outdone by a "tinkering society" on the remote British Isles in the nineteenth century' (Goldstone 2000: 7). Probably there are such periods in many societies or civilisations about which we know nothing. Goldstone argues that sharp and fairly sudden bursts of economic expansion and creative innovation occurred periodically in all pre-modern societies. These bursts never generated growth rates of total GDP of more than 1 per cent per annum and always saw a marked slowing in innovation after the initial first wave (Goldstone 2002: 354–55) – a self-sustaining element was absent. The existence of such periods is part of what must be explained and helps us understand better the process of modern economic development.

The statistical underpinning of Goldstone's cfflorescences is weak, but his argument is supported by work on recent times, when reasonably accurate statistics are available. There are plenty of what Hausmann, Pritchett and Rodrik (2004) call growth episodes. Their definition of a growth episode is precise; the growth rate in the relevant country rises by at least 2 per cent per annum and sustains a rate of 3.5 per cent, for a period of at least eight years, in the process GDP moving above the previous highest level. By historical standards, these are high rates. There are between 1960 and the present more than 80 such episodes. The unconditional probability that a country will experience such a growth acceleration sometime during any decade is about 25 per cent (Hausmann et al. 2004: 4). Of the 110 countries included in their sample, 60 have had at least one acceleration in the 35-year period between 1957 and 1992 – a ratio of 55 per cent (Hausmann et al. 2004: 21). For the 69 growth episodes for which an estimate could be made, there were 37 cases of rapid growth being sustained above a 2 per cent rate for a further eight years. In the recent past, economic growth is not an unusual phenomenon, but it is rarely sustained. It might be reasonable to assume that, whereas poverty traps may abound, a continuing absence of any economic growth is unusual. If these episodes are common now, why not in the past? It might be reasonable to see them as common throughout history, supporting Goldstone's argument.

Such a high probability of a growth episode has prompted one commentator to argue that it is easy to ignite economic growth, even through small changes in the background environment, but difficult to sustain it, provided that some minimum level of first-order economic principles are realised – protection of property, sound money, fiscal solvency and market-orientated incentives (Rodrik 2007: 35–44). A benign shock or an advantageous shift in external conditions is enough.

Governments understand the imperative of economic success, if only to reinforce their own political legitimacy: they also want the resources to deal with problems such as poverty or environmental damage. It is unclear how exactly to generate economic growth through policy measures, even whether it is possible. Sometimes modern economic development may have occurred in spite of government action, not because of it. It is a contentious issue which needs to be resolved. In order to know how economic development can be promoted, it is necessary to understand how modern economic development was achieved in the past. While circumstances are never exactly replicated, past success gives a strong hint of how to achieve future success. Yet it is not an easy task to understand past success.

There are two main approaches to understanding the past performance of economies, one exploring what is general about the process of economic development, wherever it occurs, and the other what is idiosyncratic to specific historical experiences, the former reflecting the theoretical orientation of the economist model builder and the latter the much more empirical orientation of the economic historian and development economist (for example, a Sachs (2005) or an Easterly (2002), or as revealed in the Global Research Project sponsored by the Global Development Network). Often those engaged in studying the practical problems of economic development focus on the specific. The two proponents do not often display a mutual understanding. Unfortunately, those employing the two approaches have drifted apart, without realising that this has been happening. There are worlds between the highly rigorous papers exploring the implications of the neoclassical growth model and the many attempts to provide an economic history of a particular country which encapsulates a narrative of its experience of economic development. The first of its nature simplifies, the latter tries to embrace the full complexity of the experience. Any good explanation of economic development must do both, at the same time generalising and accommodating the specific nature of all development experiences (Jones 2006: 40). The more general is any theory, the less true it is likely to be of any actual situation in the real world (Frayn 2006: 61). Since both approaches have valuable insights to offer, it is necessary to bring them back together. This book attempts to reconcile the two approaches. It is an exploration of the tension between the general and the specific in explaining the process of modern economic development. There is already a template for how this reconciliation might be achieved. Rodrik (2003: 3) has used the term analytical narrative to describe work which combines country studies with a kind of analysis 'informed and framed by the development in recent growth theory or growth econometrics'. The author believes that this approach can assist in solving the mystery of the causation of modern economic development. Although there are few pieces of work which qualify as genuine analytic narrative, Rodrik's volume of narratives points the way forward, however varied the nature of the individual contributions in the relevant book. The concept of an analytical narrative offers a starting point for such a reconciliation.

RESPONSES TO THE CHALLENGE

When the author was a student, the conventional introduction to the experience of modern economic growth was a qualitative analysis of the Industrial Revolution in Britain (Ashton 1948, Deane 1965, Mathias 1969) and its diffusion to other countries (Landes 1969), with statistical support, where it existed, which was highly specific but subordinate. It was a heroic story of innovators and innovations. The assumption was that the Industrial Revolution represented a major discontinuity at the beginning of modern economic development. Many specific economic histories were written (Kemp 1971), tracing the economic path taken by the relevant pioneer economies, culminating in the publication of comparative treatments of various European economies (*The Fontana Economic History of Europe* 1973 or Milward and Saul 1973). Traditional economic history of this kind requires a detailed knowledge of the relevant economies, with a sparing but targeted use of both economic theory and statistical data. The outcome is a country study, often a story of creative innovation and adaptation. The genre has continued, but with an increasing use of theory and quantitative data (Feinstein 2005).

There was a tendency either to see continuation of the process as one of diffusion from Britain (Kemp 1978) or to explore the way that late-comers had to adjust to the British pattern of development (O'Brien and Keyder 1978). Considerable attention was paid to the influence of relative backwardness on the pattern of modern economic development in late starters (Gershchenkron 1962 and 1968). The elements of discontinuity were greater in countries which were relatively backward when they initiated modern economic development. There appeared to be no insuperable obstacle to the spread of modern economic development within the European world, but successful economic development outside Europe was rare, an addendum to the European experience. The approach was Euro-centric, even Anglo-centric. Little was known about experiences outside the greater European area, a situation which has changed as the result of recent research, making possible a broader comparative approach.

There was a reaction against the story of progress by those who saw aspects of the process as negative. An emphasis was placed on world systems and the entire world taken as the unit of analysis, rather than particular countries or regions (Braudel 1993, Marks 2007). In this there is often a focus on the interaction of the developed with the undeveloped world (Hobson 1938, Lenin n.d., Wallerstein 1974–89, Abu-Lughod 1989, Frank 1998, Blaut 2000), perceived as an exploitative one and critical to the economic success of the leading capitalist economies. The emphasis was on global conjuncture, with a well-defined centre and a dependent periphery. Trade and foreign investment were of their nature exploitative (Prebisch 1950). The approach was often anti-capitalist and assumed the existence of viable alternative systems based on the social ownership of capital and planning. The approach continued to be largely qualitative and historical. More recently, world history has been extended to include an evolutionary worldview with a convergence of cosmic, terrestrial, biological and human history (Christian 2005).

Traditional economic history was closer to history than economics. All changed with the entry of the economic theorists. After the 1870s economic theory stressed short-term problems of resource allocation rather than economic growth. The rebirth of economic growth theory was a difficult one, with a tentative start (Harrod 1939 and Domar 1946). The groundwork for present theory was laid in the late 1950s and 1960s by the neoclassicals such as Solow (1956 and 1957) and Swan (1956), and the neo-Keynesians such as Kaldor (1960) and Robinson (1965). After a quiet intermission, the late 1980s and 1990s saw an explosion of work on the theory of economic growth (Aghion and Howitt 1998, Jones 2002, and Barro and Sala-i-Martin 2004). Much of this work is an exploration of the implications of existing theory for a growing economy. There was an attempt to confront key weaknesses of existing models of economic growth, including the failure to take full account of important variables (Romer 1986, 1987 and 1990, Lucas 1988). The new growth theory tried to confront the problems of explaining technical change within the neoclassical growth model, making that change endogenous rather than exogenous.

For the economic historians, this tendency meant a loss of independence both in an institutional sense – the location of economic history as a separate discipline within the university – and in teaching. Rostow's anti-Marxist theory of growth stages was a hint of what was about to come (Rostow 1965). It represented the first model of economic development. Other economists followed in applying economic theory to history in a simple way (Hicks 1969). The new cliometrics represented economic history as applied economics, with the rigorous use of theory and quantification wherever possible (Fogel 1964 and Fogel and Engerman 1974). Already there had been attempts to quantify, most obviously on the national income accounts and estimates of growth rates (Deane and Cole

1964).[8] There is also a persisting pattern of such work (Crafts and Harley 1992), and not just for Britain. A typical piece of economic history is now much more analytical and more empirically oriented, in a narrow way. A model of such an approach is Davis et al. (1972), which is a self-proclaimed economist's history of the USA.[9]

Some researchers set themselves up as collectors of the raw data at the global level in a useful form (Kuznets 1956–64, 1965, Bairoch 1981 and Maddison 2001), providing the empirical basis for quantitative research into modern economic development. There is implicit in this work particular theoretical orientations, if only to provide the classification of relevant variables, and often assumptions about the nature of the historical experience. Statistics for the period since 1960 have been greatly improved, notably in the Penn World Tables, by Summers and Heston (1991) (there is an updated version 6.2 produced by the same authors plus Bettina Aten at http://pwt.econ.upenn.edu/php_site/pwt61_form.php: the accessibility of the relevant data is one of its strengths). The improvement in the underlying data made possible the application of more sophisticated statistical techniques. In the 1990s, there was a growing tendency for those interested in the determinants of economic growth to engage in empirical work, the testing of theoretical propositions against real-world data, often the data in the Penn World Tables (Barro 1996, Sala-i-Martin 1997).

Economics is not monolithic, but it is a rare economist who breaks completely free of the neoclassical paradigm. One of the most productive areas in which interesting work combining a theoretical and a more empirical bent was undertaken was technical change (von Tunzelberg 1978 and 1995, Rosenberg 1972, Mokyr 1990 and 2002, Lipsey, Carlaw and Bekar 2005). Organisational change also became a focus of study. Within economics, a new branch of institutional economics emerged, which retained the premises of neoclassical economics, but offered the possibility of dealing with the institutional context of modern economic development (Coase 1937, Williamson 1985). The relevant theory was deliberately applied to history in a rigorous way (Greif 2006). One or two unusual commentators straddled the border between economics and the old economic history in discussing the issue of the role of institutions in economic development (North 2005).

The constraints of neoclassical theory, notably quantification and empirical testing, left space outside economics for the qualitative and historical. There have been many interesting studies, which sometimes stand in isolation, although some have initiated new directions of interest. Much of the work was ambitious in its aims and scope. Significant work on long-term economic development came from economic historians (E.L. Jones 1987 and 1988, Landes 1969, Snooks 1993 and 1996, Cameron 1997), from historians (Fischer 1996, Christian 2005), from sociologists (Goldstone 1991, 2008) and from biologists or ecologists (Diamond 1997, Wright 2000). Such work often took the form of narratives, pitched frequently at the global level, and sometimes merging into analytical narrative. A divide was created between the qualitative and quantitative which has tended to grow wider over time. One school, the so-called school of world history, has greatly improved our knowledge of economic activity outside Europe, notably before the inception of modern economic development, and placed the European experience in a very different light (Pomeranz 2000).

There are therefore different groups trying to analyse the process of modern economic development – traditional economic historians, economic theorists, empiricists, including development economists, collectors and systematisers of statistical data, big history narrators, and cliometricians. The approach to economic growth has become more theoretical, more quantitatively based and largely a-historical, but there were enough economic historians and practitioners from other disciplines to keep the narrative approach alive. Recently, a flood of interesting work has been published, a good sign for the study of modern economic development – some with a distinct policy orientation (Easterly 2002, Rodrik 2003, Sachs 2005), some more theoretical (Rodrik 2007, Clark 2007, Baumol 2007), some revisionist (Pomeranz 2000, Hobson 2004), some global in scope (McNeill and McNeill 2003, Christian 2005).

NARRATIVES, THEORIES AND DATA IN A COMPARATIVE APPROACH

Three different kinds of input are necessary to reach significant persuasive conclusions concerning the causation of modern economic development. The nature of their combination determines the likelihood of a successful explanation. First, there is a need for a thorough qualitative knowledge of relevant histories, a familiarity with what happened, where and when – with an emphasis on the sequence of events and the changing contextual circumstances which surround those events. Such narratives can be pitched at different levels. They can be biographies, business histories or the economic histories of particular regions, sectors of the economy or, most of all, specific countries. The writing of such histories requires much digging in the archives and in the primary sources. The relevant narratives begin well before the period for which the statistical evidence is sound and probably well before the era of modern economic development. This has traditionally been seen as the art of the historian. Unfortunately, economic theory has steadily and deliberately stripped away its historical base (Hodgson 2001).

Secondly, there is a need for theory. Theory allows the selection of a relevant narrative, since there are many possible narratives. History does not write itself. It is by no means obvious which narrative is the relevant one. Such relevance is partly a reflection of the questions asked and the nature of the mystery to be solved. The relevant theory also determines what data are required in order to test the theories and to flesh out the narratives. The theory can be grand theory, modelling in a rigorous way the behaviour of the whole economy, including the global economy (Snooks 1993), or it can be theory relevant in a more limited way to a particular time or place, of even sector of the economy. Most relevant theories are from the discipline of economics, although theories arising in other disciplinary areas can be useful. Many problems relevant to an explanation of modern economic development cry out for an interdisciplinary approach. There is a certain danger in being eclectic, but some puzzles are more easily resolved with the assistance of theory from psychology, sociology or politics, or surprisingly from even more remote disciplines, such as ecology or biology. Some argue that only an interdisciplinary approach can yield a satisfactory explanation of modern economic growth (Szostak 2006 and 2007).

Thirdly, there is the need for data, which can take two forms – what economists call hard and soft data (Easterlin 2004: chapter 2). The distinction is easy to understand, but not fully persuasive to those not completely wedded to economic models of behaviour. Soft data is the kind of evidence often used by historians or social scientists – for example, demographers, sociologists or psychologists. It consists of diary or newspaper reports, or today of survey or interview results. It reflects subjective testimony on feelings, attitudes, values, expectations or plans, in other words on motivation, a key issue in explaining economic development. The use of soft data is by no means incompatible with the use of economic theory – it expands the scope of such theory. There is no a priori reason for excluding it. By contrast, hard data purport to measure actual patterns of behaviour – for example, consumption or investment decisions. Economists prefer the latter, sometimes ignoring the real limitations of such hard data. The quantification of economic development is constrained by both the availability of relevant data and by the conceptual understandings and definitions which allow that data to be classified in a useful way. The data must be identified, subjected to a process of selection, classified and put in an accessible and usable form. Such quantification allows narratives to be fleshed out and theories to be tested.

We have two distinct general approaches: on the one side, there is a set of separate unrelated narratives, self-sufficient and specific, stressing the uniqueness of individual experiences, and on the other, a general theory in which a common set of independent variables have the same coefficients for all countries – only the values of the variables differ. Having either a set of relevant narratives or a general theory is insufficient. There is a need to compare the narratives or to differentiate the application of the theory by groups of similar experiences. Both approaches are necessary in finding an explanation of modern economic development. Just any narrative or theory will not do, nor is it a matter of simply accepting existing narratives or theories. The combination of an appropriate narrative and theory must be tested with the aid of data selected and designed for the purpose. This book is concerned with how this testing might be done.

At the heart of any such testing is the comparative approach. Narratives are of limited usefulness if they stand on their own. There should be many narratives relating the various experiences of modern economic development. With the aid of theory, these narratives should be made comparable. One commentator finds the ultimate justification in using the comparative method as hypothesis testing (Sewell 1967), with the hypotheses emerging from the theory. There are two ways in which such a comparative approach has been used – natural and counterfactual comparisons. Such comparisons are useful in the testing and measuring of the contribution of individual elements to economic development, whether they are large – institutions and technologies, or small – a particular tariff or policy measure. As Rosenberg and Birdzell (1986: 318) assert: 'Comparative economics is an enterprise made challenging by the extreme difficulty of tracing the differences in performance of different economies to their true sources'.

The first method is natural comparison (Acemoglu, Johnson and Robinson 2002: 17 ff). By preference these are similar experiences in which the only difference relates to an element being tested. The comparison is between two real experiences. For example, it is argued that the geography, culture and economic standing of the two countries North and South Korea, established in 1945, were shared, but that the only difference related to institutions. It is possible to see the different relative economic performance of the two Koreas as evidence of the importance of institutional differences, and a strong hint of which institutions might be important elsewhere. The hypothesis might be that market-based institutions promote economic growth. It might be possible to make a chain of such comparisons, both testing theory and discovering the empirical tendencies which form the basis of theory. The same exercise might be carried out to establish the importance of institutions in transitional economies – for example, comparing the experiences of Russia and China from the perspective of the speed and comprehensiveness of economic and political reform (Nolan 1995), further back in time comparing the role of the frontier in different societies, such as the USA and Russia (White 1987), or of slavery or serfdom in the economic development of the same societies (Kolchin 1987).

The second method is the counterfactual approach, common in economics but anathema to many historians. It might be argued that counterfactualism is at the heart of any explanation of historical outcomes (Ferguson 1997). It is concerned with 'what if' questions, such as, what if the Russian Revolution had never occurred. It is an escape from a determinist view of history. Instead of being just a thought experiment, it can be built into historical explanation in a systematic way. The comparison is with an imaginary or counterfactual world, constructed for the purpose with the aid of theory. If the aim is to assess the contribution of a new technology – for example, the railways, electricity or the internet, or a new policy to promote economic development such as a tariff, it is necessary to construct an imaginary world without the relevant technology or policy, and to compare the level of GDP in such a world with that in the real world in which the technology was used or the tariff introduced. The approach rests on the economist's notion of opportunity cost, assuming that there is always a choice, a second-best situation inevitably only marginally different from the actual; there is no such thing as indispensability. In such an exercise, the counterfactual world reflects the nature of the theory used. There are major criticisms of this approach, which are considered in Chapter 9.

A GENUINE MYSTERY, OR MANY PUZZLES

We need to focus on the nature of the problem. Is the economic development problem simply a puzzle, or a set of puzzles, easily solved with appropriate information? Or is it a mystery, in the terminology of the historical sociologists, a big problem (Levi 2004: 201, Pierson 2003), much more difficult to articulate, let alone resolve? The inception of modern economic development is clearly a mystery, whose solution has been elusive. Social processes, such as modern economic development, take a long time to unfold, yet the time horizons for study of the process have become increasingly restricted, focused on immediate or proximate causes, 'on causes and outcomes which are both temporally contiguous and rapidly unfolding' (Pierson 2003: 1). Social processes can be slow-moving in their causation in three main ways. First, they are often apparently incremental, but in reality cumulative. Secondly, while there may be strong inertial tendencies within social systems, there may also be thresholds or critical masses which when attained trigger major change; these are often called tipping points.[10] Thirdly, causal processes may also involve a long chain of causal mechanisms and interrelationships, in which *a* causes *b* which causes *c* which causes . . . The same considerations also hold for outcomes. There can be a significant temporal separation between the causes of the inception of major phenomena such as modern economic development and the eventual outcome. Two kinds of argument are advanced why this is true. The first involves structural change of various kinds, notably where the world is ergodic, involving movement towards some defined equilibrium state (see the next chapter). The second involves path dependency with a proliferation of feedback processes. These pathways often commence at some critical juncture, beyond which the process becomes self-reinforcing or self-sustaining.

A rather neat distinction has been made between a puzzle and a mystery, similar to a distinction made between a convergent and a divergent problem. A convergent problem has only one solution, whereas a divergent problem has a number of possible solutions. We need to ask whether the causation of modern economic development is a mystery or a puzzle, whether it is a convergent problem or a divergent one. In a puzzle or convergent problem, there is just one solution to the problem, one answer to the question. Usually the question which is relevant to a convergent problem is clear, whereas a major step in addressing any complex problem is asking the right question. What is lacking is the information needed to find a solution. The problem is gathering and processing the information relevant to finding the optimum solution. In the discipline of economics, problems are often presented as optimization problems – maxmin problems subject to given constraints: what is the lowest cost way of producing a given output? How do you maximize utility with a given income? Even in the area of institutions – what institutional arrangements minimise transaction costs? Additional information is needed to resolve the puzzle and discover a solution, the nature of which is clear, but for various reasons it is difficult to collect. It may be highly specific but unknown, or rather large since there are many possible solutions to be investigated. It is a matter of the time spent searching for the appropriate information. With historical questions, the relevant information may not have survived. Alternatively, it may be difficult to quantify a relevant concept, although sometimes excellent proxies are developed where direct information is lacking. The problem is often presented simply as a measurement problem.

In the second case, a mystery, we cross what Arthur (1992 and 1994, discussed in Lipsey et al. 2005: 72–3) has called the 'complexity boundary': problems become ill-defined. Finding the determinants of modern economic development is a complex problem. The difficulty in a mystery is a twofold one – asking the right question or questions, and selecting the information relevant to answering that question. It may be difficult to specify the problem precisely. What appears to be a simple question with an unambiguous meaning may be more difficult to interpret than initially thought. There may be a number of relevant questions or of ways of asking similar questions, as well as many valid solutions, answers depending on the way in which you define the problem and pose the relevant question. It is necessary to spend some time interpreting the question, or questions, being asked. Sorting out the relevant questions is central to the resolution of the mystery.

Contrary to the first case, there may appear to be too much information, and the researchers suffer from an information overload. There are numerous relevant narratives of various kinds already available and a surprising wealth of data. There are elaborate narratives of the experience of different countries. There is a massive amount of information relevant to the topic and a lot of noise obscuring the relevant message. Defining the big problem may result in the delineation of a series of sub-problems. Are we dealing with the same economic system in different countries and during different time periods? If the experience of economic development is a different one in each country, there may be as many explanations as there are countries. If the experience varies over time, there may be as many explanations of the experience as there are time periods. Questions appropriate to the particular context must be asked.

In order to clarify the nature of the mystery it is appropriate to take a closer look at possible questions. There are, in Mokyr's words, a number of 'deep' questions, which this book attempts to answer, sets of questions which relate to the five W questions (Szostak 2003: 27) – the who, what, why, where and when of modern economic development, supplemented with the how question, often added by scientists. The following list takes Mokyr's questions as a starting point, but groups them according to the broader issues raised above and in the relevant literature:

1. The 'who' questions: Who initiated the process of modern economic development? Who are the agents of economic development – that is, the main drivers of economic development: individuals – the innovators or entrepreneurs, or organisations – enterprises, or even groups of companies and arms of governments?
2. The 'what' questions: What is the normal state of affairs in human society – a stationary state or one of sustained and significant economic growth? What actions are at the core of modern economic development? What is the decision-making process that encourages the kind of decisions critical to the process of economic development?
3. The 'why' questions: Why are individuals or organisations motivated to take the decisions which result in modern economic development?

Why do these decisions occur in some societies and not in others? Why is economic growth not universal?

4. The 'where' questions: Where did the process of modern economic development begin? Where were the follower countries? Are geographical factors important in determining location?

5. The 'when' questions: When did the Great Divergence (Pomerantz 2000) occur, that is, when did the economic performance of the leading economies diverge from that of others, for example the economies of Europe from those of Asia? Is there a discontinuity in key variables, notably GDP per head, which can justify the use of such terms as revolution, or take-off, and mark a clear date for the inception of modern economic development? Is it evolutionary or revolutionary? Is the timing accidental? Or is there a sense in which the inception was inevitable, the result of seeds sown over the previous thousand years? Could it have occurred earlier?

6. The 'how' questions: How does capital accumulation, including human capital, technical change, and demographic factors, or institutions and culture, or government policy, contribute to modern economic development? How did positive feedback effects, which ensure that economic growth is self-reinforcing, become more important than negative feedback effects which return the system to its original state?

The mystery requires a careful consideration of all the relevant questions. There is no way of avoiding a confrontation with the complexity of the mystery. We are dealing with a set of puzzles wrapped in a mystery. Resolving these puzzles helps in solving the mystery.

THE STRUCTURE OF THE BOOK

The book is divided into five parts. Part I considers what has been achieved and how that achievement might be extended. In Chapter 2, the main argument of the book starts with the economic theory taught in all economic departments of universities, notably in the USA – the neoclassical theory of economic growth.[11] At the centre of the theory is the concept of a long-term steady-state growth rate and the notion of convergence of all economies to this rate. There is for individual countries a transitional growth path and a highly variable actual growth rate. In the next chapter, there is a discussion of the notion of convergence, so important in neoclassical accounts of economic growth. It defines and explores the two kinds of convergence discussed in the relevant literature – β convergence, the tendency for economies with lower output per head to grow faster than those with a higher output per head, and σ convergence, the tendency for the distribution of world income to become more even. The analysis distinguishes between absolute, conditional and club convergence. In the next chapter, neoclassical theory is placed in the context of a broader interpretation of the causation of economic development. It considers the particular weaknesses of the neoclassical theory, showing how neoclassical theory is concerned with equilibrium outcomes rather than historical processes. It reviews what is called growth econometrics, attempts to identify, by statistical means, the determinants of economic growth. This chapter, as its central feature, distinguishes ultimate and proximate causation and shows their relevance to the development of the analytic narrative, which is critical to understanding modern economic development.

Part II of the book considers the influence of ultimate causes as determinants of economic development, notably those whose influence can be described as fixed in the short term. It analyses four main areas of interest – resources; risk environments; human capital, including nutrition, motivation and aptitude; and finally institutions. It notes the way in which ultimate causes interact with each other and with proximate causes. The fifth chapter considers the influence of geographical context. The chapter concentrates attention on the differing circumstances in which the influence of the resource endowment on economic development is positive or negative. The sixth chapter is concerned with relevant risk environments, which differ from country to country and over time, and their influence on modern economic development. It focuses on unexpected variability in the relevant environments and on the incidence of extreme shocks. Chapter 7 focuses on human capital, which reflects the level of education, health, and aptitude. This chapter also considers the nature of motivation and the role of culture in influencing that motivation. In the eighth chapter, institutions are the focus of analysis. The chapter explores the nature of good institutions. It focuses on the partnership between market and government, the role of civil society and the influence of the international political structure.

Part III analyses other elements of ultimate causation, more immediate in driving the process of economic development. They are first, the ability to access the technical knowledge available in the world; second, the motivation and commitment of governments to economic development. Chapter 9 considers the nature of technical change, from the perspective of invention, innovation and imitation. The analysis considers the factors that encourage a rapid rate of innovation and the barriers to the exploitation of best-practice knowledge for any particular country. It uses the American System of Manufacturing as an illustration of the importance of technical innovation. Chapter 10 picks up the role of government, from the perspective of the appropriateness and persistence of government strategy. It places that strategy in a context of the tendency to rent-seeking behaviour and of relevant political economy, both domestic and international. It focuses on the role of commitment to the promotion of modern economic development by key government decision makers. It explores the significance of the policies pursued to realise the aim of economic development, in particular the use of planning and the attempt to pick winners. It explores the advantages and disadvantages of openness.

Part IV introduces three narratives which show how proximate and ultimate causes are combined in the writing of an analytical narrative. One of the key relationships in the economic history of the world is that between resources and demography, the focus of Chapter 11. Modern economic development has been interpreted as a release from the Malthusian trap. This chapter analyses what this statement means and in what sense it might be true. The relevant demographic patterns are discussed in the context of the theory of the demographic transition. The modern demographic regime is analysed and the tendency to a neo-Malthusian perspective today identified. The twelfth chapter explores the notion of an Industrial Revolution in the pioneer economy Britain. It considers elements of continuity and discontinuity in that revolution, stressing a gradual lead-up to the first transition rather than an abrupt set of changes. It considers how far the inception of modern economic development in other countries differed from the pioneer. Chapter 13 focuses on the failure of an alternative strategy different from that of the developed economies. It considers the Soviet experience in the long-term context of Russian economic history, analysing both the causes of the revolutionary change in strategy and the causes of the failure of that strategy.

Part V concludes the analysis, emphasising the need for an analytic narrative and arguing the case for a reconciliation of the approaches of those who embrace theory and those who embrace history. It establishes the requirements of an analytic narrative and shows the kind of answers already made to relevant questions.

2. The conventional wisdom of the economist

> The purpose of economic theory is to take a complicated world, abstract from many details, and express the key economic relationships in a way that enhances understanding. From this standpoint, the neoclassical model is still the most useful theory of growth we have. It will continue to be the first growth model taught to students and the first growth model used by policy analysts. (Mankiw 1995: 308)

Despite various attempts to adopt an alternative approach to economic development, neoclassical economics still provides the only developed theory of economic growth, dominating the teaching of economics and the content of articles in the relevant journals. This may seem surprising given the richness of the debates which took place in the 1960s, and again in the 1990s, concerning how to explain modern economic development and the significance of the criticisms of the neoclassical approach (Harcourt 1972). Any exploration of the determinants of economic development must start with neoclassical theory since it is the conventional wisdom on the topic and unlikely to cease to be so. The aim of this chapter is to introduce that theory in an accessible manner, appraising its strengths and weaknesses, and identifying its place in an explanation of modern economic development.

This chapter begins with the central concept of neoclassical growth theory, the notion of a long-term steady-state equilibrium growth path. Next it considers the nature of neoclassical theory, focusing on its reliance on the production function as a representation of the aggregate behaviour of an economy. The third section evaluates the role, and limits, of growth accounting in explaining economic development. Growth accounting estimates the contributions made by the different factors of production to economic growth. Such accounting leaves a large residual which is interpreted by neoclassical economists as the rate of productivity increase, which can be seen as underpinning the long-term steady-state equilibrium growth path. The final section returns to the equilibrium growth path, further exploring its place in the determination of the rate of economic development in different countries.

THE NOTION OF A LONG-TERM STEADY-STATE EQUILIBRIUM GROWTH PATH

Neoclassical theory asserts the existence of a steady-state long-run equilibrium growth path characteristic of all economies.[1] This growth path is most often represented as reflecting the movement of the frontier of best-practice technology, knowledge of which is available instantaneously throughout the world.[2] Technical knowledge is assumed to be a public good available to all. Technology improves in each period at a consistent rate, determined from outside the economic system. Such a path is best approximated by the behaviour of the most developed economy, where most relevant technical change is generated or assimilated. The long-term rate of growth in this economy approximates the eventual long-term steady-state growth rate for all economies; in the words of North (2005: 78): 'The growth in the stock of knowledge is the fundamental underlying determinant of the upper bound of human well-being'. For an economy on the path of equilibrium growth, there is at each moment a given level of technology embodied in a given amount of capital per head and yielding a given output per head. Economists prefer to view the economic world as either moving along such a dynamic path – true of the leader but no other economy – or in transition to it. The theory assumes that during a transitional period of varying length every economy other than the leader moves in an 'out of equilibrium' state towards the steady-state path. Developed economies are on, or close to, the steady-state equilibrium path and developing countries in transition to that path.

In this book, we use the term inception of modern economic development to denote the transition from a state characterised by a lack of development to one of persistent development. This transition has been called variously an industrial revolution, a take-off into sustained growth, the initiating spurt of industrialisation. During the inception of modern economic development there is a phase transition (a traverse in the words of the theorists) from an initial steady-state equilibrium, sometimes somewhat graphically called the poverty trap, to another, a situation of self-sustained growth, often in a rather long drawn-out manner. In the short-term, the focus is on transitional economics and the movement from undeveloped to developed status. The growth rate of those catching up can exceed the rate of growth of the leading economy by large amounts and, depending on their starting point, over long periods of time. Neoclassical economists seek, and expect to find, evidence that the income per head of all developed economies is tending to converge, with the implied result that all will eventually grow at the same long-term rate. Growth rates above the leader's rate will fall until they converge on that rate, except if the relevant economy becomes the leading economy, generating technical and organisational innovations at a faster rate. In the long-term, the technical, or economic, leadership of one particular country is only temporary and another economy may emerge and set the steady-state equilibrium growth path. There have been a number of such cross-overs – between the Netherlands and the UK in the eighteenth century or between the UK and the USA at the end of the nineteenth and beginning of the twentieth centuries, at an earlier date between China and Europe (Maddison). At the end of the twentieth century, there was an anticipation that Japan was going to take the position of leadership from the USA, a cross-over which did not happen. Today the possibility of a cross-over involving China at some time in the near future is often discussed.

One view of the equilibrium path is the experience of the most advanced economy, the USA (C.I. Jones 2002: 12). Throughout the twentieth century the American economy was the leading economy, particularly in size and output per head, and is seen as operating at the technical frontier (C.I. Jones 1997: 4). The American economy, given the stability of its growth rate, is regarded as having been growing at its steady-state rate. The American economy grew by a rate of GDP growth per capita of only 1.85 per cent between 1870 and 2000 (Barro and Sala-i-Martin 2004: 1). It was a very stable rate of growth sustained throughout the period, with the exception of the early 1930s; business cycles represent temporary short-term departures from the long-term rate and the 1930s downturn was dramatic. The starting point for this estimate is of significance since it may conceal an acceleration which occurred before that date. This may reflect a situation in which Britain provides the long-term rate before 1870 and the American economy was converging on this rate. However revolutionary are the consequences of modern economic development, one of its main characteristics is a relatively low long-term equilibrium rate of growth of real GDP per head, much lower than generally thought.[3] Our sense of what is high and low has been distorted by the growth of a handful of developing countries moving during the transition from very low levels of output per head, that is, from well within the frontier of the world's best performance towards that frontier. We are led astray by the high growth rates of the economies currently converging on the most developed, such as Japan from the 1950s to the 1980s or China after 1978. Currently, the maximum sustainable rate of growth of a developed economy is not 8, 9 or 10 per cent, but a maximum of 3 per cent, probably significantly lower.

NEOCLASSICAL GROWTH THEORY

The neoclassical theory of economic growth approaches the problem of growth from the supply side, ignoring problems of fluctuations in demand and the lack of full capacity utilisation of either labour or capital (Solow 1956). The Solow model has its origins in a response to the work of Harrod (1939) and Domar (1946) who first formalized a model of economic growth, but were Keynesian in recognising that any economy might be off its equilibrium growth path. They were as much concerned with the short-term behaviour of an economy, as its long-term movement, on the assumption, as Keynes is much quoted as saying, that the long term consists of so many short terms. They accepted Keynes' rejection of Say's law, that supply creates its own demand, so assumed that a divergence between ex ante savings and ex ante investment is what drives the short-term movement of aggregate output in any economy.[4] This movement influences the level of demand at any moment of time. There is plenty of evidence that it is not the supply of savings but the incentive to invest which is important and that the latter reflects potential demand (Guha 1981: 84–5). The neoclassical model abstracts from short-term demand problems. By ignoring such short-term difficulties and focusing on the supply side, it states the long-term aggregate situation in a simplified way.

In any economy, we assume a fixed aggregate capital/output ratio, v – on average there is a fixed amount of capital required to produce a unit of output (the marginal and average ratios are equal). Usually neoclassical economics assumes that the v's are potentially the same throughout the world – everyone has the same possibilities of converting capital into output, reflecting the nature of best-practice technology and organisation available in the world. At the same time, we can assume a fixed savings ratio, s – the relevant population maintains a constant aggregate savings ratio whatever the level of income. Let us also assume that the latter is ex post, not ex ante, related to outcome rather than intention, and by definition, in a closed economy, equal to the investment ratio (in practice, there is a tendency for both to rise with the level of economic development – Barro and Sala-i-Martin 2004: 15). If savings can be instantaneously converted into investment, there is no distinction between ex ante intentions and ex post outcomes. In this simple model, the rate of growth of output is s/v, the proportion of income saved multiplied by the economy's ability to generate additional output (in a closed economy, output and income are equal) from a unit of saving. This is what Harrod called the warranted rate.[5] If the savings ratio were 20 per cent and the capital/output ratio 4, the implied growth rate would be 5 per cent, or if the ratios were 8 per cent and 8, the growth rate is 1 per cent. We can play around with the relevant magnitudes to describe possible growth scenarios. The rate of growth can be accelerated either by an increase in savings or by an improvement in the capacity to generate output from that savings.

There is a second approach to the rate of growth, to define the maximum potential allowed by the growth of population and by the impact of improvements in technical knowledge on productivity. This is the sum of the rate of growth of population, which we call, n, assuming that the age structure of the population is already consistent with this rate and that the labour force grows at the same rate as the total population,[6] and of the growth in labour productivity, say m, which is the result of technical change, if we regard all organisational change as linked to technical change. The maximum possible rate of economic growth of aggregate output in any economy is $n + m$.[7] In a steady-state equilibrium state, the two rates should be equal, that is $s/v = n + m$; in Harrod's terminology, the warranted rate equals the natural rate, but this equality might be realised only by chance. In this steady state, the labour force remains fully employed. In the simplest case, all four variable are assumed given from outside – they are not endogenously but exogenously determined. The main problem is that an exogenous (independent) determination of the four variables, v, s, n and m, implies a lack of equality between the two rates of growth. Either an economy would be faced with increasing unemployment and over-capacity, if $n + m > s/v$, or the reverse, with an upper bound of full employment, if $n + m < s/v$.[8] Is there some mechanism by which the equality is attained, so that the equilibrium is a stable one, one in which a movement away leads to decisions which restore the equilibrium?

This might be achieved by making either s or v endogenous, determined by the variables interacting within the simple growth model. The initial neoclassical response was to make v endogenous. The variation in v means that the mix of capital and labour can be varied, either at the level of an individual product, through the choice of different techniques of production, or by the combination of different products with differing v's. The capital intensity of production (the ratio of capital to labour) can be increased in either way, with a resulting impact on v. Some even argue that trade has the same effect of changing v, through the different factor intensity of imports, compared with exports.

Solow introduced the production function into his account, which was absent from the work of Harrod (1939) and Domar (1946). In the words of Mankiw (1995: 281), 'The production function should not be viewed literally as a description of a specific production process, but as mapping from quantities of inputs into a quantity of output'. We can represent the productive side of the economy by a simple aggregate production function

– the level of output is determined by the level of factor inputs, usually just capital and labour, and indirectly by the level of technology, which reflects the nature of the functional relationship between inputs and output. The contribution of land or resources is usually ignored (see Chapter 5 for comments on this neglect). The assumption is that labour and capital are mutually substitutable. The rate of substitutability can range from zero – the inputs are fixed – to infinity – any increase of price is immediately met with the reduction in its use to zero. With the often-used Cobb-Douglas production function, the rate of substitutability is one, which means there is no change in the distribution of factor rewards whatever technology is chosen – a change in the price of the factor is exactly offset by a compensating change in the quantity used.[9] Under this assumption, the contribution of a factor of production to output is equal to its share of total income. This reflects an assumption made of constant returns for both factors of production taken together – output increases in proportion to the increase in inputs, but diminishing returns for each individually – output increases less than proportionately as one input increases and the other remains constant (this is often referred to as the convexity assumption). As the use of one factor relative to the other increases, the return from its use declines. The impulse to a change in the factor mix is a change in the relative price of the factors of production. Since the cost of producing output reflects the use of factor inputs and their price, the choice of technique reflects different factor supply situations, which in competitive markets influence their price. The choice of factor mix is dictated by a simple rule: use the factor up to the point at which the cost of the marginal addition of that factor is equal to the return from that marginal unit. For capital, this means that the rate of interest is equal to the marginal product of capital.

An increase in the savings ratio, by increasing the supply of capital, will tend to reduce the cost of capital, relative to labour, and lead to an increase in the amount of capital employed per unit of labour and, because of diminishing returns, per unit of output. There is an increase in v. The level of income per head will rise, but the rate of growth will only do so temporarily, and not in the steady state. On this account, the equilibrium steady rate of growth is still determined by $n + m$: given that v, and s/v, will adjust to bring about the equality. An increase in s is offset by an increase in v. Growth is represented as a series of such moments of time, as comparative statics. If we assume for simplicity that population expansion is zero,[10] the equilibrium growth path is determined solely by the rate of technical change. If there is no technical change and s rises, there is for a transitional period a positive rate of growth of output until a higher equilibrium capital/labour and per capita output is attained. The capital/output ratio has also risen. The equilibrium rate of growth of output – in this case zero – is independent of the level of s, except during the transitional period, since v is endogenously adjusting to accommodate changes in s. The equilibrium growth path is usually seen as a stable one, with any temporary departure leading to market forces restoring the equilibrium. Provided markets work as perceived, any movement away from equilibrium will encourage a return to that equilibrium through the response of decision makers responding to the movement of the relative prices of capital and labour in making decisions on the factor mix in investment projects. During the transition, growth is a result of capital accumulation, but on the long-run equilibrium growth path, it is the result of technical change.

An alternative approach to the determination of the equilibrium path, that of the neo-Keynesians (Kaldor 1963, Kalecki and Robinson 1965), was to make the savings ratio endogenous through changes in the distribution of income. There is disagreement over whether savings come out of wages or profits. On the life-cycle theory savings come out of wages. Neoclassical economics – largely utilitarian in its bias – has preferred to develop theories of optimal saving, based on Ramsey's rule (Ramsey 1928), which stresses individual acts of saving. Empirical data show it is much more likely that savings come out of profits or interest received and are to a considerable degree the result of collective, not individual, decisions. In neoclassical economics, the production function determines the distribution of income as well as the functional relations of production. Capital receives as income its rate of return multiplied by the aggregate capital input, and labour a share determined in the same way. It is assumed the savings from both forms of income are the same. Since in the real world most savings comes from profits, this is unlikely to be true and s varies with the share of profits in total income. An increase in investment must be matched by an increase in savings in a world in which all the savings come from profits (or rents). This is achieved by a distribution of income favourable to those who receive profits, through an increase in the rate of profit and/or profit margin, relative to those receiving wages. The dynamics of the economy bring about an equality between investment and savings ex post, even if they are unequal ex ante.

The mechanism has recently been shown by Allen (Allen 2005) to correspond more closely with what happened in Britain during the classic period of the Industrial Revolution. Allen has successfully reconciled a model of savings behaviour which reflects the distribution in income and changes in that distribution with the neoclassical approach, largely by recognising at the same time the limited substitutability in production methods between capital and labour – in other words, v is seen empirically as close to a constant, while s is variable. Allen emphasises the need during the Industrial Revolution for a capital infrastructure, linked with urbanisation and transportation, whatever the exact technologies chosen in particular industries. In this situation, *s* adjusts to accommodate *m* + *n*, largely through the investment opportunities created by either technical change or population growth. The rise in investment causes a rise in savings. If the value of *m* + *n* rises, investment rises, and savings adjust, given the underlying propensities to save of different income groups. This approach has been neglected.

GROWTH ACCOUNTING

Using the neoclassical production function approach, a number of economists, starting with Solow (1957), and followed by Dennison (1962) and Jorgenson (Jorgenson and Griliches 1967), sought to identify and measure the contributions of the different proximate sources of economic growth, an approach known as growth accounting. Growth accounting makes two contributions to the analysis of economic development. It identifies the long-term equilibrium growth rate as the change in total factor productivity (TFP), and it suggests the changing pattern of proximate causes of economic development. Growth accounting is a routine starting point for economists in any attempt to impute the different sources of growth.

The aim of much neoclassical theorizing has been to explain all economic development through an increase in inputs. At its simplest level, it is possible to measure the contribution of the factors of production by weighting the factor contributions by the share of that factor in total income. This is a rather heroic assumption. The contribution of labour is the increase in the use of labour multiplied by the relevant wage. The contribution of capital is the level of investment multiplied by some typical rate of interest or average rate of return. Often it is assumed that the latter is one-third, on the equally heroic assumption that the production function is the same everywhere.

There are serious measurement problems. The capital input consists in the services of a gross capital stock which results from the addition each year of investment to, and the subtraction of depreciation from, a benchmark capital stock. It is difficult to find such a benchmark figure, but the further back in time it is located, the less influence any mistake will have on the current value of stock. Labour is usually taken to be the annual hours of work, or the number of workers. In developing countries, where family enterprises and self-employment are important, it is difficult to estimate the labour input. In the augmented neoclassical model, investment in human capital is explicitly allowed for (Mankiw, Romer and Weil 1992), but this increases the measurement problems. The definition of capital is extended to include human capital and research and development expenditures (for a good discussion of how this is done, see Clark 2003). The exercise of growth accounting can be carried out, taking account of quality, with a significant disaggregation of the capital or labour inputs. Labour can be disaggregated by age, education, sex and capital, by the nature of the productive facility, by its vintage (year of construction and therefore productivity) or its position on a so-called quality ladder. In principle, technical change is subsumed within capital accumulation, all technical progress embodied in investment. In theory, with a proper definition of capital and labour, all growth should be accounted for by an increase in the inputs of the factors of production.

In practice, when the growth accounting is done, there is usually a residual, often, but not always, large. The imputation of all growth in output to the growth in inputs is not realized, despite strenuous efforts to make it so. It is usual therefore to express the growth of output in terms of three, rather than two, proximate determinants (for a discussion of proximate and ultimate determination, see the next chapter) – an increased input of capital, an increased input of labour and productivity growth, largely reflecting technical change.

There are two views of the meaning of the residual. The first is a rather pessimistic one: it is seen as a measure of our ignorance. The residual is regarded as a reflection of measurement errors, its size random. It is a catch-all concept, including 'the effects of resource allocation from structural transformation, political and macroeconomic instability, climate change, and institutional factors that may influence the overall efficiency of economic operation' (Soludo and Kim 2003: 37).[11]

On the other hand, the residual is interpreted by many as the rate of increase of total factor productivity; it is what is left when all the re-measurements are made, and reflects the dynamism of an economy, its capacity to innovate, the contribution of technical and organizational change. The exercise is usually carried out using a Cobb-Douglas function, with its assumptions of diminishing returns to increased input of different factors of production and optimisation under competitive factor markets. The exercise can be done at a given moment of time, expressing levels of output per head or capital per head, or over a period of time, expressing changes in inputs and outputs (in mathematical terms, the first difference in levels). Estimation of the residual allows comparison across time and across countries. It is appropriate to apply the technique over long periods of time, since the results are otherwise influenced by short-term factors such as changes in the level of capacity utilisation of factors of production during the business cycle or by such economic shocks as significant short-term movements in the terms of trade. The basis for the estimation can be put simply. If we take a production function in which the contribution of productivity increase is separated out, we have $Y = A. F(K, L)$, where Y is total output, A is the technical level, and K and L the capital and labour inputs respectively. In some estimates, A is linked to K or to L, that is, technical change is regarded as capital or labour augmenting. If we differentiate the equation with respect to time, the result is $dY/Y = g + (FkK/Y). dK/K + (FIL/Y).dL/L$, where $g = dA/A$ and is Hicks-neutral technical change, that is, technical change which is output augmenting and does not affect the factor contributions. g is the residual after the contributions of the two factors have been subtracted from the increase in output. The capital and labour contributions are the increase in input multiplied by their shares in total income. The terms before the increase in factor contributions represent the elasticity of output with respect to increases in the factor inputs.[12]

Let us assume that in a crude way TFP measures the technical dynamism of an economy. There are some interesting empirical results from such estimates, which allegedly provide illumination on the role of productivity increase during the inception of modern economic development.[13] The first is the behaviour of the specific growth contributions in economies which have already developed. A particularly interesting case is the contribution of different elements during the Industrial Revolution in Britain. The general tendency has been to downgrade the rate of growth of GDP per head during the Industrial Revolution. According to the work of Crafts and Harley (Mokyr 2004, pp. 8–9), total factor productivity grew at the rate of 0.14 per cent during the period 1760–1800 and 0.41 during the period 1800–1830, representing as much as 70 per cent and 82 per cent respectively of the total per capita growth. These are very low rates, which could easily disappear with a small revision of the factor contribution figures. Voth and Antras's figures, computed from income accounts, differ somewhat, but not greatly, at 0.27 per cent for 1770–1801, 0.54 per cent for 1801–31 and 0.33 per cent for 1831–60, rates consistent with the Crafts and Harley statistics. The general view is that there is a relatively slow improvement in productivity, but that that improvement accounts for most of the slow rates of growth of output per capita.

A second interesting result involves trends in the modern economic development of the USA – first, the rising importance of factor productivity increase over the long term, and second, the short-term slowing after the oil price shocks of the 1970s. During the nineteenth century, the main contribution to the economic growth of the USA came from the input of factors of production, whereas in the twentieth century it comes from an increase in total factor productivity. Between 1840 and 1900, the relevant data suggest the rise in factor productivity, at just under 0.7 per cent per annum, accounts for less than 20 per cent of output growth – most of the output growth is explained by an increase in labour and capital inputs, the former not far below 2 per cent and the latter just over 1 per cent, whereas between 1900 and 1960 the rate of increase in total factor productivity is much faster at 1.32 per cent and the proportional contribution well over 40 per cent (Davis et al., 1972: 38–9). In the period 1947–73, before the oil price shocks of the 1970s, the rate rises as high as 1.4 per cent, although this accounts for only about one third of total growth, with the capital contribution exceeding it by a significant amount (Barro 2004: 439). In the period 1960–95, embracing two oil price shocks, a period for which the statistics are much better, the rate for the USA falls to 0.8 per cent and the contribution is less than one-quarter, significantly below the contributions of both capital and labour (Barro ibid.: 439).

An interesting supplement to the USA data is the 'alleged' slowing which characterised the developed world, particularly the USA, in the 20 years after the first oil shock in 1973. This is seen as general through the developed world (C.I. Jones 2002: 47, and Barro and Sala-i-Martin 2004: 438–9). In the relevant period, 1973–95, the rate was as low as 0.5–0.6 per cent, speeding up to 1.4 per cent during 1995–8 (C.I. Jones 2002: 46). Baumol et al. (2007: 12) notes an acceleration in overall productivity growth from 1.5 per cent 1973–95, to 2.5 per cent 1995–2000 and 3.5 per cent for 2000–4. Some explain the slowing through the initial build-up of investment in relevant facilities and retraining of staff in the prelude to the communications revolution, with an increased return to that investment being received after 1995.

A third empirical result relates to the nature of the Asian Economic Miracle. There was an attempt to impute the contributions to different factors of production and to technical change for the countries of the first wave of the Asian Economic Miracle, the four little Asian tigers – South Korea, Taiwan, Singapore and Hong Kong (Young 1995, Hsieh 2002). Krugman (1994) wrote an important article for the journal *Foreign Affairs* which became the conventional wisdom on the Asian Economic Miracle. Asian economic growth was not miraculous, since the acceleration in the rate of growth of output reflected simply an acceleration in the rate of growth in inputs – high savings and more capital accumulation – and a rapid growth of the labour force, including the temporary increase in the participation rate which accompanied the rapid fall in fertility rates in Asian countries, the so-called population bonus. The result of the growth accounting exercise originally carried out by Young is an interpretation of that miracle which stresses factor contributions and downplays increases in factor productivity. In the extreme case of Singapore, the result is just about zero for the latter. The implication for future growth was rather pessimistic, since the neoclassical model assumes diminishing returns to capital accumulation.

Hsieh (2002) has used the existence of the dual approach, the flip side of the primal approach, to show that this view may be mistaken. Growth accounting can be carried out either in quantities or in values. This approach is based on the principle that the reward to factors will increase only if output is increasing for given inputs. The dual approach follows from the identity $Y = rK + wL$, which when differentiated gives $dY/Y = sk.(dr/r + dk/K) + sl.(dw/W + dl/L)$, where the s's are again factor income shares (written as α and $1 - \alpha$ below). Rearranging terms $g = dY/Y - sk.(dK/K) - sl.(dL.L) = sk.dr/r + sl.dw/w$; in other words the rate of factor productivity increase is equal either to the increase in output minus the weighted contributions of increased factor inputs, the residual as defined above, or to the weighted increases in factor rewards: the dual should give the same result as the primal approach. Hsieh believes that the return to capital has not decreased in countries such as Singapore in the way implied by the work of Young and that the increase in total factor productivity is not insignificant. Work done since has tended to favour the original Young/Krugman argument, but it has also illustrated how sensitive the analysis is to the value of α.[14] Using the conventional value of α of 35 per cent, and applying it to all countries on the assumption that the same technology was available to all, Collins and Bosworth (1996: 19) find a surprisingly small role for TFP in the success of East Asia: its growth accounts for only one-quarter of the growth in the region's output per worker over the period 1960–94. There are two minor reservations. First, the rate may be improving, since it is higher for the period 1984–94 than for the previous period. Secondly, the rate is low for all developing regions and the East Asian rate higher than for other regions; it may be part of a more general characteristic of developing countries.

A fourth empirical study relates to a comparison between developed and developing countries and between different regions of developing countries (see Soludo and Kim 2003 and McMahon and Squire 2003 for individual papers estimating the sources of growth for different regions). Soludo and Kim (2003) discuss the implications of two attempts to estimate regional contributions (Collins and Bosworth 1996 and Senhadji 2000). The results are broadly in accord. In developing regions, TFP and capital accumulation tend to move together, with a relatively rapid growth of both contributors in Asia and a much slower growth in other developing regions, actually amounting to a reduction in TFP in sub-Saharan Africa, the Middle East and both North Africa and Latin America. The population bonus is clear from the relatively high contribution of labour input in East Asia, although much less significant than the capital contribution.

Senhadji (2000: 148) also found that real output and TFP growth in developing countries is twice as volatile as in developed countries. The growth of real GDP per head varies much more than the growth rates of capital and labour (Senhadji 2000: 141). Cross-country difference in growth rates may be transitory, confirmed by increasing evidence of a volatility in short-term growth rates.

General inferences have been drawn from such work in explaining the nature of modern economic development. During the sometimes long transitional period, at a low level of economic development, capital accumulation has an independent and critical role to play. During the transition to the long-term equilibrium growth path, capital accumulation is what is really important. Since TFP grows at a slow rate in all developing countries, it appears that it cannot be easy to imitate the best-practice technology and organization of developed economies. The slow rate of TFP growth applied equally to the pioneers in modern economic development. It is possible 'that the potential to adopt knowledge and technology from abroad depends on a country's stage of development' (Collins and Bosworth 1996: 37). This viewpoint has two main implications. It means that accelerating the rate of economic growth in order to converge on the steady-state rate requires a high level of savings to finance the capital accumulation, which embodies the new technology. Secondly, it reinforces the role of positive feedback with economic development. TFP's contribution increases with development.

There are two major limitations on what growth accounting can legitimately reveal about the determination of economic development. The first involves the underestimation of the significance of technical change or productivity increase. This reflects the difficulty of separating the contribution of technical change from that of capital accumulation. Growth accounting assumes that the growth contributions are independent and additive. This raises a major difficulty. There is a strong interaction between productivity increase (technical change) and the rate of capital accumulation (investment). On the one hand, productivity increase, by making investment more profitable, stimulates capital accumulation (Helpman 2004: 26). On the other hand, most technical change is embodied in capital, in specific plant and equipment, without which it is impossible to take advantage of the new technology. Rosenberg and Birdzell (1986: 20–21) argue cogently that the rise in inputs was increasingly a response to innovation: during the period of modern economic development, 'the West has increasingly placed its primary reliance on innovation'. If technical change, expressed in the residual, only appears to account for 10 per cent of growth it is not true to say that removal of that change leaves a growth rate at 90 per cent of the original rate, since a major incentive to capital accumulation has been removed. Both are likely to decline in the absence of the technical change. Consequently, the usual calculation of TFP understates the rate of technical change. There have been recent attempts to take this into account (Allen 2005: 11). Allen estimated that as much as 65 per cent of the gain in GDP in Britain between 1760 and 1860 was due to the interaction of capital accumulation and technical change.

The growth accounting approach underestimates seriously the importance of technical change since it fails to take account of the embodiment of technical knowledge in both investment and organisation. Since most technical change is embodied in some form, the residual does not exhaust the contribution of technical change.

A second element of uncertainty in estimating the contribution of technical change follows from the existence of technological externalities, complementarities or TFP spillovers, as they are sometimes called. The constant returns to scale argument may not hold since there may be significant increasing returns to scale which follow from the external effects of investment. In other words, the social return from the application of a technique in a given investment is greater than the private return captured by the enterprise applying this technology. Some part of the technology consists of non-rivalrous ideas, or knowledge, which become public and can be exploited by others. If the technical changes are large, as with so-called general-purpose technologies or macro-inventions, these spillovers can be highly significant. Consequently, in some accounts, the simple neoclassical production function is deliberately opened up to reveal all the influences of technical change on economic performance: '. . . one cannot properly understand technology when it is formulated merely as a scalar in a production function' (Lipsey, Carlaw and Bekar 2005: 218).[15] TFP represents a minimum estimate of technical advance.

A second limitation of growth accounting is that the analysis says nothing about either the direction or the nature of causation. It may be that output growth in its turn causes capital accumulation or technical advance, or both, not the other way round. The old multiplier-accelerator models of the business cycle assumed that there was a two-way relationship between outcome or income change and investment. Even if we grant that the analysis shows that an acceleration in the growth rate is due to a particularly large increase in the capital input, to a population bonus, or to an acceleration in the rate of technical progress, all of these are proximate causes – what explains the existence of the positive contribution? This requires a treatment of fundamental or ultimate causes. The elements expressed in the production function and in growth accounting are proximate determinants – what they tell us about the nature and causation of economic development is limited. A different approach is needed to identify causation, although such analysis must be consistent with growth accounting.

A SECOND LOOK AT THE STEADY-STATE GROWTH PATH

Neoclassical theory assumes an ergodic world, one characterised by an equilibrium state to which all countries are converging. In neoclassical economics, this is the long-term equilibrium steady-state growth path. The world may be non-ergodic, a random walk to a random destination, but this is a pessimistic view, although one which some important commentators, such as North (2005) or Arthur (1992 and 1994), hold. Even if the world is non-ergodic, a useful analysis of the process of modern economic development may demand an assumption that it is ergodic in order to promote our understanding of the process.

It is necessary to explore further what an equilibrium steady-state rate of growth means. In the case of zero population growth, the rate reflects the rate of technical advance in the world at large, or more broadly, if we take into account organisational change, the rate of productivity increase. C.I. Jones (1997: 8) has argued that in the long run all countries share the same rate of growth because they will eventually grow at the average rate of growth of world knowledge (ibid.: 9). Barro and Sala-i-Martin (1995: 2) make the same point, 'In the long run, all economies grow at the rate of discovery in the leading places'. Eaton and Kortum (1994, see the abstract) argue for a common growth rate which reflects the research efforts in all countries.[16] The independent advance of that knowledge implies a rate of productivity advance which constitutes the equilibrium steady-state rate of growth. Neoclassical economics initially assumed that this pool of knowledge was exogenously given, not economically determined, but generated by non-economic factors outside the economic system. There is a strong and increasing body of argument supporting such a view (Mokyr 2002, Easterlin 2004).

In the neoclassical view, technical progress is available to all in a world in which knowledge moves freely. All technical knowledge is codifiable, consisting in sets of blueprints easily transferred – tacit knowledge is insignificant, a critical assumption if the knowledge is to be accessible. Technical knowledge is a public good, both non-rivalrous, in that its use by one person does not exclude its use by another, and unexcludable – once revealed it is impossible without government protection by patents legislation to market it and even then easy to back-engineer and to copy. However there are time lags in the uptake of new technology. The level of economic development appears to influence the capacity to imitate innovations made elsewhere. Developed economies are much better imitators than developing economies. According to Eaton and Kortum (1994) the ranking of productivity levels in particular countries reflects lags in the speed at which different countries take up relevant innovations. Domestic diffusion is faster than international diffusion, but all knowledge is eventually diffused and taken up, if profitable. Barro and Sala-i-Martin (2004) argue that the costs of copying are lower than those of invention, and that it pays to imitate rather than to invent. Yet there are a broad range of factors delaying the diffusion of best-practice technology (the issues are more fully explored in Chapter 11).

So far in the neoclassical model there are two states relevant to modern economic development – the long-term steady-state equilibrium growth path and the transition to that path from an initial situation off the equilibrium path. It is not really a theory of the transition to the path of modern economic growth, only indirectly dealing with the determinants of the transition. If we believe in a major discontinuity at the inception of modern economic development, neoclassical growth theory tells us little about the nature of this discontinuity, although neoclassical economics claims to know much about how to achieve economic growth in general. This assumes that all economies converge on the same long-term steady-state growth path. Neoclassical economists recognise that this is not always the case. There may be a long-term equilibrium path specific to the relevant economy, reflecting the particular values of s, v and m, relevant to an economy. Key influences on the specific rates are the various abilities to absorb new technology and the differing savings ratios. If technology assimilation and savings rates differ, the long-run equilibrium rates are particular to each country. Both savings and absorption of new technology hide a multitude of sins – they are not simple variables, rather variables with a multitude of different determinants which need to be fully explored.

There is a temptation to try to make s, m and n endogenous, but if they are, what possible meaning does the steady-state rate have, since it will change as the variables change? The propensity to save may differ from society to society, and the distribution of income may influence the savings ratio; it may rise with income at relatively low levels of income.[17] There may be significant differences in the efficiency with which capital produces output, in other words in the technological level, efficiencies which reflect the level of economic development. The rate of population increase, n, also varies with the level of income per head, although also reflecting whether a society is immigrant friendly, which is likely to be the case if income levels are relatively high. Both s/v and $n + m$ are therefore variable, and sensitive to income levels.

The poorer is a country, the better able it should be to grow faster than the developed economies, since there is a backlog of unexploited technical and organisational knowledge, but, if its steady-state growth rate is also low, this may not be true. It may be incapable of absorbing the pool of unexploited knowledge or to make the appropriate savings. An acceleration in the rate of economic growth may depend on an eventual increase in the steady-state growth rate particular to this economy. This path may change over time, not always in the direction of the rate of the most developed economy, since there are sometimes growth disasters. It is possible for the equilibrium steady-state growth path of an economy to decline because savings may fall and the capacity to absorb foreign innovations deteriorate. On the other hand, a growth episode may result in a rise in the steady-state growth rate since, in normal circumstances, as the income level rises, the savings ratio will rise and the ability of a developing country to access outside technological knowledge will improve. It is possible that the steady state evolves over time as its determinants and their relationship change, so that there is really no stable steady-state path. The relevant economy may be forever chasing an equilibrium growth path which never actually exists.[18]

Are individual equilibrium paths likely to converge on a common path? Over the longer term, developing countries are likely to change their institutions and policies significantly in the transition, modifying these equilibrium paths at various intervals, albeit infrequently (C.I. Jones 1997: 19). The growth path should move in the direction of the steady-state equilibrium growth path of the developed world. This is true if there is some process of selection of appropriate institutions and policies, and a main determinant of the equilibrium path is government policy. Governments at low income levels can experiment with such policies (Kremer, Onatski and Stock 2001: 35). This view sees economic development largely as a search process; '. . . society is gradually discovering the kind of institutions and polices that are conducive to successful economic performance, and these discoveries are gradually diffusing around the world' (ibid.: 23). Neoclassical economics has a clear view of what those institutions and policies might be. Jones admits that prediction of institutional change requires detailed knowledge of the relevant country and its history. On this argument, each country has its own equilibrium path, which may change. For the concept to have validity and to be useful, such changes should be rare. Making the determination of the relevant variables endogenous, that is, varying with the growth of the economy, makes the definition of an equilibrium rate difficult. Each economy has its own history of transition to a self-sustained growth path. During the transition, an economy converges on its own long-term steady-state growth path – this is called conditional convergence in the literature.

Conceptually, it is possible to identify three relevant growth rates: an extremely volatile short-term rate, particularly volatile for developing countries, since it reflects the short-term vicissitudes of an economy, such as the business cycle or shocks; a medium-term rate, which is the transitional rate, persistent over decades; and a long-term rate, the equilibrium steady-state rate, which may differ from country to country and from time period to time period, and to which in some sense an economy is converging. Such a distinction assists in understanding the inception of modern economic development.

Conditional convergence on individual growth paths means not only that the transitional growth path is different, but also the equilibrium growth path particular to a country. The steady-state growth path differs from that of other countries because of the differences in Solow's structural factors. The steady-state rate of a country with low savings and with a limited ability to source technology is itself low. The slower rate operates mainly through the level of m relevant to a particular country. Fortunately, there may be groups of countries which converge on the same equilibrium steady-state rate of growth and in a similar manner. Groups of countries with similar characteristics may share rates. The shared features include regional location, similar geographical context, similar historical background, including the identity of the colonising power or a communist background, and similar cultural or institutional backgrounds. Such groups are called convergence clubs, groups of countries with similar initial conditions and structural features and a similar steady-state rate of growth. It is interesting to ask how many convergence clubs there are and what characteristics such clubs are likely to share. This is equivalent to asking whether there are different patterns of economic growth which can be identified (an issue dealt with in Chapter 12).

The notion of convergence indicates that there is in neoclassical economics a strong assumption that, once having started, wherever in the world this happens, modern economic development diffuses throughout the world. The meaning of convergence for neoclassical economists is that 'Initial conditions: – the history of a country and the existing endowment and distribution of factors of production at each point in time – weigh a lot on the subsequent growth path, at least for some time. Growth regressions invariably confirm that there is an "error-correction" process that takes economies towards their long-run growth paths when there are deviations from the path due to shocks and shifts in the underlying conditions' (Castanheira and Esfahani 2003: 181). Only the actual existence of convergence to an equilibrium growth path can confirm this view of the world; this is dealt with in the next chapter.

3. The optimist's view: convergence

... the rule of growth in developing countries is that anything can happen and often does. The instability of growth rates makes talk of the growth rate almost meaningless. (Pritchett 2000)

In the simplest neoclassical model, all economies should be converging on a single developed state, with a high level of capital per head and self-sustaining economic growth at a rate reflecting the growth of the pool of technical and organizational knowledge available in the world. Such an expectation of convergence in income levels reflects an optimistic view of the future universality of economic development; all countries will eventually develop economically. Convergence is a short-hand for the spread of modern economic development. In other words, all countries will become developed and follow the pattern of the most developed economy, at the present the USA. Such a viewpoint accords with the optimism of the liberal perspective, which argues that, freed to make unconstrained choices, individuals tend to make rational choices which optimise their situation. In this case, it is strongly argued that they lead to economic development. Most textbooks contain powerful arguments that free untrammelled markets lead to economic success at both micro and macro levels.[1] This implication of convergence needs to be tested and the theory adjusted, if the real world does not show such convergence. A critical question to be asked at this stage is the empirical one: does any change in the economic condition of the world in the recent past accord with this anticipation of neoclassical economic growth theory?

There are four sections in this chapter. The first considers the nature of convergence. The second considers the difference between absolute and conditional convergence and what analysis of the relevant empirical data shows. The third section considers the argument that there are convergence clubs, in particular two, one distinguished by a lack of economic development and one by its presence. It considers the reasons why such convergence clubs might exist. The final section looks at an alternative conception of convergence, that relating to the world distribution of income, both between countries and between the individuals in all countries.

THE MEANINGS OF CONVERGENCE

Convergence means many different things (Islam 2003: 312). In general terms, it is the tendency for the aggregate levels of output per head in different countries to move together, in the extreme case for all to move to one common level. There is a convergence in levels. More often the convergence is taken as convergence of growth rates, sometimes of the rate of growth of total factor productivity. In the simplest models, there is a monotonic but inverse relationship between output or capital per head and the rate of economic growth. In the relevant literature, there are three different types of convergence – absolute, conditional and club convergence. Absolute convergence occurs when all countries converge on the same steady-state equilibrium rate of economic growth, independently of the initial conditions which characterise the economy, in particular the starting level of output per head. By contrast, conditional convergence exists when the 'structural' characteristics of economies differ and all countries converge on their own steady-state equilibrium growth paths. The theory assumes some persistence in these structural characteristics; otherwise there would not be differing steady state rates. More realistically, it might be anticipated that countries with similar characteristics will converge on the same growth path, so that there is a finite number of equilibrium growth paths. Club convergence occurs when countries with similar structural characteristics and initial conditions converge on the same growth path. How many convergence clubs there are is an empirical matter, but it is necessary first to explore theoretically the basis for the existence of such multiple equilibria. There is a tendency to consider two equilibria, one characterised by a lack of economic development and the other a state of significant economic development.

It is an empirical matter whether convergence is actually occurring, today or in any previous time period. A superficial review of the state of the world suggests not. A casual glance at either levels of output per head in different countries or the growth rates of the recent past disinclines the observer to accept the notion of convergence; indeed divergence seems much more likely. The world is characterised by very significant differences in the level of economic development and in the rates of economic growth. Some developing countries, notably in East and South Asia, are growing very fast and appear to be catching up with the developed world. Others have had significant periods of contraction, notably the countries of sub-Saharan Africa. Still others, such as those in Latin America, seem to have a very uneven performance. There appear to be only a few countries which are sustaining rates of economic growth sufficiently rapid to allow a significant convergence. In some cases, apparent success is rudely interrupted by a major setback. Latin America has a history of such reversals.[2] The former Soviet Union saw a major interruption to its economic growth in the 1990s.

Lucas (2000) has pointed out that a rise in world inequality is not incompatible with eventual convergence. There is inevitably a significant degree of apparent divergence inherent in the experience of modern economic development itself, resulting from the delays in its inception in many countries. Since modern economic development does not occur instantaneously in all countries, this is unavoidable. The long-drawn-out process of entry of countries into the group of developed countries, means that initially there must be an increase in inequality between countries. When there are few developed economies and the process of modern economic development is unusual, there may be an apparent divergence, which will reverse itself when sufficient countries experience the inception of modern economic development. The success of some and the temporary failure of most is bound to cause an apparent initial divergence. Until 50 per cent of the countries are members of the upper convergence club, inequality increases, which helps to explain the significant rise in inequality up to World War II. The average rate of economic growth in the world also accelerates during this first phase and then declines once the 50 per cent point is reached. A two-phase process is inherent in the graduated nature of the inception of modern economic development.

ABSOLUTE CONVERGENCE – NO, CONDITIONAL CONVERGENCE – YES!

For all economies, there is the prospect of an individual transition from a state of undevelopment to one of development. What is unclear is the nature of this transition. There may be a transition from the initial state to the developed state, involving movement through various temporary equilibrium states. The intermediate states, even the final state, may not be the equilibrium steady-state rate of economic growth of the most developed economy. During the transition, there may not be convergence in an absolute sense, rather periods of conditional convergence. Whether there is absolute convergence depends on the behaviour of individual equilibrium steady-state growth rates. Periodically, there may be absolute convergence between groups of countries sharing certain characteristics such as their initial level of development, notably but not only the group of developed economies. There may even be absolute convergence of regions within countries which share structural characteristics – similar culture, institutions, attitudes and policies.

Neoclassical economists have strong theoretical arguments in favour of absolute convergence, since rational decisions made in the relevant market transactions lead to convergence. The market for ideas, the source of innovation, is the relevant market. The diffusion of ideas is supported by rapid communication. One aspect of the communications revolution in a global world is that the flow of ideas is much faster, so that any innovation is quickly visible to all and quickly imitated.[3] This underpins the assumption of a common technology. Even if economies are closed to the entry of foreign commodities or factors of production, provided there is a free flow of ideas, and no obstacle to the adoption and application of such ideas, convergence to a common rate of growth is likely. Allowing the free movement of commodities and factors of production strengthens the tendency to convergence. Opening an economy to the free flow of commodities, with the resulting emergence of comparative advantage and the equalisation of factor returns, will, through the associated demonstration effects, reinforce the flow of ideas, in this case embodied in new products and services, and at the same time tend to equalise the level of income for all factors of production, a process equivalent to the spread of economic development – in this case through trade. Opening an economy to the free flow of capital and labour reinforces convergence. Capital flows to where it is scarce and where its return is highest, by assumption in developing countries. Labour does the same, but this time the flow is from developing to developed economies. The outcome is to equalise factor returns. Capital, in the form of FDI (foreign direct investment), embodies innovations and new ideas. FDI inflows are associated with a package of inputs, including technical knowledge and entrepreneurial know-how. The flow of FDI directly reinforces the flow of ideas and innovations.

In a neoclassical world, convergence occurs, driven by these mechanisms. Market integration and income convergence go together. The neoclassical theory of economic growth has underlying it the optimistic perspective of liberalism, notably on why the removal of barriers and the attainment of free trade and the free movement of factors are good for the world. It applies to a world in which markets are integrated and are efficient, that is, embody in prices all available information. It is a world with insignificant transactions costs and without institutional frictions. Left to their own devices, individuals will make good choices, which result in universal economic development. In such a world, economic development is inevitable, not exceptional, despite the present restriction of economic development to a small number of countries. Universal modern economic development becomes a matter of time.

Efficient markets have not always existed or been as they are today. In the words of Nelson and Wright (1992: 1933), '. . . just as markets and business have become more global, the network of individuals and organizations generating and improving new science-based technologies have become less national and more trans-national, so that convergence reflects a diminution of the saliency of nation-states as technological and economic entities'. Those features of openness which are related to and encouraged by globalisation promote convergence. Yet work by Milanovic (2003: 26) shows a persistent tendency for convergence to occur between developed economies, even during the Great Depression of the interwar years when markets were relatively closed, but convergence occurs because of cultural, rather than market, integration (ibid.: 28). Technological transfers occur, via books, private exchange of information, personal and business travel, irrespective of whether there is a lot of trade or investment between the relevant countries. Face-to-face contact is often critical to technical borrowing. The only shock which seriously interrupts this process of convergence among developed economies is war.

That there are such mechanisms is strongly argued by economic theory, that they operate in practice is more contentious. We can ask, is there evidence that these mechanisms are powerful enough to make the spread of modern economic development inevitable, and is this shown by empirical data? In the end, whether convergence is happening is an empirical matter. A second question is relevant: if convergence is a valid process, over what period of time will it occur? This is determined by the rate of convergence. How long does the undeveloped world have to wait to share the benefits of development? Unfortunately, the answer is often a very long period of time indeed. There is a desire to see convergence confirmed by the empirical data and to see it occurring within a relatively short time span. Temin identifies the transition in the USA as a growth traverse during the period after the Civil War, when the rate of capital accumulation rose (Temin 1997: 72–4). The transition lasted less than half a century, a long period of time relative to human longevity. The theory indicates transitions which are much longer. If a transition may take as long as a century and a half, the initial background conditions will have changed out of sight (Harley 2003: 812). Some commentators see the transition as much longer even than this (Kremer, Onatski and Stock 2001: 39).

If each country has a different equilibrium growth path, convergence may be on to that path. Conditional convergence occurs if there is convergence on the individual steady-state growth paths specific to individual countries. This is a pessimistic view of the world, in which structural conditions determine a decidedly limited potential for economic development in certain countries. In neoclassical theory, the steady-state level of income of a particular country and the rate of economic growth depend on a whole swathe of structural factors. It is usual to distinguish between factors which are integral to the Solow model and others introduced later.[4] The former include starting levels, both of capital per head and of productivity, of the savings ratio, of rate of growth of productivity and the rate of growth of population and, if we relax the assumption of a common production function, even the shares of income going to capital or labour. Since these elements may differ, different equilibrium growth paths are associated with different amounts of capital per head and different levels of income. There may be many other variables not included in the Solow model which influence such a rate of growth, a point considered later. The focus of interest then shifts to the issue of which elements differ and why (Islam 2003: 315). Not surprisingly differences in technological level turn out to be important in convergence studies: not unsurprisingly, if they are excluded from the estimate, there is a much greater chance of convergence. This causes some commentators to turn to the problem of a convergence in levels of factor productivity or its growth.

Testing for convergence can take many different forms (Islam 2003). In that testing, the workhorse of regression equations is most easily understood in the following simple form:

$$r_i = \beta \log y + \psi X + \pi Z + \varepsilon_i$$

Where r is the growth rate of output in country i and y the initial level of output in that country. X are the Solow factors, including the rates of growth of population, of technical change and of depreciation, which are seen as together determining the steady-state rate of growth. Z are any other variables which the commentator wishes to include but are not included in the neoclassical model, which influence such factors as the rate of take-up of new technical knowledge. They may include geographical, institutional or policy elements, what in the next chapter are included under the heading of ultimate causative factors. There is some resistance to including such factors since it moves the analysis further away from the original Solow model. ε is an error term for country i.

Convergence occurs if β has a negative value. The speed of convergence will depend on the size of β. Implicit in the usual neoclassical models, using a Cobb-Douglas production function, is a speed of about 4 per cent per year. Commonly, income per capita is seen in empirical studies as converging to its long-term value at a much slower rate, at about 2 per cent per annum; this means about 2 per cent of the initial gap between income per head and its long-term value is closed every year – a very slow transition (Barro and Sala-i-Martin 1992, Mankiw, Romer and Weil 1992). Other researchers claim to have found faster rates of convergence – 6 per cent (Islam 1995) and 10 per cent (Caselli, Esquivel and Lefort 1996). On the other hand, there is an empirical tendency to exaggerate convergence by overestimating β, because a tendency to underestimate starting output or income is usually associated with a tendency to exaggerate the rate of growth, and vice versa. Data problems lead to this bias. A slow rate of convergence throws considerable doubt on what a steady-state equilibrium growth path, attained so far in the future, might mean.

In his original study on convergence, Baumol (1986) claimed to have found unconditional convergence over the period 1870–1979 among a set of 16 developed countries. There were two problems with this argument. The first is that the convergence only occurs after 1950, not before. Before that date, for the rather longer period between 1870 and 1950, there is divergence (Abramovitz 1986). The second problem follows from the deficiencies in the original data source of Maddison (1991). Baumol et al. (2007: 45–7) acknowledges that Maddison's original data were formed by backward extrapolation, which meant that convergence was self-confirming and that USA assistance after World War II to many of the relevant countries tended to reinforce convergence. De Long (1988) pointed out that the sample of countries analysed is one self-selected for success and therefore for convergence. Only the successful have the statistical data needed for analysis. The empirical data from the Heston, Summers and Aten set show that absolute convergence does not exist for the population of all countries in the world. A graph of growth over the period 1980–2000 against initial GDP per head, in the words of Baumol et al. (2007: 47–8), 'clearly fails to support the convergence conjecture' and, if anything, shows that rich countries tend to grow faster than poor countries. Convergence might exist for small groups of developed countries or regionally within developed economies, in other words in countries or regions which share structural features – the salient economic, social and political characteristics. Baumol (2007: 46–7) detected such convergence across groups. Studies following the Baumol study have shown that there is such convergence for a lesser universe – for example, for the group of developed OECD countries, but at a lower level also for the states within the USA, or within Australia and New Zealand, for prefectures within Japan, for provinces within Canada and for regions within Europe and India, for counties within Sweden. The results for India are controversial. It is highly likely that economies which share characteristics will display convergence. The commonalities in the relevant countries make the convergence unsurprising. There is no convergence for more heterogeneous groups, such as all countries in the world.

Given a world of absolute divergence, there is a need to rescue the theory and this is done by redefining convergence as conditional rather than absolute convergence. It is strongly argued by many that there is conditional convergence, that is, output per head converges if allowance is made for other factors which have an important influence on growth rates. If we remove their influence, there is convergence. It is said that the finding of conditional β-convergence has remained relatively robust (Islam 2003: 341), since countries show a tendency to move towards their own steady-state growth path, which might be rather low.

CLUB CONVERGENCE

There may exist distinct groups of countries with separate steady states to which they are converging or transitional paths to one steady-state path which differ from group to group (Bernard 2001, Quah 2000). Certain equilibrium or transitional paths may be shared by a small group of countries, a 'convergence club'. If conditional rather than absolute convergence prevails, such clubs differ according to their levels of income per head, their implied equilibrium rates of growth and the determinants of these rates. The simplest picture sees the number of such attractors as limited to two, a high-level and a low-level attractor. The neoclassical arguments in favour of convergence to a high level have been put, but the high-level equilibrium is an attractor only for some. In each generation, some economies converge on the high-level equilibrium. It is possible to classify the group of developed economies according to the nature of their transition to the long-term equilibrium path, including its timing. Those which have failed to converge can be grouped together, but there are significant differences within this group. Conditional convergence recognises specific equilibrium paths, which differ according to such factors as the savings rate or the rate of assimilation of new technology. Recently, much more attention has been paid to the low-level equilibrium, why a decisive break-out from the low-level equilibrium is unlikely.

Discussion of convergence clubs often starts with the empirical data. Unfortunately, it is focused on the short term. Using the improved statistics of GDP and economic growth which relate to the period since 1960, Bernard (2001: 16–18) considered the nature of such groups. He suggests three putative convergence clubs, whose membership depends on whether the underlying characteristics of the economy place it at the upper equilibrium level, the lower equilibrium level or somewhere in between.[5] Collier (2007) supports such a division, seeing the world as divided into one billion rich people, another billion poor, and four billions moving from the latter to the former status. Bernard begins with tentative upper and lower bounds for the steady–state rate of 0 per cent and 5 per cent, but suggests that the upper bound is in practice rather lower than the latter figure – as low as somewhere between 1 and 3 per cent, that is, at the rate of the long-term average growth of productivity per head. Two per cent can serve as a tentative upper bound, as the long-run growth rate of the USA suggests. Once at the upper threshold, the steady-state rate of growth has attained its theoretical maximum, since further improvement in fundamentals cannot raise the rate. The lower bound speaks for itself – it is zero growth. At the lower threshold, with a particularly bad set of fundamentals, the growth is zero or close to it. Negative rates are due to transitory factors; they do not last beyond a short period. For both these clubs, change in the fundamentals do not induce a response from growth rates. Between the thresholds, the growth rate responds to how advantageous the fundamentals are.

The big question asked by Bernard, and explored in much more detail by Quah, is whether most countries fall within this third group with intermediate fundamentals or whether they have already segregated themselves into the two groups characterized by minimum and maximum development – Quah's twin peaks or a bi-modal distribution of cross-country output per head. Analysis of levels of output per head tend to emphasise two groups, a cluster around a high level of income per head and one around a low level, roughly in the way discussed by Bernard. There is a considerable literature arguing for 'twin peakedness', or in the language of the mathematician, the existence of two basins of attraction. One study (Bloom, Canning and Sevilla 2003: 366) places 85 per cent of the countries in the low-level club and 15 per cent in the high-level club, although the standard deviation is much larger in the first group than the second. Quah (1996) has shown both persistence in the ranking of countries and a growing 'twin-peakedness' or bi-modality of the distribution of income. There is a growing literature confirming that the distribution of countries by output per head is bi-modal: the coexistence of a rich mode and a poor mode. The data of Bourguignon and Morrisson (2002: Table 5, 740) are argued to support the 'twin peaks effect'. Countries which are identical in their structural characteristics – preferences, including savings, technologies, rates of population growth, government policies, and in their initial conditions – will converge on the same equilibrium growth path. There is clustering at the two extremes with the existence of persistent poverty,[6] and an asymmetry in so far as countries entering the top income group do not move down from that group, whereas for the bottom group there is movement both up and down (Kremer, Onatski and Stock 2001: 5). Since there are no reversals, projections forward of trends in the distribution see the vast majority of countries eventually entering the top group, although the transition may take a long time. At some point in the future, the distribution may become uni-modal, but this is a long time in the achieving.[7]

There is a major criticism of this kind of approach. If we regard the identification of the individual long-run equilibrium growth rates as an empirical matter, it is hard to isolate a steady-state growth path for particular developing countries. Since each is in a transitional state moving towards a long-term equilibrium position, it is not easy to read from the data what that target rate is. Add short-term shocks, both positive and negative, and their influence on actual growth rates and the problem is compounded. Fluctuations in short-term growth rates often conceal the transition and long-term equilibrium target rates. Pritchett (2000) emphasises the tendency to underestimate the importance of volatility in growth rates, especially for developing countries. He gives a highly relevant example, asking a pertinent question. 'Between 1960 and 1980 Cote d'Ivoire grew at 3.1%, an African growth miracle, while between 1980 and 1992 its gross domestic product (GDP) per capita fell 4.1% a year, a growth disaster. Ignoring this break, average growth was 0.225%. Nearby Senegal stagnated throughout the same period, with stable growth of 0.18%. In what relevant sense are these two growth experiences the same?' (Pritchett 2000: 222). As Pritchett later shows, the evolution of GDP per capita in each of the developing countries is not well characterized by a single exponential trend (Pritchett 2000: 227), since for individual countries there is little correlation in growth rates across time periods. Easterly (2006: 38–41), using Maddison's data, points out an empirical problem for the assertion of a single low-level equilibrium trap. While for sub-periods from 1950 to 2001 the poorest one-fifth of countries have per capita growth rates lower than all the other countries (after 1980, the growth rate is not significantly different from zero), for the period as a whole this is not true, since the country composition of the poorest fifth changes significantly. Some poor performers are converging from above, falling back from a temporary acceleration in growth rate. Easterly argues that the failure of the lowest fifth to grow much slower than the rest and the positive nature of growth of the group as a whole belies the existence of a single low-level trap. This is probably true, but the key issues are the time period over which the analysis holds. Eventually, many economies fall back to the low-level equilibrium, but a significant number of countries escape from the trap.

The complexity of the situation is reinforced by the empirical data. Pritchett makes much of a structural break dividing the period from 1960 into two. Pritchett, reflecting the true variety of performance, divides the countries into six groups (clubs?) according to their growth rate before and after that year. First, those countries which sustain a growth rate of real GDP per head of 3 per cent before and after he calls 'steep hills', and secondly, those who sustain 1.5 per cent just 'hills' and thirdly, those with a growth rate in both periods of less than 1.5 per cent as 'plains'. At least these groups show a consistency of performance. On the other hand, a fourth group, those who decelerate from above to below 1.5 per cent, he calls 'plateaus'; fifthly, if the rate deteriorates to below zero he calls them 'mountains'. Sixthly, and finally, the small group which moves from below to above 1.5 per cent he calls 'accelerators'. Developed countries are nearly all hills, or in some cases steep hills. These represent what might be the long-term equilibrium growth rate, if there is just one. Most developing countries outside Asia are mountains, which suggests some reversion to a low-level equilibrium position. However. there is a significant membership in each of the six groups.

It is not so much a matter of different steady state-rates but rather of different degrees and types of instability.[8] For developing countries, instability rules. In the short run, those economies which are not developed appear to be tossed around by chance events. The volatility creates a lot of noise, making it difficult to recognize any underlying rate of advance. There are both positive and negative shocks. The rapid economic development of developed economies is a positive shock, the oil price hikes of the 1970s a negative shock. This short-term volatility partly explains Bernard's desire for an emphasis on differences in the long-term equilibrium rate, and Easterly's denial of a single poverty trap. Bernard sees a need for disentangling transitory elements from long-run movements, and he deplores the over-emphasis on the transitional phase during convergence. In his words, 'The observed heterogeneity of estimated long run growth rates across countries is substantial, although smaller than the variation in output growth rates themselves' (Bernard 2001: 20). Clearly Easterly agrees. The divergence in steady-state growth paths should be the main focus of attention, as should the heterogeneity in the levels of steady-state output per head. Bernard believes both are positively related to measures of initial human capital, but there are other factors which are influential, as the next section shows. In this context, Rodrik's (2007: 35–44) suggestion that it is easy to ignite growth, but difficult to sustain it, is highly relevant. Most developing economies did not sustain growth beyond the oil price hikes of the 1970s. An analysis of longer trends is desirable but difficult, because of the weakness of the statistics.

Despite Pritchett's skepticism, there are persuasive theoretical arguments for convergence of economies in the club of the poor. This issue has been raised under different headings, such as coordination problems (Hoff 2000) or poverty traps (Azariadis and Stachurski 2004). The discussion on coordination problems goes back to a Rosenstein-Rodan article in 1943, which used their existence to justify an active role of the government in coordinating economic development. He saw pecuniary external economies as occurring as a result of simultaneous investment in related sectors of the economy. Development does not occur unless the relevant investments are coordinated; this amounts to a boot-straps argument. Made together, the investments are justified by the returns achieved on individual projects: made individually, the returns do not justify the investment. The focus today is on sectoral or technological complementarities of various sorts (Galor 1996).

Recent work broadens the problem of externalities or spillovers, including aggregate demand spillovers, well beyond the exceptional examples given in the old textbooks (see Hoff 2000: 15, table). It was believed that externalities were hard to find in the real world (Hoff 2000: 13), limited to beekeepers, apple farmers and polluting factories, and the associated public goods, for which the exclusion principle at the core of market activity is infeasible, were limited to exceptional products and services, such as those of a lighthouse and defence. These were seen as marginal in their effect on general equilibrium models of the neoclassical type. Market failure was a rare phenomenon, largely to be ignored. The situation is now perceived differently. The relevant externalities include all sorts of pecuniary externalities arising from a host of different conditions – the enforcement of property rights, informational spillovers, ownership structures and the demand effects of non-tradeables produced with increasing returns, as well as knowledge spillovers, expectations interactions, externalities in contract enforcement, search externalities and those resulting from social and political interactions. Public goods have been expanded to include equilibrium sets of prices, group reputations and knowledge – in particular, that a certain technological result is feasible. They are now considered to be everywhere. In the words of Hoff, 'Whereas we used to believe that the implication of externalities was that the economy would be slightly distorted, we now understand the interaction of these slight distortions may produce very large distortions' (Hoff 2000: 46). The important factors are not just those referred to above, but also a wide range of economic and cultural elements – various features of human capital formation, including increasing social returns to scale, capital market imperfections, parental and local effects, imperfect information and a non-convex production function of human capital; differing distributions of income, with their effects on savings rates; and endogeneity of fertility rates, that is, the dependence of birth rates on income levels. All of these prevent the free market of the neoclassical model operating to cause convergence.

There is also a growing literature on poverty trap(s). Such a trap can be defined as 'any self-reinforcing mechanism which causes poverty to persist' (Azariadis and Stachurski 2004: 33). It is not difficult to construct poverty traps from the elements described above. The classic trap is the Malthusian one, discussed at length in Chapter 12, sometimes referred to as a demographic poverty trap. Collier (2007) discusses four other traps – the conflict trap (discussed in Chapter 6), the natural resource trap (discussed in Chapter 5), the 'landlocked with bad neighbours trap' and the bad governance in a small country trap. Such traps are seen as taking widely different forms – history-driven poverty traps, a technology trap in which undeveloped economies fail to capture increasing returns, an impatience trap in which low personal savings and high consumption constitutes a problem, a low-skills trap (Easterly 2006: 41), and a globalisation poverty trap, in which increasing global competition creates barriers to economic advance. In particular cases, such traps can coexist and reinforce each other. It may be easy to break out of the trap, but difficult for an economy to sustain the break-out. For example, at low levels of income savings ratios are likely to be low, so much so that in some cases the capital stock actually diminishes, since the rate of depreciation of capital exceeds the savings rate, causing the long-term rate of growth to be slow, even zero or negative. There are numerous such negative feedback loops.

In these circumstances it is not difficult to justify the existence of low-level equilibrium traps out of which rational decisions by individuals make it unlikely that the economy will move. The existence of significant externalities and their interaction helps define alternative equilibria, some decidedly inferior to others. Economies similar in their structural characteristics have multiple equilibria if they differ in the factors indicated. There may even be a bunching of such traps at similar levels of income per head. Different countries share long-run equilibrium growth rates, reflected in multiple stable growth equilibria, in that there is a tendency for economies in the neighbourhood to converge on these equilibrium paths. Such rates become attractors and other rates are only temporary. In such a world, history matters and initial conditions largely determine which equilibrium is relevant to a particular country. Initial conditions continue to have a persisting influence on the economy, so that any improvements in output per head are usually short-lived, although short-lived may be a matter of decades, not years. The initial conditions usually result in negative feedback mechanisms becoming operative quickly. Lower-level equilibrium traps are stable in that movement away from the trap usually results in a return, although not necessarily immediately. The existence of such traps does not preclude growth episodes, but often growth episodes end quickly.

There is not necessarily an incompatibility with neoclassical economics in so far as such models allow for various effects which yield multiple equilibria (Galor 1996: 1996). The existence of such traps creates a new problem – the indication of how an economy can escape from such a trap. Clearly, a movement out of the low-level equilibrium is not impossible, otherwise there would be never any development, but escape is rare. The mode of exit reflects the nature of the trap. The inception of modern economic development means that an escape has been successfully implemented. Sometimes scale effects are used to explain the disappearance of the low-level trap, but this is to over-simplify the situation and to give escape an inevitability it does not appear to have.

Clearly, what determines the membership of any club is a commonality of fundamental determinants of the rate of economic growth. A study by Feyrer (2003) has confirmed differences in the productivity residual, rather than capital accumulation, as the main determinant of membership, in other words, the ability to assimilate foreign technology. The analysis does not take us far since potentially there are so many determinants of the productivity level. It is easy to regress the residual, A, the technical level of an economy and its change over time, on a host of variables, the fundamentals which cause the economy to operate at varying points within the world production possibilities frontier – such as the level of income inequality, political or economic stability, democracy, property rights regimes, climate, geography, openness of the economy, financial depth, ethno-linguistic fractionalization – in other words, a veritable hotch-potch of long-term and short-term factors, many of which were not envisaged as important in the original neoclassical model.

THE WORLD DISTRIBUTION OF INCOME

A second way of measuring convergence is to look for what is called σ-convergence (as compared with β-convergence), which is defined as a reduction in the level of international inequality. There are three possible concepts of world inequality, which focus on different aspects of the distribution of income (Milanovic 2005: chapter 1). The first considers the level of unweighted inequality between countries: it focuses on average GDP per head in each country, giving an equal weight to each. The second considers population-weighted international inequality, giving a weight to countries which reflects their population size. The third is the true inequality, in which the GDP of every individual is considered (Bhalla 2002). Such inequality is estimated on the basis of a worldwide random sample of household incomes. It is much more difficult to estimate within-country inequality.

From the perspective of neoclassical theory, the first is relevant, since it takes account of the different conditions and different policies in the countries of the world. It tells us whether the institutions and policies considered appropriate to promote economic development by neoclassical economists are bringing about convergence, as they are expected to do. From the point of view of the welfare of individuals, the third is relevant. It tells us about the real amount of poverty. The second concept is an approximation of the third. There is no reason why the level of inequality estimated according to the different concepts should be the same, nor that over time it should move in a common direction. It is possible for β-convergence to occur but for σ-convergence not to occur. There is quite a literature which points this out, based on what is called Galton's fallacy (Friedman 1992, Quah 1996).[9] This means that despite a tendency for countries to converge, even in an absolute sense, the distribution of world income between countries may become more uneven, although the reverse is not true – if the latter occurs, the former is bound to occur.

There is disagreement over how to measure the exact levels of inequality – it depends on what you use as an indicator to measure that inequality. A simple method is to ask whether the standard deviation of the cross-country income distribution (or variance – the square of the standard deviation, or the coefficient of variation) has declined. If it has, there is convergence. The variance in GDP has its weaknesses as a measure. There are a number of alternatives, including the Gini coefficient, the Theil index or even the changing position of different quartiles or quintiles in various populations. All the methods have been used. The indicators do not always give the same answer.

The world income distribution between individuals reflects both within-country distribution and between-country distribution. Between-country distribution gives equal weight to countries as disparate in population size as China and Singapore, India and Slovenia, but has been the basis for measurement until recently. Helpman (2004: 90), using the statistics of Bourguignon and Morrisson (2002, table 2, 734), has shown that within-country inequality has steadily declined as a source of overall inequality, moving from accounting for close to 90 per cent of the total inequality in 1820, down to just over 60 per cent in 1910 and just 40 per cent in 1950, at which point it roughly stabilised for the period through to the present. It is the rise in between-country inequality which explains most of the movement in overall inequality during the last two centuries. This led Bourguignon and Morrisson (2002: 733) to conclude: 'Differences in country economic growth rates practically explain all of the increase in world inequality . . .'.

If we consider variations in income distribution between countries, as measured by Gini coefficients, the most commonly used measure, the differences are much larger than those which occur over time within countries (Li, Squire and Zou 1998: 26). The latter changes are very small, with the income distributions influenced by structural features which are relatively stable, but clearly different in different countries. There are some exceptions, for example China, but even for China, the impact of growth rates outweigh changes in the within-country income inequality; however, there has been a worsening of income distribution since the inception of reform in 1978. The clear implication is that the variations in income distribution within countries are not being reduced, at least over the period since World War II, for which there are good statistics. Even taking into account between-country movements, the mobility of individuals between income groups is, according to Bourguignon and Morrisson (2002: 739–40), extremely low, although it increased over time.

Bourguignon and Morrisson (2002: table 1) have synthesised a mass of information over a long period of time, from 1820 to 1992. The pattern is for the most part unambiguous. World inequality became worse quickly and more or less continuously from 1820 to 1950, with the exception of the period 1910 to 1929. The worsening then decelerated, with some improvement in the 1950s and probable stability between 1970 and 1992. The standard deviation rose from 0.826 in 1820 to 1.027 in 1910, and then to 1.154 before it stabilized, but with some increase. Acemoglu has extended the analysis. Since World War II, the world income distribution has been relatively stable, with a slight tendency towards becoming more unequal. In the words of Acemoglu (2006: 9), 'There is certainly no narrowing of income gaps. Instead, there is a small but notable increase in the dispersion of incomes.' According to Acemoglu, the standard deviation of log income per capita in the world has increased from about 0.9 in 1960 to just under 1.2 in 2000. Over the past 130 years, there has been significant divergence – on this account, the standard deviation has doubled, moving from just over 0.6 in 1870 to 1.2 in 2000 (Acemoglu 2006: 13).

Put another way, the ratio of GDP per person in the fifth richest country to the GDP per person in the fifth poorest has risen from under 22 in 1960 to over 30 in 2000 – this avoids the influence of outliers. Pritchett, using historical data on about 50 countries over 200 years from Maddison, has indicated that the ratio of maximum to minimum income has gone from 6:1 to 70:1 today. The implications are clear. There is divergence, big time. As Easterly (2006: 43) asserts, 'There is a positive correlation between per capita growth from, say, 1820 to 2001 and the initial level of income in 1820', not a negative correlation, as neoclassical theories would suggest.

It is interesting to speculate as to whether a broader definition of welfare might change the picture. Critics of the impact of economic growth suggest that the statistics exaggerate a putative improvement in the standard of living. The opposite is likely to be the case. Increasing longevity would be regarded by most people as an improvement in the standard of living, since it is usually associated with improved health at a given age.

Data on inequality in life expectation show a significant equalisation from 1930, which, on any reasonable weighting compared with income movements, show a reversal of growing inequality after 1945, but the influence of this is declining, with little further scope for a push in the direction of convergence (Bourgignon and Morrisson 2002: 741–2).

The main forces explaining this movement towards greater inequality, particularly in the period up to 1950, can be summarised by two tendencies – the slow economic growth of Asia, notably China and India, in the early period, contrasted with the rapid growth of Europe and its offshoots. The forces making for a growing inequality were increasingly offset over time by a more even income distribution both within and between developed economies, particularly Europe and its offshoots, and also, more recently, by the acceleration in the growth performance of Asia. Africa then became the major influence promoting inequality.

Any aggregate change in income distribution can be viewed as the result of a complex interaction between the internal distribution of income in particular countries, the differing average rates of growth of per capita income, themselves reflecting the growth in both total income and in population within those countries, and the relative size and rate of growth of population in different countries. If we consider the distribution of income at the individual level, the influence of the interaction between rates of growth and income distributions within countries is weighted by the size of the country. For example, China and India, with more than one-third of the world's population, have a much greater influence than they do when the level of analysis is the country.[10]

Asking whether there has been convergence is a different question from asking whether there has been an increase in poverty, or whether economic development has been good for the majority of the world's population. In the absence of any fundamental socio-political change, poverty reduction, that is reduction of the number of people with income levels below a key threshold figure, such as one or two dollars per day,[11] will depend crucially on the rate of economic growth, much more than on any changes in income inequality within countries, but most of all on the rate in the largest countries such as China and India. This is what prompted Bourguignon and Morrisson (2002: 733) to point out that '. . . world economic growth, though strongly inegalitarian, contributed to a steady decline in the head-count measure of poverty throughout the period under analysis', all 172 years. On their figures, the proportions of the world population, either poor or very poor, dropped from over 94 per cent and almost 84 per cent to just over 51 per cent and just under 24 per cent respectively, but the absolute numbers rose, with the numbers of very poor stabilizing between 1950 and 1992. The number of poor was 2.8 billion in 1992. More recent estimates have shown a decline in both figures, reflecting the acceleration of economic growth in China and India. Poverty is becoming an African rather than an Asian problem.

For a neoclassical economist, it is a major puzzle why very large income differences between countries persist in an age of the free flow of technology, of expanding trade and of financial integration (Acemoglu 2006: 17). A simple answer might be that there is no institutional and cultural convergence of different economies which would produce societies which satisfy the required first-order economic principles. In other words, the institutional structure is not frictionless – it is fixed in the short term. Convergence regionally within countries suggests that such a free flow and integration of markets can in appropriate circumstances have the anticipated effect of convergence. It is easy to understand the desire for optimism, the hope that there will be, at some time in the future, convergence of all countries to the position of the most developed. Reality belies the existence of unconditional convergence: indeed, it is likely that divergence is occurring; but for how long?

4. Introducing real time with a narrative

> The empirical study of economic growth occupies a position that is notably uneasy. . . . it is also one of the areas in which genuine progress seems hardest to achieve. The contributions of individual papers can often appear slender. Even when the study of growth is viewed in terms of a collective endeavour, the various papers cannot easily be distilled into a consensus that would meet standards of evidence routinely applied in other fields of economics. (Durlauf, Johnson and Temple 2004)

There is a need to broaden beyond a theory emphasising proximate causes. Any reasonable explanation of economic growth should consider ultimate factors, those factors which influence the contribution of proximate factors. This means moving beyond conventional neoclassical theory. The capacity of the neoclassical model to explain economic development is limited by its focus on proximate factors. There is a need to consider the full complexity of the development experience and the full range of causative factors in order to produce a persuasive explanation of modern economic development.

There are five sections in this chapter. The first identifies the main weaknesses of the neoclassical model, some arising from its failure to explain the behaviour of the real world, others more fundamental – behavioural assumptions whose validity is in doubt. The second section reviews the outcome of attempts to use regression analysis to identify the determinants of economic development and in particular to test neoclassical theory. The third section explores the distinction between proximate and ultimate causation. Two sub-sections indicate the nature of proximate and ultimate causes. The final section considers the usefulness of theory and narrative and introduces the notion of an analytical narrative.

PROBLEMS WITH THE ECONOMIST'S VIEW OF ECONOMIC DEVELOPMENT

Neoclassical economics deals with the modern growth regime in developed market economies, not with the pre-modern economy, nor the transition from the latter to the former (Galor 2004: 42). It is unfair to criticise the theory for failing to do what it was not designed to do. The present chapter aims to introduce material complementary with, rather than contradictory to, the existing theory and to build upon existing theory. The neoclassical approach to economic development has been developed in an elegant and sophisticated way, and increasingly tested against empirical data. The former development is much more persuasive in terms of the strength of the model's internal logic, than the latter testing, which has produced results showing that the model does not fit the real world.

There are two particular kinds of problem. The first kind reflects criticisms which do not constitute a total rejection of the model, but lead to its further development. Often they emerge from problems of calibration, the testing of the implications of the neoclassical model against empirical regularities in the real world (Mankiw 1995: 282). In this approach, a model is set out representing the main relationships. The aim is to estimate all the parameters in the model, thereby making possible its application to different times and places by the fitting of different experiences according to the value of known variables. The model is calibrated against the real world, or those parts of the real world given a quantitative expression. It has to fit the known variables and produce a realistic view of the evolution of such variables over time for any one economy. If the model is to have any persuasiveness, the predictions of the model should be consistent with what happens in the real world, although this lacks the rigour of a thorough statistical testing.

Mankiw (1995) indicates three areas of difficulty. The first is implicit in the analysis of the last chapter, that the basic neoclassical model fails to predict the large differences in income found in the real world. The simple model assumes that all countries have the same production function, a single map from total inputs to aggregate output that holds for every country (Azariadis and Stachurski 2003: 21). Given that each country has a steady-state growth path and level of income per head determined partly by its rate of savings and population growth and that in the real world such savings rates differ by a multiple of four and population rates by two percentage points, the largest income disparity thrown up by a neoclassical model based on a Cobb-Douglas production function is about two, whereas the real world disparity is more than ten. The second problem is that the model predicts a rate of convergence to a steady state twice that actually achieved, a convergence rate of 4 per cent, compared with a rate half that, 2 per cent. The transition to the equilibrium state takes much longer than predicted and the influence of initial conditions is felt for much longer than the model suggests. The third is that the differentials in rates of return predicted by the model are much larger than any observed in the real world. The return on capital in poor countries is predicted to be as much as 100 times the level in rich countries, if the usual Cobb-Douglas production function is used. The same kind of problem emerges if an attempt is made to explain the growth of the American or Japanese economies in terms of neoclassical capital accumulation (King and Rebelo 1993). Unrealistically high productivities of capital, and rates of return, are implied for early periods of modern economic development.

The critics continue to adjust the model to remove the anomalies. Sometimes such adjustments are marginal, leaving undisturbed the basic nature of the model. For example, the latter two calibration problems were dealt with by Mankiw, Romer and Weil (1992) by broadening the concept of capital to include investment in human capital within the production function. The level of capital accumulation is increased significantly. This version of the neoclassical growth model is known as the expanded version. Sometimes the redoing is radical, as in the incorporation of less than perfect competition in order to accommodate the monopoly elements introduced by deliberate innovation-creating activity. Much of the literature on endogenous economic growth represents an attempt to make a more realistic view of technical change compatible with the neoclassical theory, in the process allowing for less than perfect competition, and in so doing dealing with the first calibration problem, explaining the significant variations in income per head in different countries.

A further adjustment of the neoclassical model relates to the limits on what an aggregate growth model of the neoclassical kind can do. In the words of Temin, 'The economic history that results from their use [general equilibrium models] consequently views the economy as a single interacting entity, not as a series of disconnected activities' (Temin 1971: 74). A model which can successfully simulate the behaviour of a national economy is useful, but the gains from such analysis seem to be reaching their limit, at least for economies such as the UK and the USA. Such an approach cannot answer all the questions asked in this book. Harley (2003: 828) has pointed out that aggregate analysis acts as a starting point for disaggregated analysis by highlighting the underlying sources of difference in steady-state growth rates. Growth accounting can be applied to different sectors of the economy.

A second kind of criticism relates to problems which arise from the nature of neoclassical theory itself. There are two different problems. The first is a methodological one, raised with some persuasiveness by Krugman in his unpublished paper of 30 May, 2009, 'The fall and rise of development economics'. Krugman argues that tightly specified models have become the unique language of discourse in economic analysis, and that a rejection of that drive to rigour condemns development economics, or economic history, to the wilderness. There is a need 'to do violence to the richness and complexity of the real world in order to produce controlled, *silly* models that illustrate key concepts (Krugman 2009: 1).' Unless they are incorporated into such models, important qualitative insights are likely to be ten-day wonders. Accepting the need for the rigorous expression of an argument is not the same as accepting the range of assumptions concerning the economic world made in neoclassical economics. Rather it prompts the asking of the following question, does the model have relevance outside the operation of a free-market capitalist system, with something useful to say about the transition to such a system, including the introduction of free-market capitalism itself?

There are two methodological weaknesses of the model which prevent it yielding an adequate theory of economic development. First, it is essentially an exercise in comparative statics, rather than a study of dynamic processes, dealing with outcomes – usually equilibrium outcomes – rather than processes. The insufficiency of neoclassical theory is illustrated by the failure to consider real time and causation in a, if not the, major decision relevant to economic development, the investment decision. Neoclassical theory fails to address the investment decision. This omission follows from the method of approach. In a timeless world, investment always equals savings, and it is only necessary to explain savings decisions. In real time, through its frequency and quality, the investment decision drives the process of economic development; investment drives savings, not the reverse.[1] This was a central point of the Keynesian revolution in economic thinking and was incorporated, during the 1960s, in a whole series of neo-Keynesian growth models, notably by Robinson (1965).

Investment reflects the level of confidence and the degree of risk aversion in a specific economy. Keynes' animal spirits is a starting point, but investment is linked with innovation, and is promoted by a potential increase in demand or a reduction in the costs of production caused by technical change. Investment embodies technical change, its determination linked to the determination of the rate of productivity increase. Investment is necessary in order to realise that technical change. Investment occurs in linked growth projects which relate to the different stages in the development of a technology.[2] Little technical change is disembodied, except in the sense that after an initial investment, productivity improves through a process of learning by doing and observing. Implicit in any technique is an uncertain potential for productivity increase over a long period of time. During the lifetime of a technique, there is often concealed investment associated with the learning by doing and observing. The initial choice made in an investment decision is more than what is suggested in a conventional production function; it is a potential trajectory of revenues and costs, which cannot be fully known and increases in uncertainty the further into the future we look. There is a continuing learning process. The neoclassical conception of the variable, v, is misguided, in that it assumes technology to be a set of blueprints, both for individual products and particular sectors of the economy, even for the economy as a whole. The notion of a technique as a set of blueprints, rather than the embodiment of a unique learning experience, incorporated in the trajectories described, is an over-simplification. A choice once made often locks an economy into a particular technological paradigm, into an uncertain path of developing knowledge. Just because investment in a given technique is profitable in one country does not mean that it is in other countries. The trajectory of revenues and costs will be different, particularly where much of the relevant knowledge is tacit.

The second weakness is the focus on proximate, rather than ultimate, causation – neoclassical theory does not explain the prime movers of economic development, often appearing as a description of the characteristics of that development rather than a genuine analysis of causation. There are deeper methodological problems. The attempt to compare across countries is based on a set of assumptions about the nature of the world and its decision making, which stress a homogeneity of the economic growth process. This is to put the cart before the horse, to assume something which requires investigation. The economic growth process is the same wherever and whenever it occurs, the only difference lying in the value of the variables seen as important determinants, notably savings or investment and fertility decisions.

There are two main assumptions underpinning such a view (Kenny and Williams 2001: 2–3). The first is epistemological universalism. Using scientifically respectable method, theories can be developed which explain economic behaviour relating to growth. 'All economic processes everywhere are, in principle, knowable' (Kenny and Williams 2001: 2). The present writer takes the view that there has been a set of events which have occurred and that in principle it is possible to both describe those events and explain them. Moreover, there is much more in common between history and science than often thought (Stuart-Fox 1999, McNeill 2001, Berry 1999, Gaddis 2002). The stance is one of philosophical realism, no different from that of neoclassical economics. The second assumption is ontological universalism, which has two levels of meaning. The first is the uniformity of nature, including human behaviour. This is the basis for any scientific research. We can assume that a large part of human behaviour is not random or arbitrary. The second level involves two more contentious assertions. First, the 'components' of all economies are in some way the same, which makes economies and economic processes comparable. Secondly, the components interact with one another in the same ways, thus producing economic 'laws' or regularities which operate across all econo-mies, regardless of time or space. All country economies are members of a single population. In the words of Szostak (2006: 2), 'Growth accounting exercises, both in their earlier time-series guise and their more recent cross-section guise, are grounded in an assumption that there is some central tendency in economic growth processes. The work is valuable but the assumption is dangerous'. In the statistical literature the same approach is adopted. Parameter homogeneity is assumed, the components or variables determining economic development and their interaction are the same everywhere. This is a particularly inappropriate assumption in studying complex heterogeneous objects, such as national economies (Brock and Durlauf 2001: 36). A common response (Rodrik 2007: 55) is that the eco-nomic principles are the same, but the context varies. The major difficulty is accepting the neoclassical world as descriptive of the pre-modern era. Within such a world, it is difficult to explain how the choices in different economies, one assumes rationally made, lead to such different results, specifically to the high and low incomes which characterise developed and undeveloped economies. If we assume a degree of rationality in such deci-sion making, as Azariadis and Stachurski conclude, '. . .the choices facing individuals in rich countries and those facing individuals in poor countries are very different' (2004: 20). It is more than differing context.

TESTING THE THEORY

The revival of growth theory in the 1990s and beyond has been marked by an empirical orientation which was lacking in the previous work during the 1950s and 1960s (Mankiw 1995: 301). As Mankiw argues, in recent times the typical empirical paper on economic growth chooses a sample of countries and runs a cross-sectional regression, seeking to identify statisti-cally significant determinants of the rate of economic growth. The statisti-cal strength of a relationship is critical. The consistency of the association is also relevant. Do we find the same association in different populations, that is, different countries or different geographical areas? Do we find the same association at different times for the same country? Do we find the same association using different research designs? In such analysis, on the left-hand side of the equation is the rate of growth of a country over a significant period of time, the dependent variable, and on the right-hand side are the regressors, the set of variables considered significant as deter-minants of this rate of growth, the independent variables. Neoclassical theory suggests a particular set of regressors, including the initial level of income per head, but testing is not limited to this set. The variables might be economic, such as the rate of investment; institutional – for example some proxy for the system of property rights; political – the degree of stability – or they might be policy measures, initial conditions, or any other possible determinant. Some are difficult to quantify. In principle, provided all the normal requirements of statistical analysis are satisfied, it is possible to use regression analysis both to test the neoclassical theory and to measure the more general influence of individual determinants, including policy actions, on the growth rate of different countries. Any such relationship tells us nothing about the direction of causation, but it identifies relevant relationships and any theory must be consistent with the relationships found.

There are two flaws in the many regression exercises carried out. First, variables are often included without a theoretical justification. The reductionist method of economic theory assumes that there are independent variables and we can know what they are (Gaddis 2002: 55). There is a need to separate independent from dependent variables and from the world surrounding both (ibid.: 60). An ecological view of reality stresses the interdependence of all variables. The main problem in regression analysis of the determinants of economic development concerns the nature of the underlying theoretical model, or what is often called model uncertainty. There needs to be a theory which indicates why a variable might be incorporated into the analysis. Discovering statistical relationships without an underlying causal theory does not move the explanation of economic development forward. Sometimes the link with the underlying economic model is made explicit, sometimes it is left implicit (Durlauf, Johnson and Temple 2004). For most practitioners, the world is still the neoclassical world, often expanded in a rather ad hoc manner.

The Solow theory does not include explicitly all the factors which influence in a significant way the rate of economic growth, so that much testing extends beyond the neoclassical theory, notably by considering factors which influence key variables in the theory, such as the level of technology or savings. With the help of regression analysis, we should be able to 'verify' the determinants of economic development, identifying the empirically salient growth variables, in the process indicating whether or not the neoclassical model provides a reasonable description of the growth process. The determinants might include structural elements such as geographical and institutional features, notably political institutions, or events, often referred to as patterns of shocks, both positive and negative, usually exogenous to the relevant economies. A common inclusion is variability of the terms of trade, regarded as an indicator of the incidence of external shocks. There is particular interest in policy measures, notably those associated with economic reforms which stimulate economic development.

The aim of such an analysis is often a universally applicable set of policy prescriptions for achieving the goal of economic development.[3]

There are strong arguments that the quest is a failure (Levine and Renelt 1992, Mankiw 1995, Kenny and Williams 2001, Fforde 2005), although there are still those who believe that such statistical exercises continue to be useful (Sala-i-Martin 1997, Hoover and Perez 2000). The results of regression analysis are not generally considered robust. The importance of one determinant often depends on what other determinants are included in the analysis, and how all of them are measured. Changing the other independent variables included in a regression often changes the significance of the targeted relationship, even the sign. There is disagreement about how robust the results should be to have any validity. There has been considerable debate over Leamer's extreme-bounds analysis (Hoover and Perez 2000: 2–3). He defines the extreme bounds as the upper and lower limits to the value of a variable coefficient, taken from all the possible regressions which include the relevant variable, with twice the standard error added at both extremes. A variable is said to be robust if its extreme bounds lie strictly to one side or the other of zero, that is, all values are either positive or negative. Levine and Renelt (1992) adopt a variation of this which reduces the number of regressions and argue that variables are robust if their coefficients do not include zero. They argue that few variables qualify as robust determinants of economic growth. Sala-i-Martin (1997) counters that this is too strict and accepts a variable as robust if 75 per cent of the values of its coefficient lie to one side of zero, consequently finding many more robust variables. There is a grave danger of a criterion arbitrarily being adopted which either excludes or includes all variables, neither of which outcomes is helpful, but a result which shows the fragility of the exercise.

A very large number of variables have been considered significant enough to be subjected to this kind of testing.[4] Selecting the subset of important variables is difficult, which often leaves the exercise as a general description of the nature of the process. Since the relationship between a given independent variable and the rate of growth usually depends on what other variables are included, such work shows conclusively that mono-causal explanations are non-starters.[5] As Mankiw (1995: 304) points out, regression analysis leaves us 'with a bunch of correlations among important endogenous variables'. The testing indicates at best possible broad patterns of relationship which can be further pursued and assists the exclusion of unlikely patterns. One problem is that relationships which are clearly important often do not appear to be statistically significant, such as those between the rate of economic growth and policy to increased expenditures on education or to open up trade. One relationship which unsurprisingly appears to be very robust is that between the rate of growth and investment.

The second weakness of regression analysis is that there are well-known statistical problems inherent in the exercise which undermine its value. The first problem is fundamental. Even if all countries in the world had the relevant data, the number of variables used approximately matches the number of countries. There are too few degrees of freedom to test properly the relationships considered potentially significant. It is almost impossible to group the countries into 'clubs' of similar countries and to apply the statistical tests to these separate groups – they are just too small. The use of panel data helps expand the number of cases, but creates its own problems, for example the influence of short-term factors such as the business cycle (Mankiw 1995: 307). Another difficulty, closely linked with the small size of the population of countries, statistically speaking, is the inadequacy of data. For example Kremer, Onatski and Stock (2001: 18) argue that only small changes in the data, well within the possibility of measurement errors, remove the presence of Quah's twin peaks. The limitations of data not only reduce the number of countries for which the exercises can be carried out, but also the time period over which such statistical exercises are possible. The large study of Durlauf, Johnson and Temple (2004) deals only with the period since 1960.

The next problem is simultaneity, the fact that the dependent variable and the independent variables are jointly determined. The procedures must be carefully organised, since there are obvious collinearity problems if both ultimate and proximate causes are included in the same regression analysis. For example, if the rate of economic growth and the rate of investment are correlated, what exactly does this mean? That the level of investment is a determinant of the rate of economic growth, that the rate of economic growth is a determinant of the rate of investment, or that there is a third element determining both? Introducing into regression analysis the ultimate causes alongside the proximate causes makes the coefficients of the proximate causes highly unstable (Brock and Durlauf 2001: 235). Simultaneity has often been dealt with using a two-stage least-squares technique. In this approach, an instrument, an exogenous variable independent of, but highly correlated with, the relevant variable within the model, is used to predict the value of the relevant variable and that estimated value is then used in the second stage to measure the correlation with the dependent variable.[6]

Often there are unavoidable difficulties of measurement, especially when the variables refer to non-quantitative features. There is no choice but to use various proxies for the relevant variables. These proxies are sometimes put together for an entirely different purpose. There is particular difficulty with using proxy variables for policies (Pritchett 2004: 231–6). A policy can be defined 'as a conditional rule, a mapping from states of the world to actions' (Pritchett 2004: 231). The variable used as a proxy for policy in growth regression needs to accurately capture difference in policies as mappings. For example, an average tariff hides the differing role of tariffs, some of which are beneficial and some harmful to economic development. Often proxies hide the subtlety of influence and mislead. The problem of measurement is particularly relevant to qualitative variables such as the nature of institutions. The attempt to validate the importance of institutions through regression analysis has produced inconclusive results, whether the focus is civil liberties, property rights, political instability or social capital. This is scarcely surprising since unobserved institutional elements can vary systematically across societies and directly influence the effectiveness of an institution. As Greif (2006: 20–21) argues, two societies which have the same formal rules specifying property rights will experience very different levels of investment if different beliefs about the enforcement of these rights prevail in each.

Measurement error compounds the difficulty of multi-collinearity. Multi-collinearity arises when there is a strong correlation between the variables on the right-hand side of the equation, which is likely if ultimate and proximate variables are lumped together. The real problems start when the residual or error terms between countries are correlated. Non-linearities arise both because of the interdependencies between variables and of the existence of an influence in individual cases which becomes active only beyond certain threshold levels. One study concludes, 'First, although cross-country sources for growth studies can point the way to important determinants of growth, they are not very adept at catching the key interactions between variables that can be critical for sustained growth to occur. Secondly, and consequently, countries with similar values of key variables often have quite different growth records' (McMahon and Squire 2003: 2). Parameter heterogeneity is another problem. In such a complex world, where 'context' determines the influence of any particular variable, the difficulties with regression analysis are not surprising.

Hausmann, Pritchett and Rodrik have stressed the unpredictability of growth accelerations since 1960. Their general conclusion is that there is a poor match between occurrences of growth takeoffs and favourable circumstances (Hausmann, Pritchett and Rodrik 2004: 20). A lot of growth episodes take place when those conditions appear not to be particularly favourable, and growth episodes typically fail to materialise when the conditions are favourable. Even where the explanatory variables are statistically significant – such as increases in investment and trade, in unsustained accelerations with real exchange rate depreciations, and in those which are sustained – political-regime change and economic reform – they explain little of the growth pattern that the data reveal (Hausmann, Pritchett and Rodrik 2004: 19). This led the authors to stress 'idiosyncratic, and often small-scale, changes' and to comment, 'The search for the common elements in these idiosyncratic determinants – to the extent that there are any – is an obvious area for future research' (Hausmann, Pritchett and Rodrik 2004: 22).

Many commentators share the view of McMahon and Squire (2003: 6): 'Sources of growth analysis can only take us so far, and this type of analysis may well have already reached the point of strong diminishing returns'. An important contribution of the regression work already done, according to Durlauf, Johnson and Temple (2004: 5), has been: 'The clarification of the limits that exist in employing statistical methods to address growth questions. One implication of these limits is that narrative and historical approaches . . . have a lasting role to play in empirical growth analysis'. McMahon and Squire (2003: 29) argue strongly for the necessity of in-depth country studies to follow up the sources of growth analysis. Durlauf et al. quote the work of Mokyr and Landes as valuable examples of the narrative or historical approach. They say that this is unsurprising because of the importance of factors which do not lend themselves to statistical analysis, such as political, social and cultural factors, despite the fact that a large number of variables used are proxies for just such factors. Brock and Durlauf (2001: 232) agree with them. In their view, an important role of regression and other forms of statistical analysis is 'the identification of interesting data patterns, patterns that can both stimulate economic theory and suggest directions along which to engage in country specific studies'. There is a persistent call in these comments for country-specific studies.

There are two alternatives to statistical testing which have been proposed – calibration, already discussed, and binary recursive tree estimation or discriminant analysis (Ghosh and Wolf 1998 or McMahon and Squire 2003: chapter 1). This approach helps the researcher to deal with the problem of non-linearities, in particular thresholds and interdependencies. The aim is to predict as accurately as possible membership of key country groups, in this case, a fast-growth group or a slow-growth group. The countries were ranked according to actual growth rates and divided into three roughly equal groups, the middle group being initially excluded from the analysis. Other divisions could be employed in a similar exercise. Each of the relevant individual independent variables was taken and threshold levels of the variables sought which produced the lowest number of errors in predicting membership of the two extreme growth groups. The predictive capacity of all the different variables was compared. The best predictor turned out to be the investment ratio, an unsurprising result, with a ratio of 22 per cent as the threshold point. The underlying notion is that there is a threshold beyond which a variable has a favourable impact on the rate of economic growth. The relationship is not necessarily linear, since the regression results suggest that the growth rate above the investment threshold level is 2 per cent higher than predicted by a simple regression relating growth and investment (McMahon and Squire 2003: 24). The productivity of investment is context specific, depending on the achievement of threshold levels of other relevant variables (McMahon and Squire 2003: 12). Investment has to be distributed to the right sectors of the economy and for the right purpose; other factors of production have to be combined with the relevant capital; and the environment must be sufficiently stable and free of disruption, external shocks and war; in other words, sufficiently low risk.

The exercise considered which other variables (with their thresholds already selected) improved the predictability of rapid growth. It developed a tree with nodes and branches represented by the relevant variables. Initially, the exercise was carried out with no allowance for institutional variables. It might be that investment in human capital and a low rate of inflation offset the impact of a low investment ratio and raise the predictability of membership of the high-growth group, or a low rate of inflation increases the possibility of membership of the rapid growth group, even where the rate of investment is above the threshold level. Groups of countries with related variables could be put together with similar patterns in terms of the causation of rapid growth. In this way, varying interdependencies, some complex, could be accounted for. For example the variable, initial income level, is only highly significant for poor countries characterised by high investment ratios, inflation which is not excessive, and moderate population growth (Ghosh and Wolf 1998: 12). The inclusion of variables for institutional quality places the risk of expropriation as the variable with the highest predictability, which is scarcely surprising since the two variables of the investment ratio and freedom from the risk of expropriation are closely correlated and freedom from such risk is clearly a prerequisite for most investment (McMahon and Squire 2003: 21–2). It is also possible to carry out a similar exercise, dividing the countries by investment ratio or by the productivity of investment, to see which variables are related to these two variables.

In this exercise, there are exceptions; for example, some countries with high investment ratios have low growth rates and some with low ratios have high growth rates. There are always outliers, countries which fail to fit any of the expected patterns of interdependency. There needs to be an in-depth analysis of the failure: this requires in-depth country studies. For the group of medium growth economies, the situation is more ambiguous, with some countries having variables fitting the high growth pattern and others the slow growth pattern. These countries also require in-depth analysis. Ghosh and Wolf argue the results '. . . caution against a piecewise focus on individual growth determinants, suggesting instead a "holistic" approach that explicitly takes account of cross-dependencies between various growth determinants' (Ghosh and Wolf 1998: 14). The revival of big push theories of economic development (best illustrated by Sachs' recent best-seller, 2005), which argue that growth occurs fastest when a synergistic advance in variables of different types occurs simultaneously, illustrates the important role of interdependencies (Szostak 2006: 3). The analysis allows some generalisation from the repetition across countries of certain patterns of variables and the grouping of countries with similar growth rates and values of the relevant variables, but emphasises the number of exceptional cases or outliers, indicating the need for particular narratives. The particular mix of thresholds achieved and interdependencies of variables marks out many experiences as unique. Both regression and discriminant analysis emphasise the importance of the context in which economic growth occurs and the need for a deeper analysis of causation.

ULTIMATE AND PROXIMATE CAUSATION

According to one authority there are four criteria for identifying a causal relationship (Szostak 2007b: 2). Another study indicates as many as seven criteria for distinguishing non-causal from causal associations, but these can be assimilated to Szostak's four (Hill 1965, quoted in Aiello, Larson and Sedlak 2007: 57).

The first step is establishing a correlation between an independent variable(s) – the putative cause, and the dependent variable – the putative effect, commonly undertaken in cross-country regression exercises. The second step is establishing a chronology, the sequence of cause and effect in real time. This requires developing a narrative of some kind. Such a narrative must comprise a time sequence which is persuasive in the time delay with which effect follows cause. It should also rule out the existence of a third cause. A further aspect of the relationship is its specificity. Is it unique or does the same effect in different cases result from different causes? Does the one cause produce one effect or more than one? A careful comparison of different narratives can tell us this. It can also provide an answer to the question, Is the effect proportional to the cause in the different cases? Is there a gradient of effects which is consistent with the magnitude of the cause? A sequence in time does not alone establish causality – you need a theoretical justification for a relationship between two events. There must be a plausibility about the relationship which reflects an underlying theoretical mechanism, economic or otherwise. Since a cause precedes an effect and is linked by a particular mechanism, it is necessary to reveal and analyse the mechanism. There may be a number of relevant mechanisms. The third step is therefore to show how the causal relationship unfolds in practice, including identifying any intermediate variables. Once an explanation is reached, the fourth step is ruling out alternative explanations of the result – the Popperian process of seeking to falsify a hypothesis and retaining it for as long as it is not disproved. This may involve experiment, with interventional and observational studies where this is possible.

Economists excel at the first, and sometimes the second in a rather mechanistic way, economic historians at the second and third. The fourth is infrequently attempted in this area, largely because of the nature of historical disciplines. There are two methods of testing relevant to the pure and the historical sciences respectively. Economists tend to choose one, that of hypothesis testing, through statistical work rather than controlled laboratory experimentation, to the exclusion of the other. The other method involves the use of concepts in a different way, such as those of evolution in biology or of plate tectonics in geology. The nature of the historical sciences has striking similarities with that of economic history in the telling of stories. Even the more experimentally oriented sciences are converging in method on an historical approach. In such research, the explanatory concepts are not hypotheses to be tested. Such concepts can only be rejected if they 'violate the sense of reasoned adequacy' (McCloskey 1991a: 101). Reasoned adequacy may involve the application of all four criteria.

There is an interesting discussion of causation in Macfarlane (1997: 378–85), who takes an historical approach to analysing demography, an important part of the story. Macfarlane points out that it is unusual for the relevant causal links to be single links, although there are some such links. The causative chains usually consist of multiple links. It is difficult to identify such chains, because they are embedded in complex social and economic systems. In different contexts, the same condition can produce multiple effects and the same effect can have multiple causes. The order, timing and 'weight' of each causative link are important – the reality is that there is a significant path dependency for each country. The causes need to be investigated in particular cases. Economic development is typically characterised by feedback of various kinds. Within the pre-modern regime the negative feedbacks predominated, in the modern regime the positive ones prevailed. Macfarlane talks of the need for a holistic approach for what are apparently narrow problems, an approach not limited to strictly economic causes, but extending into religion, law, biology and medicine. Often the effects are unintended, or random, and not directly amenable to the use of logic to understand. Often a slight tipping of the balance was enough to move from cause to effect. Thresholds need to be identified. The comparative method helps identify and trace these causal links, but the same results in different societies can be produced by very different causal chains. So much appears to be the incidental, rather than deliberate, effect of actions taken for different reasons.

In analysing modern economic development, it is sometimes useful to take a swathe of relevant variables as constituting a given context – technology, institutions, attitudes – and to consider only the proximate causes of economic growth, as neoclassical economic growth theory does. Favourable proximate causes, sometimes prompted by external shocks, ignite, but only ultimate causes sustain. Moreover, describing a process, which is self-sustaining, is easier than identifying the initiating factors; it involves a bundle of interrelated positive feedback effects, which once initiated, inevitably continues (Mokyr 1999: 30–31).This approach is not helpful in analysing the inception of the modern growth regime. Bloch and Tang (2004: 245–6) summarise the current position: '. . . there is now a general view that the neoclassical model of growth that emerged in the 1950s, particularly Solow's (1956 and 1957) path-breaking contributions, offers neither an explanation of the experience of the Third World countries nor practical guidance for sustained economic development', which has prompted the response. 'To understand why some countries have performed better than others with respect to growth it is therefore necessary to go beyond the proximate causes of growth and delve into the wider fundamental determinants. This implies that we cannot hope to find the magic bullet by economic analysis alone' (Snowdon 2002: 100, quoted by Szostak 2007: 2). This leads us to a discussion of the underlying causation of the transition and inevitably to an analysis of the distinction between ultimate and proximate causation. There has been a shift of interest to the drivers, the 'deep determinants'.

Diamond (1997), in his Pulitzer prize-winning book, *Guns, Germs, and Steel*, makes an important, but not new, distinction between ultimate and proximate causation. He did not explore the implications of the distinction, nor its history; he assumed its importance. This is not an unusual silence, since the terms proximate and ultimate, or terms with same meaning, are used frequently in the relevant literature. It is a distinction which helps an understanding of the nature of different approaches to modern economic development. Diamond's distinction derives from the work of the researcher of animal behaviour, Tinbergen. The significance

of biology as a paradigm for human history has been noted by many commentators (Berry 1999: 130–37). The distinction is between the ultimate
causes – the basic structural features of an animal and the adaptive significance of these features – and the proximate causes, the lifetime experience
of a particular individual and the mechanisms important to the survival of
that individual. Natural selection is part of an ultimate cause, whereas the
adaptive features of a species at a particular time are the proximate cause
of survival. The parallel in our case might be between the structure of
societies in general and their ability to generate modern economic development, and the nature of a particular society and how it organizes economic
life, notably how it translates inputs into outputs.

In the introduction to a book on analytic narratives, Rodrik (2007: part
A) makes a similar distinction, referring to deep, rather than ultimate,
determinants. Elsewhere, the term fundamental is used (Bloom, Canning
and Sevilla 2003, who refer to 'fundamental forces' and to 'underlying
forces'), or in some cases no short descriptor is used at all – the researcher
simply moves beyond proximate into specific causes which are clearly not
regarded as proximate. Maddison (1988) had already used the distinction
in trying to indicate the determinants of economic development in an
article more than a decade ago commenting on the work of Olson, a distinction further developed by the author (White 1992). Such a distinction
is common in the literature relevant to modern economic development,
although not often analysed. Cameron (1997: 3–4), in his economic history
of the world, argues that a historical approach has two virtues, putting a
focus on the origins of current disparities in the level of economic development and making an identification of the fundamentals of economic development, undistracted by current concerns. Implicitly, this makes the same
proximate/ultimate distinction. Hedlund (2005: 8–9), on the premise that
history matters, argues for three different levels of analysis, which move
from proximate to ultimate, further making a distinction between ultimate
causes according to their fixity (see section 2 of the book). There are the
short-run 'resource endowments, the quality of infrastructure and state of
technology embedded in available productive facilities', which encapsulate
the proximate causes. Secondly, there are the rules of the game, the organisations and skill investments made in reaping maximum benefits from
resources and infrastructure. Thirdly, there are the fundamental social
norms and values relating to private property, individual initiative and the
responsibility and role of the state. Elsewhere, he refers to coherent sets of
these norms as mental models. The relevant time scale reflects centuries,
not just generations. Likewise Gaddis (2002: 95) distinguishes immediate,
intermediate and distant causes or processes, referring to immediate as
proximate.

It is useful to give two examples of the implicit use of the concept of ultimate causation from researchers with different perspectives. Komlos uses the word proximate but not ultimate, although the latter notion is implicit. In considering the relationship between population change and economic development, such a distinction is necessary in order to explain the interweaving of the positive and negative effects of population change. Stressing the positive, Boserupian effects, he argues, 'Population growth was therefore the proximate cause of the industrial revolution, but the achievement of the previous millennia were the preconditions for sustaining the economic momentum precipitated by the rise in population' (Komlos 1989: 205). Earlier, stressing the negative Malthusian effects, he had argued that the plague might be the proximate cause of a collapse of population, as in fourteenth-century Europe, but that the epidemic attacked a nutritionally weakened population (Komlos 1989: 195), which, by implication, is the ultimate cause. Clark (2003) asserts that there is ample evidence for extensive spillovers from knowledge production and investment, following from the largely non-rivalrous nature of the consumption of ideas, despite the existence of patents. He goes on to argue (2003: 13–14), 'Thus investments in knowledge capital that generated efficiency growth not only explain most of modern economic growth at a proximate level, they essentially explain all economic growth'. The exercise in ultimate causation is to explain why no previous society before 1800 had expanded the stock of knowledge at the appropriate rate, why it happens in Britain within a 50-year period, and why some economies benefit from this knowledge expansion and some do not, although again Clark does not make explicit use of the term ultimate.

Proximate causes, as revealed by neoclassical growth theory, tell us that output deficiencies are the result of worse technology, less physical or human capital, but do not tell us why a country has worse technology, less physical or less human capital. In the words of Acemoglu (2006: 84), 'Growth theory is useful in highlighting the proximate causes, in providing us with a framework for thinking about the fundamental causes, and also in clarifying the mechanics of the process of growth, so that we can more carefully evaluate different theories and approaches'. Ultimate causation means exploring the causes behind the proximate causes. Proximate causes are 'transmission mechanisms' (Mokyr 1999: 29), but these transmission mechanisms involve 'a long and uncertain time gap' between cause and effect (Rosenberg and Birdzell 1986: 8).

The distinction is partly a matter of the time perspective adopted. In economic development, by long term we usually refer to centuries, even millennia. The medium term involves decades. The short term or proximate means the immediate past, this year or even this month. Ultimate refers to features which are fixed, or potentially persistent beyond the immediate experience of this generation and its direct antecedents. Of course, over a sufficiently long time period everything is malleable, nothing is fixed. What exactly is a relevant time perspective reflects the nature of the problem being analysed. The ultimate is often exogenous, outside the typical models used to explain the relevant variable, assumed to be unchanging. What is proximate is a variable, endogenous in any explanatory model. In the words of Bloom, Canning and Sevilla (2003: 359), '"Fundamental forces" [read ultimate causes] must be characteristics that determine a country's economic performance, but are not determined by it'. A variable is endogenous if the level or rate of economic development influences the variable (Rodrik 2003: 7), or if it is related to some other variable(s) within the model, exogenous if it does not and is given in the short to medium term, providing a context for short-term behaviour. Ocampo (2003: 3) labels the ultimate factors 'framework conditions'.

In discussing the role of culture in economic change, Jones distinguishes between two possibilities – cultural fixity and cultural nullity. The former implies cultures which are specific and unchanging and cultural nullity cultures which are instantaneously malleable (E.L. Jones 2006). Jones believes the latter is closer to reality, but that culture changes with a time-lag and can act as a constraint on economic development in the short term. The same distinction could be applied to a host of other causes, which can be placed on a broad spectrum running from fixity to nullity. For example, the accessibility of technical knowledge may be delayed, since in the short term the absorptive capacity of a society is given. Unfortunately, the degree of fixity and nullity varies from one causative factor to another and from one country to another, and the relationship of that fixity to the possibilities of modern economic development is a complex one (discussed in some detail in the next section). Geographical factors are the closest to fixity. Continental drift and the building of mountain ranges or new island chains occur over long periods of time, despite the fact that we can observe the process at work. Most aspects of geology are given in the short term, but not all. Climate changes more quickly than geology. There are natural fluctuations in temperature and precipitation. There is certainly a recognition that there is no absolute fixity in this area. It is difficult to find a clear boundary between fixity and nullity, or between ultimate and proximate cause. There is no obvious threshold or way of identifying which is which.

Another factor which is to some degree fixed is humankind and its genetic make-up. Natural selection occurs over long periods of time and in the short term the human genome is given. An issue usually avoided is the degree to which different groups in the world differ systematically in genetic characteristics. There is first of all the nature/nuture debate, whether differences in human beings are inherited or learned. The general finding of research seems to be that there is a 50/50 split, which implies that nature does matter, although some argue that the unknown part is larger than the two combined. The second issue is whether there are differences between different geographical groups relevant to economic development. Some group differences are obvious, involving familiar physical features. Others are less obvious, and more controversial, involving mental capacities; discussion of the issue is usually avoided. Our unit of study is the state. It is reasonable to ask whether there are significant differences between the citizens of such states in certain aptitudes and to ask, if there are differences, when did they appear and how persistent they are. There is a literature arguing this case, usually denigrated or ignored. This is a mistake for various reasons.[7] At this stage it is sufficient to say that differences in aptitudes are another candidate as an ultimate cause.

There is a terrible temptation to ignore fixity and the role in economic development of the long-term factors, concentrating on the proximate factors (Ocampo 2003). There are two main reasons for doing this. The first reason for ignoring ultimate causation is a belief that modern economic development is a major discontinuity, clearly due to some dramatic short-run changes, and what happens before the discontinuity is irrelevant. The discontinuity can be explained by proximate causes alone. The rest is mere context. On this argument, there are no ultimate causative factors of any significance. The focus of interest is therefore on short-term growth and on igniting that growth rather than sustaining growth, apparently a relatively easy task given the proliferation of growth episodes (Ocampo 2003: 3). The sustaining reflects factors of ultimate causation. Moreover, it is difficult to model the relevant processes, and there is a lack of relevant data, in particular of reliable statistics, which go back only a half century. Some areas, such as culture or institutions, are just not amenable to quantification, or rather, if quantified, have a large margin of error. The further one moves away from proximate causes, the more difficult it becomes to test the importance of causal factors, particularly if there are obvious feedback effects and complex interactions between different causes.

Secondly, there is a sometimes deliberately, and at other times unconsciously, an a-historical and static approach implicit in the relevant theorizing. As Snooks (1993) argues, neoclassical economics is concerned with outcomes, not processes. The outcomes change the conditions for the next choice. The static approach is inherent in the view of neoclassical economists, who see change as represented by the outcome of choices at given moments of time. At best, neoclassical growth theory is an exercise in comparative statics, a comparison of equilibrium outcomes with different values of the relevant variables. In this kind of analysis, history does not matter, in the sense of the process of change and the causation of key elements of that change.

There is another, perhaps an opposite, danger to that facing those who stress proximate causation. There is a danger in this kind of causal analysis that '. . . multiple causation and the analysis of long chains can easily degenerate into vagueness' (Macfarlane 1995: 388, reproducing an argument of Sorokin). The causal chain can become unpersuasive for two reasons (Pierson 2003: 15). The links in the chain can be weak: there must be good theoretical and empirical reasons for thinking the link to be strong. There must not be too many of these links. Even a probability of 80 per cent that a link holds leads, with only three links, to less than a 50-50 chance that the entire chain is valid (Pierson 2001: 15). There is the problem of the infinite regress, a fool's infinity, in which we go further and further back to discover the origins of modern economic development – there is always another cause behind the one under scrutiny, always a set of events and circumstances representing a further step on a unique historical path which precedes the relevant period. This is the fallacy of absolute priority. The approach implies a form of determinism, in which there is a need to go back to the absolute beginning – everything is predetermined, and the only explanatory framework is the whole set of events and circumstance as they unfold. There needs to be a careful justification of how far back any analysis goes; it has to stop somewhere (Pierson 2001: 15–16). Gaddis (2002: 96) refers to 'the principle of diminishing relevance'. At some point, there is an exercise of judgement of what is important. The chain should be broken where pathways diverge significantly, causal connections are much weaker and there is no theoretical justification for going back further. Ultimate causation is not an excuse for tracing causes back to their ultimate origin, finding the starting point of an historical tendency in the mists of time. It becomes impossible to separate the important from the trivial, everything becoming relevant. It is at this point that neoclassical growth theory becomes important. Theory is required to explain why certain causes are likely to be more important than others. It is necessary to distinguish what is important from the noise. There is too much information to resolve the mystery – there is a need for selection. Theory helps the researcher to select what is relevant. Statistical studies also help attach different degrees of importance to the individual causes.

The distinction is more than just a difference of view on time perspectives or model building. Proximate causes are really part of the description of a phenomenon, in this case modern economic development (Ocampo 2003: 4). When Jones writes, 'Industrialization was the result of intensive growth rather than its cause', he has in mind growth in GDP per head before the modern period. A high level of factor productivity, a large

accumulation of capital, including human capital, a more diversified structure of the economy, including industrialisation, are all characteristics of
modern economic development, not causes. They are part of what needs to
be explained. It is critical to distinguish carefully causes and characteristics
in order to properly understand the phenomenon to be explained.

Proximate Causation

Proximate causation can refer to the events which immediately precede
what is being given a cause. The approach of the economist centres on the
production function. The analysis of growth accounting in Chapter 2 has
explored many of the relevant issues. Output is generated by a combination of factor inputs and the technical/organisational level; a growth in
output by an increasing contribution from these inputs and productivity
increase. Any explanation of economic development is couched in terms
of the contribution of the relevant inputs and of the efficiency with which
these inputs are converted into outputs. For many, this is a sufficient explanation. In the standard approach the relevant equation can be stated:

$$y = ak^{\acute{a}} (hl)^{1-\acute{a}}$$

In this equation k denoted the capital input and l the labour input. Labour
is measured in efficiency units, including an investment in human capital,
h. a represents the technical level at which production is occurring. Or,
looking at the situation in growth accounting terms, $y - 1 = \acute{a}(k - 1) + (1 - \acute{a})h + a$, which means: per-capita GDP growth = the contributions of
capital deepening + human capital accumulation + productivity growth.
The rate of economic development is explained by the contributions made
by each of these elements.

Maddison (1988) adds to the list of proximate causes other short-term
factors – the degree of capacity utilisation – a Keynesian problem of
demand, and the net flow of funds into or out of an economy, whether
plunder (−) or foreign aid (+). The latter might include flows of FDI. The
former determines the intensity with which the inputs are used and the
latter either diminishes or increases the potential supply of capital.

Ultimate Causation

Rodrik (2003: 5) is rightly parsimonious with the ultimate determinants,
limiting them to just three, two of which he regards as partly endogenous
and one as fully exogenous. The former two comprise the role of institutions and of economic integration, by which he means integration into

the international economy, or openness to trade. Integration relates in particular to market size. Institutions are discussed more fully elsewhere in Rodrik's work, but include basic principles which must be satisfied, the enforcement and protection of property rights by an efficient legal system, the provision of appropriate services and infrastructure by an efficient and incorrupt bureaucracy, and the maintenance of law and order by government. The exogenous determinant is geography, which consists in the advantages and disadvantages yielded by a country's physical location, including latitude, proximity to navigable waters, and climate.

In discussing ultimate causation, Maddison (1988) made a further distinction between medium- and long-term factors. Using Olson's work, he extended the ultimate causes to include significant historical events with a medium-term impact, including wars and acts of social conflict, which interact with the basic social order as characterised by its developing institutions, beliefs and ideology, and the degree of socio-political conflict within the relevant social order. Maddison added as medium-term factors the macroeconomic policies for growth and stability pursued by the government and the distance from the technical frontier, whether the leaders of a country were committed to promoting economic development and whether that country was able to absorb best-practice techniques and organisation from abroad. In this account, the role of government policy commitment and effectiveness, rather than its institutional strength – in the terminology of one commentator, its infrastructural power (White 1987) – and the opportunity and ability of a society to take from an existing pool of technical and organisational method are medium-term ultimate causes. White (1992) thought it appropriate to add the resource position (a broader notion than geography) as a long-term ultimate determinant, also identifying the risk environment and the shocks which are part of that environment as other long-term determinants. In this work, the relevant institutions are classified into three – government, markets and civil society – the last a bridge between the first two. It is also necessary to add, as another potentially significant ultimate cause, differences in aptitude between the citizens of different countries. This is a factor which is usually ignored, but an honest treatment has to deal with it.

THE ANALYTIC NARRATIVE

In the literature on the search for the causation of the Industrial Revolution, there are two main approaches. In the first approach, which underpins neoclassical theory, the classical liberal assumption holds that, left to their own devices, individuals self-organize and are motivated to take actions which result in economic development, usually through the free operation of markets. Evolutionary biology, it is argued, can provide an account of why this might be so. Institutional arrangements or cultures which promote economic development emerge through a process akin to natural selection. Economic development is the natural state of affairs, as the convergence literature attempts to show. Since most countries in the world have still not begun the development process, this cannot be the whole story. There must be obstacles which prevent development occurring. The usual, alleged obstacle is the action of government, but there is no one obstacle which explains all the failures. It is necessary to select some critical obstacle(s), or in the words of Rodrik (2007: 46–48, 56), barriers or binding constraints. Country studies begin to list obstacles and the list expands, becoming more and more specific. The analysis slips into a descriptive account of the conditions which evolved before the event, rather than an analytical study of causation.

In the second approach, the historical, there was a search for both the sufficient and necessary prerequisite(s) for the Industrial Revolution. Finding a cause is sometimes seen as finding a sufficient condition, one whose realisation inevitably leads to the phenomenon to be explained, such as successful economic growth. The sufficient condition could take the form – if the investment ratio rises from 5 per cent to 10 per cent, then modern economic development is automatically triggered (Rostow 1965). The search for a sufficient cause for modern economic development is unlikely to succeed because of the complexity of the processes at work. There is no simple explanation of the unique events which constitute modern economic development. It is probably impossible to discover a sufficient cause, or a combination of causes which together constitute a sufficient cause. A second best is to find the conditions deemed necessary, although they do not guarantee the outcome under analysis. A necessary cause is one which must be present for economic growth to occur but does not inevitably result in such growth. The analysis reduces to a search for necessary causes (usually called preconditions or prerequisites). It is not difficult to elaborate a long list of necessary causes. These become more and more specific as they are related to the particular experiences of various economies. Each country's experience is likely to throw up new prerequisites, there often being little overlap between them. The Asian economic miracle has extended the list, causing one commentator to assert, '. . . scholars recently have shown that virtually every factor that its proponents have identified with the "European miracle" can be found in other parts of the world' (Marks 2007: 14). The list becomes longer and longer and the analysis of causes degenerates into a description of circumstance, each country with its own long list of causes.

Both the two approaches described above have to confront the problem of complexity, notably concerning causation. They suggest that the emphasis should be on the individual experience. The inadequacy of both shows why a narrative approach is critical to an adequate explanation. Lying behind immediate causes are chains of causation which stretch back in time, sometimes over long periods. The trouble is that there may be many combinations of specific conditions which either promote or inhibit modern economic development. This book has unravelled positive feedback loops which correspond to necessary prerequisites and negative feedback loops which correspond to obstacles. The key issue for the inception of modern economic development is the changing relative strength of the two.

Clark (2003) has pointed out that within the basic neoclassical paradigm there are three variants which seek to explain modern economic development, variants which have a different potential for development.[8] The first variant accepts the simple neoclassical model as a starting point and assumes that a shock from outside the system induces the relevant behaviour, resulting in modern economic development. This provides a mechanism for introducing ultimate causes from outside the model. This might be the introduction of the institutions which protect private property, including intellectual property rights; a change in factor input, for example a major epidemic which reduces labour supply (North and Thomas 1973); or a change in attitude to knowledge and the application of that knowledge to technical innovation – the scientific revolution (Mokyr 2002).

The second variant sees the model as generating multiple equilibria in the way described in the previous chapter. In one such approach, which focuses on the relationship between resources and population in the process of economic development, there are three relevant alternatives envisaged – a low-level Malthusian trap, a high-level homeostasis between population and resources or the modern growth equilibrium. An alternative approach defines possible poverty traps. Both approaches are consistent with the existence of multiple long-term steady growth equilibria.

Thirdly, there is a variant which makes everything endogenous and finds the driver of economic development within the model itself. It is an aspiration of all models to make every significant variable endogenous. This poses the question whether it is possible to have a theory of everything, one theory which explains different regimes, that of slow or stagnant growth and that of rapid growth, and the transition between them. In the words of one commentator: 'The discovery of a unified theory of economic growth that could account for the intricate process of development in the last thousands of years is one of the most significant research challenges facing researchers in the field of growth and development' (Galor 2004:

41). These so-called unified theories are in the early stages of development and have major problems in fitting the empirical data.

Clark favours this approach and intellectually it represents a more satisfying interpretation. If we take the third approach, the generation of economic growth does not require a series of external shocks to propel it forward. The model itself generates economic growth. The making of all causes as endogenous creates all sorts of problems of simultaneity in imputing causation, since in such a world everything depends on everything else. Once there is a reduction in the number of fixed exogenous variables providing the context, the neoclassical model begins to merge into a narrative. Within a narrative, it is much easier to include such factors. This suggests that the form of a rigorous model is inappropriate to the explanation of complex social tendencies, such as modern economic growth. It inclines the analyst in favour of a narrative approach, but a narrative of a particular kind. The problem is compounded when linked with the extension of the relevant time horizon to comprise all important causative factors, including both ultimate and proximate causative factors. Since the aim of any good theory must be to make endogenous everything which has a significant influence on economic development, there are always going to be problems in sorting out causation.[9]

It is at this stage that a model becomes a narrative, since it is impossible to contain the complexity of the relevant processes within a model. History becomes useful. Cameron argues that '. . . those who are ignorant of the past are not qualified to generalize about it' (Cameron 1997: 4). Snooks argues further, 'Economic history can make a fundamentally important contribution to an area of economics in which theory has been conspicuously unsuccessful – the analysis of dynamic economic processes' (Snooks 1993: 7). The most persuasive argument for the usefulness of history is that all the disciplines related in some way to the problem of economic development are by their nature historical – whether it is economics, management or business studies, sociology or politics. 'Economic historians, like historians more generally, must strike a balance between a study of particular times and places and broader efforts at generalisation' (Szostak 2006: 1).

McCloskey has strongly argued for the importance of narrative for human understanding of the life around us. 'Our lives are ceaselessly intertwined with narrative, with the stories that we tell, all of which are reworked in that story of our own lives that we narrate to ourselves . . . We are immersed in narrative' (Brooks 1985: 3, quoted in McCloskey 1991: 102). Or 'It is no accident that European economics and the European novel were born at the same time. We live in an age insatiate of plot' (McCloskey 1991: 102). The narrative is a preferred way of taking meaning out of the chaos of events and circumstance around us, but like theory it is still an abstraction, one portraying movement through time (Gaddis 2002: 15). From the perspective of the social sciences, including economic history, the narrative has an important role to play: an analytic narrative is an interpretation of history in which chosen historical sequences are structured by, and interpreted through, theory (Carpenter 2000: 654, but generalising away from his emphasis on game theory).[10] It combines the use of analytic tools with the narrative form, or in the words of one group of its proponents (Bates et al., 1998: 10), 'Our approach is narrative; it pays close attention to stories, accounts, and context. It is analytic in that it extracts explicit and formal lines of reasoning, which facilitate both exposition and explanation.' Put more succinctly analytic narrative is 'deductive explanation of individual historical facts' (Elster 2000: 693), or in two words, which succinctly bring out its paradoxical nature, 'deductive history' (Elster 2000: 694). The term analytical narrative gives proper attention to what is common and what is unique in the growth experience. Previous work failed to do this. It is possible to analyse without a narrative and to narrate without any explicit analysis, but unlikely. There is usually a process of iteration between the two, a process which is often important, in that the historical narrative is checked against the theory and the theory aids selection of a relevant narrative. In the words of Bates et al. (1998: 16): analytic narratives '. . . are disciplined by both logic and the empirical record'. The historical narrative provides the inductive element in the research, particularly where there is more than one narrative to be compared, and the theory provides the deductive element and the rigorous logic.

There is an important distinction made by Gaddis (2002: 62–3). Social scientists, such as economists, tend to 'embed narratives within generalisations'. The principal objective is to confirm or refute an hypothesis and the narrative is subordinated to that task. Theory comes first and explanation is entered as needed to confirm it. 'Social scientists particularize for general purposes; hence they practice general particularization.' On the other hand, historians normally 'embed out generalization within our narratives'. Generalisations are subordinated to explanation. This is called particular generalisation. Gaddis goes on to distinguish embedded and encompassing theory. This is a difference of emphasis which is important. Historians work with limited, not universal, generalisations; they believe in contingent, not categorical, causation; they prefer simulation to modelling; and they trace processes from a knowledge of outcomes.

In the recent literature on economic growth, there are three interesting examples of the use of the analytical narrative. Each assists in a different way in explaining its nature. All the relevant authors take the main tenets of neoclassical economics, principally rational choice theory, as a given. The first and most interesting illustration is the study by Hedlund (2005) of Russian path dependence. In this study (Ibid.: xiii), he claims originality in 'the use of the historical narrative as an illustration of the theoretical argument on path dependence'. His aim is to explain the persistent underperformance of Russia over its history. He is dealing with a time period which stretches for one thousand years, so it is a rather long narrative in which what is relevant is determined by the theory. The original work relates to the way in which it is possible to lock in to an inferior technology and where there is a possibility of multiple equilibria, which follow from different choices made, often influenced by apparently small factors (David 1985 and Arthur 1992). Individual choice does not produce a social optimum. Hedlund extends the argument to institutional choice, referring to formal rules, informal norms and enforcement mechanisms. In the Russian case, these revolve mainly around the persistence of autocracy and patrimonialism (see Chapter 13). Hedlund moves beyond the model based on neoclassical economics with externalities to taking account of the way in which ideology or a world view reinforces the choices made and the role of cognitive dissonance in producing behaviour consonant with the world view. It is a bold piece of work.

Of the other two examples one does not use the term, analytical narrative, but develops a procedure and methodology which fits exactly the author's understanding of what is an analytical narrative (McMahon and Squire 2003), done from the perspective of selecting policies to promote economic development. The other uses the term deliberately and then provides case studies illustrating individual interpretations of the technique (Rodrik 2003); again, the bias is policy selection. The former is overtly comparative, whereas the latter leaves the individual case studies to speak for themselves. The work of McMahon and Squire is aptly named, *A Global Research Project*, a two-stage project, in which the analysis has been done in the first stage and the country narratives are planned for the second stage. The first stage is seen as identifying the determinants of economic growth which are to be inputs in the second stage. The analysis starts on a regional basis, considering six demarcated regions characterised by the predominance of developing countries. It began with a critique of the conventional neoclassical approach, notably growth accounting and regression analysis, but moves on to consider in more detail three particular areas of interest – microeconomic determinants of relevant decisions made at the household and firm levels – savings, fertility, labour supply and human capital investment decisions; the role of markets and their interaction; and finally, the influence of political economy. It is significant that the last is the longest chapter. The analysis, while operating largely within the neoclassical model, does consider its weaknesses and how to counter them. On the other hand, Rodrik has discussed briefly and in general terms what an analytic narrative is and then provided actual illustrations of what an analytical narrative might look like. These case studies amount to essays exploring the possibilities inherent in this approach. The essays are rather different in the way in which they combine narrative and theory. Some incline to seeing history as applied theory, others stress more the significance of the narrative itself and use theory simply to choose narrative themes and analyse causative factors.

Much of what falls under the banner of economic history tends to be either one or the other, narrative or analysis, not both. Economic history has moved in recent decades from a narrative to an analytical orientation. With the cliometric revolution, there was in economic history a deliberate attempt to apply rigorous theory, for the most part neoclassical theory, and to quantify any assertions of causation made. Such history provides a valuable contribution to a more analytical treatment of historical causation. It helped rectify the balance in economic history, which moved too close to history and to narrative telling. In that sense, cliometrics assisted economic historians in applying an analytical approach and solving a number of puzzles. However, economic history is not just applied economics, nor is it just a series of puzzles. Often specific economic histories are broken up into separate thematic sections, with an emphasis on the application of relevant theory to data within limited areas (Floud and Johnson 2004). Such a history looks like a set of weakly related pieces of analytical work, each dealing with a separate puzzle or puzzles, often not linked by an appropriate narrative. Analysis has tended in this kind of approach to fragment the narratives. Cliometrics has subsequently moved economic history too far in the direction of economic analysis and away from the telling of an appropriate narrative. The development of an analytic narrative is a matter of balance.

The strengths of the analytical narrative reflect the combined strengths of theory and history. Mokyr and Voth (2006: 1) suggests three ways in which theory is useful in answering the kinds of question asked in this book. First, it focuses on the variables that matter. In the words of Cameron (1997: 4): 'Although some historians believe their function is to "let the facts speak for themselves", "facts" respond only to specific questions posed by the analyst who deals with them; posing such questions inevitably involves a process of selection, conscious or unconscious . . .'. Secondly, it points out likely, and less likely, causal connections between relevant variables. Certain outcomes can be inferred from theories which model the most important economic relationships relevant to economic development. Thirdly, it adds precision to the analysis. The strength of a theory is derived from both its internal logic and from testing its implications against the real world. Even in the use of the comparative method there is a need for an underlying theory of the processes compared. This helps in the selection of what is worth comparing.

Mokyr (2006: 2) has also pointed out the serious limitations on the usefulness of neoclassical theory in explaining the process of economic development. The problem is not irrelevance or the mistakes of neoclassical theory – it lies in the inflated claims made for prescriptions based on the model's key relationships. There are four major limitations on the theory's usefulness. The first limitation is the treatment of some key areas of causation, such as technical or population change, as exogenous. The second is the role of intangibles, which cannot be quantified, such as culture. The third is the interaction between key contributing factors, notably technical change and capital accumulation. It is difficult to distinguish between movement of the production function and movement along the production function. The final limitation is the lack of observations – the occurrence of just one great transition.

Snooks (1993: 3–7) lists a number of arguments for the usefulness of history. First, historical study is useful in providing the background to current problems. Current situations cannot be understood without analysis of that background(s). Secondly, history provides a broad canvas, in both time and space, and from a disciplinary perspective a much broader canvas than economic theory. Thirdly, it allows us to investigate whether the behavioural assumptions hold for all time or change over time, in particular whether economic rationality is genuinely universal. This is an important issue since nearly all economic theory rests on the assumption of economic rationality. Most other social science disciplines reject the universality of economic rationality. Fourthly, history provides a storehouse of data for testing economic models – it is, as some assert, the laboratory of the economist. Theory is of no value unless it is tested against the real world.

It is in this context that we can interpret the strengths of the analytical narrative: they are fourfold – first, it helps us to interpret, and generalise about, a complex world, identifying the variables of interest in a relevant explanation, and to test the strength of key relationships involving those variables; secondly, theory provides the concepts with which we understand the mechanisms of economic change and the themes which are relevant. In particular, it helps us to select a relevant narrative. There are many possible narratives, reflecting an over-abundance of information about the past and an arbitrariness in the survival of evidence. Thirdly, it assists us to give full recognition to the complexity of the causation of modern economic development; and fourthly, it lays the basis to frame policies whose potential success is not contradicted by past experience. A judicious use of narrative and theory, by allowing us to explain past successes and failures, can be used as a basis for accurately predicting individual outcomes, even the rates of economic growth of particular countries, which follow from specific policies.

As Rodrik (2007: 4) comments, 'Any cross-country regression giving results that are not validated by case studies needs to be regarded with suspicion. But any policy conclusion that derives from a case study and flies in the face of cross-national evidence needs to be similarly scrutinised. Ultimately, we need both kinds of evidence to guide our view of how the world works.' Any explanation of the inception of modern economic development requires both analysis and narrative, incorporated in the analytic narrative. It pays particular respect to the uniqueness of each historical experience, emphasising that the exact sequence of events and their context do matter. In such a narrative, timing is of fundamental importance. It is a narrative that takes full account of the chains of causation, including the sequence, the timing and the various feedback effects characterising those causative chains. The narrative provides the coherence of an historical experience.

PART II

Ultimate causes: a fixed or malleable context

In its broadest ecological context economic development is the development of more intensive ways of exploiting the natural environment. (Wilkinson 1973: 90)

Any useful analytical narrative must incorporate ultimate causes in the determination of economic development, if the aim is to explain the inception of modern economic development. The next step is to identify each separate factor, according to their apparent degree of fixity. Often individual ultimate causes are selected as the main themes in big histories which attempt to interpret global economic history. Geography is an obvious starting point and the interaction of human beings with their natural environment is at the centre of any understanding of economic development. There are two main aspects to geography – resources and risk: each is given a separate chapter, although risk has a relevance well beyond its geographical manifestation. Natural shocks do not exhaust the list of catastrophes to which humans are exposed, many conjured up by humans themselves. A second area of relevance relates to the nature of human society – humans with their experience, education, attitudes, health and aptitudes and the institutional context in which they conduct their economic business. An interesting approach is to see humans as the outcome of a process of natural selection. The influence of these factors differs sufficiently from country to country to qualify them as candidates in helping to explain different rates of economic development.

The intention is not to introduce a determinist argument since these factors interact with each other and more malleable factors in the process of economic development, their influence being mediated through the context in which they operate. The role of different causes and the nature of the interaction between them changes over time. These chapters deal with the factors separately but the interactions are important. This makes an understanding of a complex interaction difficult to achieve, particularly the changing balance of negative and positive effects which makes possible the inception. What often appears as advantages in economic development turn out to be disadvantages or to have their potential for advantage neutralised by other factors. The exact mix of factors, and their interaction with proximate causes, is what defines the uniqueness of each experience of economic development. The interaction between the various causes is specific to particular country experiences and changes over time. Negative feedback loops exist which prevent the inception of modern economic development. Positive feedback loops are in full play once that inception is achieved.

Part II contains four chapters. Chapter 5 analyses the role of geography in the process of economic development, in particular the influence of the resource endowment. The emphasis is on the complexity of the relationship between specific endowments and economic development. It shows how resources can be boon or curse. Chapter 6 considers the nature of the various risk environments in which economic development occurs, not only natural environments. It considers the incidence and impact of, and response, to 'shocks' of various kinds, many originating within human society. Risk environments, and risk tolerance, evolve in specific, sometimes benign ways. Chapter 7 considers the nature of human capital, including health, education and the controversial issue of differences in aptitude. It broadens the definition of human background beyond the usual educational inputs considered. If a long time perspective is considered, the roles of natural selection and cultural evolution qualify as another relevant issue. Chapter 8 looks at the institutional context of economic development, considering the relationship between institutions and modern economic development. It considers, in particular three different kinds of institution – government, the market and civil society – and considers the importance of a positive interaction between them in modern economic development.

# 5.	Resources as a stimulant or constraint: the role of geography

Resources do not guarantee their own development. It is not enough to be sitting on top of coal; one has to develop the technology and business practices to exploit it. It is not enough to haul back resources or engage in trade with distant regions; one has to ensure the resources are not squandered in the way that Spain and Portugal did in failing to utilize American treasure. One has to go on doing these productively and cumulatively. (Jones 2006: 115–16)

Judging by recent interest, there is little argument about the role of geography as a significant causative factor in economic development, but on careful consideration it is an example of how complex all relationships are in explaining economic development. It is extremely difficult to generalise. At one extreme are scholars who attribute the rise of Europe to mere accidents of geography (Blaut 1993 and 2000, Diamond 1997 and Abu-Lughod 1989, Pomeranz 2000, O'Brien 2006). At the other extreme, there are those who give no importance to geography, seeing it as simply the neutral venue of economic activity. It is true that there is every possible permutation of a relationship between the natural resource position of a country and its experience of economic development – countries with abundant resources displaying early and rapid modern economic development, such as the USA; countries with such resources remaining undeveloped, such as Saudi Arabia or some Latin American countries; countries with poor resources failing to initiate modern economic development, such as landlocked states in either Africa or Latin America; and countries with poor resources surmounting their disadvantage to become successful, such as Japan or Switzerland. Few countries are completely lacking in natural resources of some kind.

The first section of the chapter considers the general influence of geography on economic development. The second section analyses more systematically the main elements of geography important to economic development and shows how testing the importance of geography can be achieved. One major argument advanced is that economic development in Europe was critically dependent on the 'ghost acreage' made accessible by the colonisation of large parts of the world by the European powers – this is the theme of the third section. The last section considers a case study, sub-Saharan Africa, in which resource limitations may well have had a continuing impact in curbing economic development, but which also illustrates how an abundance of resources can be a curse.

DETERMINISM OR POSSIBILISM?

For a significant period of time, the argument that geography is a determinant of the pattern of economic development was unfashionable. Geography was seen as irrelevant to economic development, at most a background feature of little importance. Recently, largely under the influence of Diamond (1997), Bloom, Sachs et al. (1998), Gallup, Sachs and Mellinger (1999) and Krugman (1998), and of interesting attempts to explain the poor performance of African economies (Artadi and Sala-i-Martin 2003), taking into account specific geographic features, the influence of geography has come back into favour. In several accounts, there is almost a revival of geographical determinism. The influence of geography is advanced by some as the critical difference explaining differential economic performance. For example, in reviewing the causes of the British Industrial Revolution, O'Brien (2006: 7) refers to four factors, the first three of which are in some sense geographical: a highly productive and responsive agriculture; abundant and accessible supplies of minerals, particularly coal; foreign trade, promoted and sustained by massive and cost-effective state investment in naval power, which opened the resources of other countries for British consumption; and technological discovery and innovation, referred to as only a proximate cause. He also refers to the advantage of natural waterways (O'Brien 2006: 13). This prompted O'Brien to assert, 'Geography not only matters more than institutions, it goes a long way towards explanation of their form and evolution' (O'Brien 2006: 11).

Location is an important feature of economic activity and requires explanation. Most human activity is unevenly distributed across the face of the globe, and in critical economic areas, very unevenly distributed. Why do vast cities appear? Why is so much capital concentrated in so few places in the world, notably within the developed economies? Why do most financial institutions concentrate in certain cities? One explanation is that important economic resources are just as unevenly distributed, whether the relevant resource is oil, timber, fertile soil or precipitation. The two distributions are linked. People move to where there are resources, whether they are natural or man-made. The nasties are also unevenly distributed, and their distribution is also relevant to the location of economic activity. Humans avoid certain parts of the world, where conditions are too harsh for people to live or which impose costs which make economic activity disadvantageous, for example where it is too cold, where there is little rain or water, where mountainous conditions make movement difficult, or where it is excessively hot and humid. In the past, when air-conditioning and heating was either absent or very costly, this avoidance was more marked than it is today. Certain conditions repel, just as others attract.

It is easy to make assertions about the importance of geography, much more difficult to evaluate that influence. Testing of the basic hypotheses has been rather crude. Latitude, or the distance from the equator, is taken as a crude indicator of geographical difference. A test of the influence of latitude on economic development requires both a spelling out of what element linked with latitude is relevant and detailed data in a form suitable to testing. The relevant elements might be temperature, precipitation, elevation or distance from the coast, rather than latitude as such. Relevant data should be locationally explicit, rather than country based. In one research project, Nordhaus has estimated 'gross cell product', the gross value added within 1-degree latitude by 1-degree longitude contours – that is, 64,800 grids in the whole world, although most have no or little land. It is not difficult to show how far economic activity is geographically concentrated, even within the developed economies. Population and output per person within such cells can be estimated, even area cultivated. Interest is focused on the relationship between the high concentration of economic activity and geographical features. The density of economic activity is especially strongly related to temperature, precipitation and coastal proximity. Common in grid analysis is the regression of geographical factors against income per head or growth rates of income per head, the exercise done with other independent variables providing a varying context (Hibbs and Olsson 2004). For example Masters and McMillan (2001: 175) use grid analysis to support a specific argument, that 'people tend to choose to live and grow crops, where there is some frost, but not too much'. Frost kills pathogens and pests, and controls organisms in the soil (ibid.: 169). This underpins the importance of the concentration of modern economic development in temperate latitudes. Masters and McMillan conclude, 'frost frequency does have remarkable significance for economic behaviour, independently of many other factors for which data are available'.

The influence of geography need not be a continuing one, effective during the whole period up to the present. Being a potent influence at some point of time in the past may be enough, leaving a lasting legacy, and not just in the agglomerations of economic activity in certain locations. At key moments, geography comprises contingent factors which make all the difference, particularly in combination with other factors. The initial geographical advantages may have long since ceased to be obvious, but they may have been decisive at a key moment of time, when it was perhaps a significant determinant of the rate of economic advance. Hibbs and Olsson (2004) have shown that initial geographic and bio-geographic conditions, what they called environmental meta-conditions, have had a decisive influence in explaining differences in output per head, constituting 'more nearly ultimate sources of contemporary prosperity' (Hibbs and Olsson 2004: 3715). Geographic conditions are defined by three factors: how favourable climate is to agriculture, using the Koppen classification, distance from the equator – latitude, and by east-west ecological orientation – distance of a region, east-west, relative to distance, north-south. Bio-geographical conditions are defined by the local availability of domesticatable plants and animals. These factors not only largely explain the timing of the Neolithic revolution, but also 50–60 per cent of the current differences in GDP per capita (Hibbs and Olsson 2004: 3718). The inclusion of institutions raises the figure to 80 per cent, relevant since, it is argued, institutional quality largely reflects the higher output per head already given by geography, since richer countries have better institutions, rather than the other way round. In this sense, they argue that institutional factors are a proximate cause, if the most powerful one (Hibbs and Olsson 2004: 3715).

It is likely that, through the chains of cause and effect represented in the path-dependent historical experiences of different countries, geography leaves lasting influences on the diverging performance of various regions of the world. Krugman (1998) has argued strongly: '. . .aspects of natural geography are able to matter so much not because natural features of the landscape are that crucial, but because they establish seeds around which self-reinforcing agglomerations crystallize' (Krugman 1998: 24). Once initiated, the concentrations of economic activity are self-reinforcing. There are areas of agglomeration, to which economically important resources move, including capital and labour, because the return is higher than elsewhere. Economists often assume that the scarcity of a resource, such as capital or skilled labour, will push up its price and attract an inflow to the region of scarcity, a movement which eventually offsets that scarcity. This is not the dominant tendency in the world, otherwise economic activity and economic development would be much more evenly spread.

The interaction between geography and human activity is two-way. Human activity affects the geographical environment in which it occurs. The present concern with the environment is an implicit recognition of the importance of geographical factors – the finite supply of key resources, the limited availability of water, reduced biodiversity, global warming, even an increased incidence of natural shocks. Global warming has sensitised commentators to the impact of human economic activity on climate and short-term weather conditions. It is argued that global warming reinforces the impact of geography, notably the incidence of natural shocks, sensitising us to a previously underestimated strength of geographical factors. The changing conditions under which such shocks occur are usually ignored, for example, the greater amount of capital at risk, which gives them more impact. How far such activity has caused global warming is unclear and highly controversial, although there appears to be a growing consensus among scientists that it has.[1]

Environmentalists have also drawn attention to the finite supply of key resources, sometimes adopting rather crude models of their rate of exhaustion. Predictions of only 30 years of oil left go back as far as the 1880s. The Club of Rome Report in the 1960s was based on predictions of how quickly particular resources would run out, which reflected the size of reserves and a projection of current usage rates into the future.

There are two diametrically opposed arguments relevant to the theme of this book. First, the influence of geography is straightforward: resource abundance promotes the process of economic development, or resource deficiencies inhibit the same process. On the negative side, geographical contexts are seen as highly relevant to the poor performance of Africa. There is a strong case for a beneficial effect of resource abundance, but there must be those ready and able to take advantage of the resources. Since geography does not change much, an argument resting on favourable resources has to explain why those resources did not produce a positive result in the past. Resource advantages have been used to emphasise the successes both in Europe and the USA. The Industrial Revolution in Britain has long been seen by some as reflecting the availability of coal in geographically advantageous locations, often close to deposits of iron ore (Wrigley 1990). Britain benefited from such locations, France was disadvantaged by the absence or poor location of coal deposits. Belgium has abundant coal, the Netherlands did not – Belgium industrialised more quickly. The Rhineland and the Ukraine developed around the coal fields. In addition, the flow of resources which came from the newly settled Americas (Pomeranz 2000), and other neo-Europes, are seen as very important to economic development within Europe. The discovery and exploitation of 'ghost acreage' is seen as a vital part of the acceleration in economic development in Europe, since it eased a potential constraint imposed by the pressure of population on resources. The rich natural abundance of the USA has affected the speed, if not its very emergence as the leading economy. Staple theory, once a focus of much interest, has linked the success of newly settled societies to their natural resource endowments (Altman 2003). A major issue raised by such arguments relates to the factor endowment of different areas and its influence on their economic development. The staple argument stresses the role of the specific resource endowment of certain areas and the demand for exports from those areas in influencing the pace and pattern of economic development.

The alternative stands the argument based on resource abundance on its head. It stresses a process of challenge and response, arguing that abundance discourages effort and promotes corruption, and that those most lacking the relevant resources make the strongest efforts to compensate for resource deficiencies. Japan is the most frequently used example of a country overcoming resources constraints in a creative way. Its position with respect to both agricultural and industrial resources is decidedly inferior to that of Britain, which may explain why Japan did not initiate modern economic development. It has a limited amount of fertile land, almost no coal or iron ore, and very little in the way of energy supplies. Japan, like Britain, had one major advantage, excellent access to water transport. This allowed the substitution of foreign for domestic sources of the relevant resources. What you can produce and sell can be exchanged for what you cannot. Japan has been creative in compensating for any natural resource deficiency.

More generally, there is much talk of the so-called resources curse. The classic historical case is the abundance that the acquisition of the New World opened up for Spain, notably in gold and silver. The Spanish colonies were initially much better endowed with relevant resources than the British colonies. The massive flood of silver and gold into the Spanish economy initially raised income levels, but in a perverse way, this sudden injection of riches harmed the growth prospects of Spain. The government was tempted to pursue expensive ambitions and to devote resources to the military and other purposes unsuitable for promoting economic development. The resources allowed both imperial and individual pretensions to be relatively easily realised, at least in the early years, diverting effort and attention away from economic activities, at enormous cost to the prospects of economic development. As demand rose and the money supply expanded, prices in Spain rose. The inflow of silver and gold sparked an inflationary surge, with significant negative effects. Spain became dependent on other areas of Europe for the supply of cheaper manufactured goods and services. The inflow of silver and gold from the New World made Spain dependent on imports of manufactured goods and less able to produce them itself. The same argument applies to any commodity-driven economy, including today gas- or oil-driven economies (Corden 1984) and economies with a wide range of commodities such as Australia, but in these cases, other elements can compensate and allow the benefits to be received and the losses avoided.

ARGUMENTS AND THEIR EVALUATION

The geographical factors of interest are those largely unaffected by human activities, at least on a decadal time scale (Nordhaus 2005: 3). On a longer time scale, humans are shaping the geographical context. The stable factors involve physical attributes tied to specific locations – either invariable over time (latitude, distance from coastlines, or elevation) or variable over differing time periods, but not usually in the short term (climate, soil or the availability of raw materials or energy sources). It is assumed that any changes are independent of human activity (exogenous), probably not an unreasonable assumption, at least until the spread of economic development in the latter part of the twentieth century. A sensible approach is to consider the most important relevant topics, such as physical configuration, including location, climate, agricultural and industrial resources and transport access.

Successful economic development has mostly occurred within temperate latitudes.[2] It is rare in the tropics – Hong Kong and Singapore are the most striking, but recent, exceptions, the state of Queensland in Australia another. This has prompted Sachs to conclude: 'Perhaps the strongest empirical relationship in the wealth and poverty of nations is the one between ecological zones and per capita income. Economies in tropical ecozones are nearly everywhere poor, while those in temperate ecozones are generally rich' (Gallup, Sachs and Mellinger 1999: 179). Economic development is difficult in areas characterised by low soil fertility and conditions dangerous for humans and their animals. Location can be reduced to such factors as the distribution of climatic conditions at different latitudes, including their impact on soil fertility and the relative frequency of disease throughout the world, whether affecting humans, animals or plants.[3] For example, tropical areas with large rainfalls have impoverished soils beneath the abundant plant cover in the canopies of the rain forest. Stripping away the vegetation exposes poor soil to further leaching of the nutrients. In a recent study, Bloom, Canning and Sevilla (2003) linked two convergence clubs of high and low income to geography. Countries which are members of the low-level club have higher income per head if they enjoy advantageous conditions. The probability of membership of the upper-level club, and implicitly the likelihood of escape from the low-level club, increases for cool, coastal economies with heavy rainfall, evenly spread throughout the year. If the country is hot, landlocked, with low or very seasonal rainfall, it is difficult for it to break out of the poverty trap. Membership of the upper-level club frees the country from geographical influence. This reflects a restructuring of the economy away from agriculture. Masters and McMillan (2001: 182) add the benefits of seasonal frosts to the factors making for higher income per head, a breakaway from dependence on agriculture, and for convergence. 'It may be that their climate [that of the temperate zones] fostered a historical accumulation of man-made capital, whose productivity grows toward similar levels anywhere in the world'. Tropical areas lacked the advantage of the destruction of potentially dangerous pathogens and the impact of frost on soil structure.

Extremes, of whatever kind, are a problem. Some parts of the world are subject to a high incidence of storms – hurricanes, cyclones and typhoons, or floods. Others are liable to protracted periods of drought. Both heat and cold impose costs, in some cases making economic activity impossible. Permafrost at surprisingly low latitudes in such areas as Siberia, under the influence of large land masses, rules out most activities, including agriculture, and makes construction costly. There are still arguments about the impact of heat on the intensity of work. In the tropics, only air-conditioning has removed the effect of heat on economic activity, but there are adjustments which can be made, such as the siesta. Already in 1400 the world population of about 350 million was concentrated on barely 7 per cent of the dry land, since the rest of the land was covered by swamp, steppe, desert or ice (Marks 2007: 24). Astoundingly, even today, when population is greater than 6 billion, 70 per cent still live on the same 7 per cent.[4]

The world is divided by various patterns of temperature and precipitation (rain, hail, snow) into ecological zones. The Koppen classification is probably the best-known attempt to classify climatic types. The climatic type most conducive to dense human settlement is the 'humid temperate', characterised by rain all the year round, with hot summers and mild winters. The distribution of this type is interesting, favouring Western Europe and North America. There are some startling contrasts in the world, highly relevant from the point of view of agricultural productivity and the rate of new settlement (White 1987: 49). The USA in its contiguous landed area has 34 per cent of its land in this type, whereas the old USSR had only 0.5 per cent, located along the Black Sea, a contrast which influenced the rate at which these two societies initiated modern economic development (White 1987).

Geography largely determines what will grow where and how easily, what technology is required and whether it is feasible in particular regions. Climate and soils draw invisible boundaries for the cultivation of particular plants and the domestication and rearing of particular animals. Even where cultivation of a particular crop is possible, there is a need to adjust to local conditions. Because most crops have a narrow range of conditions under which they thrive, they are sensitive to both small differences and to small changes in temperature or precipitation. The pattern of rainfall moulds the environment, largely determining vegetation cover. Soils differ in fertility and in the trace elements which are present. There are also significant differences in the length of the growing season, incidence of frost or seasonal distribution of rainfall. It is tempting to assume a set of initial geographical conditions, of temperature, precipitation and of soil type, given by nature. Water, warmth and soil are resources relevant to economic activity. Even a simple notion such as soil fertility is not an unchangeable 'initial condition', but is a variable reflecting the intensity of the agricultural system, in particular the frequency of cropping and the inputs which are made to renew fertility (Boserup 1965: 13).

Physical configurations include the location of mountains, of stretches of water and rivers, and access to coastlines. Large mountains have a significant influence on temperature and rainfall. They are difficult to cross or use agriculturally, and difficult to live in. Coastlines and rivers give access to water transport, still the cheapest method for moving bulky goods. Rivers provide silt and natural fertilisation when they flood naturally and regularly. Many of the early civilisations were founded on river systems, where soil was fertile and irrigation possible.

The geographical configuration of the Eurasian land mass has greatly influenced its economic activity. There are three areas of strikingly different climate, soils and transport access – the maritime western and central European region (more or less the countries of the European Union), the continental land mass of eastern Europe and western Asia, and the monsoonal area of southern, south-eastern and eastern Asia. The Gulf Stream keeps the first region much warmer than might be expected from its latitude. There is plenty of moisture, but mainly in winter, which makes the planting of crops which can handle winter conditions essential. Soils beneath the extensive hardwood forests were relatively poor and required manure or long fallow periods to keep fertile. It is easier to turn the light soils in woodland areas than the sods of the grasslands, such as the steppe, the prairies and the pampas, which partly explains why the famous grasslands of the world were cultivated so late. For the latter, heavy ploughs are required, pulled by livestock, or later tractors. However, even the lighter woodland soils of Europe usually required ploughing with the aid of a team of animals. Agricultural productivity is lower than in areas where soil is much more fertile. Also made much of in the literature is the physical configuration of Europe, a peninsula of peninsulas. The Baltic, Mediterranean and Black Seas penetrate deep into the continent, linked by associated seas and fed by major river systems which are navigable. There are not many areas of Europe which are distant from water transport. Half of Europe is within 120 miles of the sea. The wide plains of Eastern Europe are an exception – in Russia, just 2 per cent is within a similar distance of the sea. The second is the natural divisions within Europe provided by such mountain ranges as the Pyrenees, the Alps and the Carpathians, which define the core areas of many of the nation states which have evolved in those areas (E.L. Jones 1987). By contrast, the mountainous nature of the Balkans has made for fragmentation. These two factors played a significant role in the emergence of the multi-cell country system of Europe, which reflecrted, in the words of Havel, 'a maximum of diversity in a minimum of geography'.

The central region is much drier and subject to the extremes of a continental climate. Except in the valleys of the major rivers and in mountainous areas, where there is snow, there is a lack of moisture for agriculture. This region is largely grassland, the home of the nomads and their large herds of animals. The grasslands of the world – the steppe, prairies, pampas – are a response to relatively low rainfall, their full economic exploitation retarded by mounted raiders and the absence of large ploughs. The grasslands of Eurasia were a major aid to rapid movement by peoples whose movement was often initiated by climatic disturbances (Fagan 2008). For many centuries, the movement of nomadic peoples along the Eurasian grass highway influenced the condition of the agricultural societies to the south and west, particularly those most accessible and richest. The dynasties of China rose and fell with invasions from the north. India suffered from such incursions. European empires were rocked by 'barbarian' invasions, particularly Russia, which, perhaps even through to the present, was influenced by the Mongol invasion of the thirteenth century (Hedlund 2001).

The third region is mostly within the tropics. It is influenced by a monsoonal climate which brings plenty of rain in summer. The most obvious of the physical geographical features are the vast mountain ranges in the centre of Asia, notably the Himalaya ranges, so large that they influence the nature of climate through most of Asia, notably in an area stretching through both temperate and tropical areas, from Japan to India. The huge Indian Ocean plays its role in the system, acting as a kind of heat reservoir, even to East Africa, remaining at approximately the same even temperature when the Asian land mass heats up in summer and cools down in winter (Bernstein 2008: 38). The heat produces lower air pressure and the cold higher pressure – winds move from high to low, so in summer they come from the sea bringing plenty of moisture (south-westerlies) and in winter they blow off the land (north-easterlies). A kind of monsoon determinism has influenced some commentators to see this climatic phenomenon as a major causative factor in many aspects of Asian life. The monsoons make possible the wet cultivation of rice (Oshima 1987). Rice cultivation, as compared with the cultivation of other grains, has been an important influence (Bray 1986), allowing a much higher density of population, even requiring it, given the labour-intensive nature of both the preparation of the paddies and of rice cultivation itself. Economic life has at its core the monsoon and rice cultivation. Moreover, in the words of Fernandez-Armesto (2001: 401), 'the frustration of the potential of the Indian Ocean, and the fulfilment of global ambitions in the Atlantic, have to be explained in part with reference to the inescapable facts of geographical determinism: the tyranny of the winds'. The reversal of the monsoonal winds encouraged movement within the Indian Ocean, explaining the early growth of trade and the existence of a huge trading system in Asia, but constrained any exit from that ocean (Fernandez-Armesto 2001: 384–5). Such an argument led Fernandez-Armesto (2001: 405) to comment, 'In most of our explanations of what has happened in history there is too much hot air and not enough wind'.

A maritime orientation is a potent influence for economic development. The potential for economic development is raised if you are an island, preferably one free from foreign invasion for a long period of time, as is the case for both Britain (since 1066) and Japan, and one within temperate latitudes. Macfarlane (1997: 388) has stressed the importance of the islandhood of England and Japan in influencing their demographic behaviour. Early development has occurred in areas with a maritime climatic influence – that is, with moderate temperatures and adequate rainfall, and not in areas which are land-locked, that is, relatively isolated, and free of maritime influences. Distance from the coast increases proneness to the extremes of a continental climate (harsh winters and hot summers). Proximity to the coast or to major river/lake systems, particularly linked to open seas, is highly beneficial in reducing transport costs.

Location with respect to the main centres of world population is probably the most talked-about factor. The tyranny of distance has been stressed with respect to some countries (by Blainey 1966 in his classic book on Australia). It is possible to conquer the tyrant distance, as Blainey shows. Yet it is better to be Canada or Sweden, close to major Triad centres, than Australia, distant from all such centres. Proximity to large concentrations of economic activity, and to large markets, is important in itself. Collier (2007: 56) argues that, on average in the world, a rise in the economic growth rate of 1 per cent causes an increase of 0.4 per cent in a neighbouring country. He also notes how the distance from the EU indicates the probability of an East European country becoming an economic success or a failed state: the key is the pressure to conform to European rules in order to get entry (Collier 2007: 139).

Physical, as well as ecological, barriers mean that distance is not a simple thing. There are major barriers to movement, sometimes provided by jungle, deserts or mountain ranges. The Sahara and the dense jungle of equatorial Africa are major barriers to north/south movement within that continent. Similar barriers exist in South and Central America. Such barriers render some areas, not obviously isolated, detached from the more dynamic areas, particularly when reinforced by ecological differences. Isolation is a constraint on the movement of innovations. Diamond has contrasted the east/west axis of Eurasia, compared with the north/south axes of Africa and the Americas. Such an axis, because of similar climatic conditions, encouraged contact and the transfer of plants, animals and ideas in general; movement of ideas and technology is significant. Much agricultural technology is ecology specific and not transferable across the ecological divides. A surprising amount of industrial technology is also ecology specific, as early settlers in Australia discovered (Raby 1990). The milling and brewing industries are good examples. Diamond pointed to the distribution of domesticatable animals and plants as a key element in the rate of long-term development of different areas. The range of such wild flora and fauna influenced where agriculture was independently developed and the timing of such development. It influenced who could imitate successfully. Nearly all agricultural technology is environment specific. The modern technology of agriculture was developed in temperate regions. The main food crops grow best in temperate areas. If we focus on temperate latitudes, it is clear from the historical record that there have been significant long-term fluctuations in climate, having a significant impact on economic life, and that these fluctuations have been synchronous across the world (Galloway 1986). During the last thousand years, there have been two relatively cold periods during which conditions changed rapidly – with minima reached around the mid-fifteenth and the late seventeenth centuries. It appears that the carrying capacity of the land was reduced and population growth slowed during the little ice ages or was reversed as a result of the impact on fertility and mortality rates. However, the current period has been a notably warm one in the history of the earth, at least since the last ice age, 13,000 years ago.

Water is a much neglected resource – a vital input for all human activity. Its importance is rising in significance.[5] There is a high income elasticity of demand for water in developing countries. Modern economic development is water-intensive. Irrigation is an important, and expensive, aid to agriculture. For some societies, control of the river systems is essential to agriculture and there is discussion of the notion that hydraulic empires emerged to manage the systems. Initially, annual floods might renew the fertility of the soil, but they require control, to prevent major damage to other facilities. Many older civilisations in Egypt, the Middle East, India and China were focused on major rivers.

There are a limited number of basic raw materials critical to the economic activity of human beings, beyond foodstuffs and water. Bairoch (1993: chapter 5) has shown how until the 1950s developed countries usually industrialised on the basis of local raw materials, although this general picture conceals individual divergences. The relevant materials are those which help meet the basic need for shelter, clothing and warmth, and also serve in tools and machinery of various kinds. Even before industrialization, the fibres from which clothing is made – particularly wool, flax and hemp, but also cotton and silk – and the construction materials necessary for buildings and structures of various kinds, mainly timber, were important. Leather was also an important item for a range of purposes. The relevant construction materials were wood or wattle and daub; stone and other more solid materials were seldom used. One of the great revolutions was the introduction of brick and tile into construction of housing – in Britain, during the seventeenth and eighteenth centuries. Most of these basic materials required land for their production. As important was a source of fuel. A fundamental transformation at the inception of modern economic development was the replacement of timber as a fuel, the move from an economy based on organic sources of fuel to one based on inorganic sources (Wrigley 1990). While inorganic sources of energy such as wind and water were used in the pre-modern period, and in some areas on a significant scale, and animals, notably horses, continued to be used right to the end of the nineteenth century, timber was the main energy source. A 'timber famine' is said to have preceded the quickening of economic change in Britain (Wilkinson 1973: 115). The replacement of timber by coal was central to the Industrial Revolution. In Britain, its substitution took place over a long period of time, stretching from the sixteenth century well into the nineteenth. This is a theme developed by several commentators (Wrigley 1990, Pomerantz 2000 and Cameron 2003). Cameron (1997: chapters 9 and 10) even distinguished between forward and latecomer economies in the nineteenth century on the basis of whether they had good coal supplies or not. He shows how the pattern of modern economic development in its early phase reflected the availability of coal. O'Brien (2006: 12) quotes an estimate that shows that Britain's output of coal in 1815 implied the release of 15 million acres from timber production, equivalent to 88 per cent of the arable area at that time.

The distribution of such raw materials initially reflected the distribution of flora and fauna and continued to do so for textile raw materials, but later the location of deposits of the key materials, such as coal, became much more important. Any material with a high bulk-to-value ratio, and the ratio of coal was high, could not be transported far. Industrialisation required not only food for a greatly increased population living in urban areas, but also a massively increased supply of both textile fibres and of coal. The level of the demand depended on the level of economic development and its speed, and also on the pattern of growth in different sectors. The alleged resource scarcity in Japan did not become a problem until industrialisation speeded up and militarisation changed the structure of the industrial sector (Yasuba 1996).[6] The pattern of trade shows that in the early period of modern economic growth before 1900, when trade was relatively free, Japan exported resource-intensive commodities, such as raw silk and tea, and imported manufactures including textiles. The pattern changed between 1900 and 1930 in the direction of export of manufactures and import of raw materials, but only became a problem in the 1930s, largely as a result of government intervention in the economy.

Often neglected as an energy input is a good supply of fast-running water, in the early stages of modern economic development an important energy source. This was important in both the UK and the USA. Most importantly, significant industrialisation required both energy sources and the raw materials of metal production on a massive scale – notably coal, later oil and gas, and iron ore, later non-ferrous metals and bauxite. Early industrialisation occurred largely where the raw materials were located, chiefly near the coal fields, largely because of the high bulk-to-value ratio of the main raw materials, which made their transportation very expensive. A map of European industrial activity on the eve of World War I is a map of the coal fields of Europe and North America.

A country can substitute for missing resources by importing the relevant resources. This depends on good transport access. Before the advent of the railway, water transport had an enormous cost advantage over overland transport, whether by sea, or along navigable rivers or lakes. For bulky goods, this is still the case. Countries with easy access to water transport, such as Britain or Japan, or continents such as Europe, with a heavily indented coastline and well-located rivers, had an enormous advantage in economic development. In some cases, they could substitute for missing resources by importing the necessary raw material. Even Britain imported most of the textile fibres which were central to industrialisation – cotton from the southern states of the USA and wool from Australia. Japan and South Korea have imported many of the raw materials needed for their industrialisation, including sources of energy and basic metals. Geography is still important in explaining both the level and patterns of international interaction, such as trade and direct investment. The gravity model takes into account a number of geographical features, including proximity and access to coastline. Nations tend to trade with and invest in other nations in close proximity. Landlocked countries are still at a marked disadvantage in initiating modern economic development, although some succeed

– Switzerland and Austria are examples, but in these cases the identity of the neighbours is critical. In Africa, 38 per cent of the population live in landlocked countries (Collier 2007: 54), and the influence of neighbours on economic development is almost invariably bad.

INTERACTIONS AND GHOST ACREAGE

One increasingly popular argument emphasises the differing impact of the interaction between Europeans and the outside world. European coloniza-tion and settlement is linked directly with a varying disease environment. Both the perception, and for a significant period, the reality, encouraged patterns of settlement by Europeans which reflected partly exposure to disease and immunities of different societies, and partly the institutional legacy from the colonising powers. European settlers perceived varying degrees of threat in settled areas. Studies done show marked difference in mortality regimes, and by implication in morbidity, in the early nineteenth century (Crosby 1986). Mortality rates for European soldiers, public serv-ants or churchmen show significant differences during the early period. In the tropics, the death rate of Europeans was much higher than in temperate areas, since they were exposed to diseases to which they had little immu-nity. Certain environments appeared lethal to the incomers and a major deterrent to settlement. During the nineteenth century, these differences slowly disappeared as the incomers adjusted to the new environments and learned to live there. By then, the pattern of colonisation and its nature had become fixed. Other factors influenced settlement – the existence of dense populations living in the relevant areas and lack of familiarity with such environments. In the tropics, small ruling groups were imposed on large existing populations with little influence on the general nature of economic activity, except where there were goods available which were not elsewhere – mining and plantation settlements emerged to exploit these possibilities. Sugar plantations or silver mines were introduced to exploit local resources. Often labour forces were brought in from outside to work the plantations or mines, labour forces better adapted to local condi-tions. The African and the Indian diasporas are results of this action; they replaced the white labour force, which was expensive, partly because of its high attrition rate.[7] The Europeans were usually only there temporarily and did not have a continuing permanent interest in the colonies.

In some areas, the Europeans brought in diseases to which the local population had no immunity, which emptied the areas of previously rela-tively dense populations (the Americas, Australia and Oceania, Siberia).[8] Europeans poured into areas similar to those with which they were familiar

– temperate areas well endowed agriculturally. They brought their institutions and technologies with them. Even so they experienced unexpected difficulties of adjustment; it took time to develop the colonies, but within historically short periods there was significant economic development.

Colonies of settlement and colonies of temporary sojourn were characterised respectively by very different institutional frameworks which, on the one hand encouraged a broad kind of economic development or, on the other, were based on rent extraction.[9] Geography had a powerful influence on the nature of the initial economic development and its potential for the future, one reinforced by a continuing institutional imprint which had a more lasting influence. Colonies based on the extractive model stressed large landed estates and uneven land-holding. They also tended to have highly centralised authoritarian governments. Surplus income was extracted for the metropolitan society and a narrow ruling elite. The divergent development of the Spanish Americas and British America illustrates this nicely (Engermann and Sokoloff 1994). By contrast, colonies of settlement often had decentralised political authority and a predominance of small-scale owner-occupier agriculture. A rich civil society emerged in regions which became the USA, Australia, Canada and New Zealand, and underpinned both a movement towards democracy and the inception of modern economic development, largely through the operation of the market. There is little doubt that these divergent historical paths had their roots in geographical features, and there is a growing literature which recognises this.

The colonies of settlement represented an extension of the landed area of Europe. The term ghost means that the acreage – standing in this context for land or resources in general – was not located in the relevant area, but served a function which was equivalent to land that was. The region of most relevance is Europe, principally the most densely populated parts in the west of Europe, such as Britain. The acreage available within Europe was much greater than appeared at first sight since it was supplemented by the areas opened up abroad, particularly during the eighteenth and nineteenth centuries. As already indicated, the ghost acreage amounted to a significant ratio of the domestic supply of land. The share of imports in meeting any particular demand is not the critical issue, rather the easing of particular bottlenecks whose persistence could have slowed the pace of industrialisation and even blocked modern economic development. Economic models always assume that alternatives exist – there is always a choice and an opportunity cost. In practice, this is not true. It is significant that the main raw material of the 'leading sector' of the Industrial Revolution, cotton, was imported. De Vries (2001: 428) refers to the 'ghost acreage' of cotton in 1830 as 23 million acres, more than the whole of

British cropland. The key question in this case is whether there could have been a substitute for American cotton, although the latter involved trade.

The release of Europe from the Malthusian constraint of limited resources, principally food supply, was critical to its economic development (this is discussed in Chapter 12). An increasing labour intensity of exploitation of the land in order to supply the food and raw materials needed to support a growing population can be avoided through an increasing inflow of imports. A flow of emigrants to areas of new settlement abroad relieved the pressure of population on the finite supply of land. Before World War I as many as a million people were moving annually from Europe to the USA alone. Most of the early imports from colonies were luxury goods with a high value and an initially limited market, but in some cases a market which was growing rapidly – spices, precious metals, tea, tobacco, sugar. Such products came from both colonies of settlement and those of temporary sojourn. Some of these products had an important role to play in improving health (Macfarlane 1997). The nature of these items suggests that they were catering for a demand resulting from previous economic development. Since they could not be grown in Britain, although they could in other parts of Europe, their production abroad did not directly provide 'ghost' acres. In so far as they were substitutes – tea for beer, sugar for honey – they did so indirectly. As transportation and transactions costs were reduced, more bulky raw materials were imported, such as cotton or wool, and later, foodstuffs such as meat, when refrigeration technology allowed, and grain. Some of these were direct savings. In so far as cotton replaced wool or flax this was certainly the case. A halving of international transport costs in the eighteenth century brought cotton and wool into the international trading system, beginning in a significant way in the first case at the start of the nineteenth century and in the second well into its first half. The advent of railways, the steam ship and of refrigeration allowed the same to happen to wheat and meat in the second half of the nineteenth century. Given the population expansion in Britain, these were critical inputs.

AFRICA AND THE RESOURCES CURSE

Sala-i-Martin (2002:19) has summarised the nature of the problem: 'The welfare of close to 700 million citizens of a whole continent has deteriorated dramatically since independence and the main reason is that the countries in which these people live have failed to grow. Understanding the underlying reasons for this gargantuan failure is the most important question the economics profession faces as we enter the new century'.

Africa, notably sub-Saharan Africa, has consequently become a focus of a major debate on the role of geography in this failure. The relatively poor economic performance is not new (Bloom et al. 1998: 210); Africa's poor economic growth is 'chronic rather than episodic' (ibid.: 208). After independence from colonialism was achieved in the 1950s and 1960s, there was initially a mood of optimism concerning the prospects for economic development in the newly independent African countries, a mood confirmed by an initial acceleration in the rate of economic growth, at least in the period before the first oil shock in 1973. This optimism, and the associated improvement in economic performance, was short-lived. For most of sub-Saharan Africa, the period after the 1970s was one of stagnation, and even contraction, with some notable exceptions. The exceptions, such as Botswana or Mauritius, stood apart in key respects, small economies with particular advantages such as valuable natural resources. Per-capita GDP fell on average in the whole area by about 10 per cent between 1974 and the early twenty-first century. This is a case of absolute divergence, since most of the world was improving its position. The end result is that 15 of the poorest 20 countries in the world are now located in Africa and almost 50 per cent of Africa's population lives in extreme poverty – income of less than one dollar a day (Bloom et al. 1998: 210).

There is no shortage of arguments why this failure might have occurred and a growing body of regression studies which have tried to give a quantitative weight to individual factors.[10] At least seven areas of weakness are identified: exploitative external interactions; a heavy dependence on commodity exports; internal weaknesses; poor economic policies; unhelpful demographic change; the combination of social fractionalism and poor social capability; and finally, geographical factors. Some of these have a negative impact on the level of investment and its distribution, or even the price of investment goods relative to consumer goods, others reinforce the inadequacies of human rather than physical capital, including issues of health, often expressed in poor life expectation, and educational issues, yet others are expressed in a lack of openness, an excess of public spending, or state or government failures, in particular the artificiality of borders and their lack of correspondence with tribal divisions, the prevalence of civil wars and the universality of corruption, and the failure of Africa to move into the final stage of the demographic transition with fertility rates remaining at about 5. Such arguments are by no means mutually exclusive.

The focus here is on the geographic arguments. 'At the root of Africa's poverty lies its extraordinarily disadvantageous geography, which has helped to shape its societies and its interaction with the rest of the world. Sub-Saharan Africa is by far the most tropical – in the simple sense of the highest proportions of land and population in the tropics – of the world' major regions, and tropical regions in general lag far behind temperate regions in economic development' (Bloom et al. 1998: 211). There are three main arguments. The first relates to the greater exposure of the population within African countries to debilitating diseases that reduce the productivity of workers and deter investment in education and health. Interest in this factor has increased with the spread of HIV infection and a growing death rate from AIDS. A significant proportion of the relevant populations is HIV positive, reaching as high as 30 per cent in many southern cone African countries, and these are often concentrated in the population of working age. This is the tip of the iceberg. There is a long history of disease which has inhibited economic growth in Africa. In temperate areas, populations are protected by seasonal frosts from dangerous organisms that threaten their health, which also protect the plants and livestock on which nutritional levels are dependent (Masters and McMillan 2001). In tropical areas, there is no such protection. The relevant diseases for humans include malaria, sleeping sickness and bilharzia. Malaria is seen by Bloom et al. (1998: 233) as a major, if not the major, barrier to Africa's normal integration into the world economy. In many cases, the diseases do not kill, but greatly reduce the productivity of the relevant workers. Disease interacts with poor nutrition. Poor nutrition makes individuals more susceptible to disease, and disease makes it difficult for individuals to derive nutrition from the food they ingest. Disease is a problem for both humans and for domestic animals. The value of human capital is as a consequence limited. It is possible that such factors account for relatively poor scores in intelligence tests.

There is no doubt that, in combination with other factors such as the slave trade and the general harshness of the environment, including its low agricultural productivity, disease explains a remarkably low population density, even in pre-colonial days. This sparseness of population made state-building exceptionally arduous, so that by Eurasian standards the states in Africa remained small and weak, lacking in broader political or cultural unity (Darwin 2008: 314–15). They were easy prey to the colonial powers. Moreover, the colonial state remained a shallow state and poor preparation for the post-colonial era (ibid.: 316, 465, 467).

The second argument refers to the nature of agriculture and its unamenability to technology which has been developed in different climatic zones. Agricultural productivity is chronically low. Tropical forest does not yield fertile soils when cleared. Soils are for the most part poor. Outside the area of tropical forest, rainfall tends to be highly variable, so that drought is a problem. Moreover, the climate does not encourage the planting of the crops important in Europe and Asia. Comparatively little research has been done either on tropical diseases or on agricultural technology relevant to the crops grown in such areas. Countries in tropical areas cannot tap into a pool of technology available in temperate areas.

The third argument stresses the problem of transport accessibility, which makes involvement in international trade difficult. The Sahara desert separates sub-Saharan Africa from Europe in a significant way. The problem of transport access reflects the high proportion of landlocked or semi-landlocked states, the concentration of population away from the coast, the low proportion of coastline to area in the continent as a whole, and the comparative absence of both good natural harbours and long navigable rivers. Only 21 per cent of the population live within 100 km of the sea or along navigable rivers, compared with 67 per cent in the USA and 89 per cent in Europe (Bloom et al. 1998: 239).

It is appropriate at this point to discuss 'the natural resources curse'. There has been an increasing tendency to stress the negative influence of resources (see Collier 2007: chapter 3 for a good summary of the arguments, with an emphasis on Africa). Resources are what any particular society, and at the global level, societies in general, consider to be resources, which is reflected in market value. Technologies of extraction, transportation and use and demand for the products and services in which natural resources are embodied change over time. What is a resource in one period may not be in another. Moreover, resources need to be exploited in a way positive for the process of economic development, which requires not only appropriate organisation and technology, but a distribution of the benefits which ensures that the extractors, the consumers and society at large gain from the process. Unfortunately, under disadvantageous circumstances, resource abundance reinforces various negative feedback loops. The same condition can be both stimulant and constraint on economic development. Which it is depends on a range of conditions, many of which are more likely at low levels of income per head. Moreover, the strength of the loop can vary according to changing circumstance.

Some commentators have pointed out that where resources abound in Africa, there appears to be a resource curse, well illustrated by the impact of oil on Nigeria. Such a curse summarises the possible negative impact of a good natural resource endowment on those apparently benefiting from it. There are three main aspects to such a curse. The first negative influence of abundant resources is on institutional quality, particularly where institutions are relatively weak in the first place. In countries such as Nigeria, the negative effect is most likely to occur. Such an influence is labelled a voracity effect, because the resources generate rents which encourage rapacious rent-seeking behaviour. The existence of such resources discourages the development of better institutions, by encouraging behaviour which stresses short-term returns. The good resource endowment encourages corruption, weak governance, or more bluntly, plunder, as well as rent-seeking. Evidence suggests that it is much easier to appropriate certain kinds of assets – fuel or minerals rather than other resources (often referred to as 'point-source' natural resources) (Sala-i-Martin and Subramanian 2003). It is likely that the effect is non-linear, in that the negative marginal impact of resources on institutional quality depends on, and increases with, their level, but discontinuously. Resources encourage corruption; abundant resources make it almost inevitable that corruption becomes dominant.

The second negative effect relates to the focus induced by natural resources on commodities which do not have 'a trajectory for further growth' (Goldstone 2008: 173). These difficulties are called the Dutch disease. The Dutch disease, which began to afflict the Dutch economy in the 1960s, can be diagnosed as a disease of abundance, in this case an abundance of gas, but it could be an abundance of any natural resource. The terminology reflects the impact of the discovery and exploitation of good deposits of gas upon the Dutch economy. The existence of good resources squeezes out other economic activities and prevents the kind of diversification of the economy which constitutes modern economic development, particularly at its inception. This is a problem especially where the resources at some stage run out. Without a carefully planned exploitation of recently discovered resources, there is a tendency for the real exchange rate to appreciate, that is, in the context of a fixed nominal exchange rate, prices rise and with a floating rate, the nominal exchange rate rises. The more abundant the resources, the more significant are the real exchange rate changes. If resource exploitation encourages an inflow of capital, in order to help exploit the commodity, the situation is made worse – such an inflow further encourages a rise in the exchange rate. Abundance itself can be a problem, acting as a barrier to the diversification of an economy or encouraging an over-concentration on the primary sector of that economy. Exports of other goods and services are discouraged and imports encouraged. In some cases, a selfish elite benefiting from resource abundance may deliberately block the emergence of new sectors of the economy and the specialised training required by a potential labour force for such sectors (Goldstone 2008: 173). In certain circumstances, such abundance can act as a barrier to economic development, blocking the development of other sectors. Even developed countries such as Australia have problems with this effect. Any country which has a commodity-driven exchange rate is likely to find itself faced with an exchange rate higher than might be desired.

The third negative effect is the tendency for commodity prices to fluctuate relative to other prices, causing significant changes in income. With floating exchange rates, this is linked to a volatile exchange rate. Over the longer term, the Dutch disease persists, but in a different form. In a world in which the balance between supply and demand of most commodities is volatile and subject to frequent reversal, so that the relative prices of commodities vary significantly over time, an environment of uncertainty is created for other products. Investment in other products and services is of varying profitability, since it varies with the real exchange rate and in an unexpected way. Even for products and services which are not exported, the competitiveness of imports fluctuates dramatically with movements of the exchange rate.

6. Geography and beyond: the importance of risk environments

> ... uncertainty is not an unusual condition: it has been the underlying condition responsible for the evolving structure of human organisation throughout history and pre-history. (North 2005: 14)

Survival, whether physical or economic, is the primary motivation of individuals and society, survival amidst a flux of environmental change (Guha 1981: chapter 2), both natural, including fluctuations in the availability of resources, and human, the variable relationship with other societies or individuals. The latter includes the predatory pressures of military competition, the fluctuating opportunities arising from cooperation, notably trade and transfers of knowledge, and increasingly obvious demonstration effects, which identify opportunities. Human beings wish to control risk, but the degree of risk aversion differs from society to society and from person to person. Since human beings seek to control their environment, so that it is predictable and manageable, risk, uncertainty or ambiguity, however described, are regarded as deterrents to economic development (North 2005).

A naïve view sees a monotonic relationship between the level of risk and the lack of economic development. Higher risk discourages the kind of decisions which favour economic development, particularly investment decisions. If enough people make decisions characterized by caution, an economy can become mired in a poverty trap. There are two comments to be made on such a viewpoint. The first is that both a rigidly controlled and a completely unpredictable environment are likely to be bad for innovation. In the words of Gaddis (2002: 87), innovation mostly occurs on 'the edge of chaos'. The second is that only under particular conditions do decision makers prefer less variance to more. Their attitude reflects where the expected mean return lies. If it is close to zero, it is likely that on some projects or in some years a return will be negative, but how negative? Most investments look like this if you are in a poverty trap. The influence of risk on economic development is as ambiguous as that of resources. The predominant influence of resources is positive, but they can have negative effects; the predominant influence of risk is negative, but shocks can have positive effects.

The first section of the chapter considers the nature of the general relationship and the way in which economists, particularly financial theorists, regard risk, introducing difficulties which a genuinely dynamic approach brings. The second section looks at the three main aspects of risk – the nature and incidence (frequency) of risk-generating 'shocks', their impact, notably the economic cost, and the response to such shocks, both in short-term decision making and in more long-term institutional adjustments. The next section considers a number of historical treatments of the influence of risk, generalising the way in which such influence might be understood. The chapter concludes by considering the general influence of risk environments in a long-term perspective, notably its institutional influence.

RISK, RETURNS AND CHOICE

Risk is a variation in a key performance variable resulting from an unanticipated shock or change in behaviour which has a negative impact on the relevant decision-making unit, whether government, enterprise or individual, even country. At the macro level, the performance variable might be the rate of economic growth and the relevant risk environment that of the whole economy. At the micro level, the relevant performance indicator might be the rate of profit for a particular project or enterprise. A sophisticated and elegant body of economic theory has been developed which considers risk in a market context. In such theory, risk is represented as a set of probabilities, rather than as a general uncertainty, although those probabilities may be either subjective or objective. It is conventional in economic theory to see a trade-off between risk and return. The relevant activity will be avoided unless a higher return compensates for a higher risk. On the neoclassical account, human motivation reflects a desire both to maximise the return from investment in any economic activity, and also to minimise the risk to which that economic activity is exposed, but allegedly you cannot do both simultaneously – there is a trade-off between the two, with the risk appetite of the decision maker determining the actual mix chosen. This trade-off does not appear as persuasive when a dynamic perspective is taken. There is no reason why a particular innovation should not both increase the return and reduce the risk. From the perspective of economic growth, it is critical to place the desire to control risk in a long-term and dynamic context.

From the conventional economist's viewpoint, volatility in the natural environment takes two forms: first, the variation of a key variable around some mean – at the macro level, GDP or at the micro level profit, share prices, or important quantitative indicators such as harvest yield, temperature, rainfall, or secondly, the possibility of an extreme downward fluctuation (a 'shock' or extreme event).[1] Such a shock threatens security and survival. What generates risk is unanticipated volatility. Such a view assumes that the world is ergodic: there is some equilibrium which defines the relevant mean around which it fluctuates and to which it returns. A non-ergodic world is one of great uncertainty and a high level of risk. There is no pattern, and therefore no way of measuring the volatility.[2] Fernandez-Armesto (2001: 465) has expressed this succinctly: 'The history of civilisations has been patternless. Their future, therefore, is unpredictable'. Or even more to the point (Fernandez-Armesto 2001: 451), history '. . . lurches between random crises, with no direction or pattern, no predictable end. It is a genuinely chaotic system.' It is useful to assume that the world is ergodic, as neoclassical economics does, in order to understand the processes which characterise it, including modern economic growth, whatever the truth of the matter.

The natural environment comprises a risk environment, reflecting its tendency to vary in a threatening and unanticipated way and to impose unexpected costs on economic activity. Each country has its own natural risk environment. Just as the resource position is specific to a country, so is the nature of the risk environment. The natural environment is sometimes violently variable, with tsunami, volcanic eruptions, earthquakes, storms, droughts and floods all affecting economic life, but with an infrequent incidence. Natural shocks can be dramatic in impact, and have a powerful influence on responses. Climatic fluctuations cause changes in agricultural yields and in the capacity of a society to transport foodstuffs. Living in a drought-prone area has a significant influence on farming methods.

There are two senses in which the relevant fluctuations, or 'shocks', are not simply natural phenomena. First, risk results from imperfect perception. Ignorance is often the source of this difficulty. Risk does not exist if the timetable of future 'shocks' is known with precision. They may impose a cost, but the nature of the impact is entirely different. The imperfection may be due to relevant information being inaccessible or not existing, undiscovered or even undiscoverable. Alternatively, it might be due to the nervousness of the perceiver. There is a second sense in which the volatility moves beyond the natural: the human environment itself is volatile. Humans create their own risk environments, through the patterns of behaviour and institutions which they create. There are various risk environments, in which economic players operate, which change over time with the development of the economy. Such risk environments qualify as another factor of ultimate causation to be taken into account in explaining economic development in any region of the world.

An initial position might be that the greater the risk level, the less likely is economic development to occur, since the high risk will deter the key decisions which promote economic growth. Financial theorists generally assume that the uncertainty associated with risk is a bad thing, ignoring the possibility of a positive unanticipated upward variation. A new body of theory, called the real options approach, takes into account the possibility of unanticipated positive outcomes.[3] Such theory considers an investment decision as involving three, rather than two, options – invest, don't invest, or postpone the decision until you have more information or can reduce the possibility of a negative outcome without losing the benefit of an unanticipated upturn. The ideal is to mitigate the risk in such a way that the upside is undisturbed and the downside removed.

There are two sides to risk. On the one hand, the attitude of decision makers to risk influences relevant economic decisions – how willing they are to take on some risk. Responses to risk reflect the degree of risk aversion, or sensitivity to risk, of the key decision makers in any society. On the other, there is a riskiness of the environment in which the decision is made. The attitude to risk may differ as much as the risk environments themselves. The distinction is by no means clear cut, since humans both create and perceive their environments. There is a subtle interaction between a particular risk sensitivity and the specific risk environment. The controversial issue is how far the perception creates the environment of risk. Economists assume risk aversion is general throughout all populations, associated with an assumption of diminishing marginal utility of income.[4] Individuals will reject a 50/50 gamble since they will lose more utility with a negative gamble than they will gain if they win. Yet we know that they take such gambles. There have been attempts to test whether this assumption is realistic. There is a considerable literature on the framing of decisions, identifying under what conditions individuals are risk averse and under what conditions risk takers.[5] It is usually assumed that entrepreneurs are risk takers, at least relative to the rest of the relevant population. The validity of such a rule depends on how the individuals 'frame' the choice. There is a strong degree of irrationality about such decision making and simple rules of thumb are often adopted. More importantly there are biases which push decisions in particular directions. It is an interesting question whether the general level of risk aversion differs from society to society (Hofstede 1991).

Risk relates to uncertain future outcomes resulting from today's choices in a host of decisions which together constitute economic development, not just investments in equipment – choices of occupation, decisions to expand output or introduce new products, steps in self-improvement, or even the taking of a loan to support various economic activities. Risk is usually seen as acting through the addition of a risk premium to the rate of discount applied in estimating present value, whether done explicitly or implicitly. Uncertainty of future outcomes has a negative influence on present decisions – the greater the uncertainty, the more investments will be rejected by decision makers. Economic development requires investment, but investment is discouraged either by a more threatening risk environment or even more so by a predominance of risk averters in the relevant population.[6]

In explaining economic development, the conventional approach to risk management has major limitations, not least, that it lacks a genuinely historical perspective. Financial theory talks only of a distinction between systematic and non-systematic risk and does not consider the source of risk as relevant. Systematic risk involves a common fluctuation which affects the whole market, whereas non-systematic risk is specific to an enterprise, project or individual. Non-systematic risk is dealt with by the portfolio approach, and in the extreme case can be removed completely by an appropriate choice of elements in the portfolio, provided the portfolio is large enough and the returns from individual assets independent of each other. This is the basis of insurance. Risk control is usually seen as a matter of portfolio choice, with a wide definition of what constitutes a portfolio; it might be a portfolio of strips of land in open fields with different micro-conditions (McCloskey 1991b), or a range of trading ventures to different regions. There are two significant theoretical problems. First, the portfolio assumes a market context. Secondly, the market itself cannot fully handle risk because of problems which relate principally to asymmetrical information held by the partners to a relevant transaction; these are usually discussed under the headings of adverse selection, where the asymmetry is ex ante, and moral hazard, where the asymmetry is ex post.[7] It is impossible in a rational way to build risk fully into a market-based price system. Moreover, systematic risk is not covered.

Stability and predictability of the environment is an issue in the making of appropriate decisions, particularly the making of investment decisions which promote economic development, but a willingness to take risks is as important. Variability does not exhaust the risk since there is a low probability of an extreme event occurring. The limit is conceptualised in the notion of value at risk. The 'value at risk' reflects what you might lose at an acceptable confidence level.[8] You might argue that the loss from a 'once in 100 years' catastrophe must not exceed a certain threshold level. The problem is deeper than this. Survival, at both the organisational and the individual level, may be threatened, particularly if the majority in a relevant society are living close to the subsistence level.

SHOCKS – INCIDENCE, IMPACT AND RESPONSE

It is important to consider the sources of risk and to classify those sources in a useful way. The events, or changes of behaviour, which create risk are of a varying nature and it is critically important to identify and understand the sources. There are relevant events which are natural, events which are social or a combination of both social and natural, such as war, fire or disease, economic events – market fluctuations, unexpected changes of taste or technology, and political events, involving the exercise of power in changes of regime or simply of policy, social unrest or sudden and unexpected manifestations of rent-seeking behaviour. Sometimes these events occur in clusters, different shocks reinforcing each other, together constituting a particular risk environment. The exact nature of the risk environment is specific to a time and place.

Understanding the source of risk is critical for identification and measurement. It is helpful to trace the chains of causation running from the original shocks to their impact in economic outcomes, in order to measure the incidence of shocks and their possible impact, and devise methods of mitigating the relevant risk. The frequency of incidence indicates whether a source of risk is important. The causation shows us what might be done to reduce the risk, or to spread its costs. Many chains of causation are not properly understood even today – they certainly were not in the past. Prediction can be in general terms – the probability of a shock occurring somewhere – that is, the working out of the law of large numbers and the application of the portfolio approach, or specific, why should it occur in a specific place at a specific time? Different societies accumulate a considerable knowledge of the incidence of shocks specific to them and of how to mitigate their consequences.

Each geographical region in the world is characterised by a different risk environment which changes over time; sometimes there are within these regions micro-environments with subtle variations in risk vulnerability. Focusing on the natural environment, there is a differing variability of climatic and geophysical conditions and a differing vulnerability to extreme events. So-called natural shocks occur with varying frequency throughout the world, difficult to predict with any exactness because the disasters occur rarely. Not all shocks have an exclusively negative impact. They may have a lasting beneficial effect which encourages the concentration of population in vulnerable areas. You might live beneath a volcano because the soil is rich and agricultural productivity high. You might live in a flood valley because the annual silting renews the fertility of the land. You might live on a tectonic fault line because a good natural port is located there. The higher returns offset the higher risk.

Social shocks take the form of famine, disease, war – the three horse-men of the apocalypse, and fire or acts of piracy or brigandage, where natural factors have a role to play but are strongly influenced by human behaviour. A harvest failure may have climatic causes, but only becomes a famine through the problem of social entitlements, that is, the way in which a society distributes purchasing power and the capacity to purchase grain (Sen 1977). Governnment failure allows famine to occur. There may be a natural component to such shocks but their incidence is linked with the way in which human behaviour is organized. Developed economies have the organisation and resources to deal with such shocks. There are powerful feedback effects in this area, which in turn reinforce both low- and high-level equilibria.

The emergence of a commercial economy brought its own shocks. Initially, harvest fluctuations were a major source of fluctuations in the demand for other products, including manufactures and services. Where the agricultural sector was a large part of the economy, any such fluc-tuation had a powerful impact on the demand for the products of other sectors of the economy. Such a tendency to volatility deters investment, notably in factory industry. Persistence of a proto-industrial economy could be the result. The financial sector is central to the operation of a market economy and reflects any tendency to volatility. Financial crises which characterise the history of market economies are more studied than any other shocks. These shocks often take the form of currency/banking crises. Runs on the banks were common until governments took action to control them, institutionalising protection, through lender of last resort functions for the central bank or deposit insurance. In certain circum-stances, markets are inherently unstable, since they operate on the basis of confidence. Contagion or herd effects are common. There is a tendency to overshooting, which shows itself in extreme fluctuations in the prices of various assets – property, shares or currencies for example. Bubbles are not uncommon. Such fluctuations can have positive outcomes in that they move resources from old to new areas of the economy, but there is a tendency to overdo this movement. Problems emerge if there is a failure of government leadership, as in the 1930s, in stabilising macro-economies, whether at the global or the national level. Such crises are by no means limited to particular economies. The scope of such crises has tended to increase with the internationalisation of economies. The market extends their effects to other economies with which the affected economy is con-nected. Any shock which affects part of the area can affect all parts, some-times in a massive case of systematic risk.

There are major problems of measurement of all shocks since the response to shocks determines their impact and usually the incidence is measured by some indicator of impact. Shock are only perceived, identified, and even recorded, if they have a significant impact on deaths or costs. A society which has acted to mitigate certain types of shock may appear to be free of such shocks. Two societies may be exposed to exactly the same risk environment, but one appears to be free of such risk and the other highly exposed. It is extremely difficult to discover an objective measure of incidence which measures the incidence independently of the response. The impact is important but reflects the response. Shocks impose a continuing increase in operating costs on different societies, and destroy factors of production directly, whether capital or labour, thereby reducing the inputs into economic growth. They deter investment in projects which are at the core of modern economic development. A threat to life is a qualitatively different threat to one which affects only property or the level of costs, and can limit decisively the time horizon of relevant decision making. They may also increase transactions costs generally, biasing the institutional arrangements of an economy in a direction unconducive to economic development. Often the incidence of shocks is measured by their impact, by the number of deaths or the level of costs, preferably compared with the level of GDP. Minimum thresholds might be defined before an event qualifies as a shock. In the historical record, it is difficult to detect shocks which do not have a significant impact – they disappear from the record. Shocks can constitute disasters or catastrophes if they have sufficient impact. There have been numerous attempts to credit natural shocks as the terminators of major civilisations, but the imputation is controversial in nearly all cases (Diamond 2005). As Snooks (1993) has argued, the exhaustion of a strategy of survival and material advancement is more likely to be the cause of such a decline and fall.

The impact of shocks reflects vulnerability, that is, the number of people at risk or the amount of capital exposed to such shocks. An earthquake in an empty part of the world will have no impact. As population increases and as capital accumulates, exposure increases. Human activity increases that exposure. For example, fish farms or tourist resorts which remove the natural mango swamp protection of coasts make tsunamis more potentially destructive. The economic infrastructure of an area is particularly vulnerable to earthquake damage, particularly from the fires which follow an earthquake in an urban area. It is easy to exaggerate the negative direct impact of shocks. Fires which frequently destroy parts of cities allow a rebuilding of those cities and a rebuilding which may enhance the attractiveness of the city but also improve its efficiency in the distribution of goods. Birth rates often increase quickly after a demographic crisis, rapidly restoring the size of population prior to the crisis. A crisis often takes the old and the weak. Recovery may be much quicker than often anticipated, even in developing countries. Societies differ markedly in their capacity to respond to shocks. Some societies respond positively to the challenge of a high risk environment, just as some respond positively to deficiencies in the resource endowment. Such a positive responsiveness can be seen in developed economies. There is no one-to-one relationship between risk and the rate of economic development. Both incidence and impact may appear to be insignificant, but only because the response has been positive. Low-level economic development traps may be associated with poor resource endowments and superficially high levels of risk, with a poor responsiveness to such risk. The transition out of such traps is what has to be explained.

There are five types of possible short-term response. The first response is avoidance, which may be the result of caution, a genuinely high risk or simply a lack of risk takers. Avoidance means not making decisions which lead to the relevant risk exposure: a risky investment is not made, an uncertain market not entered. There is an opportunity cost to avoidance, which is the return foregone. An overly cautious approach to risk means the failure to make the decisions which lead to the inception of modern economic development.[9] Being ultra cautious or plain risk averse can stop economic development occurring. The second response is to take no action. Information asymmetries mean that certain decision makers, insiders, have more information than outsiders. Risk is often taken on by those with a core competency in handling risk in the relevant area. For them, the risk is lower. They know more about the potential frequency of the relevant shocks and how to respond to them. In particular, they are much better able to anticipate the particular timing of the relevant shocks. Their routine activities and operations already take account of the risk environment and the frequency of shocks. They may be better able and willing to engage in the next two responses, first, to direct resources to increasing their insider knowledge, and secondly, to take the next step, to mitigate as below. A third response, therefore, is to develop an information strategy relevant to the area of decision making. This is often done implicitly. Some ignorance cannot be dissipated, since the relevant knowledge does not exist, or is too expensive to dissipate. In most situations, it is possible at some cost to reduce risk by acquiring relevant information. Most societies develop a fund of relevant information which helps them control the relevant risk. Much of this is tacit. A fourth response is mitigation, actually taking action to reduce the risk. Familiarity with the nature and causation of relevant shocks increases the potential for risk mitigation. The nature of such knowledge is often highly specialised and sometimes involves cutting-edge research. It requires a focus on the sources of risk – the incidence of the events which constitute the risk environment. Some risk mitigation simply involves anticipating the precise date of a shock and moving out of danger people (relatively easy) and capital (more difficult). Mitigation involves deliberate action. Quarantines prevent the spread of disease. Building levees protect against floods. The lender of last resort of a central bank prevents a run on the banks. A sprinkler system prevents fire. Negotiation with a government and the extraction of a visible and firm commitment can protect a foreign investment. Such action always has a cost.

The fifth response is management. Management involves the spreading or redistribution of a given risk. The risk level is not reduced, but someone else takes on at least some of the existing risk. The spreading may be commercial, as in insurance or hedging, where another party is paid to take on the risk. They make a profit by putting together an appropriate portfolio of insurance policies or forward contracts/options. The role of a third party is to assist in offsetting different risks. Diversification within an appropriate portfolio is a mechanism for distributing risk and making it possible to use the market to manage the relevant risk. There is a significant cost associated with risk management – the costs and profit of the insurer or relevant financial institution. The further into the future the vulnerable transaction, the more difficult and expensive it is to hedge. Alternatively, risk management may be cooperative – strategic alliances are often formed to voluntarily share both returns and risk. Or it may involve the government, which provides back-up assistance, perhaps to farmers in a drought or to those who have suffered losses in an earthquake, thereby forcibly redistributing the costs of the relevant shocks from the victims to taxpayers in general. This is a much more frequent occurrence than usually admitted.

In the risk literature, the emphasis is almost invariably on risk management, which from an historical perspective is only one of the possible responses and not necessarily the most important.[10] Often risk management is used to reduce the level of incidental risk, that which is not central to the core activities of the relevant organisation. For example, traders often insured against loss of a ship, but not against fluctuations in market conditions for the products in which they traded. The latter is a risk in a core area of activity. Also, except for financial institutions specialised in currency transactions, foreign currency risk is incidental. The most popular mechanism of risk management is the portfolio approach, that is, a reliance on diversification. Diversifying does not mean that the risk is reduced for any individual decision or asset. With a large enough portfolio of assets whose returns are independent, it is possible to remove all unsystematic risk. This is the principle on which insurance operates and why insurers can make a profit. The same holds for financial institutions and hedging. The losses are spread among all those sufficiently exposed to take out an insurance. Systematic risk, defined as the risk affecting the whole of a market, is not removed. An excess of systematic risk, especially where major shocks occur, can ruin the best of insurance companies and overwhelm a whole system, including market systems. Where there is a danger of significant systematic risk, the government is inevitably involved in attempts to control that risk.

A key issue relates to the relationship between the consequences of risk control, whether by government or private decision makers, and the conditions which favour economic development. Both policies and institutional structures designed to cope with risk can inhibit economic growth. Where risk is high, risk control itself may act as a barrier to economic development. Such an argument has been developed to explain the failure of Australian aborigines to develop agriculture (White 1992) and the differential economic performance of the USA and Russia (White 1987). This is most notably the case where risk management predominates over risk mitigation: the redistribution of risk under risk management inhibits risk mitigation, hence the origin of the term moral hazard. Key decision makers redistribute risk in exactly the same way as they redistribute income in rent-seeking. The trick is to reduce the risk level to a manageable level, but not to create obstacles to those decisions which are at the heart of modern economic development. The relevant risk environment comprises all segments of the general environment confronting decision makers which cause volatility in returns, whether political, cultural, economic or technical, as well as natural. North (2005) believes that the key transition is from accommodation to a natural risk environment to one which is man made.

RISK AND ECONOMIC HISTORY

The neglect of risk in any account of economic development is a serious omission since risk is universal and affects strongly the key decisions significant for economic development. Some historical interpretations give a prominent place to the role of risk in influencing the inception of modern economic development in specific economies, noting the way in which the risk environments in those societies evolve over time. There are three possibilities. First, a successful risk-control strategy reduces risk to a level that allows economic development to occur. Secondly, there is no such strategy and the contribution of a hostile risk environment and/or a strong degree of risk aversion prevent economic development. Thirdly, risk control permeates the whole of society, itself acting as an obstacle to economic development. In some cases, risk is so important that it has a powerful impact upon the institutional structure of a whole society, polity and economy, one which can block the process of economic development. An obsession with risk, and the resulting radical institutional adjustment, may prevent significant economic development. Elaborate institutions and behavioural patterns of risk control can impede economic development, if the level of the relevant risk type is high and requires a strong response.

There is a growing genre of historical interpretations which puts the emphasis on the destruction of different civilisations by unexpected shocks, often resulting from a poor ability to mitigate the consequences of such shocks. Diamond has made such an approach respectable (Diamond 2005). In human history, such outcomes are unusual and often controversial in causation. This section is concerned with less dramatic denouements. Eric Jones, in his path-breaking book, *The European Miracle* (1987), articulated a theory about the differential impact of shocks, and of risk in general, on the divergent historical development of European and Asian economies. He was seeking to explain why the economic miracle of accelerated economic development first occurred in Europe rather than in Asia, and why there was a significant delay in the Asian case. There were two main arguments in the book, one of which is directly relevant to risk; the other, relating to the nature of political systems, in particular to a varying proneness to rent-seeking behaviour, is dealt with in a later chapter. The latter is relevant, since the absence of a legal system which protects property and enforces contracts is often seen as a significant source of risk. If those who make investment decision are exposed to the predatory actions of those who are engaged in rent-seeking activity, then the risk level may be too high for such decisions to be made. This issue is dealt with at length in the chapter on institutions.

Jones argued that it was possible to distinguish shocks by the factor intensity of their destructiveness, that is, by whether they were more labour or more capital destructive. Earthquakes, fire, flood tend to be capital destructive, whereas epidemic, disease or war are much more often labour destructive. The environments of Europe and Asia were characterised by the prevalence of shocks, differing according to their factor destructiveness. In Asia, the tendency is capital destructiveness. Such a regime tends over the long term to deter capital accumulation. By contrast, the risk environment in Europe is relatively benign to capital but not to labour. This encourages the accumulation of capital, but gave considerable economic power to labour. There was a tendency to labour-destructive shocks in Europe, such as the Black Death in the fourteenth century, which killed at least one-third of the population, but also wars, which have been particularly frequent (Tilly 1992). Such a theory emphasises general patterns of response to particular kinds of variability in the environment. There has been significant criticism of the theory, but directed at whether two such distinct patterns exist. The notion of influence from the risk environment is not rejected.

There are other interpretations which stress the influence of risk factors in history. One set of political theories focuses on the impact of floods, arguing for the frequent existence of hydraulic societies, that is, societies concerned with controlling the use of water from important river systems. Many societies in China, India, the Middle East or Egypt were focused on major rivers. Sometimes the theory was linked to the notion of Oriental despotism, autocratic political systems which required central control because of the requirements of water control. Such control moderates the destructiveness of the rivers in years of flood. The annual variability may be critical to the enrichment of the soils, which are regularly flooded, but the key is to keep such a flow under control. Since floods threatened to destroy the river control systems, they were potentially capital destructive. Significant capital investment was required to regulate water flow and this involved a considerable administrative effort by the relevant governments. The centralisation of government authority made it unlikely that there would be scope for the making of the decisions at the core of economic developments. All risks of this kind tend to encourage a centralisation of authority. At the eastern boundaries of Europe, the persistence of Russian autocracy is also linked to a high risk environment (Wittfogel 1981, Coe 2003).

Given its historical importance, it is necessary to consider how in specific cases risk is controlled. There are some illuminating examples. The first relates to the incidence of fire. Urban conflagrations were a common feature of the pre-modern economy. Western Europe, beginning in England and the Netherlands, in the seventeenth and eighteenth centuries went through a significant transition when it became much more protected from the fires which everywhere periodically burnt down towns and cities. Jones notes for England that between 1500 and 1700 local data show that the frequency and size of conflagrations more or less reflected the pattern of urban growth, but between 1700 and 1900 the conflagrations gradually diminished, despite the continuation of urban growth (Jones, Porter and James 1984). Building, formerly constructed of combustible materials such as wood or wattle-and-daub, were now built mainly of stone, brick or tile, and became much less flammable. Massive conflagrations which destroyed thousands of structures become much less frequent. It is interesting to ask why and how this happened, how Europe became protected against this kind of capital-destructive shock, whereas elsewhere there was no such protection. Prompted by Jones' argument, Goudsblom comments on the pre-modern fire regime, 'The resulting destruction of capital could hardly fail to curb economic growth' (Goudsblom 1992: 150). Previous economic development made possible the transition, but the transition made possible more economic development, yet another feedback loop. There are two aspects of the transition worth commenting on. First, the transition consists of a multitude of individual decisions, many involving an investment commitment, which have a much larger benefit taken together than they would as individual decisions, if others fail to make a similar decision. There are clear network effects, and a problem of coordination. An individual whose house is constructed of non-flammable materials is not in an improved situation if the house is surrounded by buildings made of flammable materials. Some government or community agency is helpful in encouraging the making of appropriate individual decisions. That action is easier if others, usually the rich, have already established the precedent. When that happens, the government can intervene to regulate and impose a cost on those not participating (Goudsblom 1992: 144–6). Secondly, the initial capital cost of less flammable structures is higher, but the continuing amortisation and maintenance costs lower, so that a lengthening of the time horizon by reducing the implicit risk premium included in the rate of discount would make the transition more likely. Perhaps the decisions should be placed in the context in which risk aversion was reduced for other reasons.

There is no doubt that in Britain there was a dramatic reduction in interest rates during the period, which must reflect a greater tolerance of risk and/or a less hostile risk environment. A dramatic reduction in interest rates is relevant to this phenomenon, indicating as it does a longer time horizon. This might also be related to the emergence of a more developed capital market. The evidence from estimates of interest rates reveals a large fall in the risk premium from 15 per cent to 7.5 per cent. It is difficult to explain (Clark 2007, McCloskey 1991b), but it must relate in some way to an improvement in security – less danger of expropriation and less risk from civil unrest. Homer and Sylla (1996) have noted the saucer-like shape of the curve graphing the behaviour of interest rates during the rise and fall of empires, very much in accordance with changes in the risk environment associated with the establishment and extension of a stable environment and its breakdown later. The fall in England could be simply a greater willingness to bear risk in risk environments which were no more benign.

One argument has it that the key change is genetic, although it is difficult to distinguish genetic from cultural change: typically, they reinforce each other. This argument is put both as one which characterises all of human history – a tendency everywhere to an increase in the proportion of risk takers in the overall population (Galor and Moav 1992) – and as one which characterises English economic history – the rise in the proportion of risk takers explaining why it achieved its pioneer status (Clark 2007). This issue is further explored in the next chapter. The decline in interest rates is linked to another phenomenon – the enclosure of the open fields and the disappearance of scattered strips, which occurred simultaneously with the 'stonification' or 'brickification'. McCloskey (1991b) has argued that the persistence of the strips was an example of risk mitigation, allowing individuals to even out natural fluctuations in yield by diversifying the micro-conditions to which they were exposed. An alternative response to the risk of harvest fluctuations was to store grain. Substitution of the latter for the former indicates a clear acceptance of a higher level of risk. McCloskey has shown than the riskiness of holding grain, arising from fluctuations in its price, rose.

The second interesting case relates to disease. Changes in the European disease environment or disease environments relevant to European settlement outside Europe are interesting. Some diseases are endemic, others epidemic. The former may be debilitating, the latter may burst on the scene afflicting populations without natural immunity in periodic *crises démographiques*. Diseases thrive in different conditions and have a particular geographic coverage, which changes over time. The density of population has a critical influence on the nature of disease, so towns are particularly prone to infectious diseases. Towns are associated with the commercialisation of an economy and an increase in income levels. In urbanising societies, death rates in the cities were higher than in rural areas, yet did not stop the process of urbanisation. At an early stage of development, urban population grew by migration rather than by natural increase. As we have already noted, different areas have different disease incidence and their inhabitants differing immunities. Some diseases, such as malaria, are restricted in their incidence largely to the tropics. Other diseases are closely linked to nutritional problems and to the supply of food. The relationship between disease and human society is a changing one, and involves an extremely complex process of accommodation which occurs over a long period of time. As the pathogens adjust to the host through a process of natural selection, locals develop immunity and many diseases become childhood diseases. Diseases, whether of humans, animals or plants, mutate, becoming more or less threatening. Most diseases change their nature over time, as the hosts gather an immunity. Particular once epidemic diseases often become endemic, although they may become epidemic in populations previously unexposed to them and lacking immunity.

The freedom from epidemic disease, notably but not only the plague, which accompanied the inception of modern economic development is not fully understood. The disappearance of intermittent *crises démographiques* and the steady increase in longevity, following the understanding of the pathology of infectious disease, both occur with the inception of modern economic development. In the case of plague, some commentators believe it was the result of a mutation of pathogens or even a change in the density of carriers, but some point to the improved application of quarantine by governments. Both a more reliable supply of food and better hygiene are also advanced as reasons for the growing freedom from disease. Once more, positive feedbacks were at work. There are two examples of epidemic shocks which greatly influenced Europe and its path of economic development.

The first occurred within Europe itself. The Black Death of the mid-fourteenth century which killed a third of Europe's population is a particularly potent example of a labour-destructive shock. The disease is endemic within certain rodent populations within the steppe areas and has tended to erupt into both Asian and European societies at different times over a long period of time, going back to the famous plague in Athens, described by Thucydides in *The History of the Peloponnesian War*. It exists there even today. After a long history of epidemic outbreaks of plague, its incidence suddenly ceased in Western and Central Europe, the last major outbreak being in Marseilles in 1721 (in Britain in 1688). North and Thomas (1973) have argued that the impact of such a shock was to dramatically change the factor endowment in Europe, in particular the mix of land and labour, and to hasten institutional changes which ended the feudal system and promoted the operation of the market. Labour became scarce and more valuable – it gained a freedom to move not previously held. Land holders who needed labour were prepared to offer all sorts of inducements to attract labour away from existing attachments to both land and lord. The relationship became a commercial one, as markets for land and labour developed. The Black Death hastened the dissolution of feudalism and the arrival of a commercial economy dominated by markets of various kinds, including labour markets. The second example, already discussed in the last chapter, occurred in regions to which Europeans moved abroad, previously isolated areas in the Americas, Siberia, Australasia, where the native populations had no immunity to the diseases brought in by the newcomers. The introduction of smallpox, influenza or measles led to mass deaths. The existing populations were destroyed and the lands in temperate areas emptied for European settlement.

Almost purely social is war, since it has an obvious human agency. Internal conflict acts a barrier both to a central monopoly over the use of force and to economic development. Lawlessness in general is closely linked with the emergence of the modern state (Rosenberg and Birdzell 1986: 96). The process by which central control was asserted was long drawn out. War also occurs when other shocks have weakened a society, making it vulnerable to civil war and outside attack. Tilly (1992) has shown how the national state emerged in Europe because of its success in combining the use of coercion and capital. The national state grew largely because of its success in waging war and assembling the means to support a war-making capacity. It replaced arbitrary and unanticipated levies and expropriations by the authorities with regular taxation, often granted with the approval of those taxed. Snooks (1993) has argued that the strategy of conquest is one of the mechanisms by which societies improve their level of well-being. The extraction of tribute, slaves, taxes represents the motive for such action. Collier (2007: chapter 2) has pointed out in the recent past the relationship of civil wars and coups with low levels of income and poor rates of economic growth, and in the case of civil wars, with the domination of an economy by primary commodities; they help finance such wars. Rich countries do not tend to have civil wars or coups. It is a vicious circle, in which the lack of development in the bottom 50 countries makes them prone to civil war and to coups and the occurrence of the latter imposes large costs on the economy, preventing economic development. The occurrence of one civil war also makes more likely a recurrence. This general picture is unlikely to have been very different in the past.

In other works, the authors have traced the evolution of relevant risk environments (Moss 2002, White 1987), particularly the role of the government in controlling those environments. During the process of economic development, the relevant risk environment changes its nature, and dramatically. At the critical phases in the development of economic activity – entry into the agricultural revolution, including the transfer of European agriculture to areas of new settlement, the rise of a commercial economy, and the industrial and service phases of modern economic development – there is a rise in the level, and a change in the nature, of risk. Established economies adjust to the risk characteristics of the previous phase. The risk associated with the new phase is too high to allow the transition to happen. Movement into the new phase requires either a reduction in the risk below a threshold level, through risk management and mitigation, and/or a greater willingness to take on risk, with a growing number of the risk tolerant. The risk mix changes over time, and in a systematic way. The defining type of risk changes with the growing complexity of the relevant societies.[11]

As societies become more complex institutionally, the sources of risk increasingly are found in social elements rather than in fluctuations in the natural environment. A significant transition is to a market-based economy. In some cases, this occurs quickly. As Abu-Lughod (1989: 177) argues, 'It is difficult for us today to appreciate the extent to which trade depended on risk reduction, or the proportion of all costs that might have to be allocated to transit duties, tribute, or simple extortion'. Protection costs were a continuing constraint on the development of trade. Any rise in protection costs can reduce the level of trade, as Abu-Lughod suggests happened with the break-up of the Mongol Empire, itself the result partly of the shock of the Black Death (Abu-Lughod 1989: chapter 6). As societies commercialize, the significance of market risk rises. Unified trading areas, and later investment clusters, require policing, and imperial control has often provided the relevant security: witness the Pax Romana, the Pax Britannica or even the Pax Americana (Guha 1981: 76–7). The risk of expropriation declines in such an area.

There is a synergy between the nation state and the market because the market offers an expanded opportunity for raising revenue, but the government is critical to building the infrastructure necessary to market operation, including the control of market risk. Market instability is always a possibility. In certain conditions, markets are inherently unstable, characterised by overshooting or by bubbles and crises of various kinds. The rising importance of the financial sector creates its own risk. Financial crises represent major economic shocks.

The transition to industrialisation raises the importance of a different kind of risk, which involves unexpected changes in technology – the 'creative destruction' which Schumpeter so vividly reminds us of – dramatic shifts of taste and unexpected changes in the pattern of demand or unanticipated changes in technology. The rising level of investment creates a vulnerability to these unexpected changes which constitute another kind of risk. It increases the significance of risk aversion, notably as expressed in the level of interest rates. More modern economies where the emphasis is on the service side of the economy involve what has been called power risk, which applies both internally and externally, or in Galbraith's terminology (1967), the exercise of countervailing power. Such risk arises from rent-seeking behaviour at both the international and the domestic levels. Such risk, since it is implicit in the political economy of different societies, has always existed, but it can act as a particular barrier to economic development in modern societies. Even in developed economies, rent-seeking coalitions can proliferate in stable times (Olson 1982). The political invades the area of the economic, not always in order to extract rent, sometimes simply to exercise power.

As economies and societies develop, they become exposed to different risk environments. There is a path dependency, in that the events and the responses to those events are specific to particular societies. Each story is unique. Attempts at risk control may impede the key transitions which characterise economic development, for example the transition from a hunter-gatherer society to an agricultural one, or from a self-sufficient economy to a commercial or market-based one, or the transition which is most relevant here, to an industrialised society. There was a prevalence of clusters of shocks during key transitional periods in various societies, particularly those which were autocracies, for example, in the so-called Times of Troubles in Russia or during dynastic changes in China. Such periods highlight the problems such societies have in handling the shocks and the dependence of their resolution on a strong central authority. Once the central control weakens, as it inevitably does during dynastic cycles, the significance of risk control is revealed. Sometimes the shocks act independently, propelling the system through the transition, and sometimes a weakening of the relevant systems during the transition makes them more vulnerable to such shocks and they appear to experience more shocks. Often famine, epidemic disease and war are linked: the whole is greater than its parts. The history of most societies is inevitably a catalogue of shocks of various kinds, the history of the successful a story of the positive response to such shocks.

THE LONG-TERM INFLUENCE OF RISK

The influence of risk on institutional and organisational structures is significant. In some cases, the whole panoply of political and social organisation, as well as business institutions, has been influenced by the need to control risk. Military security is one of the key factors explaining the nature of a polity, but other shocks are relevant and reinforce the military needs. For example, the centralisation of the Chinese state reflected the ever-present danger of a nomadic incursion from the open north (Guha 1981: 92–6). Defence needs alone largely explain the monistic political system, the solidarity of the ruling class and the nature and importance of the Confucian ethic, emphasising a doctrine of obedience. Equally, the service state in Russia was a response to external threats, which were often real (Coe 2003). A defensive militarisation became a feature of Russia's path-dependent historical experience. Military risk may predominate in certain societies, but it by no means exhausts the impact of risk. The danger of famine was another threat encouraging centralisation. Because the military threat influences the nature of the polity, which in its turn influences the nature of the economy, it is highly significant. Its absence is highly relevant to the inception of modern economic development, particularly in island societies such as Britain or Japan, where institutions could develop free of the influence of frequent outside intrusion. An excessively rigid system may control risk at the cost of removing the flexibility required for economic growth.

The first argument involves a top-down influence, the role of the political system and the government in assisting in risk control. Risk not only influences private decision making; it is a strong influence on the nature of government strategy and policies, since governments often see one of their roles as controlling such risk. Deliberate action, notably by government, is critical to the risk control that allows a society to reduce risk below a threshold level which makes possible economic development. Government has a very important role to play in this area, notably in the early stages of economic development, whether accumulating grain reserves, restraining piracy, organising a quarantine, discouraging what is called diversionary or rent-seeking behaviour, maintaining law and order and protecting property, controlling financial crises, or simply in maintaining macroeconomic stability. Sometimes that action of government was self-conscious and deliberate, at other times it was unconscious. There is a whole infrastructure of risk control which is put in place by government, beyond the organisation of the military. It is one of the main functions of government to do this. Government policies with respect to risk control are critically important to the whole process of economic development, and at different levels of the economy, whether it be direct or indirect in laws and regulations influencing how other non-government, particularly commercial, organisations were constructed. The various stages in economic development require a measure of appropriate risk control. The role of the government is critical in controlling risk to the degree necessary to allow economic development to occur at all. This is a matter of the structure of government, with an emphasis on infrastructural rather than despotic power, the commitment of that government to appropriate policies and the successful implementation of those policies. This argument is relevant even to the USA, where government was active in controlling the kind of risk which was relevant to the stage of economic development at which the economy was operating (Moss 2002).

The reason for government intervention is market failure. There are numerous examples where individual decision making does not produce a socially beneficial result, considered from the perspective of economic development. Government intervention is needed to reduce the level of risk to one which promotes a significant increase in the number of individual investments. The most common market failure results from information asymmetries. Moral hazard involves an ex post asymmetry. The taking of an insurance, or covering risk in general, reduces the incentive to mitigate risk. If you have a fire insurance, you no longer have a strong incentive to incur the costs involved in putting in a sprinkler system. Adverse selection involves an ex ante asymmetry, uncertainty concerning the quality of a product or service being provided. The receiver of a loan knows much more about his/her creditworthiness than the giver of the loan. The provider of medical insurance knows less about the health of the insurer than the insured knows. The potentially large impact on price of these asymmetries is obvious. For this reason, as well as others, successful economic development requires a positive interaction between government and market. There are both government and market failures which make necessary this interaction and positive feedback effects from such an interaction. Pursuit of the relevant policies over a sufficiently long period of time is necessary. The government puts in place an infrastructure which decreases the risk to which private decision makers are exposed. In some cases, it takes action to increase the return to compensate for higher risk, as with the monopolies granted to chartered companies which operated abroad, such as the East India Company. The action taken was appropriate to the times and to the conditions of the place.

The second influence involves the indirect route, a rather different institutional response – the adaptation of the structure of economic organisation to the risk environment, in particular the emergence of the modern business enterprise. The main features of the latter are strongly influenced by the need to control risk, notably for the stakeholder groups who provide the finance needed for investment. There is some truth in the tendency of more efficient organisations to emerge as a result of political and economic competition. There is no random walk in the way in which economic activity is organised within a market economy. Initially at the international level, the regulated companies, such as the East India Company, were given a monopoly and the scope to intervene politically in the areas in which they had dealings. This helped compensate for the high risk of their operations. They were the first multinational companies. As governments took over the control of political risk and competition increased, the business enterprise changed its organisational basis. It is no accident that the limited liability public company emerged as the vehicle for business activity. There is now a recognition of the problems of economies which were information-deficient and risk-high and the way in which business organisation accommodates these features. Until recent times, this was the general case. Whether it was during the Industrial Revolution in Britain (Harris 2004) or during the Asian Economic Miracle, notably but not only in China (Haley and Tan 1996, who talk of a black informational hole), there appeared highly specific pathways of business organisation based upon different mechanisms for minimising risk. Institutions other than government are often moulded by the risk environments in which they evolve. The modern business enterprise has as two of its defining characteristics limited liability and clear procedures for bankruptcy, although the latter tend to vary subtly from one developed economy to another.

Both features have emerged to encourage the supply of investment funds to and the continuation of entrepreneurial activity in the modern enterprise. Limited liability emerged with the rising capital requirements of the modern economy in the context of a high level of 'industrial' risk. In this, the construction of the railways had an important role to play. In the USA, where there was significant competition for investment funds between the states, limited liability was introduced earlier than in the UK.

Limited liability is the norm for the modern corporation, but not for private companies or partnerships. Anyone buying a share in such a company is only liable for the amount they put in, not for the total debt of the company. Alternative arrangements might have been unlimited liability or an amount of liability negotiated with the individual suppliers of capital. The limitation reduces risk for the shareholder, increasing it for other providers of credit. Such an arrangement, whereas it increased risk for creditors, both voluntary and involuntary (those with tort cases), by reducing the risk of those who provided equity, allegedly had the net impact of increasing the supply of equity and or capital in general. It is difficult to show that this was the outcome, but it is highly likely that it was. Since alternative systems of liability did not operate in parallel, there was no natural experiment showing the outcome of the introduction of limited liability. The rising importance of tort cases and the danger of those responsible escaping the consequence of that responsibility have led some to question the role of limited liability, in current circumstances with good reason. It may no longer be necessary in order to generate the investment funds needed for modern economic development. Bankruptcy laws are necessary to ensure an orderly division of the remaining value of an enterprise and to ensure that individual entrepreneurs have a means of returning to business activity. A proper ordering of claims makes it possible to prevent a rushed break-up of a company. Such arrangements differ from country to country. Chapter 11 in the USA allows companies to continue trading when bankrupt and bankruptcy judges to change contract arrangements in order to make the company solvent.

Such influences are obvious, but they are only part of the story. The whole institutional structure of a society reflects its risk exposure. The subtle ways in which risk manifests itself can be identified by individual country studies, of which there have been until now very few.

7. Human capital: education, health and aptitude

It is a truism to say that modern economic development results from the acts of human beings, but the statement has real meaning. Destroy all the physical capital, burn all relevant technical blueprints, and the human beings of developed societies will bounce back, although without outside assistance, it might take some time to achieve. This is exactly what happens after major wars. What is now commonly called human capital is the key. Endogenous growth models have focused on the positive relationship between a country's growth rate and its stock of human capital. Recent theoretical analysis stresses the need to incorporate into the inputs of the neoclassical production function an allowance for human capital, either as a separate item or as part of one of the other factor inputs – labour or an expanded capital input, thereby combining the investment in people with the investment in machines. The two types of investment are often complementary and linked by technology, which requires investment in both.

The various elements which increase human capability – education, health and aptitude – are factors of ultimate causation, influencing the proximate cause, the input of labour. Also relevant are the motivation of decision makers, including the culture, or attitudes and beliefs, which influence that motivation, and the opportunities available for the employment of human capital. A society endowed with individuals of good motivation and health, with attitudes which favour the kind of behaviour which promotes economic development and aptitudes which assist in solving the problems thrown up by economic development, and characterised by a good fit between the supply of and demand for human capital, is one in which modern economic development is likely to begin. On the other hand, all elements of human capital are deemed by some as malleable, adjusting according to the changes which occur in society, notably the economic ones; they are the result of economic development, not its cause, providing a positive feedback in the virtuous circle of economic development. Others argue that such changes cannot be used to account for a revolutionary inception, since they do not work quickly enough. They are much more persuasive in helping to explain a long-drawn-out evolutionary transition to modern economic development or the gradual achievement of a threshold level critical to economic development.

There are four sections in this chapter. The first considers the general notion of human capital, putting the emphasis on education, where it is normally placed in neoclassical economic growth theory. The second section reviews the connection between health and human capital, focusing in particular on the role of nutrition. The third section considers the argument that one aspect of human capital, aptitude, is a factor differentiating the growth experience of different countries. The fourth section addresses the question of motivation in human decision making. It introduces the issue of culture and its significance, particularly in influencing motivation, and the incentive structure which persuades people to undertake certain kinds of activity rather than others. The final section considers the opportunities for the employment of human capital.

THE MANY MANIFESTATIONS OF HUMAN CAPITAL

Neoclassical economists see an increase in human capital as caused by particular kinds of investment, notably in education.[1] Such investment may be difficult to identify and measure. Commonly, the amount of the human capital input is seen as increased by the process of education, quantified through some measure of the average education undergone in the relevant country. Such human capital is viewed from a quantitative rather than a qualitative perspective: years of primary, secondary and/or tertiary education, or the resources devoted to education. Alternatively, some measure of literacy can be used as a proxy. Human capital grows with the number of years that the average person spends in the educational system. There is argument whether the early years of study develop more capital than the later years. It is usual to add to this the opportunity cost of having people studying rather than working. In terms of proximate causation, a simple way of interpreting the effect of such an investment is an increase in the number of units of labour input. There are a number of attempts to allow for differences of quality. Just as the quality of investment in physical capital is as important as the quantity invested, so the quality of human capital is as important as its quantity. At a micro level, this should be reflected in the additional income received by those with more education, provided the labour market is operating efficiently. In this context, quality refers both to the nature of the inputs into the investment in human capital – educational or otherwise – and also to the quality of use of that human capital. There may be social returns to investment in human capital, beyond the private returns, a justification for public provision of education.

It is useful to explore the way in which human capital influences the level and growth of productivity. The complementarity between physical and human, and between both and the application of new technology, complicates the economic growth picture and makes a production function approach inadequate as a description of the process of economic development. It affects a country's growth rate in two main ways. First, it contributes in the same way as physical capital, with the qualification that there are unlikely to be diminishing returns to human capital, as there are to investment in physical capital. This assumes a complementarity between the two forms of investment and a return to the joint investment. Human capital is a source of new ideas, which are non-rivalrous and available to all, and of a social return not captured by private individuals or enterprises who invest in that form of capital (Romer 1986). Secondly, human capital influences the rate at which a country accesses the existing pool of technical knowledge in the outside world, speeding up this process.

Attempts to measure the impact of educational expenditures have produced paradoxical results. Increases in education, or schooling, are not strongly correlated with economic growth, which has puzzled those who have placed human capital at the core of their theoretical treatment of modern economic development. Two particular problems stand out for these theorists. The first is the paradox of a stable long-term rate of economic growth in the developed countries in the context of a massive increase in expenditures on education, knowledge or R&D (C.I. Jones 2002). In theory, such an increase should have produced an acceleration in the rate of economic growth. The second is the big increase in schooling in a large number of developing countries which has failed to sustain an acceleration in their growth rates. Such problems reinforce the argument that schooling as such is not an adequate measure of the input of human capital. There is a need to take into account three considerations (Pritchett 2004: 217). The first involves learning outcomes from the schooling provided in specific countries – there are enormous disparities in the quality of the educational process. The second consideration is the job placement of the schooled – what they actually do – and implicitly how relevant the schooling is to the skills and aptitudes required by jobs relevant to modern economic development. Third is the relative demand for schooled labour as well as its supply. It does not help producing large numbers of unemployed graduates. Those qualified need both an incentive to find employment in areas conducive to economic development rather than in rent-seeking activities and the possibility of doing so because there are jobs available.

On the other hand there is plenty of evidence that the general level of education of a society, its human capital defined in this sense, does matter. Work on the UK shows that there was little improvement in the education input over the period allegedly relevant to the inception of modern economic development (1770–1860), which confirms other studies measuring the contribution of education, but that the level of education, whether at the beginning or the end of the relevant period, made a significant contribution to economic development (Mitch 2004: 356). It is difficult to identify periods of discontinuity in the contribution of human capital and unlikely that a major educational effort of itself can trigger the inception of modern economic development. It is therefore not surprising to discover that the increase in expenditures on education appear to have had little impact on growth, whereas overall levels of education or literacy do seem related to economic performance. A simple method of estimating the overall contribution is to engage in a thought experiment, comparing the actual contribution of labour with that which would be made, in the words of Mitch, by 'unschooled Eskimos' (Mitch 2004: 332), by which he means any workers without skills relevant to a modern economy. You estimate the difference between the average income per worker and that of an unskilled (Eskimo) worker – that is, the skill premium – multiply by the size of the relevant labour force and calculate the proportional contribution of labour skills to total income. The results vary from 15 to 35 per cent, clearly a non-trivial contribution (Mitch 2004: 333). It is difficult to show by 1860 any major improvement in the overall contribution (Mitch 2004: 353, 349), but it remains non-trivial. Such an exercise assumes that all the increase in income can be imputed to education. Such a relationship speaks loudly for a role of human capital as an ultimate cause and at the same time for an evolutionary view of the inception of modern economic development in the UK. The accumulation of human capital is likely to be an incremental process, although improvements in health and education can follow a discontinuous rise in investment in these areas: public health programmes in the nineteenth century appear to have had a major impact. The general build-up of human capital to a critical threshold level appears to be a long-drawn-out process.

It is useful to distinguish the skills and aptitudes specific to particular jobs and particular levels of economic development, and the general ability of an individual to learn.[2] The former can take a multitude of different forms. Those living in pre-modern societies may have a range of skills no workers in a developed economy have, which leaves them well equipped to survive in very different, but highly specific, environments (Diamond 1997). The latter, the general ability to learn, is not a given. It involves literacy of various kinds and a whole range of tacit knowledge essential to living and working in a modern economy. It differs considerably from one society to another. The degree to which individuals can benefit from education varies, although it might be that with appropriate preparation the benefit can be raised. Education is built on an accumulating level of literacy in a range of activities. Today computer literacy is increasingly a sine qua non of modern society. Intelligence can be used as an indication of the quality of the trainability or educatability of the relevant individuals. How far this starting base is itself a social construct is uncertain. A basic level of literacy may be necessary for any training, if only to understand simple diagrams. Economic development once more creates a virtuous circle in which the ability to benefit from education is linked to previous development.

To focus only on education is to limit greatly the concept of human capital, since education and training are inadequate as a full representation of human capital. Human capital has many different features. It involves health and aptitude, as well as the experience and skills developed in learning by doing and observing, sometimes institutionalised in apprenticeships[3] or even in self-improvement through relevant civil society institutions. The latter reflects the operation of civil society, which is discussed in the next chapter. There are therefore two other major sources of an increase in human capital – improvements in health, which raise the productivity of labour and can result in improvements in aptitude, if the improvement occurs during the early years of life, and the experience which is either passed on in families and general upbringing or through 'on the job' experience or training, such as apprenticeship schemes. The last is job-specific and usually dealt with directly by labour economists. A general-purpose human capital is relevant, not just to the accumulation of specific skills and expertise. There are few proxies for the average quality of such experience. It is an area largely neglected, but the impact of experience is cumulative. Societies making the transition to economic development generate a pool of experience which steadily increases the availability of human capital.

There is another important issue, often ignored, which involves the degree to which aptitude varies systematically from country to country – it is an empirical rather than an ideological matter whether it does, although ideology often determines whether differences in aptitude are considered at all. There is a significant body of evidence which shows such difference, although there is much debate on how aptitude might be measured in a culture-free way. It may be that IQ tests of any kind are bound to be culture-orientated, measuring the capacity to operate effectively in a developing economy. In one study (Hanushek and Kimko 2000), international mathematics and science test scores are used as a direct measure of labour-force quality and show clear national differences. The possible relationship between intelligence and economic development needs to be addressed. Nationally, intelligence appears to rise with economic development, another positive feedback loop.

Human capital accumulates in various ways, not always as a result of a deliberate intent. Immigration, where it is of the skilled or experienced, can save on a significant educational expense, but it is yet another example of a positive feedback loop since emigrants move from lower income to higher income countries or countries with a higher growth potential. It helps that immigrants are usually both young and healthy, and tend to self-select for the adventurous and imaginative. There is a natural tendency for immigration to improve the fit between the supply of and demand for human capital.

HEALTH AND NUTRITION

The absence of disease, particularly debilitating disease, and better nutrition promote healthiness. Average life expectancy can be used as an indicator of health. In a stable population equilibrium, where the fertility rate equals the mortality rate, life expectation is the reciprocal of the mortality rate. Lower mortality is linked with greater longevity. Longer lives are also usually healthier lives. One study (The Soap and Detergent Association 2007: 9) concluded, 'Infectious diseases, violence, and traumatic accidents that didn't kill exhausted the productivity and quality of life of the survivors. For every recorded death, 20 to 30 persons became ill and weak, and they suffered.' The statistic comes from a study by Shattuck (1972), which summarised the situation in the USA. If we conservatively take an average mortality rate of 30/1,000, the lower morbidity figure suggests that each year as many as 600 out of 1,000 people were seriously sick, and this in a relatively healthy society. In some societies, debilitating sickness may have been close to universal. Usually, an extension in life expectancy can be interpreted as an improvement in health, meaning that at a given age individuals are healthier.

The dramatic increase in life expectancy which began in Western Europe and in North America in the second half of the nineteenth century, and then followed at a remarkable pace in the rest of the world in the twentieth century, resulted from a much better understanding of the transmission of various diseases, notably infectious diseases, their causes and a discovery of methods of curing those diseases. Less dramatic earlier declines reflected more reliable food supply, better hygiene and in the case of reduced threats from epidemics, improved quarantine. An important characteristic of modern societies has been a steady increase in longevity of two years a decade, sustained over a long period of time. Much of this could be seen as a result of the inception of modern economic development and is part of a positive feedback effect. The increase in life expectancy was also accompanied by an increase in stature.[4] One extreme claim (Fogel 2004: 34) asserts, 'The available data suggest that the average efficiency of the human engine in Britain increased by about 53 per cent between 1790 and 1980. The combined effect of the increase in dietary energy available for work, and of the increased human efficiency in transforming dietary energy into work output, appears to account for about 50 per cent of the British economic growth since 1790'.

Child mortality is another measure which qualifies as a good proxy and is sometimes used in this way. There has been a massive drop in child and infant mortality. Some periods of life are critical in terms of the impact of nutrition on healthiness and even aptitude. The earliest periods are particularly important, since any deficiency at this time can have lasting effects throughout life. A high level of child mortality indicates a high potential for lasting damage to health for survivors. There is a reinforcing cycle, particularly important in the earliest years of life. Nutrition improves immunity to disease. In the young, it helps avoid damage to vital organs, which can have a lasting effect. On the other hand, the avoidance of disease allows healthier individuals to benefit from improved nutrition. There is plenty of evidence to show that illness seriously affects the capacity of the body to retain nutrients (Easterlin 2004: 110), so that an improved supply of food does not always yield the expected results. A growing literature has established a relationship between nutrition and height/weight and between nutrition and productivity. The influence of improved nutrition is partly a matter of the energy which a given diet allows a worker to expend, partly a matter of mental alertness and aptitude.

Once more, the effects are cumulative, since human capital increases with the process of economic development, which generally raises nutrition and reduces vulnerability to disease. An important aspect of investment in human capital is what Mitch has called biological or population maintenance (Mitch 2004: 334–5). Biological maintenance includes the provision of nutrition, the development of language skills and the instilling in children of formative habits in a variety of dimensions, including diet, eating habits and standards of hygiene. This is normally carried out by the family rather than the school, but where this is impossible, it might be the responsibility of other institutions, such as the parish in England early, before and during the Industrial Revolution.

A key issue is accessibility to, and the reliability of, a food supply. Over time an increasing proportion of the population becomes independent of agriculture, even within the rural sector. Proto-industrialisation meant that large numbers of workers in the countryside were generating income from industrial pursuits and services: in Western Europe, this became significant from the sixteenth century.[5] Most industrial workers initially worked in the countryside. Access to food reflected entitlements, that is, the income available to purchase food, transport effectiveness in moving foodstuffs and the proximity of areas of food surplus. The reliability of the food supply is a critical concern. Modern technologies made the harvest less volatile and agriculture more diversified, and less subject to disasters.[6] Some societies operating at or close to the subsistence level have had significant proportions of the population malnourished, even at the best of times. The most advanced of societies had a minority of their population operating at or below the subsistence level. Marx called this group the lumpenproletariat: it is the underclass, who are destitute and often criminal. The size of this group tends to be much higher in urban than in rural areas. This proportion might amount to as much as 20 per cent of the population, but is usually less in an advanced society. This group was largely unemployed and because of poor nutrition unemployable. There are definite limitations on the amount of work which many could do – they lacked the input of proteins to give them the energy to do more than survive. Even societies such as England or Japan had an underclass, working below the poverty level and suffering from malnutrition, especially in the rapidly growing cities and towns. The poorest of Britain either did not reproduce themselves, in London, or barely did so, as in the smaller towns (Clark 2007: 115–16). The members of that class did not work, partly because they could not work, a vicious circle. Poor nutrition resulted from a lack of income, which resulted from a lack of gainful employment and in turn prevented them from engaging in sustained physical labour. In these two pioneer societies, the vulnerability to harvest fluctuations was much less severe and the incidence of *crises démographiques* ceased much earlier than elsewhere. It is also likely that the relevant populations were much healthier than elsewhere. This is linked with control over fertility. Where fertility varied with economic conditions, it was possible to moderate the impact of a bad harvest, for example, by having fewer mouths to feed. There was a natural tendency for fertility to decline in overcrowded and costly accommodation in the cities. The productivity of the rural sector determined the potential size of the urban sector.

Nutrition levels in pre-modern societies are highly variable, both seasonally and annually. The proportion malnourished rose with the time since the last harvest was collected. In Russia, by late winter and early spring a significant proportion of the population were struggling to survive.[7] This is not untypical of pre-modern societies. Bad harvests, which might occur once every five years, brought forward the time of suffering or more

accurately the time of starving. A series of bad harvests, or an exceptionally bad year, might massively increase the number in distress, and at
an earlier time in the year. Whatever the causes, it is not difficult to link
famine with serious harvest failures. Some commentators see the cause
of all famines as social rather than natural (Sen 1977). The occasion for
such a shock was almost always some significant climatic fluctuation. In
theory, such disasters were regional and grain could be transported from
other areas where the harvest was better. Higher grain prices could speed
the process, but where it was slow because of poor market development
or a slow response of government, severe malnutrition would become
a major problem with a mounting number of deaths and continuing
negative effects. Certainly, many pre-modern societies, particularly those
which were isolated or relatively closed, or those where government was
not as efficient as it might be, were highly vulnerable to natural climatic
fluctuations – too little or too much rain, premature frosts or excessive
temperatures – or to human shocks such as war and civil disturbance. The
potato famine in Ireland during the 1840s is an example of what could
happen, with the impact compounded by a monoculture and a reliance
on the market where the population had little means of purchase.[8] The
government of China was at great pains to ensure an emergency supply of
grain in such times.[9] In the worst of times in such societies, the numbers
suffering malnutrition increase markedly, hence the importance of the
state of the harvest and the role of the government in dealing with extreme
shocks. Malnutrition made the population vulnerable to disease, of both
the endemic and epidemic varieties; a vicious circle results.

APTITUDE

Weede and Kampf (2002: 377) assert 'Intelligence matters!' 'Differences in
general intelligence are real, stubborn, and important' (Gottfredson 2000:
76). Intelligence 'is a highly general, biologically grounded capacity for
processing information' (Gottfredson 2000: 83) and can be interpreted as
the ability of humans to adapt to their changing environment. This ability
reflects three important adaptive mechanisms (Christian 2007: 5). The first
is natural selection, a genetic process which characterises the development
of all animals. The second is individual learning, mostly achieved as one
generation passes on its knowledge to the next through both horizontal
and vertical transmission (Cavalli-Sforza 2000: chapter 6) – just as cultures
are learned so is the ability to learn itself. This can be described as cultural rather than genetic evolution. The third is collective learning, which
Christian regards as the key to human success, since it is cumulative. As

Christian asserts, 'Humans no longer function just as individuals. Almost every object or idea we use today represents the stored knowledge of previous generations.'

Intelligence, notably as expressed in IQ, has been interpreted in three ways – as 'a person's capacity for complex mental work', embracing various intelligence factors, which are linked to an underlying general intelligence, referred to as g; by behavioural outcomes, as a common property of successful people, including of course the economically successful; and as an arbitrary quality, whatever valid intelligence tests measure (Weede and Kampf 2002: 363), the last being closely linked with the second, particularly if it is argued that most measures are culturally orientated. There is a lot of evidence in favour of a correlation between intelligence and achievement criteria, at least in developed Western countries. Weede and Kampf argue that there is no other measurable human trait which is so closely correlated with as many criteria of achievement as intelligence (ibid.: 364). G can be defined as 'a highly general information-processing capacity that facilitates reasoning, problem solving, decision making, and other higher order thinking skills' (Gotfredson 1997: 81), a view shared by nearly all intelligence researchers. It is the most significant variable explaining individual educational, occupational, economic and social outcomes. It is reasonable to extend this to national achievements, such as the inception of modern economic growth and the maintenance of high economic growth rates.

Jones and Schneider (2006: 91) put the argument succinctly. 'A key lesson . . . appears to be that the health and vigour of the human brain is likely to be a key determinant of national economic performance. The ability of human to adapt to the appropriate environment is critical to the achievement of modern economic development'. Clark (2007), implicitly taking the second of these definitions, focuses on an improvement in the ability of a population to problem solve in a way which promotes economic development. There is just one comprehensive attempt to test the relationship between national intelligences and output per head or growth rates in output per head (Lynn and Vanhanen 2006).The national study has been carefully analysed in two papers by Jones and Schneider (2006) and Weede and Kampf (2002), from both theoretical and empirical perspectives.

The first of the studies establishes a clear and robust relationship between intelligence and both the level of output per head and rate of growth of output per head, showing that a 1 per cent increase in national IQ is associated with a 0.11 per cent increase in the annual average growth rate (Jones and Schneider 2006: 72). On a preliminary analysis, Jones and Schneider see this influence as transitional, with IQ raising steady-state income, that is living standards at a given moment of time, but not affecting the steady-state rate of growth. A one point increase in IQ raises steady-state living standards by 6.1 per cent. With a 30 point plans span in national IQ rates shown by the available statistics, a considerable part of the cross-country differences in living standards can be explained by this one variable. The second study confirms this conclusion, showing that IQ explains much more growth than the usual measures of education, such as literacy or school enrolment rates (Weede and Kampf 2002: 376–7). It also has a much stronger effect than catch-up opportunities, investment levels, or such institutional factors as the degree of freedom, however measured. The relationship is both robust and highly significant. As the study points out, if nutrition increases IQ, as seems likely, there may be a virtuous circle between intelligence and economic growth. Intelligence raises the growth rate and the growth rate raises intelligence (ibid.: 378). The conclusion is that regressions show a stronger relationship between economic growth and measures of intelligence than any other variables considered relevant by those who engage in regression analysis (Jones and Schneider 2006: 91). This is a rather startling finding. Either the regression approach is flawed and to be rejected entirely – and we have put some arguments for this, or there is good reason to include measures of intelligence in the analysis of the determinants of economic growth.

It is necessary to evaluate both theory and evidence, justifying the use of the national averages of IQ used by Lynn and Vanhanen. This is largely an empirical matter, requiring the collation of various measures of intelligence and their use to explain performance differences. The first problem is measuring intelligence. IQ tests are usually condemned as being culture bound.[10] The aim is often to measure general intelligence, *g*, by means of a broad and diverse set of cognitive abilities, but abilities which do not include language comprehension and can be applied where illiteracy is high.[11] General intelligence might be relevant to economic performance because it is correlated with trainability, but where the job is not amenable to training it helps with the practices which are most associated with modern economic development – creative problem solving, independent decision making, and innovative adaptation. General intelligence may also assist a country to absorb technology from outside. Independence of the influence of specific cultures may not matter if intelligence is defined as the ability to be successful economically. Jones and Schneider conducted their tests removing the data for OECD countries, that is, countries which are already developed, and focusing on only the undeveloped and developing countries. This has the effect of excluding the influence of the cultural characteristics of developed countries. It is possible to use culture-reduced non-verbal intelligence tests to assist in the removal of the influence of culture, although that may not be sensible if our focus of interest is the influence on economic development. Jones and Schneider (2006: 79) note that there is a strong positive correlation between measures of IQ and the two measures of cognitive ability used by Hanushek and Kimko (2000) based on maths and science scores. The latter also found a strong relationship of their measures with rates of economic growth.

The debate is part of a wider disagreement. In the nature versus nurture debate the general conclusion amongst scientists has been a 50/50 split, although some argue that the unexplained proportion exceeds the postulated shares of nature and nurture. American studies of the IQ of adopted children show a third of the variation in IQ among individuals can be explained by cultural transmission, one third by biological heredity, and the last third by other unspecified causes (Cavalli-Sforza 2000: 189). However empirical studies have shown that the heritability of IQ increases with age: typically from 0.2 in infancy (in so far as g can be measured), to 0.4 in the pre-school years, 0.6 by adolescence and 0.8 by middle to late adulthood (Gottfredson 2000, 89 and 2008: 558). Much has been made of the fact that the human species is genetically a remarkably homogeneous species, with differences smaller than among chimpanzees (Berry 1999: 133). About 80 per cent of the diversity occurs within local and regional populations, and only 10 per cent within and between continents, which causes Berry (ibid.: 133) to conclude, 'Any attempt to relate different histories to different genes is bound to be futile'. However it has been pointed out that the same is true of dogs where there is considerable diversity of characteristics (Cochran and Harpending 2009: 17). 'Modest genetic difference between groups could cause big trait differences' (Ibid. 19).

Clearly not all differences are inherited: there are important environmental influences which differ from individual to individual or from country to country. It is likely that genetic differences reinforce cultural differences. There is a subtle interaction between cultural and biological evolution (Berry 1999: 136). Cavalli-Sforza (2000: 178) summarises the situation nicely: '. . . cultural selection acts first through choices made by individuals, followed by natural selection, which automatically evaluates these decisions based on their effects on our survival and reproduction.' There is a positive correlation between these two forms of selection (the relevance of this to the determinants of economic development is put by Clark 2007). In the world of Cochran and Harpending (2009: 31), 'Biology keeps culture on a leash'. Even Lynn concedes that there are environmental influences on intelligence, notably nutrition, but not so much education. He points out that, if this is the case, the mix of influence on intelligence is different in undeveloped economies, with much more environmental influence, than in developed countries, where genetics reaches its peak influence. Explanations of differences in national IQ between countries include differences in nutrition during early childhood, difference in family size, differences in the healthiness of the general environments, in educational opportunities themselves and in parental literacy, or we might summarise, in the general quality of biological maintenance.

Intelligence therefore raises the broader issue of the nature and influence of biological adaptation but such adaptation is 'both autoplastic and alloplastic: it involves changes in the gene pool of the species as well as manipulation of the environment' (Guha 1981: 7). The usual focus is on the latter, on an analogy between economic growth and organic evolution. Some commentators not only believe 'economic growth is best interpreted as an extension of the evolutionary process' but even see economic growth as 'an integral part of evolution' (Guha 1981: 8). The emphasis on world history is making such a process part of the human story. Although humans, through social control of breeding, have greatly accelerated the rate of genetic change among plants and animals, because of slow breeding in humans the evolution of the genetic base remains sluggish and the primary mode of adaptation is seen as alloplastic. Since natural selection, by acting on fertility and mortality, is the greatest evolutionary factor in human biology, any cultural factor, such as the qualities linked to economic success, which is associated with significant differences in either, notably lower mortality or raised fertility, can spread through the population at a rapid rate, but exactly how fast? With a realistic time perspective genetic change can account for both the inception of modern economic development and the identity of the pioneers? It appears that the rate of genetic change has accelerated over the last few thousand years, now 100 times greater than the rate over the last few million years since humans separated from chimpanzees (Cochran and Harpending 2009: 23). Cavalli-Sforza (2000: 45–46) concludes that a gene which presents a strong selective advantage can be spread by natural selection in only thousands, even a few hundreds, of years. In the animal world the classic case is the peppered moth which after industrialisation changed from a white colour to brown or black within decades. For humans the classic example is the spread of lactose tolerance which enabled a significant improvement in nutrition and which must have appeared after the first domestication of animals about ten thousand years ago. Usually children lose their ability to digest milk when they are weaned from their mother's milk, but herding populations quickly develop a 100 per cent lactose tolerance beyond that age. Lactose tolerance of Europeans emerged within the past 7000 years but most of the world's population is still lactose intolerant. In an article in *The Australian*, 28 February: 10, University College London academic, Mark Thomas pointed out, 'the ability to drink milk is the most advantageous trait that's evolved in Europeans in the recent past.' Populations which depend on animal inputs for a significant part of their food tend to be healthier than those not. The evolution of lactose tolerance is significant since it suggests the possibility of evolution towards an increased ability to innovate, like the introduction of agriculture, which is seen as initiating the acceleration in genetic mutation, together with the development of language (Cochran and Harpending 2009: 23).

There is one finding in intelligence tests which is highly significant. There appears to have been an increase in national IQ in countries which have measured IQ over a significant period of time (Lynn 2006: 5–6). During the second half of the twentieth century measured IQ rises on average by two to three points per decade, a phenomenon known as the Flynn effect, after its discoverer. Some have argued that this is due to an improvement in test-taking skills, others that there is a genuine rise in intelligence, due to a cognitively more stimulating environment or more likely to improvements in nutrition (Lynn 2006: 6). The increase appears as an increase in the lower part of the distribution of intelligence.[12] There is some evidence that the Flynn effect has run its course in developed economies, that the improvement in IQ has ceased. Again, it is tempting to conclude that much of the improvement in intelligence is a result of modern economic development. Apart from the issue of what is being measured, it appears that the population within those countries which have developed has raised its intelligence by a variety of means and that this has helped the process of modern economic development to become self-sustaining. This might be regarded as another example of a positive feedback loop. Developing countries may converge in measures of intelligence as in the process of accelerating economic growth they improve the environmental factors – those related to the impact of nurture rather than nature.

MOTIVATION

There are two additional problems relating to the role of human capital in economic development and its appropriate use. Just as physical capital must be used in an efficient way in order to promote economic development, the same is true of human capital. The first problem relates to incentives for such efficient use and the associated motivation of the possessor of the human capital to use that capital in a socially optimum way, one that promotes the process of economic development. The second problem relates to opportunity. A lack of opportunity means that human capital remains dormant. There may be those who are willing, but not able. Since it is necessary to match human capital with appropriate positions, the existence of a high level of human capital is a necessary but not sufficient condition for modern economic development.

Motivation in key decision making is critical. There are two diametrically opposed approaches to the issue, one assuming a universal motivation, the other that motivation is culturally determined and differs from society to society. In the words of Hedlund (2005: 312–13), who is referring to a cleavage stressed by Elster, 'On the one side we have Adam Smith's homo economicus, who is supposed to be guided by instrumental rationality. On the other is Emile Durkheim's homo sociologicus, who is driven by norms. Where the former is constantly looking for new opportunities, being "pulled" into the future by prospects of rewards, the latter is "pushed" from behind by "quasi-inertial forces". To the former, history simply does not matter. To the latter, history is everything.'

Neoclassical theory rests upon a narrow definition of rationality, implying maximising behaviour. We are all maximisers – of profit, income, utility or whatever is relevant, or alternatively cost minimisers, which amounts to the same thing. This reduces economics to a set of optimisation puzzles. Rationality is seen as universal – characteristic of all societies at all times. If there is an ultimate cause in neoclassical growth theory, something fixed for all time and places, it is this universal psychological propensity to maximise, with the associated rationality displayed in pursuing the relevant objectives. Regardless of time and place, individuals are assumed to be imbued with this motivation; it is part of mankind's natural makeup.[13] Even if profit maximisation is accepted as rational, and a reasonable motivation, there are all sorts of problems with such a motivation. The first involves risk. How do you maximise in conditions of risk? The neoclassical answer is maximisation subject to the constraint of an acceptable level of risk – in the extreme case, survival, whether of the individual or organisational unit (Wright and Kunreuther 1975). Too high a level of risk elicits an avoidance response. The second problem is the relevant time horizon over which the maximisation occurs. Action which maximises short-term returns often threatens long-term profitability. A longer time horizon increases the level of risk and makes it important to build risk into the relevant analysis. Given the importance of investment in the process of modern economic development, the time horizon becomes of paramount importance. There is another issue – the relevance of such disciplines as psychology, sociology or genetics, to understanding motivation. There are a multitude of specific influences on the decision making of individuals. The relevant psychology is more complex than simple rationality. Key decisions are made by individuals embedded in particular social situations. We can view the different identities of actors as imposing constraints on maximisation. If it can be shown that human beings today do not act in a rational way, it is appropriate to take a different approach, and relax the narrow assumption of rationality, defined in the neoclassical way. It is possible to tackle the issue from a theoretical rather than an empirical perspective.

The first constraint is psychological. There has been an attempt to devise laboratory tests which both test the validity of the neoclassical assumption and try to show the nature of the decision-making rules or biases adopted. The work of Tversky and Kahneman represents a major step away from crude notions of economic rationalism. It explores the psychology of decision making, emphasising that an important cognitive influence on decision making is the way a problem is 'framed'. One part of the approach is to consider the biases which decision makers bring to their decisions. For example, prospect theory considers any decision about the future in the context of the present, the starting point or initial status. Future outcomes are assessed in the context of the status quo. For example, risk taking occurs most frequently when the prospect is a deterioration in the status quo and vice versa. There are weaknesses to the work. One objection to these experiments is that they are made in artificial conditions, which do not correspond to real world business conditions. The approach addresses the psychology of decision making, rather than its sociology. It fails to represent how individuals would have chosen to act in the past.

The second constraint is sociological. There has been a major effort to introduce some realism into the assumed motivation by focusing on the notion of 'bounded' rationality – even cognitive constraints (Simon 1955). There are two difficulties with a universal rationality. First, maximising behaviour may be characteristic only of capitalist market economies which have already developed; it is one expression of a fully developed bourgeois or modern man. The way in which motivation manifests itself differs from one society to another and over time. The emergence of such motivation is critical to the inception of modern economic development. One weakness of neoclassical economics is its timelessness. As already indicated, the neoclassical approach does not consider processes, only outcomes. Simple formal rules are introduced to explain the process of decision making in all societies and at all times. Historically, the issue is much more complex. A second problem is the neoclassical emphasis on the deliberate decision making of a representative individual. If individuals differ in motivation and in opportunity, reflecting group influences, the aggregation of individuals is not simply a multiple of representative individuals. Individuals are partly moulded in their motivation by their communities or the organisations and associations of which they are members.

The idea of a bounded rationality includes less than perfect information, a limited ability to process existing information, and the universal activity of bargaining in decision making. There are various trade-offs in bargaining between different groups, which is often conducted in less than perfectly competitive markets or in contexts which are decidedly not market contexts. The result was to introduce the notion of 'satisficing', aiming for a satisfactory rather than a maximum return, a much more realistic way to describe motivational aims. Satisficing allows the retention of an economic motivation. It is difficult to disagree with the assertion of Clark (2007: 4), 'Over the long run income is more powerful than any ideology or religion in shaping lives. No God has commended worshippers to their pious duties more forcefully than income as it subtly directs the fabric of our lives.' A sensible approach is adopted by Snooks (1993), that human beings have as their main motivation survival and then the maximisation of material well-being. To achieve this, they adopt different dynamic strategies. What differs is not motivation but the strategy chosen to satisfy the economic motivation. The choice of strategy reflects the relative return from different strategies for different societies and the pressure of competition on those societies. The main strategies comprise family multiplication, technological change, conquest and commerce. There is a stage at which any strategy becomes exhausted, in other words the return from that strategy declines significantly. There is in each period a dominant strategy, but other supporting strategies are relevant. During the modern period, the dominant strategy is technological change. It becomes a matter of analysing when and why this is so.

The role of culture is sometimes summarily dismissed (Mokyr 2002), sometimes dismissed with reservations (Jones 2006), sometimes elevated to great significance (Landes 1998), and on occasion regarded as the ultimate cause (Harrison 1992). Fernandez-Armesto (2001: 414–15) has summarised the dilemma, 'Culture is part of an unholy trinity – culture, chaos, and cock-up – which roam through our versions of history, substituting for traditional theories of causation. It has the power to explain everything and nothing.' The debate is focused mainly on the degree of fixity of values and attitudes. There are three possible positions. Many economists see values and attitudes as malleable, responding to changes in the economic environment which are the result of other factors. They are therefore irrelevant to the causation of economic development. The second possibility is that they are to some degree fixed and represent static world views which reinforce social stability, including a fatalism about the possibility of improvement in this world. Such a position is clearly not good for economic development and may have a role in explaining the absence of modern economic development in most of the world, but cannot be universally true. The third possibility is that individuals are socialised into particular societies with cultures characterised by attitudes, values and behavioural patterns which differ markedly, some conducive to the kind of economic decisions which promote economic development, others not. Equally, in some societies there may be a change over time in favour of attitudes and values conducive to economic development.

OPPORTUNITY

There is a fascinating account of how the Ashkenazi Jews (the Jews of Europe) developed an IQ which underpinned their disproportionate intellectual achievement in recent times (Chapter 7 of Cochran and Harpending 2009, 187–224). That intellectual achievement was linked with occupation of entrepreneurial and managerial roles which were complex but offered significant financial rewards. The process of natural selection which favoured higher intelligence rested on three tendencies. The more prosperous you were the more children you had. Economic success was linked to roles which demanded appropriate cognitive and personality traits. Intelligence was heritable. The argument can be broadened, although the speed of evolution may be slower since Britain, Japan or wider regions such as Western Europe or East Asia are much less closed than the Ashkenazi.

The key development is the emergence of bourgeois or modern man (Clark 2007: chapter 9). This emergence is the result of either cultural or genetic mechanisms, or both. The relevant characteristics can be passed on through socialisation of children by their parents or through genes. In the British case, Clark argues strongly that conditions were conducive to the passing on of the characteristics that made for economic success. Three particular elements promoted this – the great stability of English society over a long period of time, starting at the latest in 1200; the slow growth of English population between 1300 and 1760; and the extraordinary fecundity of the rich and economically successful, with a survival rates for children double those of the poorest groups. In a largely static economy there were not enough positions for the children to step into their parents' shoes, so the relevant attitudes and ambitions diffused through the working population. While the same process was occurring in Japan or China, in England the process was much quicker: there was a significant downward social mobility and the reproductive success of the economically successful meant that English society was rapidly becoming middle class, with an almost universal economic orientation. There is more than an emphasis on intelligence, or IQ. With such an argument, Clark does not have to specify the exact nature of modern man, nor to trace the nature and timing of his emergence. It is interesting to consider the nature of the relevant characteristics which are being passed on. The translation into behaviour is a dynamic process, in which there is change, although, as Clark rightly indicates the changes are muted by Malthusian mechanisms, which ensure that even in England there is no trend increase in income per head right up to the nineteenth century and that the slow improvement in efficiency is translated into an increase in population, albeit a slow one. The traditional social norms are steadily loosened despite the Malthusian mechanism (Clark 2007), so that within an apparently static economy there is important social and cultural change occurring. Thrift replaces a tendency to be spendthrift, prudence impulsiveness; an emphasis on hard work displaces a love of leisure, and a pacific tendency a violent one. Hours of work increase very significantly, the incidence of homicide declines massively. When appropriate, caution and rationality prevail; when not, ingenuity and innovativeness. The levels of numeracy and literacy rise, as does the amount of education. Curiosity and a desire to understand become common. Discipline, conscientiousness and engagement prevail, cooperation and trust extend their influence.

There is a need to focus on the ability to innovate which is linked with the willingness and ability to invest in relevant assets, 'by taking unknown risks on novelty' (Goldstone 1987: 119). This is the key to modern economic development. In narrow economic terms, there are three elements relevant to the investment decision seen – the prospective return, the cost of capital and the appropriability of the return. We need to expand on this. If an organisation, or individual, were investing its own funds, the exercise becomes one of estimating the current value to see whether it is positive. In such an exercise a discount rate is applied to future revenue or cost streams, one which includes a risk premium. Just before the period of the Industrial Revolution there was a very significant decline in interest rates, from 10 per cent or above to just 2 per cent. The dramatic decline in interest rates (discussed at length by Clark 2007) is linked to either a reduced risk aversion or a decline in the riskiness of the environment, for which there is plenty of evidence, or indeed a combination of the two. This gives an enormous boost to investment of all kinds. The cost of capital reflects this decline in the rate of interest.

Appropriability is a matter of making available a reward for taking a risk and the retention of that reward. The reward is not only pecuniary, it includes broader psychic or social benefits. It might even be desirable to give positive incentives to individuals to try their hand at business; at minimum, it is necessary for obstacles to be removed. Typically, societies act to stigmatise innovation and deviation from cultural norms. It is rare to do otherwise. A key issue in any society is what activities or professions are valued. Individuals will only innovate if there is a prospect of improving status relative to others. In most societies, social status and power are distributed in a way which discourages involvement in commerce or business life. In many pre-modern societies business is looked down upon, even derided. This is true of most civilisations which failed to 'take off'. The classical European civilisations of Greece and Rome are good examples.[14] The social pecking order relegates those associated with commerce or business to the lowest level. It is acceptable to serve in public life, to enter the armed forces or the official religion – it is even acceptable to be associated in some way with farming, if only through land ownership. However, those already having social status avoid any taint from business. As a result, those who succeed in business, particularly the upwardly mobile, seek as quickly as possible to be free of the stigma attaching to the origins of their wealth. They are likely to move their investments into respectable assets not associated with business life – into land or the maintenance of a way of life in keeping with high status. They may pursue a strategy of marriage which conceals the background of their success. Successful entrepreneurs are lost to business life. This is even true of the first pioneer, British society.

A key question for any society is whether there is scope for entrepreneurial or innovative activity – is it encouraged and rewarded?[15] Goldstone argues that the conditions that favour innovation are historically contingent (Goldstone 1987: 133), they emerge as a result of a political crisis in which marginal groups make space for their preferred activities, activities which potentially have an economic orientation. The numerous cases of business success of minority groups in various societies provide an insight into the conditions for success. The Chinese for a long period of time were very successful outside China compared with a lack of success in mainland China. For some minority groups, progress in occupations which give high status, such as the army, the church, or government service, is blocked. They have only business open to them. This often accounts for the high representation of such groups in entrepreneurial groups, whether we are considering the Jews, minority Indian or Chinese populations outside the home country, Armenians, Quakers or historically non-conformist groups in Britain, or non-believers in Russia. It is not difficult to find such groups everywhere. It is possible to include immigrant groups in various societies. Success in the business area is reinforced by the network benefits within groups, the members of which know each other well and are forced to trust, each other. Their very survival may depend at some stage upon others within the group. There are economic benefits which derive from the nature of the networks. Because of this trust members of the networks help each other; they employ each other; they extend loans to each other. They provide all the services which are critical to economic success. For that reason, access to the critical resources needed for business success is linked to the very existence of such minority groups. The role of such groups tells us much about the preconditions for business success. The communalism which makes such minority groups successful also limits their ability to extend the success to the majority societies, unless they can become part of the civil society which links its members in a looser but more wide-ranging way. Unfortunately, there is a negative feedback loop, since the presence of minority groups in such activities often increases the disapproval attached to them. This negative loop may be released only by unusual historical circumstances.

8. The institutional setting: government, market and civil society

> The danger lies in assuming that economic growth is natural and that if it does not take place, arbitrary human actions (usually thought of as politics) must be interfering. By closely identifying a theoretical ideal with a 'natural' state of affairs, neoclassical economic theory loses its potential to explain how economic change is in fact historically created through the building of economic institutions. (Bin Wong 1997: 62)

The consequences of institutional weakness can be illustrated through the prisoner's dilemma, which shows the dangers of predation (Easterly 2006: 87–8). There are two potential partners to a joint investment. The entrepreneurs have a choice between cooperation in the investment, which requires a minimum investment of funds beyond the capacity of either of the individuals alone, and using the same resources to buy a gun, which allows one partner to seize the funds of the other, redistributing existing resources. It is assumed that the strategy of predation precludes that of productive investment. The gun costs 1 unit, the investment yields 2 units and each player starts with 3 units of funds. The returns from the different strategies might look like this:

Player 1 Player 2	Buys a gun	Does not buy a gun
Buys a gun	2,2	0,5
Does not buy a gun	5,0	4,4

Each player is worse off if they fail to buy a gun and the other does. The strategy of buying a gun without the other player doing so yields the highest individual return, so it is rational for each to buy a gun and hope the other does not; this is the preferred strategy. The dominant strategy is that they both buy guns and retain their original funds, minus the cost of the gun. Such a strategy is inferior to a cooperative strategy of investment which maximises the combined income of the players, that is to refrain from buying a gun and to invest cooperatively. The example reveals the high probability of a low-level income equilibrium. An institutional arrangement which avoids the prisoner's dilemma is clearly desirable.

Unfortunately, the historical record shows that there is no one set of institutional arrangements which guarantees the inception of modern economic development, achieving aims including the avoidance of predation. Institutions evolve in a specific and often path-dependent way and have a persistence which qualifies them as ultimate causes. The mechanism of their development needs explanation. From one perspective, societies are engaged in a process of trial and error in identifying and implementing the specific institutional arrangements which support modern economic development.

The present chapter starts by defining exactly what is meant by an institution. It analyses the persistence of institutional arrangements and their influence on economic development, focusing on the problem of identifying the right institutions. The second section discusses the partnership between market and government, noting the way in which they interact, either positively or negatively. In the third section, there is a discussion of the role of culture and civil society. The final section considers the influence on economic development of political organisation at the international level, such as systems of states or empires.

FINDING THE RIGHT INSTITUTIONS

Greif (2006: Chapter 1) begins his exploration of the role of institutions in the path to the modern economy by defining institutions broadly, as any non-technological feature of a society. He goes on to argue that 'an institution is a system of rules, beliefs, norms, and organizations that together generate a regularity of (social) behaviour' (Greif 2006: 30). Behavioural patterns become institutionalised or routinised: in other words, they persist. There are two perspectives on institutions – the agency perspective, largely that of economists, and the structural perspective, that of sociologists (Greif 2006: 40–41). The former stresses that institutions express intent, reflecting the aims of their founders, the latter that institutions are exogenous, imposing constraints on the way people behave. Those who stress agency see institutions as deliberately constructed for different purposes – to provide incentives, to reduce uncertainty (North 2005), to increase efficiency (Williamson 1985) or to distribute gains (Knight 1964). Those who stress constraints see institutions as preventing economic development. Greif's aim was to integrate the two perspectives. In North's more limited conception, institutions are the formal and informal rules which constrain human behaviour.[1] Institutions, whether formal or informal, are 'the underlying rules that govern transactions between agents in an economy, both transactions between private parties, as well as between private parties and the government' (Beck and Laeven 2005: 8).

Institutions are manifested at one extreme as loose conventions or customs and at the other as organisations. Typically, economists see organisations as comprising loose forms of market activity rather than hierarchies (Rosenberg and Birdzell 1986: 1x–x). It is difficult to conceive of government or the enterprise simply as systems of law or informal convention, since in both hierarchy directs communication and channels cooperation. The structural definition of institutions as organisations is still an important one, since these are the framework in which decision making, problem solving and the interaction of relevant stakeholder groups occur. Even markets take on an organised form which has a considerable continuity of existence.

It has been common recently, even among economists, to argue that institutions are one, if not the most, important influencing factor in modern economic development (North 1981, 1990 and 2005, Rodrik 2003, Acemoglu et al. 2001 and 2002, Engerman and Sokoloff 1994).[2] For some they are the ultimate cause. Many studies purport to show a general relationship between good institutions and successful economic development, but in individual experiences it is difficult to trace the specific influence of institutions, which is often indirect. It is easy to list particular institutional arrangements, which appear to have played a positive role in at least one experience of economic development, often in combination with other factors, and to list those which have been obstacles, the no-no's of economic development, institutional arrangements which are causes of the poverty traps preventing the vast majority of human beings from sharing in the positive consequences of modern economic development (Azariadis and Stachurski 2004). Institutional structures have a persistence which justifies their inclusion among ultimate causes. In normal circumstances, institutions change slowly and are difficult to reform in a deliberate and systematic manner, largely because there are so many groups with a vested interest in the status quo. Major institutional change is rare and usually occurs in revolutionary circumstances, accompanying a radical shift in political power, for example with the collapse of an existing structure. Sometimes radical changes are the result of outside interference. More often institutions evolve, developing in unexpected and idiosyncratic ways. Institutions differ dramatically from country to country. They both mould the patterns of behaviour which prevail in different societies and reflect those patterns – from an economic perspective, they help establish the rules of the game.

The role of institutions is complex. In the opinion of one authority:

'That "institutions matter" is not . . . obvious, . . . as successful countries have very different institutions and countries with exactly the same institutions have very different outcomes' (Pritchett 2004: 229). There are interesting paradoxes, for example two striking examples of economic success achieved with very different institutions – the expanded group of OECD economies and the early successful Eastern Asian economies, the four little tigers. An example of the same institutions with different economic outcomes is that of the colonies of former colonising powers, notably Britain, which often share the same institutional inheritance but have very different economic performance. What then are good institutions? They are those which promote economic development and the decisions relevant to such development. There are complicating issues. Szostak (2006: 11) makes an interesting point, reflecting the work of Kohli (2004), that the key difference in terms of the prospects for economic growth is between 'countries that can manage/enforce any institutions well, and countries that can manage/enforce no economic institutions well'. Such a viewpoint plays down the importance of particular institutions. The emphasis should be on the quality as much as the nature of institutions, which makes rigorous analysis of the role of institutions extremely difficult and a simple testing of institutional contributions to modern economic development impossible. Particularity is the name of the game. Rodrik (2007: 15) agrees with this viewpoint, arguing that there is no unique correspondence between the functions that good institutions perform and the form that such institutions take. Superficially, the kaleidoscopic relationship between institutions and economic performance seems to confirm Szostak's view.

From an economic perspective, good institutions are those which perform well in solving standard business problems, and enabling relevant transactions by keeping their costs low. They promote the implementation of the following tasks – securing property rights, enabling individuals or organisations to retain the returns made on their investments, making and enforcing contracts and resolving disputes. The problem in evaluating precisely the role of institutions is threefold. First, the institutional structure of any particular society is sui generis, since the relevant institutions differ subtly but radically from society to society. It is easy to label institutions as the same when in reality they are different. It is difficult to generalise about the nature and role of such institutions. Secondly, the performance of the same institution differs from one society to another and is hard to measure. Even bad institutions perform at different levels of effectiveness in different societies. Thirdly, it is unclear how far there is path dependence in the evolution of institutions. Once again, an analytic narrative would take full account of the specific form of institutions and their performance.

How do you measure the good performance of institutions? In recent years, the focus has shifted to the level of transactions costs; good performance means low transactions costs.[3] Such costs are assumed to be zero in the economic systems embraced as optimal by neoclassical theory – there are no frictions in the operation of a market system. According to the new institutional economics, they are positive in all economic systems and their level an important determinant of the nature of institutions. Different institutional arrangements imply different levels of transactions costs. A significant level of transactions costs makes important the choice of appropriate institutions within which economic activity can be organised. Some structures involve high levels of institutional costs, as the centrally planned physical planning systems of the communist countries showed. It is difficult for such systems to survive in a competitive world, in which it is impossible to ignore a high level of transaction costs. How far institutions are deliberately chosen or evolve in a way which minimises transactions costs is controversial. There may be some randomness in the evolution of institutional structures or they may evolve for different reasons than the level of implied transaction costs.

There are highly desirable outcomes of well-functioning institutions which make for low transaction costs, such as a low degree of corruption, the rule of law, insignificant political instability, and a credible commitment by the state (Castanheira and Esfahani 2003: 167). However it is usually to the protection of property rights and enforcement of contract that reference is made when institutions are argued to be important. To operate effectively, a market system requires protection of property and enforcement of contract. It is necessary to see which features of institutions promote these beneficial effects and which don't. However, this is not enough. There is also what Keynes described as animal spirits, the confidence to look to the future and to take a sanguine view of the possibilities of business success. The risk to property, which can suppress Keynes' animal spirits, can arise from two sources – from private disorder – war, crime, ethnic violence, squatter takings, torts, monopoly, bribery and investor expropriation or simple theft – or from government itself. Governments can expropriate or confiscate in a variety of ways, including the use of the tax system. Well might it be asked, who will guard the guardians? It is common for the theoretical literature to argue explicitly, often to assume implicitly, that a particular set of institutions comprising representative democracy and a capitalist market system promotes modern economic development by producing the desired outcome. Without appropriate institutions to protect property and enforce contracts, and impose checks and balances on the governors, modern economic development is impossible, largely because the market cannot operate effectively in such a context; the relevant transaction costs are too high and the incentives to appropriate decision making removed.

There is a tendency to focus on over-regulation by the government or its various arms as a source of high transactions costs, to see a lean government as favourable to economic development. Any regulation creates vested interests in the monopoly profit created (Olson 1982) and since the costs are often diffused and the benefits concentrated, there is a tenacity in preserving the status quo which is absent in the attempt to remove the relevant regulation. There may be a tendency for such institutional distortions to accumulate over time and to steadily reduce economic efficiency.[4] On the other hand, regulation may be critical to the operation of any market system, certainly to its acceptance by the majority of the population. There is good regulation and bad regulation.

The historical evidence for the role of these arrangements in the inception of modern economic development is problematic, since a study of Britain shows no clear improvement during the critical period of the inception of modern economic development. There are some who provide persuasive arguments that the appropriate institutions existed long before the Industrial Revolution, in societies which did not begin the process of modern economic development (Clark 2007). Perhaps the situation in Britain was already more favourable in this respect than elsewhere at the beginning of the relevant period. Institutional change is rarely sufficiently radical to offer an explanation of a turnaround in economic performance; it is much more likely to account for a favourable evolution.[5]

Confirmation of the appropriateness of the institutions associated with representative democracy and the market system to modern economic development is vividly displayed in recent history, which, it is claimed, made its own judgement. The Cold War was, and still is, seen as a conflict between two clearly distinguished institutional systems, a conflict which yielded a decisive winner – it validated the arguments in favour of choice models based on the market and free elections. On the one side were one-party communist countries organised in a centrally planned economic system which used the market mechanism sparingly, on the other were developed democratic states mainly using the market mechanism to allocate resources and to distribute income. The latter triumphed; the 'end of history' in the Hegelian sense represents the culmination of a long historical process and the final triumph of both democracy and the market (Fukuyama 1992).

The distinction between the two political and economic systems in contention during the Cold War rested on the respective roles of the government and the market, often seen through textbook models rather than through realistic descriptions of what occurred.[6] Government intervention in the economy has acquired a bad name, but the market has been vindicated: there is a stress on government rather than market failure. The task in communist or ex-communist countries is seen as restoring the operation of efficient markets. In the radical systems change experienced throughout the communist world – in some countries imposed by events and in others deliberately adopted, the greater effectiveness of the institutions associated with the capitalist market model was seen as both cause of the collapse in Europe – communist economies were out-competed – and also as inevitably the core of the reforms needed to rescue both the collapsed polities and economies, and any others, from a similar fate. Institutional reform is intended to improve economic performance where communist regimes have survived. Initially, the significance of institution building in the transition was largely ignored, but the differing role of institutions is now used to explain the differing outcomes of reform in the relevant countries, notably divergent economic performance. The attempt to effect a successful transition from an economic system based on planning to one which is market-based offers valuable insights into the role of institutions in economic development.[7] In the words of one pair of commentators, 'The experience of transition economies offers a unique historic experiment in institution building' (Beck and Laeven 2005: 2).

The key issue is the effectiveness of the newly created institutions in the reforming societies (Murrell 2005). The experience of the transitional societies has been very different. The apparent success of gradual reform, usually adopted within an authoritarian political context, notably in generating rapid economic development, is seen as a legitimation of the market model, particularly if the Asian experience is considered, but also recognition of the difficulty of introducing the new institutions required by a systems change.[8] The transition from a planned system to a market system highlights the difficulties of identifying the general relationship between institutions and economic development and displays all the problems of institutional reform, including the degree to which it is difficult to implement. Some examples of success are seen as showing that rapid institutional change is not impossible given favourable conditions. Where such favourable conditions do not exist, it is best to deploy a set of transitional institutions, much more suited to the particular circumstances of a country and its capabilities (Murrell 2005: 11): such as institutions are usually regarded as second-best. Murrell sees this as having particular validity for the experience of China. It is always possible that the relevant institutional structures are specific to particular countries and likely to be more lasting than often thought.

THE PARTNERSHIP OF MARKET AND GOVERNMENT

What kind of institutional system is promotive of economic development? One answer, based mainly on the European experience, is a capitalist market system with a strong government and a dense civil society.[9] There are a number of preconceptions about what is needed for the successful operation of such a system. First, an emphasis on the innovative role of small enterprises is a common theme in the economics literature (Rosenberg and Birdzell 1986). Baumol (2007: 60–61) distinguishes four types of market capitalism: state-guided capitalism, in which there is significant government intervention; oligarchic capitalism, in which there is a strong concentration of wealth and income; big firm capitalism, in which large enterprises dominate; and finally entrepreneurial capitalism, in which small innovative firms play an important role. The last one is favoured by Baumol as most conducive to modern economic development.

Secondly, there is a tendency among economists to stress the emergence of an autonomous economic sphere, one firmly outside political and religious control (Rosenberg and Birdzell 1986:24), alongside other relevant spheres similarly autonomous, such as science. It is worth quoting Rosenberg and Birdzell (1986: 256) at some length. Although the reference is to science rather than to the market, it is valid for both: 'We are so far accustomed to think of organisations solely in terms of hierarchical bureaucracies like armies, governments, or corporations that it is difficult to realise that an enterprise so individualistic and non-hierarchical as a modern science can properly be said to be highly organized. But such a narrow impression of organization would have to be dismissed as misleading on the basis of the history of science alone. Without a hierarchy, Western scientists formed a scientific community within which they pursued shared goals of understanding natural phenomena with dedication, cooperation, competition, collective conflict resolution, division of labour, specialisation, and information generation and exchange at a level of organisational efficiency rarely matched among large groups, hierarchical or non-hierarchical.'

There is a clear distinction between a patrimonial state, in which there may be a struggle between those who hold such patrimonies, to exercise coercion over each other, extending the assertion of patrimonial rights to take what income they are able and desire, establishing in the process new property rights, and a modern state in which there is a monopoly over the use of coercion exerted by a central authority, often an absolutist monarch or emperor.[10] In a patrimonial state, private property is politically constituted, consisting of all sorts of government-created offices, rights and monopolies which can be exploited profitably. In a modern state, property is economically determined and its ownership and use expressed through contracts, and its value and use determined by the market. In some strong states, not all, central power is used to defend private property rights. In the former, there is a fusion of sovereignty and property, in the latter they are clearly separated – this is the basis for autonomy.

Thirdly, it is common, noting the lack of hierarchy and bureaucracy in such market systems, to stress the significance of both experiment and diversity in autonomous systems. The emphasis is on the decentralisation of responsibility and the predominance of relatively small hierarchies in developed economies (Rosenberg and Birdzell 1986: 297), and on the fact that the great part of economic activity, notably that involving change and adaptation, is conducted on a small scale, largely because experiment – of its nature best conducted on the smallest scale, is so important to such economies.

There are two qualifying comments. Nearly all decision makers, including scientists, belong to large hierarchical organisations, although many of their productive interactions may not be strictly within those hierarchies. At the time of the writing of the quotation above, a branch of economics, institutional economics, was emerging which showed that in certain conditions, including market failure, hierarchies existed because they were more efficient that non-hierarchical organisations. Moreover, in practice, there seems to be a relentless march in the direction of larger hierarchical organisations – the iron law of oligopoly seems to rule.

Such a viewpoint seems to imply the absence of a role for government. In principle, it is possible for a market to emerge endogenously without exogenous government intervention, but only under rather special conditions, some of which are analysed by Greif (2006). The historical experience shows that government and market are not alternatives, nor in conflict with each other, but rather interact in a positive way when economic development is taking place at a significant rate and in a negative way when economic development is absent or weak. They also interact in a variable way as conditions change, notably of the general environment and technology. It is this interaction which is critical; it must be neither too close nor too distant, since there needs to be information transfer and cooperation. Any deficiency in one institutional arrangement will act as a brake on economic development; it is generally recognized that there are both government and market failures.

The market, like government, is a social construct: it is 'instituted process rather than natural equilibrium' (Dugger 1989: 607). As Dugger (1989: 607) graphically puts it. 'The market is not a natural phenomenon. It bears no resemblance to the Grand Canyon or the Rocky Mountains.

Instead, it is a man-made phenomenon. It resembles the Panama Canal and the Empire State Building.' This has further implications. As Rodrik (2007: 154) points out, markets are 'not self-creating, self-regulating, self-stabilising, or self-legitimating'. It is impossible to introduce a fully fledged market system overnight; it usually evolves over a long period of time. Moreover, the market evolves simultaneously with the emergence of government, preferably one with strong infrastructural power, able to assist in provision of the infrastructure required for effective and efficient market operation (White 1987). The market cannot be introduced to good effect without the support of an appropriate infrastructure of institutions and attitudes, whose nature is specific to the particular market. Again in the words of Rodrik (2007: 155), the market is '"embedded" in a set of non-market institutions'. Market development requires government action since the government typically provides most of this infrastructure; it also uses its sovereignty to resolve disputes in the evolution of the market (Dugger 1989: 613–14). Such an infrastructure helps to keep the relevant transactions costs low. If transactions costs are too high, the market will not grow; all sorts of other administrative arrangements will be substituted for it. The market is not a neutral venue for economic transactions, rather a mechanism by which income and costs are distributed in a way desirable to those with market, and political, power, whether they are large enterprises, governments or groups with large ownership stakes (Dugger 1989: 610–13). A promotive market is one which both operates with low transactions costs and provides an income distribution yielding appropriate incentives to entrepreneurial activity.

Some argue that merchants themselves are capable of enforcing the rules of the game (Ridley 1997, Greif 2006), but this is unusual, constituting only a beginning. Such relationships are fragile. Appropriate law must exist and be enforced. Predictability is highly desirable, although the law should be flexible enough to adjust to the requirements of a changing environment. Everyone is subject to the same law, even those who govern. The rule of law provides protection to property, or rather rights of control over property (Rodrik 2007: 156), and a means to enforce contract, whether explicit or implicit. It provides space for the entrepreneur to operate without too much risk of expropriation of any assets that he/she has created. It prevents too much rent-seeking behaviour and a winner-takes-all politics. For the rule of law to be effective, there need to be authorities willing and able to enforce the law. Law and order require not only a body of law appropriate to the time and place, but law courts and police to enforce the law. The writ of government must run in all the areas under the sovereignty of that government. Honest police, an impartial judiciary and good laws are all highly desirable. Law and order is a pure public good, although some aspects of the law can be privatised by security firms, private lawyers and protection rackets. The consumption of law and order, just as defence, is non-rivalrous, since consumption by one does not prevent the consumption by another. Nor is it true that the law must be regularly accessed. It stands as a back-up rather than as a regular recourse, its very existence as a last resort usually sufficient. Litigiousness has high costs. The law establishes, at one level, the rules of the game. A society where agreements are kept, provided they are reasonable, is one in which transactions costs are likely to be low. The infrastructure supporting market operation includes a set of attitudes conducive to honest and fair dealing. Preferably, attitudes must be such as to make recourse to the law usually unnecessary and therefore unusual; a handshake suffices. Attitudes of honesty, industry, thrift and sobriety are often rightly associated with economic success, and are regularly promoted. These attitudes are often seen as associated with certain religious beliefs. Christianity created a set of attitudes which were highly conductive to economic development (Stark 2005, Weber 1958 and Tawney 1962).[11]

Order is a second requirement, usually associated with the law if viewed from a domestic perspective. Inside a country, it is a matter of suppressing brigandage and crime in general. The fall in the level of violence in countries which have developed economically is significant (Gurr 1981). Outside a country it is often the case that the navy, or other countries' navies, play an important role in controlling piracy, which in some cases merges with privateering supported by foreign governments. International relations and international agreements provide the framework within which piracy is controlled, but in the end it is the strength of one's own government which is important. It is usual for dominant powers to provide the policing which might favour their own, but indirectly assists commercial activity by others. The extension of the reach of the merchants of a particular country is closely linked with an extension of the reach of its navy and army. The level of risk within the British Empire was low because of the Pax Britannica and the application of English law. Sometimes commercial organisations, like the chartered companies, are given a monopoly over both commercial activity and political control (the East India company is a prime example). They are even allowed to mobilise their own armed forces. Sometimes both economic and political activity is conducted by the same organisation, sponsored and supported by relevant governments.

Other areas vitally important to the market include communications and transport infratructures. The former is critical to the transmission and distribution of information relating to prices. Initially, the physical development of markets provided a venue at which relevant information was exchanged. Public regulation was critical in this process. In the nineteenth century, the telegraph effected an enormous acceleration in the speed at which information moved both within countries and from country to country. Previously, communication depended on face-to-face contact. The law of one price is supported by the rapid communication of information regarding changes in market conditions. The telegraph was far more revolutionary in its consequences than the internet. Telephone and postal services were also critical to the transfer of information. Transport involves a variety of media. Initially, water transport was much cheaper than overland movements. The improvement in the efficiency of sailing ships was critical to the expansion of foreign trade. The expansion in cargo space with the reduction in the necessity of carrying guns was an important factor, aided by the protection of the navy. The cost of transportation is important in determining which goods can be traded on markets. In most countries, canals were dug and railways constructed either by the government itself or with the help of a government guarantee of the return on the capital raised for this purpose. Turnpike trusts and the roads require government regulation and assistance in their construction and maintenance.

The government has a responsibility to counteract obvious market failures, where they have occurred. Such failures were more pronounced in the past when information asymmetries were common and uncertainty greater. The further back in time we look, the more extensive is this role, a role already discussed in the context of the need to control risk (Chapter 6). In the pivotal early modern period when the economic environment was extremely precarious, large investment in trade and investment was only made when government acted to avert as many risks as possible (de Vries 2002: 72). Most government policy is in some sense concerned with the aim of controlling the multitude of different risks confronting decision makers. This involves government action to restrict the potential destructiveness of natural shocks, to regulate the nature of business enterprises, or to limit the volatility of markets by preventing financial crises. Today government also seeks to provide macroeconomic stabilisation, since a failure to do so can lead to the most extreme manifestation of market failure, an economic depression, like that of the 1930s. It also deals with the social insurance function, the problem of those who lose in the process of economic development. It regulates the abuse of market power. While the usual focus in analysis of economic growth is on the impact of government on the efficient allocation of resources, governments need to take into account the equity implications of the operation of markets, notably the influence of income distribution on incentives. Social instability is a result of an excessively uneven distribution of rewards, or a sudden worsening of the distribution. There is a need to prevent unrest by actions which counteract the impact of poverty or of such shocks as temporary harvest failures. Conflict management is another function of government vital to efficient market operation.

Markets can only blossom in the context of the emergence of this kind of infrastructure, which brings us to the role of the government. The main concern of many governments, right up to recent times, was warfare in all its different guises, notably its conduct and finance. As one commentator has said, 'The British state between the years 1700 and 1850 was indeed a warfare state, not a welfare state' (Harris 2004: 219). To some degree this was a matter of defence but also of offence, particularly for the strong states. Mercantilism equated economic and military strength. The aim was to accumulate gold or silver by means of trade and even more by naked force and to use that wealth to increase military power. In the words of de Vries (2002: 79): 'The mercantilist idea of trade implied a heavy backing by force, passively and if need be actively. Many a market literally was conquered and defeated.'

There is a tendency in neoclassical economics to see government as invariably bad for economic development. In particular, despotism, or authoritarian government of various kinds, is regarded as harmful. In the words of one pair of commentators: 'One of the oldest themes in economics is the incompatibility of despotism and development' (de Long and Shleifer 1992). Rodrik (2007: 8) argues, 'democracy is a meta-institution for building good institutions'. On the historical record, both propositions seem valid with strong reservations. There is no incompatibility between authoritarian government and modern economic development. By modern standards, authoritarian governments have been the norm for the economically successful, at least at the time of their inception of modern economic development. Hobson (2004) has pointed out how late the franchise was extended, even to a majority of the people.

Our concern here is the structure rather than the policies of government and what those structures allow a government to do. Structure is the configuration of units within a political framework and the institutionalised channelling and repetition of behaviour which establishes that framework, and as a result guides economic activity. In one sense, a government is what it can do. Policies can only be implemented by a government which has a structure which is strong. According to de Vries (2002: 101): 'In the West, with industrialisation, the amount of money available for governments for supporting the economy, directly and indirectly, increased sharply, which in its turn had its positive effects on national income' – another significant positive feedback loop. The origins of such an advantage can be traced back in time. Britain had such a strong government in the early modern period, standing apart from other European states because of the nature of its government. Elsewhere in Europe, the breakthrough came in the nineteenth century. Britain early and Europe later had infrastructural rather than despotic power. One aspect of infrastructural power is the ability to raise tax revenue or to borrow – in this, Britain was precocious. This includes the efficiency with which tax is raised (the difference between gross imposition and revenue received by the government). In the words of one analyst (Brenner 2003: 661): '. . . it was in their goals (in practice, not easily combined) that both of building a strong state, mainly for the achievement of international military, commercio-colonial, and religious objectives, and of defending parliamentary liberties, that leading sections of the English parliamentary classes, most distinguished themselves from their counterparts throughout most of Europe'. The state was strong in that it monopolised the use of coercion, in that it was 'precociously unified' (Brenner 2003: 714), and had a tax-raising and borrowing capacity that vastly exceeded any other European power. Increasingly, over time it also had an unequalled administrative capacity. Britain, often lauded for lean government, had more public servants per head of population than even the most centralised of European states, Russia. At the same time, the use of the coercive power came to be limited by parliament, which protected the property rights of citizens by controlling taxation and forced loans, and generally preventing the creation of non-parliament-approved sources of income, such as monopolies or offices (tax or customs farms for example). It is the blend of strength and constraint which is the key to its role in promoting economic development.

Government is a multi-dimensional institution, with hardly a part of the economy unaffected by its activity. The bureaucratic structure of government administration has been built up over time, as the ability of the government of a modern developed state to frame and implement policies steadily expanded. In recent times, there is a tendency to an expansion in government activity and the ability to finance that activity, whatever the nature of the political system (Peacock and Wiseman 1961). Harris shows how in the wide-ranging areas of government regulation – public ownership and operation, if sometimes only in partnership with private ownership; fiscal policy, including the raising of taxes and loans and expenditures; and the action on property rights – government had a significant influence on the decision making which constituted the inception of modern economic development. One achievement of the British government was to separate coercion and capital sufficiently to allow, for example, a dramatic economic change to occur within the group of landowners who recognized their interest in using their property to generate additional income, leading to significant improvement in agriculture. To further their economic interests, the ruling group turned from military activities to more productive use of their resources. There are therefore different aspects of government relevant – the interaction between various interest groups and a state which tries to articulate their goals; the various activities of the different sections of the bureaucracy and the judiciary, overseeing a range of different services; and the role of local government as well as central government, or even provincial or state government in federal systems.

Many of the conventional wisdoms about government are over-simplifications of a complex reality. The first is that there is usually too much government. The major problem of many undeveloped societies is 'under-government' (de Vries 2002: 109). Often government used to be indirect, unsalaried individuals carrying out government functions, to a varying degree under government control, but both expensive and corrupt. The premise of two distinct arrangements, of market and government, as in some sense alternative methods of organisation, is itself a distortion of the true situation, since the two overlap and interact. The two are so intertwined that it is difficult to make a clear-cut distinction. At a date early in the industrialisation, the role of the government is so ubiquitous, even in Britain, traditionally regarded as a market-based economy, that it prompted one commentator to say, 'It now seems more appropriate to speak of the state within the economy rather than of the state and the economy' (Harris 2004: 235).[12] The market provides the finance to build up the state and the state provides the public goods critical for market operation; there is a strong symbiosis. The financial apparatus allows government to expand its purview and to do things not previously thought feasible. In Asian economies, the role of the government is more active than in Europe.

There is bad government. Many economic systems today are highly regulated, which often means that a considerable part of economic activity is illegal or semi-legal. The regulation is not of the kind which buttresses a flourishing market system. Where economic activity is illegal or occupies a grey area, where its existence is not officially recognized – whether it is the Soviet Union or Peru – but made possible by official corruption, it is difficult to use ownership as a basis for securing loans to expand a business (de Soto 1989). This imposes a severe constraint on economic expansion. Over-bureaucratic regulation leads to slow and expensive granting of relevant permissions and to an increase in the level of illegal activity (de Soto 2000). A significant cost is imposed on business. After all, corruption simulates the operation of a market system – if an unregulated market would make an activity profitable, a bribe is clearly worth making; it is just another cost. This is true of Peru (de Soto 1989), the Soviet Union (Boettke and Anderson 1997), or any other regulated society. Corrupt systems may have transactions costs lower than fully regulated systems. Each regulation requires a careful justification.

Both weak and strong governments can therefore harm the prospects for economic development. Weak governments cannot protect property and enforce contract nor provide the many other public goods required for efficient market operation. They cannot ensure that there is no extortion from those who are economically successful. Strong government can provide both, but does not necessarily choose to do so; it may be able but unwilling. Worse is '. . . the fundamental political dilemma of an economy: any government strong enough to protect property rights, enforce contracts, and provide macroeconomic stability is also strong enough to confiscate all of its citizens' wealth' (North, Summerhill, and Weingast 2000: 6–7). Many strong governments may be unmotivated to do what is necessary to promote economic development. Until the modern period, political systems have been largely authoritarian, but often weak in an important sense; they are capable of despotic but not of infrastructural power (White 1987).[13] The ability to satisfy the whims of the autocratic says nothing about their ability to implement relevant policies. Their writ only runs to a limited degree. They may not have the resources to implement relevant policies, or they be obstructed by key groups. Such governments would find it impossible to implement the range of policies undertaken by governments in modern developed societies. It is difficult for them to increase the revenue collected by government by encouraging the creation of new income. It may be impossible to achieve stability at the macroeconomic level, to educate the population, to ensure law and order in frontier areas, to improve the transport system or generally to invest in an appropriate way. They fall back on rent-seeking to win support from key groups, often the already powerful.

CULTURE AND CIVIL SOCIETY

Successful economic development is often associated with a strong civil society and a significant accumulation of social capital. Civil society is both source and product of social capability. For Putnam, social capital 'refers to connections among individuals – social networks and the norms of reciprocity and trustworthiness that arise from them', and for Fukuyama, it is 'an informal norm that promotes cooperation between individuals' (Putnam and Fukuyama, quoted in Allik and Realo 2004: 34). Some societies have the capacity to self-organise in the economic or the political arena. They are characterised by a mix of government and market with civil society acting as a bridge between the two. It is the bridge between autonomous individuals who are agents of civic engagement in the networks needed for modern economic development and therefore the promoter of the efficient operation of both government and market (Allik and Realo 2004).

Civil society reflects civic engagement through the multitude of initially small organisations that emerge in societies where there is space for them. It is neither government nor commercial organisation, although there may be some role for government in their establishment and continuing operation, and a necessity to generate the funds to finance the organisation's activity, achieved in a variety of ways, including self-help and government assistance. Many such organisations do not deal directly with economic or business problems. They are religious – notably non-conformist, political – mobilising support for particular reforms, positions or parties, recreational – sport has been a common focus, educational – assisting in the provision of education in the government or commercial sectors, or charitable – dealing with those who 'lose' in a market economy. Some grow to be large, or become parts of much broader associations. Many are directly relevant to the solving of economic problems. For example, in the early Australian context there were numerous agricultural societies, mechanics institutes, friendly societies, all active in areas highly relevant to economic development (White 1991). Also of great importance elsewhere, including in Britain and the USA, were popular scientific and technical institutions (1987).

A rich civil society makes possible the transition from a society based on *gemeinschaft*, small community, to one based on *gesellschaft*, the large impersonal organisations of a modern economy. 'The limits of communalism . . . lie in their prevention of networks of civic engagement that cut across social cleavages. Strong ties based on blood bonds sustain cooperation within small groups, whereas weak ties that link nonrelatives nourish wider cooperation and sustain greater social complexity' (Kuran 2004: 142–3). Civil society reflects the attitudes of trust, honesty and reciprocity necessary for the build-up of the networks which in modern society replace the face-to-face organic unity of traditional societies. It is part of participatory politics, in its broadest sense, and of the infrastructure of market operation. It is critical to the ability of individuals to take risks in an environment in which such activity does not result in disaster. Surprisingly, there is a clear relationship between individualism and social capital (ibid.: 42). In the words of Allik and Realo (2004: 44), '. . . individualism appears to be rather firmly associated with an increase of social capital, both within and across cultures'. Institutional structures which encourage cooperation are good for economic development. While a stress on the market usually emphasises competition, successful economic development requires cooperation at many different levels.

Some societies are rich in civil society, having an abundance of social capital, others are not. There is considerable path dependency in the divergence of different regions within one country and between different countries, according to their density of civil society. As Putnam (1993) has shown, history carried out a neat natural experiment in the differing histories of civil society in the North and South of Italy and the relationship between a dense civil society and the potential for democratic politics or successful economic development. The strength of civil society both reflected the ability to self-organize and reinforced that ability. Developed economies are characterised by the richness of the non-government, non-commercial sector. We are all familiar with the strong association of high income per head in such developed economies as the USA, UK, Australia or Northern Italy with dense civil society, but there are numerous smaller examples. In the words of Rodrik (2007: 167, quoting Miles), 'Mauritius is a "supercivil society", with a disproportionately large number of civil society associations per capita'. Mauritius is one of only two sub-Saharan economies which have been striking economic successes over the last quarter century.

Sometimes the civil society is seen as a result of the modern economic development, but this book sees the former as a determinant of the latter. This is yet another virtuous circle. The increase in income and wealth resulting from modern economic development increases civic engagement and social capital, and the increase in the latter promotes modern economic development. Such a process rests on a strong relationship between trust, notably that beyond the family, and per capita income (Easterly 2006: 80, based on the work of Knack and Keefer (1997), and Fukuyama 1995). High-income societies have a wider radius of trust, and less of an outsider/insider mentality, than low-income societies. There is a suggestion that the ability to cooperate reflects the selection process that Clark (2007) emphasises: the appropriate attitudes are hardwired into humans (Ridley 1997). Alternatively, it is a matter of the culture inherited in different societies.

In some societies, a highly centralised and authoritarian government discourages civil society, in others decentralisation of authority allowed a free flowering. The aim in the first case is to avoid the subversion of central authority. Autocracy often sees civil society as subversive of its power and legitimacy and deliberately undermines the relevant networks and associations. Where strong, civil society achieves a number of purposes. The relevant associations provided solutions to particular problems – in newly settled regions, ways of adapting to different environments, but also a training in the cooperation at the centre of modern economic and political institutions. They improved the transmission of information relevant to market activity. The bonds created by civil society helped bind societies together, avoiding winner-takes-all politics and rent-seeking behaviour. They help create the encompassing aspect of government activity, providing a mechanism through which the government can inform and influence. The trust and group loyalty of civil society keeps transactions costs down.

Networks are part of civil society, loose associations of people with common interests (Szostak 2006 and 2007 makes much of the role of networks). It is unclear whether they are substitutes or complements for institutions (Szostak 2006: 14), probably at different times both. Networks have a major role to play in the process of modern economic development, being critical to the development of trust. Increasingly in recent times, management theorists have been focusing on the cooperative rather than the competitive aspect of enterprise interaction, focusing on strategic alliances and in this context on commercial networks or clusters.[14] Networks exist at the individual level and are important in the transfer of relevant knowledge so necessary to technical innovation and to the raising of capital necessary for the investments which underpin economic development. Such networks may be critical to the process of economic development, their role in the Asian miracle rather different from that in Europe. There are certain conditions under which networks are weak (Szostak 2006: 14), conditions under which civil society is also weak. This is likely when social divisions of various kinds are sharp – whether ethnic, religious or regional; when there is significant poverty with no safety net; when the rule of law is weak; when the exercise of politics is not free, without real choices; when different groups in a society do not have shared goals; when war, famine or other shocks undermine a sense of stability; and when minorities are deliberately discriminated against.

THE STRUCTURE OF EMPIRES

For many, the European miracle is linked with political structure, not the internal political structure, but the interaction between states, empires or other political units at the international level. Darwin in his global history of empire sees empire as 'the default mode of political organization throughout most of history'. He further comments, 'imperial power has usually been the rule of the road' (Darwin 2008: 23). In the literature, there is an emphasis on the nature of the multi-cell system of competitive independent states in Europe. Europe is seen as exceptional in its internal configuration, although there are other areas in the world where small competitive political units existed, such as South East Asia, and often India. Mercantilist theory describes accurately the nature of this competitive world. Economic success brought political and military success, but never enough in the European context to destroy the competitive national system.[15] In such a world, the ability to coerce came to depend on the ability to accumulate capital, in which individual units were highly competitive. A precarious balance of power prevailed. The intermittent efforts at a landed empire were all miserable failures.

Economic success depended on a degree of openness to innovation. Across the boundaries of the European states, there was a relatively free movement of people, capital and commodities, and most of all, ideas (E.L. Jones 1987). In the competition between states, there were serious negative effects for the laggard countries. Fortunately, markets overlapped the national boundaries. If an idea was rejected in one polity, it was always possible for the innovator to move to another, where it might be taken up and result in a more competitive polity and economy. People, capital and commodities tended to move where opportunities were greatest or oppression least, and competition between the rival political units encouraged imitation of the successful idea. The system promoted innovation in both economic and political life, without squeezing out the advantages of having large and active markets.

By contrast, there is allegedly always the possibility of an authoritarian regime with wide sovereignty suppressing innovatory behaviour, including many of the manifestations of civil society, which are regarded as subversive of central control itself. The key factor is lack of competition. This problem is compounded when the regime is an empire, such as the Mughal Empire in India or the various Chinese dynasties (Levathes 1994). Measures damaging to economic development are valid over all the empire, although there may be an offsetting advantage in economies of scale. The inherent logic of such empires is first expansionary and then contractionary, with constraints on expansion imposed by the increasing cost of extracting tribute at the frontier and contraction resulting in increasing taxation of the population. Such empires, often on the scale of Europe as a whole, can, if they wish, suppress competition and the movement of ideas, people and capital with relative impunity. Any temporary encouragement of economic development is easily reversed (the case of the voyages of Chen He in the fifteenth century is often quoted).

de Vries (2002: 68) has explored the argument. As political entities, the Western European states were 'structured and governed differently from empires'. In a mercantilist world, power and wealth, coercion and capital went together. But power had a priority over plenty, the aim being to increase the wealth of the state, not the nation. Moreover, coercion could get the upper hand, especially in attempts to ruin competition: government projects do fail (de Vries 2002: 74). In commenting on the zero-sum nature of mercantilism, de Vries asks, 'How can the economy of Western Europe *as a whole* have profited from a policy by Western European governments that was explicitly intent on "beggaring thy neighbour", and that was driven by economic jealousy. What were the beneficial effects of constant strife?' (de Vries 2002: 76). A negative aspect of the multi-cell system is that the competition in Europe usually resulted in war, notably in the pre-modern period before 1815, and again between 1914–1945 when Europe nearly committed suicide. 'Warfare . . . was the first business of European Old Regimes, consuming up to 80–90% of the tax revenues of most states' (Malia 1999: 32). In Britain it might have been an astonishing 83 per cent so that military expenditures far outstripped private capital formation (Findlay and O'Rourke 2007: 351). In such a situation, the costs of competition might exceed its benefits. For some European states and in some periods, the negative clearly exceeded the positive. The main justification offered is that most of the British expenditure was on the navy which was critical to the expansion of foreign trade, but a positive contribution can only result from an important role of foreign trade in the Industrial Revolution (this is a core argument of Findlay and O'Rourke 2007).

Conquest is a zero-sum game (very well described by Snooks 1996), in which the benefits of one side are matched by the losses of the other, just as domestic rent-seeking simply redistributes income. The return from conquest includes booty, slaves, continuing taxation or tribute taking, access to and control over natural capital, that is, over resources of various kinds. As an empire expands, the costs of continuing conquest mount and the opportunities for a significant return decline until the momentum of expansion is lost (Elvin 1973). Communications and transport become more demanding and absorb more resources. There is a limit to expansion. Kennedy (1987) has described this as an expression of imperial overreach. Once the point at which the costs exceed the returns is reached, there is likely to be an implosion, sometimes sudden and sometimes much more drawn out (as with the Roman Empire, whose demise lasted centuries). On the whole, Europe avoided this path within Europe, but diverted its energy outside.

The nation states of Europe created their own empires, largely overseas. In recent centuries, all developed countries have been involved in this process, unless they were too small to exert any such control. European powers such as Britain, France, Spain, Portugal, Holland, even Germany, created maritime empires outside Europe from the fifteenth century onwards, although Britain's first colony was Ireland. Russia was the last of the European powers to retain an empire, in this case a landed empire, different in its nature from the maritime empires and longer lasting. Non-European powers such as the USA or Japan became imperial powers, perhaps by default in the first case. Japan held Taiwan as a colony from 1895 to 1945, Korea from 1906 to 1945, and various parts of mainland China from 1931, so colonisation is not a European monopoly. Most of the countries of the world were at some time colonies; moreover, many regions within countries were once colonies. Colonisation is always a competitive process, colonies often changing hands with the ups and downs of military conflict.

The process of colonisation, which reached its peak in the late nineteenth century, influenced the pattern of modern economic development and its spread, but not in obvious ways. While military success reflected economic success, it is more controversial whether military success and colonial expansion promoted economic success for the coloniser, although it might for key business groups. Goldstone (2008: 69) notes, 'It was not colonialism and conquest that made possible the rise of the West, but the reverse – it was the rise of the West (in terms of technology) and the decline of the rest that made possible the full extension of European power across the globe'. After initial conquest, the degree of central control differed markedly from colonial power to colonial power, and even between colonies of one colonial power. The general argument is against a major influence from empire to the inception of modern economic growth, although some elements of empire may have helped and some hindered. Goldstone (2008: 67–8) summarises the argument against the influence of empire and the institution of slavery associated with it, 'If slavery and empire were a means to industrialisation and modern economic growth, then the Romans of Italy, the Mongols of China, the Ottomans of Turkey, or the Spanish colonists of Latin America should have led the way to the modern world. They did not. It was small and slave-free regions and countries, Britain, New England, Switzerland, Belgium – that did so'. Overall, the influence of colonialism on the colonisers was insignificant, whether the focus is the source of relevant raw materials or the target markets for production. Paradoxically, the fact that the West did not need the Third World to support modern economic development is good news for developing countries today (Bairoch 1993: 97).

On the other hand, the economic impact on the colonised reflected the nature of the relationship between coloniser and colonised and the nature of economic activity by key groups from the coloniser – it is once more highly specific. There are three possibilities. In the first case, the colony is completely assimilated into the colonising country, its previous nature leaving few traces. This happens most frequently where the relevant landed areas are contiguous and there is significant migration. The degree of assimilation depends on the relative size of the migrant and native populations and on the degree to which a local economy is integrated into the overall economy. Secondly, the colony remains a separate unit, eventually receiving its independence. The influence of the colonising power can be profound, even where there are few settlers from the coloniser. It might include the acceptance of the language of the colonisers as a lingua franca, the adoption of the political and legal systems of the colonial power after independence, and the legacy of a particular economic system, for example a market system. In other words, the institutional structure, even the attitudinal set, of the coloniser is inherited. It is interesting to contrast the ex-colonies of Spain with those of Britain in the Americas.[16] Thirdly, the colony is briefly under colonial control, a historically short period, and the influence of the coloniser is slight. The short-term influence may be negative because of a severe disruption to old ways, with little, if any, positive influence. Africa closely fits this model.

Most migrant movement occurs within empires which are contiguous and subject to direct central control – the Chinese first to the south and then into Manchuria, the Russian into the southern steppe and then Siberia. The usual focus is on maritime migration and in particular on European movements into new areas and other movements associated with European colonial control, of Africans into the Americas through the slave trade or of Indians into various parts of the world, as workers in the sugar plantations or as traders. In the latter case, absorption never occurs and a native population remains dominant in numbers and ultimately regains political control. Decolonisation has not freed the former colonies from a continuing influence of the former colonial powers, so that international economic relations continue to reflect the influence of the colonial past, sometimes in a powerful way. Patterns of language use, of religious attachment, and of common institutional structures reflect the colonial imprint and the previous histories of conquest, for example the spread of Islam by the sword. For example, India uses the English language and British political institutions.

Empires, like countries, often represented expanded, but controlled, areas of openness – there was a Pax Romana or a Pax Mongolica as much as a Pax Britannica or Americana. Of course, colonies also represented a form of closure, in so far as they excluded outsiders from certain kinds of interaction, such as trade or investment. In some cases this more than offset the potential openness. There are cultural clusters in the world which reflect previous conquest and colonisation. Familiarity and previous connections are important. Trading and investment relations reflect past histories, often occurring largely within these cultural clusters.

It is controversial how many cultural clusters there are: a number of about seven, eight or nine is commonly referred to in the relevant texts (Huntington 1996). For example, Latin America shows the continuing influence of its Spanish past. Colonisation has created modern states as well as cultural clusters. The boundaries of these states, however irrational in terms of previous groupings of peoples, have had a surprising degree of resilience, notably in Asia and to a lesser degree Africa. In Africa, the legacy of state boundary drawing without regard for tribal divisions has led to considerable friction and frequent civil war. Elsewhere, there has been both a fragmentation of former imperial units – in Latin America, although not Brazil – or a consolidation of independently created colonies – North America and Australasia – yet the imprint of former colonial control is clear.

During modern times, decolonisation came in two waves. The first wave was in the late eighteenth and early nineteenth centuries and comprised the Americas, both North and Latin America, as a result of the French invasion of Spain during the Napoleonic Wars in the early nineteenth century. In the case of Latin America, there was considerable political instability as the new states emerged during the nineteenth century. The results in economic development were mixed. One set of ex-colonies did well economically and another less well. The second wave of decolonisation came in the second half of the twentieth century, following World War II. The process was relatively peaceful and in some cases quickly effected – Britain – but more protracted and painful in others – French North Africa and Indo-China and Portuguese Africa. The whole process lasted little more than 30 years.

Controversy has arisen concerning the influence of colonisation on the prospects for economic development of the colonised. There is in some circumstances net damage done by colonialism and in others a net benefit derived. The balance of advantage and disadvantage differs markedly from country to country; it is highly specific. The overall results in economic development have been mixed. There is an increasing tendency to stress institutional legacies, notably the structure of government and its relationship to markets. Clearly the USA inherited many of the favourable institutional arrangements of the UK. It is consistent to argue against the morality of colonial political control, but to point to beneficial economic effects which outweigh obvious losses. A classic case is the Japanese influence on Taiwan and South Korea and their later successful inception of modern economic development. Some countries have managed to develop economically despite a colonial background, while others have not. In the first wave, North America has fared much better than Latin America. After the second wave, there was an initial acceleration in the rates of economic growth, but the period of 20 to 30 years following the oil shocks of the 1970s was a bad period for ex-colonies, with the exception of the East Asian nations, which began a period of rapid growth in the early 1960s which has continued with a relatively minor interruption during the Asian economic crisis of 1997, in retrospect a minor setback for most. Countries which avoided colonial control have not done consistently better than those subjected to such control; one or two have, the outstanding example being Japan. A contrast is often made between the semi-colonial status of China and its delayed economic development, and the startling success of Japan. Other countries, such as Ethiopia or Thailand, which retained their independence have not been so successful, at least until recently. It is reasonable to assume that the economically successful make economically beneficial colonisers, at least from the perspective of the inception of modern economic development. However, American colonisation does not seem to have helped the Philippines. For Britain, the outcomes are mixed. The former British colonies in North America and Australasia have done well, but most African colonies have a poor record. In Asia, the record is also mixed, with Hong Kong and Singapore doing well, but India and the other parts of the old Indian Raj waking up slowly, in an economic sense.

There is a proximate influence, the immediate impact of colonialism on the flow of funds in or out of the economy, and an ultimate influence, notably on the institutional structure of a society. Resources can be extracted through the tax system, through charges imposed for administrative services or for the defence of the relevant country. It might be through the terms of trade, through a flow of interest or dividend payments resulting from deliberately advantageous investments. For a colony, or an economy indirectly under the control of a stronger power, a transfer of real resources should show itself in a trading account surplus of the colony. The obverse is that the dominant power runs a deficit on its trading account. There are attempts to estimate the size of these flows, but the data to provide the answers are difficult to find, and interpret. Generally the answer is that they are not very large, but the answer differs from coloniser to coloniser, and from colony to colony. Contrary to frequent assertion by some commentators, there is no long-term deterioration in the terms of trade of developing economies (Bairoch 1993: chapter 10).

There is interesting work done on the relationship between the Netherlands and its main colony, Indonesia. The nature of the relationship changed from a focus of trade in the nineteenth century to one on finance in the twentieth. There are benefits for the colony as well as for the colonising economy, for example access to the Dutch capital market, which supplemented Indonesian savings. At its peak, total direct income from

Indonesia contributed a considerable 9–11 per cent to the small Dutch economy (van der Eng 1998: 32). This is not trivial, but independence, which broke the colonial link, occurred just before a surge in economic development in the Netherlands, so clearly the income was not critical to the performance of the metropolitan economy. A comparison with the interaction between Britain and India shows a contribution of income to Britain of less than one-tenth that from Indonesia to the Netherlands (Maddison 1989: 646), so the link is not large enough to have a discernible effect on modern economic development.[17] Nevertheless the impact on the colonised was usually negative in other ways, notably in deindustrialisation for key countries such as India, which had formerly had a highly competitive textile industry, an emphasis on export crops in agriculture and the stimulus given to population expansion (Bairoch 1993: chapter 8).[18]

In some cases, colonialism was associated with a radical restructuring of society, even with the construction of a modern state with its institutional trappings where none existed before, or the import of a legal system. The specific influence depended on who colonised, and where and when. There are no general tendencies, either favourable or unfavourable, rather highly-specific relationships. It is possible for there to be a negative short-term flow of resources from colony to coloniser, but a positive long-term influence, if the institutional changes are favourable to modern economic development.

PART III

The driving forces

> . . . a growth system is like a living organism with impulses of its own.
> (Rosenberg and Birdzell 1986: 331)

At the beginning of the book, three separate concepts of growth were identified – a long-term steady-state equilibrium rate, a transitional rate and a
short-term rate. This section focuses on the transitional, or medium-term,
growth rate, which provides the bridge between long and short terms. In a
notional transitional growth path, the influence of short-term fluctuations
is removed and we can get some sense of whether an economy is converging on its long-term rate. It indicates whether a short-term spurt will
eventually be translated into economic growth at the underlying long-term
growth rate. In the inception of modern economic development, the crux
is a sustained acceleration in the rate of economic growth accompanied by
a change in the structure of the relevant economy. Such an acceleration is
the result of many individual acts of innovation by entrepreneurs, usually
acting in a market context, backed up by governments which not only
abstain from acts harmful to the process of economic development but
initiate deliberately promotive policies, providing helpful infrastructure
and policies.

There are a number of elements relevant to the medium-term transition
rate, more variable than the long-term factors, but less malleable than the
short-term factors comprised within the proximate causes. Particularly
relevant are two factors – the ability of a society to innovate, which reflects
the collective entrepreneurial dynamism of individual decision makers,
and the commitment of key decision makers in government to the promotion of economic development, through a wide variety of relevant policies
and the creation of a context favourable to economic development, one
giving maximum scope for entrepreneurial activity. An appropriate mix

generates modern economic development. For follower societies, innovation is really imitation, the extraction from an existing pool of knowledge of relevant technologies and organisational methods. Such economies operate well within the frontier of best practice and as a consequence can grow at a rapid rate during the transition. The initiation and maintenance of such a rate requires a commitment by government to give priority to policies which favour modern economic development.

The way in which a society divides into different groups, and the ability of these groups, notably the entrepreneurial group, to realise their aims, is critical to the process of modern economic development. The nature of both domestic and the international political economy, and their influence on government, determines the scope for entrepreneurs to innovate. The government, as a result of the interaction of various groups within the political context set by government, lays out the domestic rules of the game, including formal laws and informal conventions. At the international level, there is an interaction between countries which establishes the international rules of the game. These are elements which emerge slowly, having an influence over a significant period of time.

There are therefore two chapters in this section. The first deals with the act of innovation and the way in which knowledge relevant to economic development grows and is exploited. The second chapter considers the degree to which governments are committed to stimulating economic development and the policies they pursue in trying to realise this commitment. It is easy for government action to remove the incentive to innovate or to fail to introduce policies which provide a positive stimulus.

9.   Innovation as a prime mover

The invention . . . of technologies that facilitate or encourage non-zero-sum interaction – is a reliable feature of cultural evolution everywhere. New technologies create new chances for positive sums, and people manoeuvre to seize those sums, and social structure changes as a result. (Wright 2000: 22)

This chapter develops a number of important arguments: first, innovation is at the core of modern economic development and technical change at the core of innovation, although for followers imitation is critical; secondly, innovation is linked in a complex manner with the growth of knowledge; thirdly, the rate of innovation is more important than its factor-saving bias; fourthly, that innovation is usually embodied in investment; fifthly, while innovation and the associated investment are jointly determined by the demand and the cost sides of economic activity, the rate of innovation is a function of the size and growth of the market – demand is the active element, cost constraints a passive element; sixthly, that the same opportunity can be viewed differently depending on the risk tolerance of the key decision makers – some societies are more sanguine about positive outcomes arising from innovation than others; and finally, that imitation is subject to a series of powerful constraints so that best-practice technology is not freely available to all.

There are four sections in this chapter. The first section discusses the issues raised by the role of technical knowledge in economic development, particularly the role of innovation and the difference between innovation and imitation. It explores the difference between a macro-invention and a micro-invention, also analysing the meaning of a general-purpose technology. The second section analyses the role of technical change in economic development, how the contribution of technical change can be measured, by social saving as a measure of the contribution of a particular innovation and by an increase in total factor productivity as a measure of the contribution of technical change in general. The third section focuses on imitation, considering the degree to which the pool of existing knowledge of technologies is accessible by all. The final section presents the American system of manufacturing, a logical development of the innovation at the core of the Industrial Revolution. As a result America defines the long-term steady-state growth path.

THE NATURE OF TECHNICAL CHANGE: INVENTION, INNOVATION AND IMITATION

Some commentators (Lipsey, Carlaw and Bekar 2005: 68) argue that human beings are by nature innovative. Christian (2005) sees innovation, notably the introduction of technologies using more intensively existing resources, as a characteristic of all human society: '. . . humans seem to have a highly developed capacity for "innovation"' (Christian 2005: 145). This is a reasonable supposition based on the human record. As the McNeills (2003: 11) comment: 'Humanity's modern style of persistent technological changeability seems to have emerged only about 40 000 years ago'. The assertion of universal innovativeness has its difficulties, the biggest of which is that most societies do not reveal such an obvious technical innovativeness, societies differing significantly in their innovative dynamism. Clearly something constrains the natural innovativeness. Since the next step is to argue 'that technology was invented by people in order to make money' (Allen 2006: 20), the obvious obstacle to innovativeness is that relevant conditions prevent money being made. It is also clear the knowledge accumulates independently of economic stimuli and that innovation requires a significant investment, which is risky in that costs are incurred now in the hope of future benefits. The key stage is when all constraints dissolve and the willingness to innovate in developed economies becomes widespread throughout economy and society. In the words of Goldstone, what is to be explained is '. . . the emergence of a generalized and functionally widespread willingness or propensity to innovate, resulting in myriad minor innovations whose interactive result was a dramatic shift of the production frontier, a propensity that was nonetheless sharply localized in space and time' (Goldstone 1987: 120).

It is the locale of a culture of innovation, and the timing of its appearance, which present the biggest challenges to explanation. A characteristic of a developed economy is that it generates a stream of innovations that are quickly and widely diffused. In this process, there is new knowledge – what is often called invention or the discovery of new principles, and the innovation which sometimes follows – the application of those new principles; and secondly, there is the accessibility of such knowledge by followers – the degree to which there exists a pool of pre-existing knowledge upon which imitators can draw, sometimes across international frontiers. It is necessary to consider why some societies can innovate and imitate successfully, and why some can do neither of these things.[1] Even if we assume universal innovativeness, there is the issue of its focus. Snooks (1996) has argued that the dominant strategy in a particular society at a particular time determines in which areas it concentrates its innovative activities

– innovation might be relevant to a strategy of conquest – focused in the area of the military or in logistics supporting the military, or to a strategy of commerce – and focused in shipping, insurance and the organisation of large companies. However this is simply a matter of emphasis since developed economies are characterised by the eventual universality of innovativeness and their ability to access knowledge developed elsewhere.

The inception of modern economic development in the West is seen as 'a qualitative jump in the rate of innovation' (Goldstone 1987: 119). As Christian argues, the key to explaining the inception of modern economic development is to explain a sharp acceleration in innovation. Technical change is at the centre of many theories of economic development and of narratives told for countries which have successfully developed, including attempts at a grand narrative. A powerful case has been put for its centrality by a large number of commentators (Rosenberg 1972, Mokyr 2002, Christian 2005, Goldstone 2008). A common interpretation of the Industrial Revolution by economic historians (Landes 1969, Mokyr 1990, Lipsey, Carlaw and Bekar 2005) puts the emphasis on a series of significant technical changes comprising mainly a switch from organic sources of energy to inorganic, notably coal, and a quantum leap in the replacement of the human hand and muscle by machines. The main feature of innovation, according to Christian, is the tapping of larger and larger energy flows, graphically captured by a photograph of the earth at night, showing the strikingly different amount of light generated by different regions. An increase in factor productivity, assumed to be a result of technical change, is seen as explaining most of the increase in per capita output in the successful economies.

It is generally agreed that a significant divergence occurred in the nineteenth century, when industrialisation involved a dramatic acceleration in the rate of technical innovation within the European world and stagnation in the East. However, there is some agreement that there was already a significant divergence in 'dynamism between technological culture and practices in the West and the East in the seventeenth and eighteenth centuries' (de Vries 2001: 416). Although some authorities see Europe's technical lead as appearing very early, as early as the eleventh century, the much more likely timing places its beginning in the sixteenth century (ibid.: 416). At this stage, it was more momentum than level which differentiated Europe, and in particular Britain, from the rest of the world, notably China, often seen as the initiator of many new technologies. Underpinning this, Britain's exploited energy fund in the early modern period must have been substantially higher than for example, China's (ibid.: 414). After all, Britain had be creative enough to learn to use its coal resources well, a process which began in the sixteenth century (Neff 1943, Wrigley 1990).

The later innovations fitted into a long process of continuing and self-sustaining invention and innovation in Western Europe, with the evolution of a wide-ranging Western lead in technology during the eighteenth century (ibid.: 437). Elsewhere the technology and technological drive were 'simply lacking' (ibid.: 439).

The key to technical innovation is the nature of the pool of knowledge in any society. Mokyr (2002) focuses on the relationship between propositional (*episteme*) and prescriptive knowledge (*techne*), a rather complex but linked relationship. The changing interaction between science and technology has been a focus of interest for a long time. The mutual reinforcement of each, and therefore the origins of a technological momentum, depended on the sources of justification for knowledge, particularly with respect to the techniques actually used. They can be classified under five headings (Goldstone 2008: 150–1). Traditional knowledge, revered for its long use, is stored informally in conventional behaviour and existing methods of production and more formally in the myths and expertise passed on from parents to children. Secondly, religions, the holy books or sayings of spiritual leaders, embody and underpin a stock of knowledge, often comprising an overall world view, but one usually consistent with traditional knowledge. Both these justifications tend to be conservative, but not always. The third source is reason – the application of logic and the deductive reasoning of the human mind in solving any puzzles which arise in particular societies. Such knowledge may be an attempt to explain the creations of God, but it can on occasion be hopelessly out of touch with the real world. Sometimes this is supplemented by an empirical approach in which knowledge is derived from repeated observation and experience, a useful check on purely deductive knowledge. The final and critical source is deliberate experiment. In this, instruments are important to careful measurement, and public demonstrations and rapid communication of such knowledge through publications and lectures also occur.

The vital step in the inception of modern economic development was developing a culture in which the final source of knowledge became dominant. This is the role of what Mokyr has called the industrial enlightenment, a phase intermediate between the scientific and the industrial revolutions. This step was taken relatively early in Britain (Goldstone 2008: 155), but it was a Western phenomenon (Mokyr 2002: 76). During this phase there was a real emergence of scientific method, scientific mentality and scientific culture (Mokyr 2002: 37ff). There was a focus on building knowledge in the Baconian way by programs of experiment, often using instruments, such as telescopes, microscopes, prisms, vacuum pumps or scientific apparatus. There were two key conditions for the achievement of this step; first, the existence of tolerance and pluralism, as against the imposition of conformity and a state-imposed orthodoxy – the lot of most civilisations and societies and often the response to a political crisis – and secondly support for the entrepreneurs who will apply the knowledge (Goldstone 2008: 160–161). In innovative societies there is plenty of space for an easy interaction between entrepreneurs, scientists, engineers and craftsmen. In Britain experimental research became widely dispersed through society and scientific engineering a normal part of good business, which resulted in the growth of knowledge moving beyond the theoretical level (largely the sticking point in continental Europe) and becoming self-sustaining, occurring in waves rather than in isolated technical breakthroughs (in Asia, isolation was the norm).

The process of collective learning, reflecting the use of symbolic language, implies a much faster rate of change than genetic adaptation alone would permit. Learning is the result of a powerful positive feedback loop, as population growth stimulates the increased information exchange which arises from the operation of more complex information networks (Christian 2005: 253). There are both scale and diversity effects which induce intellectual synergies, as the exchange of ideas, alongside that of commodities and people, widens. The context is global, although the level of global interaction may be low. The feedback resulting from the increased interaction dominates the long-term history of human societies, but does not prevent reversals for relatively short periods of time. Innovation creates more resources which makes possible, and therefore highly likely, further population growth. Within world systems the scale of the intellectual interchange becomes striking. This is the long-term context of the acceleration of knowledge growth which accompanies modern economic development. In the words of Christian, 'We have seen that accelerating innovation is in some sense implicit in the notion of collective learning, so the Modern Revolution really represents a gear shift in the pace of collective learning in the last two centuries' (Christian 2005: 352). However it happens in a certain locality – Europe, notably its Western extremities, and at a certain time – reaching its fruition in the nineteenth century.

Seen from this perspective every technique, and the technology underlying it, has a long history of development. A particular technique emerges as an idea and finishes as a final product or the process for yielding such a good or service, usually at a much later date, sometimes at distant venues. From idea to final form, there is a long process of learning – this is even before the innovation itself. The process continues. 'There is typically a long lag between the occurrence of changes in technology, even those of fundamental importance, and the time they start affecting aggregate statistics such as industrial production and national income per capita' (Mokyr 1999: 9). A number of commentators have indicated the global nature of such technical histories. Merchants carried with them along important trade routes a portfolio of resources, including technical knowledge as well as new products or innovative institutional arrangements. Technical knowledge does not consist solely of blueprints, discovered early and faithfully realised, showing the explicit relationship between inputs and outputs. A body of tacit knowledge appears, which as it unfolds raises the level of productivity. This tacit knowledge underpins the knowledge which can be represented in a blueprint and which is codifiable. It is really part of human capital. There are often complementarities between techniques or even technologies, so that an advance in one area assists an advance in another. Such complementarities take on surprising forms.

Technical change should be seen in a dynamic context. There is great uncertainty about the direction of future trajectories, but more is probably known about direction than the rate of technical change (Guha 1981: 40–1). As Mokyr (1990: 301) has commented, 'The essence of technological progress is its unpredictability', a remark supported by Wright (1997: 1561), '. . . there is something intrinsically unpredictable about new technologies'. It is easy to underestimate the legion of changes which improve the quality of a product or service by vast multiples over long periods of time (Nordhaus 1998). Technology is both uncertain in its development and complex in its interconnections. There is at each stage in its development significant uncertainty about the way in which a technology will develop and whether it will be successful. The further into the future you look, the greater is the uncertainty. Historical accidents may give such trajectories an apparently random nature, which is the source of a significant path dependence. There is sometimes a lock-in to inefficient technologies. For each technique there is a trajectory of particular product paths with their implied revenues and costs, but with a limited definition ex ante.

There is an interplay between the 'autonomous' drift of technology (within the boundaries defined by the prevailing paradigm and, more indirectly, the evolution of the science explaining this) and a particular set of inducement factors of an economic type, such as factor prices (Dosi 1982, Nuvolari 2001). The critical debate concerns whether the autonomy of knowledge or the tyranny of economics predominates in influence.

In the timeless world of neoclassical economics, there is a range of choice for techniques of production, which comprise varying combinations of the factors of production, and it is assumed that replacement of one technique by another is costless, and the key variables such as revenue and cost known.[2] Choice is dictated by the relative prices of the relevant factors of production. In the view of some (Snooks 1993), the causation of technical change is always the same – changes in the factor endowment of a society and in the associated relative price level. Sometimes this results from population pressure, particularly on resources. It is certainly the case that for the developed countries technical progress has been resource-saving, in the sense of saving land, but both capital- and energy-using. An increasing pressure on resources encouraged a resource-saving technology. Equally, a rise in the cost of labour encourages the substitution of capital for labour. More accurately, it is the expectation of a continuing rise in the cost of a factor relative to other factors that encourages a bias in technical change which saves on that factor (Habakkuk 1962). It is not simply a matter of choice of technique, it is more a matter of the direction of technical exploration, the nature of new technologies and the direction in which they are developed. The bias may not be in invention, but in innovation, the choice of which inventions should be developed and imitated. So economic inducement factors are likely to play a determining role in the direction of a technological trajectory, particularly in the early development of a new paradigm, such as the application of steam power (Nuvolari 2001: 5).

The focus should be, not choice at a given moment of time, but movement of the production function over time, with an implied change in the likely combination of the factors of production. Such a view focuses the spotlight on the nature of the technical trajectory (Lipsey, Carlaw and Bekar 2005: appendix to chapter 2), that is, the path by which a technology evolves over time. There is a major difference of view on the nature of the trajectory (Easterlin 2004: chapter 4). 'What is at issue here is the extent to which the trajectory of productivity growth can be altered by economic signals and the extent to which it is determined by the internal logic of science and specific technologies. . .' (Lipsey, Carlaw and Bekar 2005: 54). A conventional interpretation of technical change during the Industrial Revolution saw it as the repeated creation of bottlenecks and their release by technical innovation. Mokyr, on the other hand, believes macro-inventions, the big or extraordinary breakthroughs (Dosi 1982), have origins that are largely exogenous and often have a sudden and unexpected impact. Inventions can be exogenous in their source, but innovations occur guided by profitability. Whereas in their origins macro-inventions can be exogenous, their later development is invariably economically driven and endogenous (2005: 94–96). In this sense the neoclassical assumption that the long-term equilibrium rate of growth is exogenously given has some justification. The trajectories by which technologies develop reflect the changing relative factor endowment of an economy, but they may be limited both by history, the actual exploration of only a narrow band of variants close to the ones chosen, and by the direction of scientific enquiry.

The bias in the development of technology may not be a deliberate one:

it may be the result of what Lipsey et al. call the evolutionary hand (Lipsey, Carlaw and Bekar 2005: appendix to chapter 3). If different enterprises make different choices in terms of factor combinations, the movement of relative factor prices will favour some and not others. Some of those who have made the wrong decision will go out of existence. This produces the same result as a deliberate bias in innovation. In this way there is a positive feedback loop acting through markets on the nature of technical change. It is highly likely that some economies took a path which precluded the capital-intensive, energy-intensive path of the successful developers.

If inventions are exogenous, where do they come from? During the British Industrial Revolution, they represent the product of an emerging scientific milieu, highly favourable to technical change, of which both economic innovators and scientists were increasingly part. The relevant scientific community was both domestic and international, representing part of an expanding informational network. The relationship between science and technology was a changing one and the centre of much debate. One authority has it that, 'Western economic innovation owes much to interaction between the economic and scientific spheres' (Rosenberg and Birdzell 1986: 333). Both spheres became increasingly autonomous, operating independently of the political or religious spheres, but there was a positive symbiosis between them. There was 'a wide diversity of research institutions, comparatively free of political interference and controls, and yet – or rather, therefore – providing a growing, cohesive body of knowledge about our universe' (ibid.: 333). The development of scientific thinking provided a series of significant advances, which solved problems which sometimes had been a focus of interest for a considerable period of time.

A variety of institutions transmuted the growth in scientific knowledge into growth in material welfare. A multitude of technological experiments sorted out the economically useful from the economically inapplicable scientific discoveries. In the words of Rosenberg and Birdzell, 'This growth of scientific knowledge has shaped, nurtured, and fuelled Western economic growth. It offers a key to understanding the growth process'. The key notions are autonomy, experiment and diversity. The acceleration in the rate of innovation in Britain, and other societies which succeeded economically, reflected the growth of attitudes and institutions favourable to a rational and scientific approach to problem solving in the economic area. There was a significant change of attitude, broadly termed the scientific revolution, at the heart of which was the application of empirical testing in an effort to understand the workings of the natural world. Inventions could occur anywhere, but systematic innovations are much influenced by the emergence of scientific communities favourable to technical advance, themselves part of the civil society so critical to success in all areas of activity.

The terms describing the introduction of new technology – invention, innovation, and imitation – invite attention.[3] They express important distinctions but are sometimes ambiguously used. In some time periods, notably the period of the Industrial Revolution, innovation and inventions are fused, occurring simultaneously, implemented by practical people deeply involved in production. However invention can occur independently of innovation. In the words of Anderson (1991: 43–44), 'Invention may be defined as conceiving an idea for some change and demonstrating its feasibility. Innovation is the incorporation of an invention into the production process.' Later pure and applied research became separated. Technology is usually embodied in specific investment, in plant and equipment, human capital and particular organisational forms. This makes such technologies hard to access. Innovation is often used in a broader sense than technical change, including organisational change or change of a business model. The interaction between technical change and organisational change is of particular interest, innovations being often associated with radical organisational change. Imitation is a process by which enterprises introduce methods new to them but not to the outside economy, copying the true pioneers, the inventors/innovators – the Darbys, Watts and Arkwrights. This does not preclude marginal or incremental improvements in the course of innovation – these go on all the time in dynamic societies. In the neoclassical model it is argued that a technology is diffused without friction or cost. The process of imitation is not simply a replication of innovations made elsewhere, the usual assumption, one which underpins convergence within the neoclassical theory of growth. In practice, diffusion requires adaptation and adaptation requires relevant investment.

Another distinction is significant, that between major breakthroughs and minor ones. For Mokyr (1990: 293) genuinely creative societies are rare, and even their bursts of creativity usually short-lived. There are long periods of stasis. The analogy is 'punctuated equilibrium' in evolutionary biology, with its macro-mutations and its micro-mutations (ibid.: 289–291). Mokyr distinguishes two streams of technical advance, the first a sudden macro-invention, followed by a series of micro-inventions that modify and improve it to make it functional without altering its basic conception, and the other a sequence of micro-inventions that eventually lead to a technique sufficiently different from the original one to make it a novel technique rather than an improved version of the original one (ibid.: 294). He argues that without the former there would have been diminishing returns to the latter (ibid.: 297). Macro-inventions come from outside the economic system, embodying radically new ideas and merging 'more or less from nihilo' (Mokyr 1990: 13). They often come in clusters, partly because at certain times inventive activity gains a critical mass and a greater receptivity in a favourable institutional and social environment (ibid. 298). There are various attempts to classify technical change, selecting those transformations of particular importance to the process of economic development, and to the acceleration in the rate of innovation. Two concepts – general purpose technologies and macro-inventions, describe the big leap forwards. Both put the emphasis on the unevenness of technical change and the particular importance of changes in technology rather than simply in techniques. Macro-inventions are major paradigm changes leading to major innovations and a powerful wave of imitation. Whereas micro-inventions have an easily understood economic determination, macro-inventions come from outside the economic system. The term is narrower than that of a GPT since it does not include organisational changes.

A macro-invention helps to define the nature of economic development during a particular period of time, a period which may be as long as a half century or more. It is possible to talk of waves of 'creative destruction', associated with the periods of upturn during long cycles or logistics, as they are sometimes called (Cameron 1997). Such upturns are differentiated by various events closely associated with the big technological changes which are taking place. On the Schumpeterian argument, growth is built into cycles, notably the upturns. The criteria for inclusion are complex, including a significant contribution to GDP. Such changes may contribute to growth in a unique way. In the old terminology there are linkages with various sections of the economy – backward, forward and even lateral. Macro-inventions can have a major impact in raising the productivity of the economy as a whole, since they often involve such basic inputs as transport, communication or energy, required by all sectors of the economy. It takes time to implement the micro-inventions which make the new technology relevant to the various sectors. Macro-inventions often involve high levels of investment, with a tendency to booms and bubbles, particularly where there are large networks involved, such as rail and road systems, transmission and communication networks. Growth in such systems tends to become exponential since there are externalities arising from the extension of the network; the larger the network, the greater the benefit derived by an individual consumer.

The term general-purpose technologies implies the same distinction and the same acceleration in the rate of introductions. A GPT is a single generic technology, recognizable as such over its lifetime. A technology can refer to a product, a process or an organisational principle, such as the factory system, mass or lean production. There are four main features of a GPT – improvement over a long period of time, wide use of that technology across the economy, its multiple uses for different purposes and the many spillover effects, notably those encouraging the development of other technologies. Lipsey et al. (2005) recognise as many as 24 GPTs extending back to the Neolithic Revolution, seeing technical change as a phenomenon affecting all human history, although the rate at which they appear and the likelihood of more than one appearing simultaneously increase over time.

An emphasis on either macro-invention or GPT reflects a view of innovation as coming largely from outside the economic sector, and in surges, of its nature uneven, both in its temporal and its sectoral distribution. The rate at which macro-inventions were introduced quickened with the inception of modern economic development. The big leaps are large in their implications, both in what is required to make them work and in their impact. There is often a pause before a major change begins to have a positive effect on the economy.[4] The pause allows an improvement in understanding of the potential of the new breakthrough, but also a gaining of mastery over the new technology and its embodiment in specific equipment and human skills, and the establishment of related enterprises providing vital inputs. There may be a fall in productivity and rise in costs for a preliminary period of time. The process of diffusion takes more time than usually thought, particularly if it involves the application of the new principles in different sectors of the economy. Both the preparation and the later upturn in productivity resulting from the macro-invention is accompanied by an investment boom, whose economic function is moving resources from the old to the new economy. There are a myriad of small improvements and adaptations which follow from the original macro-invention, and often many micro-inventions required for its successful completion, each of which generates profit for the relevant entrepreneur, but requires the commitment of further resources.

It is possible to look back in time, to see technical change as a long-drawn-out process, just about as old as human beings. According to Lipsey, Carlaw and Bekar (2005: 132), the first transforming general-purpose technologies were the domestication of plants and animals. The first use of tools, at some unknown date, could also play this role. On this account, there were many general-purpose technologies introduced before the Industrial Revolution, a view which tends to play down the size of the discontinuity experienced at the Industrial Revolution.

Since technical change appears ubiquitous it is better to explain its suppression than its presence. There are various reasons why innovation is absent from, or of slight importance in, whole societies, despite the inventiveness of individual human beings. Lipsey et al. (2005: 70–72) identify five main ones. The first is a lack of motivation. In some cases humans adjust too successfully to an apparently unchanging environment – they live in comfort with much leisure, controlling the risk characteristic of that society in a way which discourages any change which introduces new risks. Often hunter-gatherer societies are described in this way before the transition to agriculture (Sahlins 1972). Secondly, the world view prevalent in a particular society prevents its members even perceiving relevant opportunities or challenges. It is a matter of how they see and interpret the world around them. The issue is a cognitive one. Thirdly, those innovating cannot capture benefits from the innovations, including non-pecuniary benefits. This is a matter of the distribution of power. A society is organised in a way which diverts the benefits to others, although the costs are concentrated on those innovating. As a result, private benefits fall below private costs and there is no incentive to innovate. The same may apply to the distribution of risk, with a significant mal-distribution from the perspective of an innovator. Fourthly, there are various institutional constraints on innovation, notably in societies in which power is centralised and where the key groups threatened by change oppose it. The forces of the status quo overwhelm any desire for change. Finally, the desire to innovate may be stifled by the poor physical conditions of individuals or by an unconducive mental state, such as an extreme other-worldliness. Poor nutrition and endemic disease may be the source of the problem, or a set of religious beliefs encouraging fatalism and a focus on rewards in another world. For all these reasons, it is unsurprising that the pace of innovation in the past was slow, despite the inherent inventiveness of human beings.

Snooks (1993) has argued that a, probably the, major characteristic of the period of the Industrial Revolution is that for the first time a strategy of technological change rises to dominance. A key threshold is crossed. Previously, significant technical change had taken place but the pursuit of technical change had never before been the dominant strategy. How did this happen? The new growth theory has simply made technology and knowledge an input in a knowledge-creating production process governed by rational economic decision making. In other words knowledge creating is motivated by profitability. This once more focuses on the proximate – revenue and cost streams – not on what made the process likely to be profitable and generated an awareness of, and sensitivity to, profitability. This is a step forward, but by no means an explanation of why the growth in useful knowledge became the moving force in economic change after 1800. Most economically-focused accounts hang in the air concentrating on proximate causes and failing to account for the increased sensitivity to opportunity and the heightened motivation for intellectual exploration.

The most persuasive explanation lies in the conversion of predominantly negative feedback mechanisms into predominantly positive ones. In the pre-modern regime even macro-inventions were characterised by diminishing returns, often, in the words of Mokyr, 'singletons', incapable of generating the flow of micro-inventions, which typically followed during the modern regime. The limits of the knowledge base severely restricted the technological potential. There are two contextual elements which led the change from negative to positive – a reduction in the costs of accessing existing propositional knowledge and an increased feedback from technology to propositional knowledge. The former resulted from the industrial enlightenment, the latter involved three positive mechanisms. First, technology itself became a 'forcing device' (Rosenberg 1972) for the growth of propositional knowledge. Innovation became less random and more directed. Three examples illustrate this – the steam engine's impact on the development of thermodynamics, that of long-distance telegraphy on knowledge of electricity, and canning on bacteriology. A second mechanism was 'artificial revelation', the development of instruments, techniques and laboratory equipment, such as telescopes or microscopes, which promoted experimentation. A third is the rhetoric of technology itself, which showed that the technology based on propositional knowledge actually worked. These prompted Mokyr (2002: 117) to conclude: 'The interaction between propositional and prescriptive knowledge grew stronger in the nineteenth century. It created a positive feedback mechanism that had not existed before, not among the scientists of the Hellenistic world, not among the engineers of Song China, and not even in seventeenth-century Europe'.[5]

THE ROLE OF TECHNICAL CHANGE IN ECONOMIC DEVELOPMENT

The centrality of technical progress to the process of economic development implies a significant contribution to the growth of GDP. The benefits take a range of different forms, particularly since different technologies complement each other. There are two ways of approaching the problem. One is to try to measure the contribution of technical progress in general, an issue already touched on in Chapter 2, in the section on growth accounting. The second approach is to measure the contribution to GDP of the introduction of individual techniques. In principle, an aggregation of all such contributions would equal the rise in TFP. For example in an ideal world 'rail social savings as a proportion of GDP are . . . the percentage change in total factor productivity (TFP) in the rail industry multiplied by the ratio of rail output to GDP (Crafts 2004: 7). We start with the latter.

A typical approach in cliometrics is explicit counterfactual history, creating an imaginary world without the event, innovation or institution whose contribution is being assessed, which is to be compared with the actual experience. This approach is at the heart of economics.[6] The argument is often circular in that the constructed world yields outcomes built in through the assumptions made. One assumption, often made but seldom noticed, is that nothing is indispensable – there is always a substitute, an easily defined opportunity cost. On this account, individuals do not matter. Somebody else would have done what Watt or Gates did, there would have been somebody who performed the role of Napoleon or Lenin if they had never been born. There are always alternative players, maybe not as ambitious as Napoleon or as tenacious as Lenin, but playing a similar role. If there is no railway, there is always a ship or a cart; if there is no electricity, there is always steam power or natural sources of energy. There is always an alternative supplier, or an alternative customer – all that differs is the cost. Switching costs, real or psychological, which often lock an economy into an inappropriate technological or institutional choice, do not exist.

The series began with the railways. The railways qualify as an obvious candidate as a macro-invention, since they had a range of significant beneficial effects, from cheaper, more reliable and faster movement of people and goods, through the stimulus given to steel production, engineering or construction, to the promotion of the capital market and the shaping of the modern business enterprise. In different treatments, each of these influences has been assessed. At the birth of the new economic history, there was an attempt to measure the contribution of the railway to the growth of GDP, initially for the USA (Fogel 1964 and Fishlow 1967). The initial application of the technique was followed by its use for numerous other countries (England – Hawke 1970 and Foreman-Peck 1991, Russia – Metzer and White 1976) and by a developing critique of the approach. The core technique measures the impact of lower cost and greater speed. This requires a comparison of the cost of moving the goods which were moved in a particular year, preferably at a time when the full effects of the innovation have worked themselves out – say 1890 in the USA – first, with the existing transport system including the railways and then with an imaginary system without the railways, but using the next best facilities available at the time, in some cases allowing for feasible improvement and adjustment of the old transport system. An allowance is also made for differences in the value of working capital caused by differing speeds and by differing risks. The social saving, which is the difference in costs, adjusted for other factors, is compared with the level of GDP, in order to get a sense of whether it is large or small. The same method has been applied to other techniques in a number of studies.

Almost invariably, the results have been small relative to either GDP or to the growth in GDP, but increasing over time. Fogel's estimate of the social saving for the USA in 1890 yielded a figure of less than one year's growth, less than 5 per cent of GDP. Fishlow (2000) has argued that this is a serious underestimate (by twofold). Hawke (1970) estimated a figure of 4 per cent for Britain in 1865, but recognized that this was only a partial estimate, but even this figure rises to over 10 per cent by 1890. Von Tunzelman calculated the social savings of all steam engines in Britain in 1800 at a ridiculously low value, some 0.2 per cent of GNP (von Tunzelman 1978: chapter 6). Attempts to estimate the contribution of the personal computer have produced rather larger estimates but they are still insignificant compared with overall economic growth (Crafts 2004). Estimates of the proportion of demand for the products of downstream industries, such as the steel or engineering industries, accounted for by the railways also show relatively low contributions (Fishlow 1967). The results are seen as contradicting Rostow's notion of the railways as a leading sector, including in Britain and the USA. Such an assertion rested on the strength of the various linkage effects, which it argued are much weaker than usually thought. The conventional wisdom emerging from these studies is that in the modern period no single technical change accounts for the higher level of economic growth. Economic growth reflects a multitude of different innovations. Such a critique argues for balanced as against unbalanced growth, that is that modern economic growth is growth along a broad front of different sectors and different technological trajectories.

This railway exercise illustrates all the difficulties which are inherent in such an approach (O'Brien 1983). There are two main problems. The first is that all hinges on the nature of the counterfactual world which is to be compared with the real world: this predetermines the result. The accuracy of the estimates rest on the assumption of constant returns to scale and perfect competition in the economy outside transport. Only transport facilities survive which are competitive with the new facilities and do not necessarily represent a fair comparison. The estimate of social saving also makes the heroic, but rather dubious, assumption that there is always a substitute for an innovation, that therefore there is a counterfactual world in which the same services are provided by another existing technology. Even Fogel recognised that where there was a lack of water transport, as in Spain or Mexico, the result might be different. The estimates for economies at a lower level of development are almost invariably significantly higher than for the most forward, for example figure of 18 per cent for Brazil, in 1913, 26 per cent for Argentina at the same date, and as high as 31.5 per cent for Mexico in 1910 (Crafts 2004; 20). An alternative approach would be to consider the bulky goods which would not have been transported without the railways and the production which would not have occurred (Ville 2004: 329). Fishlow recognised this difficulty by considering what land would go out of production without the railways, an approach taken up but in a somewhat different form by Pomerantz. Foreman-Peck (1991) sought to estimate the loss of income in this way and reached a different conclusion from Fogel about the role of the railways. The second shortcoming is that the exercise is static and badly neglects dynamic effects. In this world there are no technological or organisational/ institutional spillovers. There may be all sorts of interdependencies which can only be identified by a careful analysis of the chains of causation and the actual impact of particular railway systems, for example economies of scale in the transport-using sector of the economy (David 1969). There are other investments which would not have been undertaken without this innovation. The mass-consumption and mass-distribution system of the late nineteenth-century USA would not have existed without the construction of the railways. Had the capital market not developed as a result of the floating of railway paper, had the modern business enterprise with its limited liability and specialised divisions not appeared, then a host of other innovations promoting economic development would not have occurred.

Despite the assertion that most estimates are upper-bound, because of an assumption of demand inelasticity for transport services, and therefore represent a two-fold overestimate of the true social saving (Crafts 2004: 21), there are serious elements of underestimatation – due to imperfect competition outside the transport sector, improvement in the quality of product or service such as to make that product a different one (Nordhaus 1998) and considerable externalities (Crafts 2004: 8-9). 'Market failure' is the cause of these miscalculations and makes such an analysis highly tendentious.

There are alternative approaches. One has been referred to already. The substitution of an inorganic source for an organic source of power, coal for timber, is seen by many as the core innovation of the Industrial Revolution. It is possible to estimate the vast area which would have been devoted to the production of timber in a world which continued to rely on timber as a fuel. The social saving is measured by its 'ghost acreage', the amount of land for growing timber that would have been needed to supply the amount of heat and energy coal actually supplied. In 1815, Pomeranz's estimate (2000: 275–6) for Britain is already 15–21 million acres, whereas the total arable area in 1800 was about 17 million acres. Moreover, the contribution of coal could also be expressed as 'ghost labour' (de Vries 2001: 424), although labour is not a potential bottleneck, as is land. Some qualities of coal, such as the ability to provide steam power, cannot be equalled by timber. Both the quantitative and the qualitative considerations reveal the sheer infeasibility of such a situation – this bottleneck could have obstructed the unfolding of the Industrial Revolution.

In neoclassical theory, the rate of technical change in a national economy is equated with the productivity increase indicated by the growth of TFP found by growth accounting exercises – the famous residual. Differences in the residual reflect real differences in levels of innovatory dynamism in different societies. On many estimates, the residual appears comparatively large. If the estimate is done for GDP per head the residual in conventional growth accounting is typically 50 per cent and may be as high as 80 per cent. It is large in estimates done for the period of the Industrial Revolution in Britain. In other cases, where imitation is relatively more important, the growth of TFP at the inception of modern economic development is modest.

Despite the shortcomings of both approaches, there are some interesting conclusions. There is no doubt that there are macro-inventions which have a profound effect on the rate of innovation and productivity increase. However, the key issue is the eventual universality of innovation throughout an economy.[7] The inception of modern economic development reflects a general dynamism, which is expressed in waves or surges. There is no doubt that at the core of sustained modern development is technical dynamism, but it is almost invariably embodied in specific investments and organisational arrangements.

IMITATION AND THE EXISTING POOL OF KNOWLEDGE

Easterlin (2004: xiv) asks the right question: '. . . Why Isn't the Whole World Developed?' His answer is: '. . . the enormous diversity in the capabilities of societies to master the new production methods when they first came into use. . .'. This is equivalent to asking a second question: why are some societies more inventive and innovative and better able to imitate best-practice world technology than others? It is tempting to point to the expansion in a given country of the pool of 'propositional knowledge', but it is as much access to such knowledge, or the cost of such access. The pool of knowledge is global. There has been over a long period of time a continuing accumulation of ideas (technology) used by Europe from China and other Asian sources, and an increasing readiness to assimilate from outside. Moreover, within Europe there was considerable positive interaction. The relevant ideas were at different stages of development. After the initial development and application of a new technique, technical advance reflects a process of imitation or diffusion, both domestically and internationally. Imitation is critical to the inception of modern economic development. Societies which operate inside the frontier of best-practice technology can generate rapid economic growth by applying techniques already developed and put into place elsewhere. Key decision makers aspire to move from within the frontier to the frontier itself, to catch up, as a result generating economic growth from both movement to and movement of the frontier, since they can leapfrog obsolescent technologies.

Is the neoclassical assumption of a common pool of technical knowledge instantly accessible by all a reasonable one? In principle, all knowledge is immediately accessible to all economies, that relating both to techniques within the frontier and to techniques appearing at the frontier. As McNeill (2001: 12) has commented: 'Ideas . . . are among the most contagious aspects of human culture, even though, when translated into a new language and required to fit into a different social context, they have a chameleon-like capacity to change meaning, sometimes only slightly, sometimes radically.' Specifically, 'Technological innovations often meet human needs also, and are therefore almost as contagious as ideas; and they, too, alter their meaning and importance when crossing linguistic and cultural boundaries'. In practice: '. . . there is nothing "simple" about the processes through which firms come to adopt and learn to control technologies that have been in use elsewhere for some time' (Nelson and Wright 1992: 1929).

There are three factors influencing the pace at which innovations developed elsewhere are taken up. The first relates to the preparedness of a society to receive the new knowledge and apply it. Appropriate decision makers must identify relevant knowledge, understand its implications and master any practical problems. This reflects the engagement of these key decision makers in relevant information networks and their sensitivity to the usefulness of new knowledge, and is a matter of both ability and willingness to use such knowledge. Such information networks exist at both the domestic and international levels. For involvement in any kind of network location is a key issue. Christian (2005) has identified hubs which are advantageously situated for the reception of ideas, commodities and people. Britain has a particular advantage in both respects, with the development of the link between Europe and the Americas. Many of the technical innovations adopted during the Industrial Revolution in Britain were first developed elsewhere in the world. Cultural clusters assist in the transfer of information.

Mokyr (2002: 66) focuses in Britain on a small group of at most a few thousand people who formed a creative community based on the exchange of knowledge. By the end of the mid-nineteenth century, there were 1,020 associations for technical and scientific knowledge, with a membership of around 200,000.

The second factor relates to the degree to which individuals are pressured to adopt innovations in order to remain competitive. The degree of involvement in commercial networks determines the pressure. In order to compete, enterprises have to innovate. The relevant decision makers absorb existing technology by exploiting existing knowledge and imitating what is present elsewhere. In an extreme case, it is possible to purchase the associated machinery and hire the managers and skilled workers to operate it.

A third factor is the political economy of technical change (Mokyr 2002: chapter 6). It is a matter of who benefits and who loses and their access to the political decision-making process. Since the costs are often concentrated and the benefits widely distributed, the inertia of the status quo often prevails, provided they can influence government decision making. Parente and Prescott (1994) have introduced the notion of technology adoption barriers. For various reasons, there may be resistance to the introduction of the new technology. This may be a matter of religious orthodoxy and cultural conformity. Technical change is also, as Schumpeter indicated, a process of 'creative destruction'. The destruction involved the undermining of the value of existing capital and skills and the position of those wedded to the status quo and gaining from existing ways of doing things. It may not be simply a matter of inability to access a technology, but also a matter of unwillingness. Parente and Prescott refer in particular to '. . . regulatory and legal constraints, bribes that must be paid, violence or threats of violence, outright sabotage, and worker strikes' (Parente and Prescott 1994: 299). The emphasis is on the resistance to technology adoption by key stakeholder groups with an interest in the status quo. Not all of these are Luddites or machine destroyers. They include 'environmental lobbies, labour unions, clayfooted giant corporations, professional associations, reactionary or incompetent bureaucracies' (Mokyr 1990: 302). Parente and Prescott argue that considerable unmeasured investment takes place to remove these barriers, an investment to be added to that in the productive facilities embodying the new technology.

Gerschenkron (1962) argued that European economies developing in conditions of significant relative backwardness could grow more quickly than the forward economies, because of the import of best-practice technology from abroad. Within Europe, the constraints on the absorption of technology from elsewhere were relatively weak and diffusion could occur quickly. The costs of access were relatively low and declining. In practice, the movement to the frontier is unlikely to be instantaneous, although in principle feasible. Europe was part of a cultural cluster, one that could be divided up into sub-clusters. Even in Europe there was a time lag in the take-up of new technology, measured from first use in England to first use in the relevant country. Clark (2007: 303–305) has estimated the time lags in the take up of three core new technologies, cotton mills, Watt-type steam engines and steam railway in various countries. There was a diffusion lag of about 13 years for Western Europe, about 22 years for southern and eastern Europe, but much longer outside, 35 years for India and 52 years for Latin America. Technologies are clearly inaccessible over a considerable period of time, but why? It is tempting to assert that the ability to take up technology is inversely related to location within the technical frontier; the further away from the frontier, the more difficult it is to imitate. The present section shows when and how this might be true.

Patents may act as an obstacle in the short run, since they create a temporary monopoly. Allen (2003) and Nuvolari (2001) have shown persuasively how this happened in the development of the iron industry and the application of steam power during the British Industrial Revolution and how collective invention settings in which pertinent technical knowledge is freely exchanged can accelerate the rate of innovation. Some observers have noted the early introduction and importance in Britain of a patent system, which gives the holder a monopoly for a fixed period of time and the possibility of earning a monopoly profit over that period. The advantage in a high risk activity was to guarantee a return to the successful: it removed some of the risk from the investment, both in developing and in operating a new technology. It acted as an incentive for interested individuals to invest time and money in the pursuit of new knowledge and new techniques. There is a trade-off in influence on economic growth between the incentive to invention given by a patent system and the constraint placed on the diffusion of innovations by such a system. The contradiction can be moderated by licensing in which the inventor licenses for a fee the use of the new knowledge. This was introduced in Britain after 1800. The patent system in Britain was not perfect. Some did not bother to take out patents or were proscribed from doing so by the rules; others preferred secrecy as a protection of their monopoly position. There are alternative forms of protection, such as the rewarding of inventors by government, but such rewards become subject to the whims and political manipulations of the relevant players. A patent system has the advantage of being free from such political influence. The result of a successful patent system is to stimulate innovation and to prevent others from quickly imitating, at least provided they do not backwardly engineer and subvert the patent, activities which have been common in late starters.[8]

The obstacles are more varied and persistent than this. There are two relevant problems. The first is that there is so much to choose from in the pool of knowledge. There are countless new products and new sectors of the economy, countless new processes and techniques, and countless associated organisational changes, all in principle available for imitation. As the number of developed countries increases and the level of development of the pioneers is raised, the pool increases enormously in size. Initially economic development involves diversification, that is, the introduction of a wide range of new sectors, but this does not involve imitation of everything. In the words of Rodrik (2007: 77), there is a process of self-discovery in which an economy selects from the many products and processes what it is good at. There is an information problem at this stage, since the apparent costlessness of information hides the real costs of identification and selection. The process requires self-discoverers who must be motivated to do this, and usually without the benefit of patents; by definition, they are themselves in limited supply. The relevant knowledge can be drawn on, but only with a time lag imposed by the process of self-discovery. This accounts for the diffusion lag even with Europe.

Since it appears that much of the process of diffusion occurs as a result of face-to-face contact between innovator and imitator the process can be interpreted as a learning process (Easterlin 2004: 59–60): learning by observing rather than doing. For example, large numbers of 'Foreign dignitaries, industrial spies, adventurers, and prospective manufacturers' (Clark 2007: 303) swarmed round the modern facilities seeking to imitate best-practice English technology, despite the attempts in England to prevent diffusion, by stopping the departure abroad of skilled artisans (until 1825) and the export of machinery (until 1842). After this, large numbers of British managers and workers were instrumental in building cotton mills or railways in various parts of the world. The same encouragement of face-to-face confrontation with innovations happened when, after the Meiji Restoration in 1868, Japan sent out experts to a variety of relevant countries in which best practice prevailed.

There are costs to the use in a different environment of any technology – what we might call adjustment and learning costs – but in principle these costs are lower than the initial costs of developing and implementing the new technology by the pioneers. The level of adjustment costs varies from society to society, only in an extreme case being zero. There is considerable evidence to suggest that the level of costs is inversely correlated with the level of economic development and with the degree of cultural affinity with the originating society. Developed countries have both best access and least adjustment cost. The assumption is still that all technology, wherever developed, is accessible in all countries, but at a cost which is significant.

The problem is not necessarily in gaining access to the new technology in a cognitive sense; it is in applying that technology in a different environment. Clark (2007: 337–40) shows how the new textile technology current in 1914, if applied in poorer countries in the same way as in England, should have been very profitable because of the much lower wage levels, the ability to run plant for longer hours per day and in many cases the local availability of cotton. The problem of exploiting these potential benefits lay in the use of labour, not the machines. The number of workers employed per machine differed by a factor of 6:1 (Clark 2007: 340). The railways also used very much more labour than in the forward economies. Clark sums up the situation (ibid.: 345): 'Thus in both cotton textiles and railways around 1910 we observe the same picture. Poor countries used the same technology as rich ones. They achieved the same levels of output per unit of capital, but in doing so they employed so much more labour per machine that they lost most of the labour cost advantages with which they began.'

The second problem is that much of the relevant knowledge is irrelevant to the developing economy. Conditions in developing countries are very different from those in the developed economies which produce the relevant technology. The important issues may not be on the supply side – the number of self-discoverers, or indeed initiators, but on the demand side, the profitability of the imitation. There may be a hazy notion of what the return on a new investment might be (Rodrik 2007: 104) – the level of risk is high, usually in circumstances in which risk tolerance is low. Technology is developed and applied to suit particular conditions. The relevant techniques are induced by economic factors such as prices of factors of production since the main incentive is potential profit (Habbakuk 1962). The key variables are the particularities of the natural environment, with its specific resources and conditions, and the relationship of the natural environment to the factor endowment. Both of these elements differ from place to place and influence the profitability of different technologies. There is a tendency to choose technologies which are profitable in particular conditions.

A second argument involves the ability of a potential labour force to put in place and operate a technology, its social capability or learned aptitudes. The effectiveness of application of the existing technology by managers and workers is the result of three main factors – intelligence, learned aptitudes and incentives (Easterlin 2004: 60). It is possible to regard intelligence as a variant of learned aptitudes since there is a tendency for intelligence to rise over time. Both factors are a matter of human capital. Learned aptitudes can be broadly defined to include the nature of the work ethic. If workers do not attach importance to regular and meticulous completion of work tasks, labour costs per unit product rise, because of either inadequate quality of output or the need for additional workers to compensate for the deficiencies. The productivity of modern technologies is much lower where there is a lack of human capital. Extending the argument to supervisors and managers compounds the problem.

A failure of a technology to be suited to a local environment is more obvious for the primary sector of the economy, notably agriculture and mining than for manufacturing, but by no means insignificant even in manufacturing. In the case of agriculture, climate, soil types and natural vegetation are highly relevant. The agricultural technology, which appears in a technical sense best-practice, is relevant to the conditions for which it was initially developed but not to very different conditions. Diamond (1997) argued that for this reason certain climatic zones can act as a barrier to the transmission of technology, particularly in a north/ south direction. The technology of developed countries is often capital-intensive, whereas the factor endowment of developing countries stresses labour. This is not only true for agriculture but for manufacturing or any other sector of the economy. The importance of agriculture in the pre-modern period invites an emphasis on this sector. The extensive agriculture of developed countries, particularly those in temperate regions, differs markedly from the intensive agriculture of undeveloped economies in the tropics. Output per worker is relative high in extensive agricultures, and output per hectare or acre high in intensive agricultures. This reflects the land/labour ratio in the two zones, but also the availability of capital. It is partly because the amount of capital used per worker is much higher in extensive agricultures, a factor linked to the nature of technology. Sometimes it is difficult to mechanise agricultural processes in the tropics or to adjust the technologies of developed countries to make them more labour intensive and more suitable for use in tropical agricultures. An obvious comparison is between the cultures of wheat and rice and the history of the development of technology relating to both. The geographical conditions in which they grow are very different, the one dry, the other wet. The factor endowments of the areas in which their cultivation is concentrated differ significantly, with the labour availability in rice-growing societies good and in wheat-growing areas tight. Rice cultivation has been mechanised much more slowly, which partly reflects the differences indicated but also the lesser incentive and the lesser capability to develop appropriate technology.

A second aspect of the factor endowment of a specific country is the high cost and limited availability of capital for investment in the relevant technology. For example an estimation of the price of labour relative capital in England (Allen 2006: 6) shows a significant gap within Europe as early as the second half of the seventeenth century which growth to be very large a hundred years later. The different factor proportions are advanced as an explanation for the lag in the assimilation of the new industrial technology on the on the continent (Allen 2006: 11). More generally low incomes mean low savings. High risk limits the availability of foreign capital. Even in the contemporary world, capital is only available from abroad with a risk premium included to cover country risk,[9] which can be high for developing countries. As a consequence, capital is much more expensive, and in the extreme case unavailable. The problems of accessing sufficient affordable capital may make it difficult to embody the techniques in the appropriate plant and equipment, and meet the adjustment costs, including the development of relevant human capital. The capital requirements of a modern economy are high.

A second argument relating to social capabilities implies a particular view of technical change. Often capabilities are seen in the light of particular kinds of educational, organistional or financial system, the absence of which delays the application of the relevant technology. It is possible to take a much broader focus, and to see technical change as a type of learning and learning as a network phenomenon, involving a collective endeavour (Wright 1997: 1564). In the words of Wright, 'To engage in these activities, you first have to gain access to the network, by learning the language, its formulae, its measuring instruments and machinery, perhaps even its culture and folkways'. Some of this is tacit knowledge, some more easily codifiable. The gaining of access to such knowledge implies a path dependency in the evolution of technology which makes it difficult for others to access the same knowledge, without going down the same path. Different communities will have different social capabilities, which reflect the way in which technology and the economy have developed in the past. There is a subtle interaction in any given economy between the path dependent growth of knowledge and the path dependence of the way in which this knowledge is applied. Before the modern period technological networks strongly overlapped with nationhood. 'In an era of pre-scientific technology, technical knowledge tended to be much more tacit, informal, and location-specific, and therefore national in character' (Wright 1997: 1565). This makes it possible to talk in terms of a national technology (Nelson and Wright 1992: 1935–6). Technologies were complex, requiring a lot of learning by doing and observing. Advance was often local and incremental, building from and improving on prevailing practice. Many interacting individuals and enterprises were involved. Face-to-face contact was important in this process. As a result, there were likely to be all sorts of network externalities. This prompted Wright to assert, 'A striking historical feature of these networks of cumulative technological learning is that down to recent times their scope has been largely defined by national borders' (Nelson and Wright 1992: 1936). This was a matter of geographical proximity and the development of technical trajectories within established linguistic and cultural communities. Imitation was much easier domestically than internationally. It was also much easier in cultural clusters where there was much individual contact and common-alities such as language which assisted communication. With increasing internationalisation, the national bias is disappearing.

Most technology requires the existence of a specific human capital for its effective operation – a range of skills, aptitudes and abilities, which may be beyond the present competence of the relevant workforce, at least without a significant amount of retraining. The relevant human capital is built up by an appropriate education, training and experience (Goldstone 2008: 173). As we have seen, even the trainability of workers differs from society to society. It is difficult to make leaps in social capability, although some societies such as Japan have succeeded in doing so. The feasibility and cost of the retraining may be beyond the capability of the relevant society, because there is a body of tacit knowledge which is inaccessible to the labour force. Much of the knowledge required to operate a tech-nology effectively is tacit knowledge, which it is difficult to transfer and difficult to learn, without repeating the learning process which occurred in the country of origin. Again, the acquisition of this tacit knowledge may require a high level of familiarity with similar technology and a high level of scientific and technical education.

Perhaps more controversially, we can talk about differing cultural atti-tudes. Products, and even the processes of production, are perceived in different ways in different cultures. This may affect the degree to which particular innovations, and the products and processes they are associated with, are regarded as desirable. This also influences the way in which a technology is applied. McNeill (2001: 13) contrasts the impact of printing in Europe, where it disrupted the old society, creating new networks of communication and 'a tumultuous republic of letters', with its impact in China, where, by encouraging the widespread dissemination of the clas-sics, it consolidated Confucian orthodoxy, and the Muslim world where religious scruples even inhibited its use.

Technical advance is both systematic and accidental. It is systematic in that it occurs more frequently under certain favourable conditions. These conditions relate to natural resource and factor endowments, to the changing nature of risk environments, to institutional structures, notably informational and commercial networks, even to location. The random element in all of this relates to exactly which areas might be developed and their leverage on the rest of the economy. Imitation can only follow the first act of self-discovery, if it is successful. Whole industries arise out of the experimental efforts of self-discovery by lone entrepreneurs, whose access to the relevant technology occurs in a variety of ways. The existence of entrepreneurial opportunity is a key condition for modern economic development.

THE AMERICAN SYSTEM OF MANUFACTURING

The United States is an interesting example of imitation becoming initiation. The USA differed from the pioneer in most of the factors indicated in the previous section, but not in the existence of an industrial enlightenment. In the words of Wright (1997: 7): '. . . what mattered most was the emergence in the nineteenth century of an indigenous American technical community, pursuing a learning trajectory to adapt European technologies to the American setting'. There was very considerable face-to-face contact and communication.

Simple imitation was both impossible and undesirable; adjustments had to be made. In the American case these adjustments amounted to innovations in themselves. The USA carried the first phase of modern economic development to its logical conclusion in interchangeable parts and production line methods. It then innovated in completely new technologies, being at the vanguard in the development of new sectors of the economy, new products, new business models, and generally in the push into the age of mass consumption and high technology. In many sectors of the economy, the USA emerged with a clear technical lead over other forward economies and by the second half of the nineteenth century, from a technical perspective, it had become the most dynamic economy in the world. Much of the basis for this was laid earlier as the illustration of the successful use of interchangeable parts at the Crystal Palace Exhibition in 1851 showed. By the end of the nineteenth century, the USA had a significant technical lead in a series of traditional sectors of the economy, including agriculture, mining and metal-working industries, and this lead was about to be extended to another group of sectors where scientific inputs and research and development expenditures were critical and where consumer durables were to lead to a revolution in consumption. This lead was reinforced both by international events – the sequence of wars and depression between 1914 and 1945 – and by domestic actions, right through to the 1960s, when a process of convergence, defined here as a convergence of technology, became obvious for the group of developed economies, amongst whom the exchange of technology became more easily achieved.

The early estimates of Abramovitz and David (1973), perhaps surprisingly, show an aggregate US total factor productivity growth close to zero for the entire nineteenth century. Recent estimates have raised this only slightly. This is another indication of the limits of this measure of technical change or productivity increase. This does not mean that there was no technical change. Had this been the case, the high rate of capital accumulation sustained during this period in the USA would have quickly brought the rate of return on capital down to zero (Wright 1997: 1564).

The achievement of technical change was to maintain the return despite the massive capital accumulation.

The American system of manufacturing, which gave the Americans dominance in mass production industries, emerged, as might be expected, in a path-dependent way, influenced by the particular conditions of the American economy. The system differed from that which characterised British manufacturing in a number of important ways (Wright 1997: 6). It represented a development, but also a transcendence, of the British system. First, there is the greater use, relative to both capital and labour, of natural resources, with which the USA was extremely well endowed. This has been widely identified as a critical feature of American technical superiority. It is not difficult to establish the resource abundance of the USA (White 1987); in many ways, this was the most striking characteristic of the early American economy. Some uses of the resources are obvious, for example, the use of wood, which was in increasingly scarce supply in Western Europe. Because of its abundance, it was possible to use high speed machinery which was very wasteful – it literally chewed up a signifi-cant amount of the wood, converting it into sawdust. The better resource endowment is obvious in retrospect, but to impute technical superiority to that alone is an over-simplification. The exploitation of minerals in which the USA became the main producer in just about every area, from coal and oil to copper and iron ore, and a consumer well above its com-parable share in the world's exploitable deposits, involved investment in a learning process relating to exploration, training and the technologies of extraction, refining and utilisation, just as in agriculture there was 'a vast learning experience in biological adaptation' (Wright 1997: 6). Such resources, while they certainly existed, had to be exploited intelligently, in a resourceful way. The resource curse shows us that there is no automatic translation of resource abundance into technical superiority or even eco-nomic development.

Secondly, there was the use of special-purpose machinery, allowing long production runs of standardised commodities. This required the mechanisation of all the basic processes of metal working. Two points are relevant. Interchangeable parts are one aspect of this, pioneered in small arms production, but then extended to numerous machines from sewing machines to the Model T Ford. The machine tool industry, which eventually separated out from its origins in the textile industry, was at the centre of this process, extending similar methods to sector after sector of the economy, including agriculture, prompted by the lure of profitability in a competitive environment. The spread of the market encouraged this penetration of the machine. Process after process in sector after sector were mechanised. The standard commodities, whether firearms, sewing machines, clocks, boots and shoes, locks, bicycles, agricultural machinery, suited the tastes of a population with relatively high incomes but a relatively equal distribution of that income, and suited an integrated market in which the consumers were quite widely spread out and transport costs not insubstantial. The market was a very large one by any standards, offering the full range of economies of scale. An enormous marketing effort was required, and modern marketing become initially very much an American phenomenon.

Thirdly both the speed of machines and pace of work were high, making for a high throughput, a necessary precondition for mass production. The utilisation of capital and labour was at a high level of intensity. The cheapness of raw material inputs and energy encouraged this. You could afford to waste natural resources and use plenty of energy. This tendency was a precursor of the production line and of mass production, beginning with the meat-packing works of Chicago and finishing with the Model T of Ford. Mass production and continuous flow were the culmination of this tendency. Fourthly, early on, mechanisation did not so much substitute capital for labour as often claimed, rather it allowed the use of unskilled labour in the context of the high turnover and mobility of male labour. Women, child labour, immigrants were all used on an extensive scale, and not just in the textile industry. In conditions of a scarcity of skilled male labour, this substitution was critical to success.

It is possible to add to these the organisational strength of the USA in developing the modern business enterprise, largely a consequence of the railway, and the way in which management was professionalised, culminating eventually in the development of managerial education, including the MBA. The size of enterprise became a defining feature of the American scene, particularly in the trust movement at the end of the nineteenth century.

Towards the end of the nineteenth century new sectors rose in importance, such as the chemical or electrical industries, or the motor industry. They required both significant investment by research institutions, both public and private, and the education and training of engineers and scientists. The human capital requirements were high and the American educational system was well adjusted to this need and well suited to the new sectors. In both areas, the USA stood out as a remarkable performer. The sheer scale of the American effort carried it through to a later dominance in the so-called high tech sector of industry, in aeronautics and computer technology. As a proportion of GDP, research and development in the USA exceeded anything achieved elsewhere until well after World War II.

10. Government provides the context: motivation and policies

> ... few policies lead to good outcomes and many lead to bad outcomes. All happy countries are alike, but there are many ways to be unhappy. (Kremer, Onatski and Stock 2001: 340)

There are three possibilities concerning the role of government in modern economic development. The government pursues policies inimical to economic development and by its actions creates obstacles to economic success. Secondly, its strategy is neutral, designed to have the government provide a framework for others to make the appropriate decisions while stepping back from deliberate intervention. Thirdly, the government adopts policies directly promotive of modern economic development – it intervenes actively. The first is only too common; the second is the stance recommended in economics textbooks for governments; and the third is, in the view of the author, a key factor in the successful inception of modern economic development. This chapter develops a number of important points: first, that the role of government is critical to successful modern economic development in a number of ways; secondly, that a significant degree of government intervention in the operation of the market has been universal for economies which have developed successfully; thirdly, that successful intervention reflects both commitment and the expression of that commitment in an appropriate strategy; fourthly, there are no policies which are effective in all places and at all times: the policies adopted must be specific to conditions in a particular country at a particular time; fifthly, that a policy of picking winners is often pursued successfully.

The first section of the chapter reviews the possible roles of government in promoting economic development. It discusses the nature of government involvement and possible strategies, noting the way in which both change over time. In the second section, the alleged trade-off between disorder and despotism in institutional arrangements of government is analysed and the danger of rent-seeking behaviour discussed. In the third section, there is a review of the political economy of economic development, in both a domestic and an international context. The penultimate section assesses the importance of a persistent commitment of government to the promotion of modern economic development. It analyses how that commitment is translated into policies, including attempts to plan at the government level. Attention is focused on government attempts 'to pick winners'. The final section considers the role of openness as a policy.

THE ROLE OF GOVERNMENT

The conventional wisdom is against a positive role for government in the inception of modern economic development, but there are persuasive counter-arguments (Guha 1981: chapter 3; Rodrik 2007: chapter 4). From a theoretical perspective, it is easy to show the desirability of government intervention in a range of policy areas, usually based on market failure, potential or actual. The break-out from poverty traps and solution of coordination problems have already been given as reasons for such government action. The most cogent argument is empirical, since it is easy to show the universality of a significant degree of positive intervention of government in all successful inceptions of economic development. In the European context, the simultaneous rise of the nation state and the market is a significant theme of any narrative explaining the economic rise of Europe. This institutional combination was critical to its economic success. There has also been debate about the role of government in the Asian Economic Miracle, showing once more how government and market interacted in a positive way (World Bank 1993). An important task is to identify ways of building the specific role of government into the relevant narratives. To make a positive contribution, possibly a critical one, to the inception of modern economic development, key parts of government must have a relevant commitment to the broad aim of economic development, appropriate strategies to realise that aim and the ability to implement them, persuading key decision makers outside government that they can and will continue to do so.

A defect of neoclassical theory is a neglect of the role of government. The focus on a rational pursuit by individuals of a narrowly defined material self-interest ignores alternative motivations, such as the acquisition of power or the significant role of ideas, both often pursued collectively.[1] Government is the obvious place for both the exercise of power and the systematic application of ideology, whether the ideology be socialism or a market-based capitalism. Ideology is the application in a systemic manner of ideas, to the process of decision making, notably those about the appropriate organisation of society. There is sometimes a tendency for the application of those ideas to be carried further than justified by pragmatic economic outcomes.[2] Any dynamic account of decision making respects the differing motivation of key players. Snooks (1993) has indicated dynamic strategies pursued in different societies, all in his view pursued with the intention of realising the same universal motivations – surviving and then maximising material well-being. He picks out family multiplication as the typical defining strategy of the pre-Industrial Revolution era, one which can result, as we see in the next chapter, in a stationary economy with no secular increase in income per head. More relevant to government are the strategies of commerce and conquest, or, in the terms used by Tilly (1992), the accumulation of capital and exercise of coercion. One of the key transitions in the history of developed economies is from a situation in which coercion dominated capital, to one in which there is a more equal balance between the two.

There are two dangers in treating government. First, there is a tendency to anthropomorphise government as one intelligence and one voice. Government is a many-headed beast, different parts of government and different individuals holding divergent views about economic activity and often engaged in contradictory activity. Over time the size of government and the range of activities in which government engages have expanded enormously. In the medium term, there is a ratchet effect which raises the role of government during wars and similar crises – that role never diminishes symmetrically when the crisis is over (Peacock and Wiseman 1961). The bureaucratic revolution changed the nature of government and enterprise. Government has become much more specialised. The modern bureaucratic state consists of politicians and officials/bureaucrats, the former determining strategy and policy, the latter implementing both.

Secondly, it is dangerous to take an anachronistic approach, reading the nature of modern government into earlier periods of history. Government has changed its nature significantly over time, notably ceasing to be patrimonial. Leaders were once *primus inter pares* – like others, only richer and more powerful. In previous times, superior force was often a means for gaining control over economic resources, such as land. Typically, coercion was more important than capital (Tilly 1992).The assertion of a government monopoly over the use of force within a geographical area of sovereignty is itself a recent phenomenon. It is also associated with a decline in the level of domestic violence, in itself helpful to economic development (Gurr 1991).

In the pre-modern era, governments knew that military or political strength was associated with economic strength, but they did not have a clear view of the meaning of economic growth nor how to measure it. Until the putting together of national income accounts, the concept of GDP and its growth was unknown. Explicit concern with the rate of economic growth is a recent focus of governments, partly a consequence of the Great

Depression of the 1930s. Attempts to measure the level of economic activity or wealth in Britain go back to the Domesday Book in 1086, but they were fragmented and linked with government policy only in an indirect manner. Leaders were aware that government revenue was related to the level of market activity, particularly across national borders and had an interest in extending the level of market activity, and thereby increasing the potential tax revenue and ability to borrow. They were also aware that the prosperity of business was partly related to their own activities. Where there is a focus on stimulating modern economic development, there is often a fierce debate within government itself (witness Japan after it was opened up in 1853 by Commander Perry or Russia during the late Tsarist or early Soviet periods). Some parts of government are more obviously engaged in activities relevant to economic growth, for example, ministries responsible for industry, finance or trade. They may even be deliberately set up to oversee actions which promote economic development.

All governments require legitimacy. Traditionally, royal birth and the divine right to rule were sources of legitimacy. Coercion can be used to achieve a kind of legitimacy, but eventually undermines its own potential for its future exercise. Representative democracy, or the use of elections, seen as an expression of popular sovereignty, is another source. Governments gain legitimacy largely by satisfying the wishes of significant individuals or groups in the population and assisting them to realise their aims. Even in the modern period, most governments have been authoritarian, deriving their legitimacy from control of the sources of power, including economic resources. It is possible for political parties to manipulate elections and to remain in office almost indefinitely – this is common in the Asian context and a significant characteristic of communist systems. Increasingly, economic success has become a significant form of legitimacy, particularly for authoritarian regimes: a benign dictator is probably best able to provide the commitment needed for modern economic development. A common measure of economic achievement today, even for developed countries, is ranking in the league table of GDP per head, and changes in that ranking. The movement of countries in the league table of the world income distribution is accounted for by the search for policies which are effective in stimulating economic growth (Kremer, Onatski and Stock 2001: 26–39). The richer countries have in the past found successful policies (ibid.: 32), although arguably by accident. The movement up and down reflects the variable success of the policies adopted. At lower levels of income, the governments of countries are prepared to take risks, which richer countries do not need to take. There are infrequent possibilities to correct mistakes (ibid.: 33). The success of governments is measured by their capacity to deliver increases in consumption, whether private or public, especially true in conditions of high (South Africa) or potentially high unemployment (China). Expectations in the past were more modest. In modern economies, demonstration effects, partly the result of modern communications, have led the mass of people to expect improvement in their standard of living as a natural and continuing state of affairs, including access to the consumer goods which the citizens of developed countries enjoy.

THE TRADE-OFF BETWEEN DISORDER AND DICTATORSHIP: RENT-SEEKING AND 'WINNER-TAKES-ALL' POLITICS

An interesting idea is the notion of an institutional possibility curve. It represents the trade-off between the costs of disorder and those of dictatorship (Djankov et al. 2003: 6), put another way, the trade-off between the risk of private and of public expropriation of property rights (Greif 2006: p. 6, footnote 3). The costs can be interpreted as the transaction costs associated with different institutional arrangements. Economists of a neoclassical inclination place the problem in a choice framework in which institutions are chosen to minimise those costs. There are a number of strategies, which locate a society on the institutional possibility curve. The strategies describe a progressive movement in the direction of more control, and therefore towards dictatorship. There are four possibilities: an emphasis on private orderings and the assertion of market discipline; private litigation, or a reliance on enforcement by courts; regulation by government, backed up by the full paraphernalia of the government; and state ownership (Djankov et al.: 6). The success of private orderings rests on the ability of a society to self-organise and the strength of civil society. Private litigation implies the rule of law and order, with all its requirements. Both regulation and state ownership require an efficient public service.

There are two main issues. The first is the general level of such costs for the various institutional arrangements associated with disorder or dictatorship. There is the possibility that in some societies the relevant costs are lower for all institutional arrangements – this may be much more important than differences in position along the curve. The location of the relevant curve reflects the level of civic or social capital in a particular society, which fixes the general level of costs. The usual focus of attention is the slope of the notional curve – the trade-off between the two. Dictatorship helps remove disorder with its costs, or putting it differently, disorder is the cost of having a potentially more benign government. The removal of disorder is a public good. The slope of the curve represents the marginal costs of reducing disorder, which in turn reflect the quality of bureaucracy, the accountability of the executive generally and the level of corruption or graft affecting government activity. Infrastructural power of government is reflected in the steep slope of the curve – it is relatively easy and cheap for government to solve the problems of disorder. Despotic power is not necessarily associated with infrastructural power, the ability to implement relevant policies, including those relating to law and order. It might be assumed that there are diminishing returns from increasing the role of government, so that the slope of the curve steadily diminishes. Beyond a certain point, despotism becomes self-reinforcing with no compensating gain in public order.

Efficient location on the curve depends on the specific characteristics of countries (Djankov et al.: 17). If civic capital has a strong degree of fixity (Putnam 1993), it could be regarded as a constraint rather than a choice element (Djankov et al.: 10). There may not be a deliberate choice, as the usual analysis seems to suggest. The successful operation of politics can move the curve by increasing government effectiveness. The path of the curve over time is idiosyncratic to particular societies and is more important than choice at a given moment of time, although the latter may limit choices in the future and perhaps produce a slower movement of the curve. Costs might decline rapidly in some societies. Institutional arrangements can be transplanted, either voluntarily, as in the transition from a planned to a market-based economy, or by compulsion from outside, as in colonisation.

In the past, most political orders have been authoritarian; the default arrangement is clearly authoritarian. However, authoritarian regimes can fall into dictatorship. According to Gregory (2004: 11–12), there are four alternative economic models of dictatorship – the 'scientific planner', Olson's 'stationary bandit', the 'selfish dictator' who wants to accumulate and maximize his power, and the 'referee dictator' who mediates among powerful vested interest groups. Unhappily, many dictators slip into the third kind – there may be few checks and balances to prevent this. Gregory argues that the first cannot exist because scientific planning itself is infeasible (this is dealt with later in Chapter 10). Even if the dictator begins as the second, the stationary bandit, with a long-term goal of maximising the growth of overall income in order to maximise his own income, he slips into becoming the fourth, as the political and economic systems mature and various interest groups coalesce to put pressure on government. Yet, as we show below, it may be in the interest of the dictator to try to maximise the rate of economic growth, and not just because of ideological reasons. Authoritarian governments can be interested in promoting economic development, but there is always a danger that that interest will dissipate over time. 'Most of human history and even some of humanity's progress has occurred under autocratic rule, and this record of survival and occasional advance under autocracy cannot be explained without reference to the encompassing interests of autocrats' (McGuire and Olson 1996: 81); the notion of encompassing interests is discussed below.

There are two bases of political order – a consensual and an authoritarian basis (North et al., 2000: 9). In a consensual system, four features are important from the perspective of economic development. There is a self-reinforcing shared belief system about the legitimate ends of government, including economic development, and the extent of citizen rights. In other words, there is agreement on how to limit the intervention of government and define its purposes, including a realisation that this is in the interests of the majority. This limitation means secondly, that the stakes at risk in politics are limited. Political power offers small personal rewards. There is a lesser incentive either to win or to retain power. Thirdly, there is an absence of the kind of rent-seeking behaviour which may reduce the net social return from an asset, and logically from investments in new assets, ultimately to zero. Finally, it is imperative that the state makes credible commitments to protect citizen rights and to reduce the stakes of political decisions. A system of checks and balances on the use of executive power limits the potential damage a government can do and increases the credibility of government intention, notably by building in commitment which reduces time inconsistency.

The consensual system is realised to a varying degree in a democracy, but many authoritarian systems share some features – there are degrees of benignity in authoritarian political systems. Clearly, over time, with modern economic development, there is often a transition from an authoritarian to a consensual basis of government; therefore there are numerous intermediate states. It is even possible for some democratic systems to slip into a form of authoritarianism, for example, through the persistence of one-party rule, which may result from the charismatic rule of an outstanding individual.

In many societies, the aim of the main players in the political arena is to redistribute existing income rather than to create new income. Government often becomes a focus for rent-seeking activity. At worst, there is a winner-takes-all politics in which those who win political power use that power to gain access to as much income as possible, even to destroy their enemies. Where the stakes are high, and such stakes are relative to the level of income within the relevant society, there may be every incentive to engage in this kind of behaviour.[3] The resource curse has its origins in such behaviour.

Rent-seeking behaviour takes place at both international and domestic levels. Similar strategies can be pursued internally and internationally, redistributing existing income rather than creating new income. The former can promote the latter, and vice versa. The development of the ability to coerce a country's own population is linked with a capacity to coerce others. In many cases, significant resources are invested in the infrastructure of coercion rather than in other areas relevant to alternative strategies. At the international level, such behaviour is often described under the headings of conquest or colonisation, although whether any net rent is acquired depends on the nature of the acquisition. A strategy of foreign conquest can be lucrative for individuals involved in the process, but less often for the relevant country. The instruments of coercion are used in the same way to support such domestic action.

While statistical studies have shown that there is in recent times a relationship between democracy and the level of economic development, there seems to be general agreement that this is the result of economic development promoting democracy rather than the other way round, although Rodrik (2003) refers to democracy as a meta-institution, one which should underpin actual institutional arrangements and modern economic development. Economic development creates social changes which provoke a demand for the kind of personal empowerment inherent in democracy. The general experience is that modern economic development has occurred in polities which have authoritarian biases: this is even true of the modern democracies, but particularly true of the countries of the Asian economic miracle. There are shades of despotism. Even those countries which later became democratic started with severe restrictions on that democracy. Almost all developed economies have emerged from political systems which had serious limitations on the amount of democracy practised – in some cases, proneness to military or other interventions; in others, limitations on the franchise or the authority of elected bodies, often a bias towards strong or even absolute executive power, and often, where there are elections, a tendency for one political party to remain in power and to take measures which ensure the continuity of that power (this is particularly true of Asian societies which have grown rapidly).

Fortunately, there is no particular reason why authoritarian regimes cannot stimulate significant economic development, nor any particular reason why such regimes should ignore the benefits of economic development and neglect to take a long-term viewpoint. Democracies can be short term in their orientation, just as capital markets are today inclined to stress short-term returns. They are also very messy in their process of decision making and in the encouragement they give to the activity of groups opposed to any change which threatens their self-interest. It is necessary to examine the nature of authoritarian regimes, analysing in particular why it is that the process of modern economic development, despite the negative inclination of the literature towards them, has almost invariably started there.

It is easy to take a narrow conception of government and its representatives as a selfish interest group. In conditions of political instability – external and internal wars – most of the revenue of government is devoted to the military. In this situation, coercion is used to maintain the political system. Even in good times, absolutist rulers have an interest in maximising the income of government, that is, their own income (Louis XIV – l'état –c'est moi), rather than the income of the economy as a whole and in particular the merchant or commercial sector in that economy (de Long and Shleifer 1992: 4). In the words of one commentator, '. . . rulers resembled racketeers: at a price, they offered protection against evils that they themselves would otherwise inflict, or at least allow to be inflicted' (Tilly 1992: 75). Merchants, entrepreneurs, industrialists and traders are vulnerable to policies of expropriation which deter investment. It does not pay to have visible wealth which can easily be confiscated. Even lending to a government is dangerous, since the government can repudiate its debts and the tax system is also used as a significant confiscatory mechanism. Such a viewpoint assumes that absolutist rulers with both narrow interests and a short time perspective (ibid.: 31) are usually driven by the need for current revenue to secure and improve the position of the relevant dynasty or regime, certainly a shorter time horizon than any commercial group. It also assumes that government does not encompass the interests of other key groups in society, whatever the nature of its selection.

The situation is by no means as pessimistic as this suggests. Authoritarian governments which lack the legitimation of democratic elections often need the support of economic interest groups. Economic success legitimates all sorts of governments. There is an invisible hand which operates to cause authoritarian governments to act under quite common conditions in the interests of economic development, even if their sole aim is to maximise their own rents (McGuire and Olson 1997). The key issue is the existence of encompassing rather than narrow interests, that is, interests which the government has in the general health of the economy. These encompassing interests arise, first, because of the gains derived for the governors from the increased output which results from the provision of relevant public goods, and, second, because of the negative impact on output of the deadweight losses resulting from the extraction of rent, notably through some form of taxation, a loss which is shared to some degree by the governors. The greater the impact of either public good provision or rent extraction, the greater the encompassing interest dictates a lower level of extraction and a greater provision of public goods, that is, policies which promote economic development. The existence of authoritarian government is therefore not incompatible with the promotion of economic development. This beneficial result assumes the adoption of a long time horizon. Where the time horizon is short because of political instability and the insecurity of tenure of those in power, or an uncertainty of succession, there may be an incentive to expropriate even capital goods and to minimise the provision of public goods. Despite this tempering of the extreme version of rent-seeking, de Long and Shleifer (1992) show how throughout Europe before 1800 the existence of princely autocrats, rather than of broader-based polities, was associated with a slower rate of urbanisation and by implication a slower rate of economic growth. Sometimes the changes in prosperity were striking, as autocracy was introduced, as for example in Sicily. Property became liable to expropriation, if only through the tax system. Polities with checks on the exercise of autocratic power, of whatever kind, generally fared better, so the ideal political arrangement may be authoritarian, but constrained by various checks and balances.

THE POLITICAL ECONOMY OF MODERN ECONOMIC DEVELOPMENT

It is impossible to give an account of economic decision making without considering the process of political decision making, since the latter establishes the rules of the game for the former (Guha 1981: chapter 3). The distribution of power is an integral part of any political system, and therefore of any economic system, and dictates which groups or individuals have an influence on decision making. In this sense, the political comes before the economic – it makes a treatment of the political economy of modern economic development critical to understanding the process of modern economic development. Even a decision by government to step back and allow discretion in decision making to private interests needs to be explained. Power is valued and exercised for various reasons, a consideration which makes relevant the notion of political economy, both domestic and international, focusing on the context in which decision making occurs and the motivation of the various interest groups influencing government.

Economists have selected three aspects of political economy as important for economic development – representation, coordination and commitment (Castanheira and Esfahani 2003: 167–70). The first, representation, considers the relationship between government officials and those they purport to represent, in particular how far the political system reflects the interests of different groups and determines what public goods beneficial to economic development are provided and what rents for politicians are allowable. How far does government encompass the interests of the public at large, taking in the interests of a large number of different interest groups, but most notably the entrepreneurial group? Autocracy and democracy are compared, usually to the detriment of autocracy, on the assumption that the interests of the supporters of autocracy are narrow and that most interests in such a political system are neglected. As we shall see, this is not entirely true.

The second aspect, coordination, highlighted by the prisoner's dilemma, raises the problem of how individual decisions are reconciled to produce a social optimum – this involves avoiding the exploitation of the commons, or free-riding in general, and taking account of externalities of various kinds, situations where the social return from decisions exceeds the private return. Coordination may be essential in solving such problems. In such coordination, it is almost inevitable that government plays an important role, if only in providing public goods which are critical to economic success, such as law, order, defence, transportation, physical marketing systems, checks and balances against rent-seeking and risk control in many areas, and in providing those goods in which there are significant externalities, such as health or education. Government intervention in directly promoting economic development is not unusual, nor always a failure.

The third feature involves the credibility of the commitment of government not to renege on pledges given, explicitly or implicitly, in all significant policy areas whether tax, monetary or trade policies are involved, when others have made investments on the strength of these pledges – this is called rather graphically the 'time inconsistency' problem. How is it possible to stop government acting in an inconsistent and opportunistic manner? Will present policy be maintained? The focus is often on the investment decision and the impact on it of a tendency to rent-seeking behaviour, particularly by government. Such behaviour reduces the incentive to invest.

Unfortunately, it is unclear how the particular mechanisms adopted to deal with the problems of representation, coordination and commitment interact with other elements in an institutional system. The interactions which occur are extremely complex and highly specific; they require specific country studies to unravel the way they work.

Government decision making often represents an attempted resolution of the clash of different interests, represented by various groups in a population, some organised, others not – it involves both cooperation and conflict. For any decision, there are many stakeholder groups with a varying interest in the outcome. In reality, each decision is the result of a complex and dynamic interaction of influences. The role of government is usually perceived as encouraging cooperation between stakeholder groups and resolving disagreements, but also acting in an encompassing way, including the interests of a silent stakeholder group, future generations. Government strategy often represents an attempt to put into practice a set of ideas on how to construct a decent society, in other words, an ideology. Encompassing policies often reflect that ideology.

There are weaknesses in the neoclassical approach. It puts the emphasis on deliberate choices, on the assumption that groups are simply aggregations of individuals. The individual maximises an objective function which summarises his/her own welfare or self-interest; the group does the same. Further, the common assumption is that given half a chance, individuals, acting on their own, and probably most of all in groups, will be rent-seeking (Olson 1982). However, cooperation among individuals within groups and between groups is as important to modern economic development as competition between atomistic individuals.[4] Most social sciences recognise the universality of groups and the complexity of decision making within such groups. Individual citizens are members of many different groups, whose membership may be fluid rather than fixed. Some groups are formal, others informal.[5] The group is more than the sum of its individual parts. There are also networks and clusters, aggregating different groups. Neoclassical theorists also regard government as another set of interest groups, a rather complex set, but one motivated just as any other group. In the neoclassical approach to political economy, it is usually assumed that all groups are trying to divert rents to themselves.[6] Sometimes regulators are captured by those with an interest in the regulations. In the neoclassical literature, there are today three groups of particular importance in political economy – political groupings of ordinary citizens, organised to represent and promote their interests through the political system, notably through elections, lobbying or other mechanisms for influencing key decision makers; interest groups in general, systematically pursuing a variety of single aims directly rather than through the political system; and political elites, organised in parties or as part of the administration of an economic system (Castanheira and Esfahani 2003: 160).

Decision making involves the role of groups of interested individuals and their motivation. Particular problems are addressed and solved by group action.[7] It is often unclear who is making a decision and many individual decisions are obviously influenced by interactions within and between groups. Decision making in such a context involves processes of bargaining and negotiation and the articulation of a range of different aims and objectives in a kaleidoscope of changing groups and their interactions. In some simple models of conflict or cooperation, it is possible to make crude divisions such as those between government and workers, managers and owners, or merchants and landowners. In practice, social differentiation is much more complex.

The definition and influence of the public interest differ over time and place, as do the ways in which it is pursued. It sometimes comprises promoting economic development, increasingly so in recent times. In a dynamic context, even the pursuit of increased rents may involve actions which promote economic development and a resulting increase in income. In conditions of relative backwardness, demonstration effects force various interests to push for the inception of modern economic development, notably those linked with the business world, but including interest groups in government concerned at the associated weakening of international influence. Both economic interest and ideology help determine whether key decision makers in government are likely to pursue policies which are encompassing or narrow. Not all individuals or groups behave solely on the basis of a narrowly defined self-interest, many taking a broader view of what is in the interest of society as a whole, and not always because they are forced to. Economic success is a matter of the right motivation of key decision makers and the ability of government to pursue consistent policies which provide the right incentives to the entrepreneurial group – increasing the benefits of relevant economic activity or reducing its costs.

There is a supplementary approach, the historical approach, often influenced in the past by Marxism, which analyses the evolution of various social groups and their motivation, and their influence on the process of decision making. There are excellent studies of the dynamics of historical decision making which take a rounded view of motivation and a broader conception of political economy than that adopted in neoclassical theory. In this approach, there is more emphasis on the desire to acquire and exercise power for a variety of different ends, which might be economic, but also political or religious. The historical approach is a more realistic one, but it can become drowned in a detailed tracking of the influence of individual groups on key economic decision making by government, if it does not use theory to isolate the key events and influences. The use of both theory and history is essential in good studies in the political economy of decision making.

It is useful to provide an illustration of the historical approach. A neat marriage of economic theory and historical data underpins an intelligent application of political economy. Chapter 4, 'Investment, Wages and Fairness', of Gregory's aptly entitled (2004) book, *The Political Economy of Stalinism*, seeks to explain how a non-market economy still produced during the 1930s distinctive investment cycles, in which investment fluctuated more than consumption, a puzzle originally highlighted by R.W. Davies. In a table indicating investment levels, Gregory (2004: 92) shows a rise in investment from 1928 to 1932, a fall in 1933, and a renewal of a rapid rise in 1935 and 1936 after a cautious increase in 1934, followed by a further fall in 1937. In a simple reading, output is given in the short term and is either invested or consumed – the implied consumption per head of workers is equivalent to the wage. The government can try to fix either the level of consumption or that of investment – in the Soviet Union of the 1930s it chose the latter. The model makes use of a theory, fair-wage theory, applied to developed market economies by Akerlof (Akerlof and Yellen 1990). The key relationship is between the government headed by Stalin and the workers as a group. The government wishes to maximise investment for the current year, knowing that the higher is investment, the higher will be output in future periods, and in turn the higher will be future investment, and incidentally future consumption, a positive feedback effect. There is also a negative dynamic effect. The workers have a clear perception of a fair wage. If they are paid less than the fair wage, they reduce their work effort (they pretend to pay us, and we pretend to work). There may be a point at which they strike, engage in sabotage or withdraw their effort completely. The fair wage perceived by workers is not fixed – it may change from period to period with the level of output or the mood of the workforce, in particular with the rising investment effort. In the short run, the worker response is muted. The government can increase investment directly without losing all the increase, because the resulting fall in output is not large at a consumption level immediately below the fair wage. Already the economy is producing below its possible maximum output as a result of the worker response to negative incentives. The government's problem is to find the optimum level of the wage which maximises investment. There is a danger, if the government becomes over-ambitious, that in the short run the level of output will decline significantly as a result of the non-cooperation of workers. As always, there are time lags in the response to changes. Government tends to increase the investment effort, partly reacting to regional and industrial lobbyists trying to push up their own investment allocations. The result is labour discontent, an eventual reduction in effort and fall in output, which at some point becomes large enough to reduce investment below what it might have been. When this is seen to be happening, there is a reversal of policy and an easing off of the investment effort. This generates the kind of investment cycle visible in the data. The application of theory shows how the relationship between government and workers explains the existence of an investment cycle.

There are moments, what Gerschenkron (1982) called *Sternstunde*, critical moments, at which support for policies which promote commerce and economic development becomes very strong. For example, under the Commonwealth in Britain during the 1650s, the legitimacy of the regime was linked closely to the success of commercial policy, prompting one commentator to say, '. . . government support for commercial development tended, under the Commonwealth, to be raised almost to the level of a principle' (Brenner 2003: 580, and also 627). Such critical moments arise because of the specific conditions under which different groups influence the exercise of political power, and in particular the influence of merchant groups interested in commercial policy. Such conditions are often a critical aspect of path dependency. In this case, government policies favoured and encouraged certain merchant groups, notably those connected with the Americas. Brenner devotes a book of over 700 pages to explaining the developing influence of new merchant groups over policy making, stretching over a century. Government policy was important in taking full advantage of the commercial opportunities that presented themselves, and the group of merchants and project organisers interested in the external policies was an important interest group. If the international role of Britain, and the policies pursued by its government, are important to its economic development, it is important to analyse the influences which resulted in the commercial policies evolving, during the seventeenth century, the formative period for commercial policy. Any account of the evolution of commercial policy during the revolutionary period in Britain during the mid-seventeenth century must decide how to classify the different groups that changed in significance rapidly and dramatically, notably merchant and commercial groups, and how to indicate their different and changing motivation. In this case, the groups are influenced by a mix of political, religious and commercial aims. This is a case study in the difficulty and importance of articulating the political economy of any important decision (Brenner 2003).

One approach explores the relationship between the groups representing different factors of production and the nature of trade policy. In a simple model, groups representing the relatively abundant factor dictate policy. International political economy expands the approach further, considering the way in which the governments of relevant countries interact, and the way in which key groups from these countries, such as traders, investors or even migrants, interact and influence governments in the extension of their international activities. International political economy also involves the exercise of power. The most blatant exercise of power was by countries which, because of economic leadership, could exercise a military superiority, a process broadly described as imperialism.[8] The policies pursued at any given time are the result of an interaction between various interest groups, and between the strategies of different governments.

COMMITMENT TO ECONOMIC DEVELOPMENT

In economic theory, a particular meaning is given to the notion of commitment. Commitment is expressed in a stability of policy making which renders the context of decision making predictable. With commitment, decisions have a persistence which gives a guarantee that a government will not act opportunistically or inconsistently in the implementation of a policy, in particular failing to honour a pledge to retain a policy over a relevant period of time. This has particular relevance to investment decisions which take into account, and perhaps depend for their success on, such a commitment. Since the investment expenditures are sunk costs and cannot be later undone – the time-inconsistency problem – they create a hostage to bad behaviour on the part of government.[9]

There is a more important meaning of commitment, a broader meaning which comprises a continuing commitment to the promotion of economic development in general. This is partly a matter of ideology, reflecting the values and beliefs of the ruling group, often nationalistic in its orientation. A government deliberately pursues the inception of modern economic development. The key issue is the encouragement given to entrepreneurial activity. This is not necessarily an argument in favour of a strategy focused on government intervention, rather the government makes room for the entrepreneur who wishes to innovate, fostering an atmosphere in which the economic innovator is honoured, at least respected. This is not just a matter of avoiding the danger of expropriation but of giving the entrepreneur real status. Low status encourages a deliberate switching of assets and activity out of the business area. It introduces and retains policies which encourage economic activity, implying the provision of public goods critical to economic development. There is a need for a consistency and persistency of approach, not only in the general commitment to take actions which promote economic development and in the status given to the innovator, but in the specific policies selected.

Observers often have a preference for a 'hard' state, one which does not alter its agenda because of pressure from various interest groups. It persists over a significant period of time in advantageous policies and does not pander to interest groups seeking short-term advantage. Particularly where the inception of modern economic development is late and where rapid growth produces significant social and political upheaval, there is need for a supportive government, one capable of withstanding the pressure of various interest groups opposed to modernisation. The governments of Asian countries which have been successful in promoting economic development have been hard in their approach, and often because of the continuation in power of one party, the approach has been a persistent one. Key groups who might have opposed this aim, such as landowners and even workers, have been weakened at key moments in the evolution of government policy. A typical case is the development of a triangle of common interests represented by the leaders of large corporations, such as keiretsu in Japan and chaebol in South Korea, senior public officials in key ministries such as the Ministry of International Trade and Industry or the Ministry of Finance and various planning bodies, and politicians, typically belonging to parties that have been in power for long periods of time. The triangle allowed the easy transfer of relevant information, but also established a credible commitment to the government policies which were instrumental in pursuing economic development.

General instability of policy creates a risk for those who invest. It can arise because of a change of regime or policy, which itself may result from pressure from those wedded to the status quo or from those who are suffering from the policies being pursued. There may be social and political instability resulting from a clash of economic interests or conflict between different ideologies. The government may cease to promote economic development and to create an environment favourable to the entrepreneur, if it is exposed to too much pressure from those threatened in some way by the process of economic development or those who have an entirely different agenda.

There are a range of policies now considered important to the process of modern economic development. In strategies, Rodrik includes both reform of institutions and policies, although many policies do not involve institutional change.[10] Rodrik (2007) points out that there is no clear mapping of what he calls first-order economic principles (property rights, sound money, fiscal solvency, market-oriented incentives) into institutions nor into specific policies.[11] There are a variety of institutions consistent with the achievement of the first-order principles and a variety of policies which map into the required abilities or capacities. There are therefore a range of institutional arrangements and policies consistent with the achievement of these principles. Policies are likely to be effective when institutions, as defined in Chapter 8, are strong and when policies are appropriate. The weaker are institutions, the more unlikely it is that government can introduce and implement policies which can promote modern economic development. Attempts to do so can backfire badly. Ocampo (2003) points out that most of the mechanisms sustaining growth result from growth itself, in other words, the process is self-sustaining. We can only recognise the successful institutional arrangements and policies associated with the inception of modern economic development with hindsight and even then are uncertain whether the relationship is a causal one. It is possible that inception of modern economic development has itself generated the relevant institutions and policies.

The discussion usually revolves around policies commonly regarded as good for economic development, such as macroeconomic stabilisation policy (Alesina and Drazen 1991) or trade policy (Fernandez and Rodrik 1991). The latter note how common it is for authoritarian governments to institute reforms which, despite being widely regarded by economists as desirable for business, are resisted ex ante but are only popular ex post. In this, authoritarian governments have an advantage over democracies. Some policies represent a deliberate attempt to stimulate economic growth, either to perform some functions directly, for example to build railways or conduct research in public institutions, including universities, or to encourage others to take action which promotes economic growth, by providing appropriate incentives, often through the price system. Typically, the policies most talked about involve attempts by governments to deliberately pick winners, that is, to reconstruct the economy in a way which the government thinks desirable. In Asian economies, industry policy has been seen as a deliberate 'coordination device' to counter the tendency to a shortfall of private below social returns, leading to underinvestment (Rodrik 2007: 27).

Sometimes government becomes directly engaged in economic activity, but this is not necessary, nor always desirable. The most common form of continuing direct participation is obviously damaging to economic development: it relates to war – the employment of armed forces and their supply and provisioning. There is now a consensus among economists that, whatever its nature, direct public participation is a costly form of intervention in an economy, only justified in exceptional circumstances – it has negative incentive effects. In market economies, there is a deliberate attempt to restrict the size of the government sector and to abstain from picking winners. Public owners lack the incentive to efficiently allocate resources provided by private ownership, notably competition in a market context. The conventional role of the government has been institutionalised in what is sometimes called 'the golden straitjacket' or Washington Consensus (Rodrik 2003). An emphasis is put on the protection of property rights and enforcement of contract. The advice is to stabilise the macroeconomic situation and to privatise and deregulate where possible. Monetary policy is intended to keep down the rate of inflation. It is virtuous to run surpluses on both the current account and in the government's budget. The currency should be kept strong, but its value determined freely by supply and demand. In such a policy package, any promotion of economic development is achieved indirectly through minor elements of fiscal, monetary and even trade policy; it is not prominent. The general view is that the set of policies of the Washington Consensus, or even its expanded version, has not resulted in a better growth performance (see Rodrik 2007: chapter 1). As a consequence, there is a tendency to expand the number of relevant policies, extending the area of intervention. This is not unexpected, since it reveals the tendency in the analysis underpinning such policies to move towards the specific, in particular the failure of more general approaches to produce results and the need take into account the particularity of individual experience.

There are many methods of government intervention alternative to direct participation in the economy. By bringing together different individuals and groups in an exchange of information, notably about intentions, by creating different laws and regulations encouraging productive economic activity and discouraging rent-seeking behaviour, and by using the tax and credit system and the mechanism of transfer payments, the government can influence both the flow of information and the level of prices, in this way, guiding the allocation of resources. Government also oversees the nature of the relationship with outside economies. Regulation of markets is a device by which governments pursue their aims and objectives. The government often takes action to influence price or the conditions of demand and supply. As a consequence, government has a potent influence on the scope for innovation and the rewards which result from such activity.

There is a broader issue – that of the place of planning, at various levels. A loose definition of planning as guidance makes planning almost universal. Planning is the striving to achieve given objectives with limited resources in a rational way. Everyone and every organisation has in mind targets and prefers to use resources in the most efficient way to achieve these targets. In modern management studies, this kind of activity is analysed under the heading of strategy.[12] Much planning does not spell out in detail the targets and the resource needs. There is no doubt that private organisations plan in this sense. At one extreme, planning at the national level involves the discussion and putting together of a strategic framework in which different organisations communicate their intentions for the future and their need for resources to realise these intentions. Exactly the same process occurs at the enterprise level, a perspective which reflects the view that the enterprise is a coalition of stakeholders. The transfer of such information about future intentions is at the core of planning. It is not always the case that the market transfers the relevant information. The main gain from such planning is the removal of major incompatibilities of intention and the harmonisation of such intentions with the availability of relevant resources. This is part of what Rodrik (2007) describes as a process of discovery, in which the various parties participate.

What is commonly understood as planning is national planning, in particular the centralised physical planning system adopted by the Soviet Union, and later imitated by other communist states, including China, and even some non-communist states, such as India, where it reached a level of sophistication greater than in the communist countries. The drawing up of detailed and comprehensive plans for various time periods, most typically in the five-year plan, is an extreme form of planning. In the Soviet Union, it was as if the whole economy was swallowed up in one state enterprise. Modern economic development had priority over nearly everything else and was planned to occur at the most rapid rate possible. Such planning eventually proved a failure, although it would be wrong to give a wholly negative account of the outcome of the planned system in the Soviet Union.[13] The critical weakness of this kind of planning is that it involves the transfer of a massive amount of information and the labour of a vast bureaucracy to identify and effect the transfer. Even with modern computers, this is infeasible. Market systems achieve this with much lower transaction costs. The main virtue of a market system is that it summarises a mass of information through both the level of price at a given moment of time and movements of price over time and transfers that information at enormous speed and minimal cost.[14] However, there are still deficiencies, implicit in the notion of market failure.

The adoption in the modern period of some form of planning is more common than often thought. Developed economies such as France and Britain tried a different kind of planning. There are a number of labels given to the process – indicative and guidance planning are the most common. The French in the 1950s pioneered indicative planning. Such planning did not take place within the context of a command economy. The term indicative means that it did not instruct, it indicated. The aim of the exercise was to anticipate the broad outlines of the future development of the economy and to ensure that the intentions of individual enterprises and government organisations were consistent with these outlines. So-called guidance planning was employed in the countries of the Asian miracle with the same aim of transferring relevant information. Guidance planning was made easier by the existence of large enterprises controlling strategic parts of the relevant economies. The planning was used to assist the relevant governments to identify policies which would guide the economy in the desired direction. It is argued that the Irish government has used a kind of guidance planning in generating the acceleration in the rate of economic growth which has characterised that economy over the last 30 years.

Often planning is used to change the structure of an economy and to change it more quickly than the market alone would allow. The government has a clear view of a desirable structure for the economy and takes action to ensure that it is achieved: '. . . it is increasingly recognized that developing societies need to embed private initiative in a framework of public action that encourages restructuring, diversification, and technological dynamism beyond what market forces on their own would generate' (Rodrik 2007: 99).The government is not necessarily any better than the private sector in anticipating future changes in taste or technology. What it can stimulate is a discovery process where critical information is lacking. It can also help resolve all sorts of problems which hinder cooperation within a market context. There are coordination problems which require government action; certain kinds of investment are required which are unlikely to occur without government support.

Any price pattern is not a given. The pattern of demand in any economy reflects the distribution of income, which in its turn reflects the price structure. For different price structures and income distributions, there are different patterns of demand and different allocations of resources. Prices do not play a neutral role in allocating resources: they distribute income, sometimes in a way regarded as unacceptable. The pattern of demand may not be regarded as desirable: because the social returns and costs generated by current output diverge from private returns and costs; or, because of the impact of demand on the consumption of future generations, with the private sector too severely discounting the future; or because of desired changes in technology, anticipated by the government. There may be lack of incentive to invest in sectors crucial to the inception of modern economic development. As a consequence, the government may wish to encourage production in certain areas of the economy and discourage it in others. They often do this through price signals, including the manipulation of relevant taxes, or through credit policy, ensuring that a sector receives investment funds at a low cost.

OPENNESS

Much attention has been focused on the desirability of opening an economy to the outside world and on the importance of trade and foreign direct investment to the process of modern economic development. Neoclassical theory favours openness of the economy, arguing that both trade and investment promote modern economic development. Mokyr comments: 'Trade . . . liberates nations from the arbitrary tyranny of resource location' (Mokyr 1999: 34). Some see the growth of external trade as the trigger for the inception of modern economic development, as in the pioneer Britain (Guha 1981; chapter 7). One approach emphasises the influence of trade in increasing both the price elasticities of supply (of necessary inputs such as cotton) and of demand (for the products of the Industrial Revolution, such as cotton cloth or yarn), and increasing the return from industrial innovation (Findlay and O'Rourke 2007: 343-4). The California school (Pomerantz 2000) has argued that at a key time the external conjuncture was highly favourable to European economies which developed successfully – their successful inception of modern economic development was dependent on the nature of their relations with the outside world.

There are significant criticisms of the argument in favour of an open economy. Many commentators firmly locate the source of modern economic development in the domestic economies of developed countries. Unfortunately the debate has come down to one about the degree to which the profits from outside economic activity has financed industrial investment or investment in general, during the Industrial Revolution. We might call this the ratios argument (O'Brien 1980, Hobson 2004). All hangs on which ratios you use.

First, on any measure, the contribution to economic growth of the internal economy is much greater than that of the external economy. Ghemawat (2007: 11) assets, 'most types of economic activity that can be conducted either within or across borders are still quite localised by country'. In the past they were even more localised. The role of the external factor is a matter of the size of any positive contribution of external interactions to the success of developed economies and the hindrance provided by external interactions to those unsuccessful in beginning modern economic development. The first requires answering the following questions. What share of the growth in output during the inception of modern economic development was sold in foreign, notably colonial, markets? For individual economies, it is an empirical matter, involving the number and size of such transactions, compared with domestic transactions. It should be supplemented by another question. What share of investment could have been financed by the flow of profits from the plantation, mines or trade of colonial economies? The second involves answering different questions. What mechanisms were involved in the exploitation of the unsuccessful? Was the size of the burden imposed sufficient to prevent the inception of modern economic development?

The overwhelming weight of the evidence on the quantitative aspect of the external trading sector, and the specific experiences of those countries which have seen the inception of modern economic development, favour a largely internal determination of a successful transition. The existence of a universal home country bias, and even today the low share of output internationally traded and of capital formation internationally financed, focus attention on the internal rather than the external economy. Even today Ghemawat (2007: 12) has referred to the 10 per cent presumption, with 10 key indicators of the degree of internationalisation still showing an overwhelming predominance of the domestic economy. The general case is that the external sector represents a market which is small relative to the internal market. During the period 1800–1938 total exports from Europe were just 8–9 per cent of the GNP of the developed countries (Bairoch 1993: 72). The figures for both the USA and Japan are even lower. The general ratios, while supporting an increase in the level of internationalisation accompanying modern economic development, show that the external sector is much smaller than the internal sector in most countries. If double-counting is excluded, the trade-to-GDP ratio globally is today close to 20 per cent (Ghemawat 2007: 11). There are one or two exceptions, where the ratios are much higher, but these are for small states, often entrepôt city states. The nature of the interaction is again highly specific to particular experiences. As in other areas it is difficult to generalise on the basis of the experience of all countries. However even in the most favourable cases, the contribution of the external sector does not seem decisive, being at best, only supportive.

Nor does the empirical evidence support the contention that the act of opening an economy stimulates more rapid economic growth. Rodrik (2007: 215–16). summarises the evidence, 'Essentially, there is no convincing evidence that trade liberalisation is predictably associated with subsequent economic growth'. There is no robust relationship between open trade policies and economic growth. However, a rapid rate of growth of world trade is generally associated with a rapid growth of world GDP, with the former exceeding the latter. Periods of contraction of the international sector have been periods of poor growth. Correlations of such a kind establish the existence of a relationship without indicating its nature. It is impossible to say whether the growth of trade is driving the growth of GDP or whether the growth of GDP is driving the growth of trade. A third factor, say the growth of productivity which is at the core of modern economic development, is probably driving both.

Economic historians recognise that successful economic development is usually associated with some degree of closure. Generally rich countries embarked on modern economic growth behind protective barriers, but dismantled their trade restrictions as they got richer (Rodrik 2007: 217). Bairoch (1993: chapter 4) has shown that protectionism is associated with industrialisation and faster economic growth and more liberal trade with a poorer performance, with the exception of the two decades which followed the repeal of the Corn Laws in Britain in 1846. Such a policy is justified by the infant industry argument, developed by Alexander Hamilton

(Cole 1968) and Friedrich List (2005) in the early nineteenth century. It is not accidental that this was done in the USA and Germany, since these follower economies had to compete with the already established industries in Britain. The existence of scale effects and significant learning by doing means that incumbent players in key sectors of the international economy have an enormous advantage, which it takes a large effort by government to offset.[15] It is not unusual for governments to use protective trade policies to deliberately promote the development of key sectors and to encourage an inflow of investment which helps set up new industries. In order to allow an infant to grow to adulthood it is necessary to provide some kind of protection. Protection is needed to allow sectors of the economy regarded as indispensable to modern economic development to grow and mature, such as textile industries, the iron and steel industry, engineering of various kinds and the motor car industry. Such a policy of import substitution has its weaknesses; it restricts the size of the market and reduces the impact of competition, sometimes encouraging the survival of uncompetitive sectors of the economy. There is a vested interest in maintaining the protection. Direct assistance may be preferable if an open policy is pursued which shows which sectors are genuinely competitive and which are not, a combination which characterises the Asian Economic Miracle. Protection of such industries existed: in Britain – cotton textiles; in the USA and the continental European economies – all the major sectors.[16]

During the process of economic development inflows of foreign direct investment tend to exceed outflows. Such investment is more than an increased supply of savings available to a country. It usually involves a package of inputs which include technological know-how and entrepreneurial contributions. Such an input can have an importance disproportionate to the size of the associated inflow of financial resources,[17] but it is easy to exaggerate the contribution of the inflows to capital formation. Even in the case of China, in the recent past the inflow of FDI represents less than 10 per cent of the gross domestic capital formation. The ratio of FDI to overall fixed capital formation, which appears less than 10 per cent for the period 2003–2005, a not untypical recent period, is much less, if acquisitions and mergers, which do not represent new investment, are excluded (Ghemawat 2007: 11).

The second objection to the argument in favour of an open economy questions the argument based on specialisation according to comparative advantage which results from a growth in external trade. Such an argument ignores the evidence on a general pattern of economic development. Economic development initially involves a diversification of economic activity and specialisation only becomes important at comparatively high levels of income per head (Rodrik 2007: 103, quoting the work of Imbs and Wacziarg 2003), well after the inception of modern economic development. The trade model focusing on specialisation is not a good description of the early pathway to modern economic development. Rodrik points out that most instances of productive diversification are the result of public-private collaboration (Rodrik 2007: 104). The diversification is linked to a significant role of government. This is not hard to explain, since entrepreneurs bear the full costs of failure in discovering which products or processes existing abroad offer a profit in a developing economy, whereas success is likely to stimulate a wave of imitators who compete away the profit which justify the initial investment. There are investments which depend upon a range of simultaneous investment in linked activities, activities offering economies of scale, the implementation of which involves government action in allowing a network or cluster to capture the coordination externality.

Thirdly, there are various meanings to openness. More important is a broader meaning of openness, openness to new ideas and knowledge and the ability to assimilate technology developed elsewhere. Theory and experience show that it pays to be discriminating in what one is open to. A discriminating openness appears the best policy, one reflecting the particular conditions of the relevant economy. It is difficult to identify and apply a discriminating policy which works. That is why the default option for most economists is openness. Some economies are open in certain respects but closed in others. Many of the Asian economies are relatively closed to foreign acquisitions but open to imports. Openness is not simply a matter of openness to imports or FDI. It is openness to the movement of ideas and knowledge, in particular innovations in technology and organisation, and of people, as well as the inflow of commodities and investment. Often people carry knowledge and new ideas, particularly if they come from economies already on the path of modern economic development.

International demonstration effects are a key to motivation to participate in modern economic development. They operate through the responses of government, and at different levels. An external shock which reveals the vulnerability of a country to outside interference is sometimes enough to kick-start the process of modern economic development, provided other internal conditions are appropriate: the case of Japan illustrates this. International demonstration effects may also involve the introduction a new scale of tastes – new products or old products differentiated and sold at a lower price (Guha, 1981: 26–7), affecting some groups before others, notably a middle class in urban areas, and spreading through the population. Such an effect shifts the focus to the demand side of the economy. The process is likely to be rather slower than for abrupt military threats.

It reflects the activity of traders, often protected and backed up by their home governments.

One area where there has been a retrogression in openness relates to labour. Before World War I there was less restriction on the movement of people than today. The relevant restraints today relate mostly to long-term labour movements. One way of maintaining significant international income disparities is to limit such movement, so it is tempting for rich countries to stop the movement of people from poor countries; there is likely to be strong pressure from working groups to retain this closure. Even in this area, it is desirable to pursue a discriminating openness. Where there are shortages of particular labour skills or a low density of population, pro-immigration policies are often pursued. Short-term movements are different, since the movement of business people promotes both trade and investment and is desirable from the perspective of modern economic development. It certainly promotes the transfer of technology. Tourism and international education are also major contributors to national income and are encouraged.

Once more openness is an aspect of a self-sustaining process. Once initiated economic development takes on a momentum in which international connections become another positive feedback loop. There is a strong interaction between increasing GDP and the growth of international flows and a virtuous circle in which the external and the internal interact positively. Trade grows, foreign capital flows supplement domestic savings, borrowings of technological and organisational know-how, selective immigration, all become important. Key ratios increase – international trade grows faster than output and foreign investment grows faster than total capital formation. The economy which has crossed the critical threshold is better able to compete in trade, to attract FDI through a growing market or better skilled workers and to assimilate technologies developed elsewhere, even to generate its own multi-national companies investing abroad. Beyond a threshold level of income per head which is quite high, there is an increased tendency to concentration of economic activity in areas in which an economy has a comparative advantage, a tendency based on higher productivity (Imbs and Wacziarg 2003), an effect reinforced by the advantages of agglomeration.

There are several mechanisms encouraging the rising importance of the international economy and the growing integration of relevant markets (O'Brien 1997: 79–82). The first relates directly to the stance of government. A stable and peaceable international political order is a first requirement. The periods from 1815 to 1914 and from 1945 to today are periods of relative stability. Governments actively pursued the removal of barriers, suppressing piracy, removing tariffs and quotas, and opening markets generally. Cheaper, quicker and safer transport has made the world economically smaller. There have been a series of macro-inventions which have revolutionised transport – railways and the steamship, and the motor car and airplane, in the implementation of which government has played, and still plays, a significant role. The ratio of trade to total output has risen significantly.[18] Whereas in the first half of the nineteenth century the ratio of output exported, or the share of consumption accounted for by imports, was 1–1.5 per cent, by 1914 it was about 15 per cent (O'Brien 1997: 77, 82). It is not much higher today. The ratio of gross world capital formation financed by international investment has risen. Some argue strongly that the barriers to technological diffusion have come down significantly (Wright 1997).

A counter to the argument focused on the small size of the external sector highlights the nature of the early transition, the concentration of rapid growth on a limited number of sectors of the economy and the significance of external trade to these sectors. The role of cotton textiles in the British Industrial Revolution is the classic case, accounting for almost a quarter of the TFP contribution to British growth between 1780 and 1860 (Harley 1999: 184). However, it is argued that the wage and price structure conducive to modern economic development was the result of a long process of commercial expansion (Allen 2006: 2). Even the proponents of this viewpoint admit there is a significant role for import substitution – notably in cotton textiles and porcelain for Britain (Allen 2006: 9). Certainly about 50 per cent of cotton production was eventually exported, accounting to at peak in 1834–3 48 per cent of all exports (Findlay and O'Rourke 2007: 325), but the negative impact of this expansion on Britain's terms of trade could easily have been critical. The price of cotton goods relative to other goods fell from 6.3 in 1770 to 2.7 in 1815 and 1.0 in 1841, and Britain's terms of trade went from 196 in 1801 to 108 in 1851 (Imlah 1958: 94–6), almost a halving. According to Cuenca Esteban (1997) the decline was even more dramatic (Findlay and O'Rourke 2007: 232). High elasticities of demand only just prevented the Industrial Revolution from being aborted.

The process of internationalisation has been more gradual than often suggested, a process which has been developing over centuries. There have been reversals, the last major one being between 1914 and 1945, with two world wars and the Great Depression. Such reversals reflect a combination of government and market failure, for example during the 1930s beggar-my-neighbour policies in the context of a lack of international leadership (Kindleberger 1973) and/or a massive and mistaken contraction in the money supply (Friedman and Schwartz 1963). Markets are not as integrated as they appear (Helliwell 1998, White and Fan 2006) and trade and investment flows less than anticipated in an open world. There is plenty of evidence for the existence of major barriers to the free movement of commodities, factors and ideas, some visible, some hidden.[19] Hidden barriers persist, not as visible as those which are the usual focus of attention, – tariffs, exchange controls, or even transactions costs. The market segmentation reflects cultural affinities and other links, some of which may be the delineators of convergence clubs. Rose (1999) found that sharing a common currency implies a trade three times the level when the trading partners have separate currencies, a disparity he could not explain, since the relevant transactions costs appear low. A common currency often goes with common cultural norms, a common legal system, and a common history, whose influence might be cumulative but difficult to quantify. Helliwell (1998) finds that trade between two Canadian provinces is 20 times the level of trade between a Canadian province and an American state, despite physical and cultural proximity.[20] Country risk encapsulates many of these invisible barriers. FDI flows are constrained by high levels of country risk. Financial markets show national savings and investment closely linked and the portfolios of financial institutions seriously underweight in holdings of international financial assets. The exact direction of such flows reflects the level of face-to-face contact and therefore the countries with which a country trades or from which it receives investment. It is likely that the flow of ideas is also strongly constrained.

PART IV

Devising appropriate narratives

> No economic model can capture the intricacies of economic growth in a particular society. (North 2005: 165)

The aim of this part is not to write relevant analytic narratives – that requires much more space and preparatory work; rather it is to explore important issues raised by the attempt to write such narratives. As a separate narrative, each of the following chapters warrants a whole book. The aim is to consider the way in which theory, tested by data, opens the way to the selection of an appropriate narrative.

The narratives are chosen for their significance: they offer general lessons. The nature of the inception of modern economic development which has emerged so far in this book is discontinuous in obvious ways. It is also continuous in the sense that it is the result of a long-drawn-out process of change over the pre-modern period, notably in Britain and Japan. In a state of undevelopment, negative feedback loops predominate in all sorts of areas of the economy, polity and society. It is not difficult to identify the poverty traps already described. Over time, positive feedback loops emerge and multiply. For some, there are thresholds beyond which the process of change accelerates significantly after a long period of gentle change; for others, there are interactions between positive loops which are mutually reinforcing. At a critical stage, the positive loops predominate over the negative and the rate of economic change accelerates. Once this happens, development becomes self-sustaining. The release from the Malthusian trap is a good illustration of this process. This transition constitutes a major discontinuity which is partly context, partly characteristic of the inception of modern economic development. The pioneer case of transition, Britain, is an obvious focus of interest. By historical standards, change occurs at a rapid rate, but the element of discontinuity was less than often thought: it needs to be defined carefully. For later starters, the element of discontinuity has increased with startling effects in terms of the political and social tensions engendered, as illustrated by the Russian experience. The Soviet experiment dominated the twentieth century and required a careful treatment of its mix of the continuous and discontinuous, of the general and the specific.

The topics chosen for the three chapters in this section are major mysteries. Chapter 11 focuses on the release from the Malthusian trap. It is organised around the demographic transition, a description, albeit imperfect, of the way in which demographic behaviour changed in the release from the Malthusian trap. It vividly illustrates the way in which positive feedback loops overwhelm negative ones to assist in the inception of intensive economic development. Chapter 12 focuses on the most frequently told story, that of the Industrial Revolution and the degree to which the relevant narratives for other developed economies share features in common with the British experience. Chapter 13 considers the failed experiment of communism and of a rival strategy for modern economic development as it unfolded in the Soviet Union. For a time, it offered a decidedly different path to modern economic development.

11. Release from the Malthusian trap

. . . the Industrial Revolution meant, above all, an escape from the Malthusian trap'. (Komlos: 19)

A central element of the discontinuity which marked the Industrial Revolution at the end of the eighteenth and the beginning of the nineteenth centuries was a release from the Malthusian trap. 'The great span of human history – from the arrival of anatomically modern man to Confucius, Plato, Aristotle, Michelangelo, Shakespeare, Beethoven, and all the way to Jane Austen indeed – was lived in societies caught in the Malthusian trap' (Clark 2003: 1). There are three main characteristics of that trap. First, technological change resulted in an increase in population, not an increase in the level of income per head. The view is put succinctly by Clark, 'In the Malthusian economy that preceded 1800 all productivity growth is absorbed by population increases' (Clark 2003: 5). Secondly, over time, income per head oscillated around a subsistence level, although not necessarily a starvation level. Thirdly, technologically superior countries had denser populations to match the higher yields of land or of material products in general. After release from the trap, productivity growth began to raise income levels, although initially population growth accelerated dramatically and the main achievement of the first phase of the Industrial Revolution was to maintain incomes despite this increase. Clark believes that world economic history has three interconnected features which need to be explained: the long persistence of the Malthusian trap, the escape from that trap during the Industrial Revolution, and the consequent Great Divergence between developed and undeveloped economies, with Malthusian pressures persisting among developing economies. He emphasises that explaining the Industrial Revolution requires explaining both the release from the Malthusian trap for some and the Great Divergence for others (Clark 2003: 2). Such a perspective forces us to focus on ultimate rather than proximate causation (Komlos n.d.: 20).

This chapter starts with an exposition of the Malthusian model and a review of its alleged universal validity. The second section addresses the question, what releases an economy from the Malthusian trap? The next section, on the theory of the demographic transition, considers historical tendencies in the behaviour of population and their determinants. The following section focuses attention on the modern demographic regime and its main characteristics, including an analysis of the relationship between economic development and population change. Finally, there is an analysis of theories which revive the Malthusian model in describing the current difficulties arising from the finiteness of resources and damage done to the environment by economic activity.

THE MALTHUSIAN MODEL

An important issue raised in earlier chapters (5 and 7) is the dynamic relationship between population and resources and the change in the nature of that relationship at the inception of modern economic development.[1] The Malthusian model assumes that the link is central to the growth experience of any country. There are two possibilities on what drives change: first, that resources are independently determined but population responds to the supply in various ways, sometimes running ahead of resources and sometimes lagging behind; secondly, that population is the independent variable and that the pressure of population on resources can act either to increase the misery of the population by reducing their standard of living or as a stimulant to economic development, inducing innovations in technology and organisation which change the resources position for the better – this has been called the Boserupian position.[2]

Malthus believed that everywhere there was a tendency for population to grow at a geometric or exponential rate and resources to grow at an arithmetic rate – or in the words of Macfarlane for resources to act as the tortoise and population the hare. In normal circumstances, the former grew faster than the latter. The Malthusian position is to emphasise the repeated pressure of population on resources as a major obstacle to a sustained increase in income per head. During most of human history, agriculture has dominated economic activity and income levels have been low, determined in the short term by the state of the harvest and in the longer term by the relationship between population size and the agricultural resources available.[3] The latter is often referred to as the carrying capacity of the economy, and varies according to soil fertility and climate, technology and the availability of different food sources.

The trend rate of population expansion before the Industrial Revolution was slow.[4] Evidence on height indicates no improvement in nutritional status in Europe over two millennia, but a fluctuation in population density, as a Malthusian model would suggest (Koepke and Baten 2005). This operates through the sensitivity of mortality and fertility to nutritional levels, reflected usually in income levels. The Malthusian argument is that population fluctuations are density sensitive, that is, sensitive to movements in the ratio of population to the land and its carrying capacity. Provided at any given time that births rise and deaths fall with income, and therefore nutrition, there will be an equilibrium level of income which stabilises population size. In an extreme case, where the sensitivity is acute, the level of income rarely moves away from the equilibrium subsistence level, since such a movement causes a rapid adjustment of population. Usually, because of time lags in the response of births and deaths, there are longish periods of adjustment and periodic swings in both population and the availability of food. The swings reflect long periods of population either running ahead of food supply or vice versa. In the language of cycle theory, there were time lags and a tendency to overshooting.

Does the population/resources relationship dominate the pre-modern economy?[5] There are autonomous elements of both resource availability and population growth which can weaken this link. For example, it is argued that climate varies over time, with an alternation of warmer and cooler periods of three to four centuries and associated variations in the occurrence of drought. The cooler period called the Little Ice Age, from 1300–1800 (Fagan 2008), had a direct impact on the productivity of agriculture and an indirect impact through the increased incidence of natural shocks (Goldstone 2008: 21). The climatic changes also had an impact on the incidence of disease and on the level of conflict, both through the increased movement of people. There are long cycles in economic performance, reflected in the impact of resource availability on the behaviour of population and prices and even on the level of political instability (Fischer 1996). There are autonomous elements in the behaviour of population, beyond the secular climatic changes; mutations of disease micro-organisms and carriers, changing the ecological equilibrium between them and humans; improvement in medical technology, particularly when developed abroad; exchange of diseases through intensified contact between societies; acquisition of new foods which can be fitted into the existing productive system; and fluctuations in the infrastructure of security leading to alternation of periods of violence and anarchy and of peace (Guha 1981: 45). Such elements complicate the relationship, and are seen by some as more significant than the population/resources relationship.

The approach emphasising equilibrium takes a static perspective. A superficial analysis of particular histories suggests that typically societies were never at the stable equilibrium. There was overshooting and always a movement of population, upwards or downwards. Over time the equilibrium changes. Either the fertility or mortality schedule, or the carrying capacity of an economy, shifts, implying that an economy is never in equilibrium. The schedules change their position over time, meaning that equilibrium is never achieved. Whereas in Britain there may be clear evidence at different moments before the Industrial Revolution that fertility rises with income, in the period after the Industrial Revolution there is an inverse relationship: the birth schedule is clearly moving downwards. The equilibrium is a moving one, affected by factors other than the strictly economic. The static approach means that there is always an equilibrium level of population and income per head at which birth and death rates are equal, and population stable (Clark 2007: 26). Such an equilibrium is a stable one, if there is a downward-sloping mortality schedule – deaths fall with rising income – and an upward-sloping fertility schedule – births increase with rising income. The carrying capacity of a society then determines how many people there will be at this level of income. The level of income is a subsistence one, not a starvation one. A society with a high mortality and a low fertility schedule can have a relatively high subsistence income level, explaining why some societies appeared in the pre-modern period to have significantly different income levels. There is some confusion over the meaning of an equilibrium subsistence income. Fogel (2004) has noted the ambiguity. Rather than there being one level of subsistence, there are numerous levels which correspond to differing body sizes, notably height and weight. Smaller size means lower calorific needs and is consistent with a smaller food supply. It is possible, for example, to compare English and Japanese needs, taking account of the different sizes (Macfarlane 1997: 103–4).

A diagram of the subsistence ratio for labourers (that is, income/cost of a subsistence basket) shows a clear movement of most of Europe and Asia towards a subsistence level in the late eighteenth and early nineteenth century, that is towards a ratio of one (Allen 2006: 5). Britain moves in the opposite direction from a level of 3–4 which had prevailed for the period since the Black Death in the fourteenth century to the 5–6 in the nineteenth century.

During a Malthusian interval, per-capita food supply can fall below the subsistence level. Such a situation results in what Malthus referred to as positive checks, an increased prevalence of war, famine and disease, prompting the calling of such intervals *crises démographiques*, crises which periodically appear to have characterised all pre-modern economies. Large numbers of people died, and often simultaneously large numbers of births failed to occur. Mortality rates rose dramatically (to above 100, 200 or even 300 per 1000 of population). There might be a bunching of 'shocks', with war, famine and disease taking turns in acting as prime mover. During times of trouble, as they were called in societies like Russia, the resilience of societies to such shocks declined in a cumulative manner. China during the nineteenth century is seen as a society in the midst of such shocks. The demographic history of any pre-modern society was allegedly punctuated by such times of crisis. After a significant contraction of the population in another overshooting, there was an eventual renewal of the tendency of population to grow faster than resources when the smaller population saw its real consumption of food move well above subsistence. Improving living standards encourage an increased number of births and a decline in the number of deaths, notably infant and child deaths.[6] The number of births rises significantly above the number of deaths and population again begins to grow. There is therefore a cycle of population expansion and contraction, the length of the relevant periods varying by locality and time.

Malthus believed that preventive checks, such as contraception, abortion, delayed marriage, infanticide, the need for bridal dowries or periods of extended lactation, were too weak to change the relationship, preventing any society from controlling its population growth sufficiently to avoid periodic crises. Societies were incapable of controlling their fertility levels sufficiently to keep population within the size appropriate to the carrying capacity of the economy. Fertility rates were allegedly unresponsive to economic conditions, in some sense exogenous; women had as many children as was feasible, given conditions of health and social mores, although a large proportion of the children died young, even within the first year. The control of population came through periodically increased mortality rather than through a reduction in fertility.

If this view of demographic behaviour is linked with Ricardo's prediction of diminishing returns to the land, the prospect for economic development is a bleak one. Taking a production function approach, there is a fixed factor, land, with diminishing returns to the application of the other factor inputs, notably labour. In this context, land is a catch-all term for resources in general, not just foodstuffs. If population increases faster than the supply of agricultural land, there will be pressure not only on the availability of food, but on the supply of any land-intensive good, as for example timber, used for fuel and construction, or textile fibres. Even more important, the supply of feed for livestock, the main energy source in many pre-modern societies – whether within agriculture, transportation and even manufacturing – was limited by the supply of land. The size of population per unit of land is a proxy for the ratio of population to resources, but the quality of land for food production, its natural fertility, varies greatly from region to region. The productivity of the land may also increase as methods of production change. The Malthusian model assumes any tendency to an increase in productivity in the exploitation of the land would be modest, easily swamped by population change. Put in a dynamic context, as the supply of unexploited land runs out, following an increase in population, the rate of growth of agricultural output slows. In Boserup's words, the supply of food is inherently inelastic and this lack of elasticity is the main factor governing the rate of population growth (Boserup 1965: 11). As the labour to land ratio rises, the return from the additional units of factor input decline; there are diminishing returns. As the pressure on the supply of land increases, rents absorb an increasing share of the income generated by agricultural activity and of income in general, putting pressure on wages and profits. The fall in profits discourages investment in non-agricultural activities. The potential of both organisational and technical change to raise agricultural productivity is therefore considered extremely limited.

A major question arises: if the carrying capacity expands, for whatever reason, does this inevitably cause population to increase, if sometimes with a considerable time lag, so that the level of income can never rise above the subsistence level for more than a short period of time? For example, Chinese agriculture over the centuries has been characterised by a capacity to increase output, both as a result of greater intensity of cultivation – improved drainage, the introduction of new crops or multi-cropping – and as a result of an expanded area of production, mainly in the rice-growing south (Perkins 1969). This long-term increase in agricultural supply was associated with a parallel increase of population, not an increase in average output per head. Over the centuries, there was an impressive increase in agricultural output which resulted in the growth of Chinese population to the very high levels of today. Equilibrium population density rose simultaneously. Why did this occur? Was it a deliberate choice? Was it simply the case that the growth of agricultural output was never fast enough to release the Malthusian constraint? Clark argues that it is inherent in the logic of the Malthusian trap: in his words (2007: 32): 'In the pre-industrial world sporadic technological advance produced people, not wealth'.

Is all the pre-modern world Malthusian? Some argue that the constraint was eased in certain societies at dates well before the Industrial Revolution, notably in societies which were the pioneers in the inception of modern economic development. Such an argument might be combined with an interpretation of the inception of modern economic development as gradual. The obvious cases are Britain and Japan, but some argue that China also was in a very restricted sense Malthusian (Lee and Wang 1999). There is a significant literature showing that in these two societies fertility control kept population from expanding to exhaust the potential for an increase in output per head. This control, when combined with the changes which led to an improvement in productivity in the agricultural sector, shows a preparation of the relevant societies for the inception of modern economic development.

If Malthus is right, the transition to a situation in which population increases less than food supply and average income per head starts to rise significantly and persistently is unusual, the result of special circumstances. The obvious focus of interest is the nature of these circumstances. To explain the achievement of the release from the Malthusian trap, it is necessary to relax one, or both, of the main assumptions which underpin the theory – either the notion of a limit on the rate of productivity increase in agriculture, and in the rural sector in general, or the notion of the inability of any society to control its fertility rate. How and when were such relaxations achieved?

RELEASE FROM THE MALTHUSIAN CONSTRAINT

As described above, the Malthusian trap involves a situation of homeostasis, that is the existence of stable equilibrium levels of both income and population. There are mechanisms which return a system to the equilibrium levels when it departs from them, even if they are on occasion weak and the return delayed. In such a closed system, population size determines the level of income per capita, and the level of income determines the rate of change of population. Two issues arise – in what sense does the historical experience before modern economic development conform to a Malthusian world? The second question assumes a positive answer to the first – how is a release from the Malthusian constraints achieved?

The equilibrium level of income is not necessarily a subsistence level and the rate of growth of population zero, which is generally interpreted as the Malthusian position. Goldstone (2008: 72) is right in arguing that people did not typically live at death's door before the modern era. The equilibrium could involve low population density and high income (a low pressure system in the terminology of Wrigley and Schofield). This would be true, if fertility was relatively low, mortality high and the distribution of income uneven (with a high proportion going to rents and profits). The world might consist of regions characterised by different ratios of population to land and different equilibrium levels of income per head. Clark (2007: 49) notes that wages of the unskilled differ by as much as four to five times in Malthusian regimes, which he assumes existed in 1800. Inclusion of income on assets such as land or capital increases the disparities. There is no inconsistency with the Malthusian model.

Before the era of modern economic development, there are exceptions to the Malthusian situation. In a comprehensive comparative treatment of the demographic position of England and Japan, Macfarlane (1997: chapter 2) has shown a surprising, though not complete, absence of

Malthus's positive checks from the two islands, beginning at an early date.[7] Not only did *crises démographiques* involving war, famine and epidemic disease disappear, average mortality was low and longevity impressive by the standards of pre-modern societies. Typically, mortality rates in both England and Japan were well below the average rates of 35–50 per 1000 which characterise pre-modern societies. England may have had a rate of about 25 per 1,000, and Japan close to that figure, perhaps even lower. An even more important feature of the demographic history of these two societies is the ability to control fertility, albeit in different ways – in England largely through the varying incidence of, and date of entry into, marriage, Japan through changing level of abortion and infanticide and the cessation of child-bearing with widowhood. Before the inception of modern economic growth in England and Japan, fertility rates adjusted to economic circumstances, at levels close to mortality rates, but higher in better times. Lee and Wang (1999) have detected a similar tendency in China. The adjustment meant that income levels could be maintained well above starvation levels. Population expanded if economic conditions were advantageous, reinforcing a tendency to an acceleration in economic growth when it eventually began. In these two societies, preventive checks had become more important than positive checks. Some argue that all societies had the capacity to limit population growth and that England and Japan show how this could be achieved, either through limited access to marriage or through practices within marriage, including forced separation of spouses (Goldstone 2008: 75–6).

There is a second point important to the Malthusian argument. Not all income is absorbed by the consumption of food. There are goods and services unrelated to the needs of subsistence, in particular public goods. An increase in GDP per head may be largely captured by the government and result in the provision of improved government services, for example, those necessary to reduce risk levels, or provide law and order and transportation, health services and education. In such a situation, the increase in GDP per head does not result in a rise in fertility. It may result in a further rise in GDP per head because of externalities, the positive influences on investment of the provision of these services. In particular, there may be Smithian growth with the extension of the market, as government provides the relevant infrastructure. It is not irrelevant that England was the most heavily taxed country in Europe at the time of its inception of modern economic development (Goldstone 2008: 111; Hobson 2004, chapter 11).

Four important conclusions follow from this analysis. First, not all societies remained fully in the Malthusian trap. The two economic leaders in Europe and Asia had begun the release from the trap well before the inception of modern economic development, and others such as China wavered. The initial population surge in Britain at the traditional dating of the Industrial Revolution was largely a result of a rise in fertility. The higher mortality in urban than in rural areas postponed the revolution in mortality levels to the latter half of the nineteenth century when it was simultaneous with an improvement in living standards and an increase in average stature. Secondly, the demographic situation of the two forward societies is highly complex and they differ in the detailed way they achieved that release. They look similar in aggregate behaviour, even in their island home and temperate location, but the detail is different, as are the ways in which the chains of causation work – there is a lesson here for other aspects of the development model. The divergences between the two ranged from the relative absence of livestock in Japan to the nature of its housing, from the differing pattern of the incidence of disease, such as plague, to the prevalence of abortion and infanticide, from what was eaten and drunk in the two societies to the intensity of work, and also from the date of entry into marriage to the date of 'exit'. There is also the influence of the two different risk environments. Thirdly, the demography of England and Japan is relevant to the broadening of the concept of capital to include human capital. There is one straightforward gain, 'In 1800, women spent about 70 percent of their adult years bearing and rearing young children, but that fraction has decreased in many parts of the world to only about 14 percent, due to lower fertility and longer life' (Lee 2003: 167). Longer life expectations, more stable mortality rates, generally healthier populations have a dramatic effect on the supply of human capital and through that on productivity in the two societies, particularly in an age when physical labour was much more important than it is today. It is also possible to see a growing stress on quality rather than quantity of children. Fourthly, China shows how preventive checks, many similar to Japan's, can break down and positive checks reassert themselves.

China (Lee and Wang 1999) is an interesting variant on the Japanese experience. Here there was a collective control of fertility exercised through the family. The rates of abortion and infanticide were high, marriage was universal among women but not men, marital fertility was controlled and adoption of both males and females was common. The result was slow population growth and a sensitivity to economic circumstance. However, increasing economic opportunity, notably on the frontier, released the control during the seventeenth and eighteenth centuries when population growth accelerated – possibly pushing China into a Malthusian crisis in the nineteenth century. All controls vanished after the revolution and population reached a dramatically high rate until a different kind of collective control, exercised by state and party, appeared – the policy of one child per family. The Chinese experience is similar in some regards to the Japanese, but shows that control is everywhere possible but the Malthusian trap never far away.

Such an analysis makes it likely that the Malthusian homeostasis is weaker than sometimes assumed, operating only over the long term (Lee 1987), or it may not exist at all. However, the release is critical. The release of the two main Malthusian constraints occurred in a number of ways. The first release consists in a sustained increase in the supply of food and of other resources, one which ran ahead of the increase in population. The second release is an increased ability and desire to restrain fertility and therefore the rate of growth of population. The two were linked.

One line of argument links technical and organisational change directly with population pressure. When population rises beyond the ability of current technology to support it, people are induced – even forced – to innovate, a variant of the challenge and response approach to economic development, which sees resource deficiencies in a positive light, as the driving force of innovation and productivity increase. For example, in the words of Hirschman (2004: 5), 'The pressures of growing populations have probably stimulated large scale migration around the globe, the origins and spread of agriculture, the shortening of the fallow, irrigation, and most other development that we associate with civilisation in traditional pre-industrial societies'. The argument is applied not just to the agricultural sector (Boserup 1965, 1981) but to all parts of the economy (Wilkinson 1973). In the words of Wilkinson, 'Development is needed when society outgrows its resources-base and productive system' (Wilkinson 1973: 5). According to Wilkinson, a major disturbance to the ecological equilibrium, expressed in pressure on the natural environment, is what prompts economic development.

There are two ways in which the supply of food was expanded. The first is by raising the productivity of land already in use, the second by tapping supplies of land not previously exploited, notably outside the relevant region, even abroad. The chance of release was usually regarded as low because the degree of possible agricultural expansion was underestimated and the capacity of an economy to provide a regular and plentiful supply of food underrated. In practice, there were no diminishing returns. Both organisational and technical change was strong enough to cause agricultural output to rise at a significant rate, although still not fast enough to meet all the demands of a developing economy. An agricultural revolution began in England well before the Industrial Revolution, most obviously in the late seventeenth and early eighteenth centuries, although there is a tendency to exaggerate the amount of productivity increase, which appears to be about 20–30 per cent (Overton 1996). The forward economics could rely on both a more productive domestic agriculture and an increased supply from outside. It was touch and go in Britain in the release from the Malthusian trap since the share of industrial output exported rose dramatically, to 49 per cent in 1831 (Cuenca Esteban 1997 and Findlay and O'Rourke 2007: 330) in order to make possible imports of food and raw materials, and prices fall dramatically (Crafts 2004: 11 and Imlah 1958: 94–6). In 1868, at the time of the Meiji restoration, Japan had an agriculture already the most productive in Asia.

Not only has the food supply in a typical developed economy run ahead of population growth, but this holds at the world level, so that individual countries do not have to rely on their own agriculture for the necessary supply of food; they can either export people – as in nomad movements on the steppe in response to drought or in the great exodus of Europeans to new areas of settlement, or import food and other resources required as inputs in the process of modern economic development. They exchange goods and services they themselves produce for food, although the continuation of protection for the agricultural sector today shows how nervous the governments of different countries are about such a dependence. The biggest boost to supply came from the opening up of new areas of supply abroad, in particular, but not only, in the so-called Neo-Europes, areas of European settlement in temperate regions, such as North America and Australasia, but including parts of Latin America. The sources of supply included Eastern Europe and tropical areas in Africa, Central America and Asia. Eastern Europe provided timber, livestock products, furs, even honey, and increasingly grain to the more populated parts of Europe. The plantation economies provided products which could not be produced easily or cheaply in Europe, either because of climatic infelicities or because of shortages of labour; sugar is the best example, but tea or tobacco also qualify.

In the regions of European settlement, agriculture became much more extensive, using relatively little labour and a lot of land and capital: it was characterised by high productivity per worker, but low productivity per unit of land, certainly relative to the old centres of population in Europe and Asia, where much more intensive forms of agriculture prevailed. Economic development consists in a widespread application of land-saving technologies which use either labour or capital more intensely than previous technologies and substitute them for land. In the old centres of Eurasia, there was a bias in innovation which reduced the importance of resources in general. This is true even within agriculture, where typically today the contribution of land to agricultural production is estimated to have dropped to about 10 per cent (Lee 1987: 458). The main contributors are capital and technical change. It is interesting to consider how far such a bias was induced by the factor endowments of different regions of the world. It is logical to substitute when increasing scarcity raises the price of a factor, in this case land, notably where there is the expectation of such a movement of prices continuing into the future (Habbakuk 1962). In Asian rice cultivation, the relatively abundant labour was substituted for both land and, where possible, capital. Yields per hectare were extremely high, supporting a dense population. Moreover, there were insignificant economies of scale, unlike in European agriculture. Over a long period of time, there was also considerable capital investment in water control and terracing to make the maximum use of scarce land. In European agriculture there was more emphasis on livestock and equipment. New crop rotations increased the usefulness of previously marginal land. In North America, where labour was scarce, land abundant capital was substituted for labour. Highly mechanized methods, such as the cotton gin and later harvesting machinery, were introduced. The rapid growth of population in frontier areas reflected the creation of a new homeostasis in the settler societies, one characterised initially by high fertility and low mortality rates, and a Boserupian response to the population pressure in Europe itself. Sometimes the improvements in transportation and extension of the cultivated area caused the supply of basic foodstuffs, such as grain, to run ahead of population, as it did in the 1870s and 1880s, when transport improvement gave a major impetus to supply on world markets and agricultural prices fell dramatically.

The best-known innovation of the Industrial Revolution is the change in the nature of energy used in most human activities, away from organic sources which indirectly require the products of the land, to non-organic sources, initially to water and wind exploited by mills, eventually to carbon fuels, the products of coal mines and oil or gas fields which require much less land, although the deposits are finite in supply. Timber as a construction material and as a fuel declined in importance, as did tallow as a lighting source, as first whale oil, then oil and electricity, were adopted. Late in the process of modern economic development, natural fibres were replaced by artificial fibres. All of these changes were massively resource-saving.

Nor are food needs infinitely elastic. The income elasticity of demand for food at higher levels of income is low. There is an obvious limit on the food one person can consume. The contribution of agriculture and the rural sector to both the level and growth of GDP has been much reduced with the process of economic development. The first phase of modern economic development involved the rise of the secondary sector of the economy – manufacturing, and the associated decline in agriculture and the primary sector. The second brought the rise of services. Within a modern economy, agriculture, and the rural sector in general, contributes only a small share of output and employs a very small proportion of the labour force. The influence of population density on incomes has become insignificant.

The other release from the Malthusian constraint involves the response of rates of population growth to income levels. Recently, the ability of a society to control fertility rates has moved into the spotlight. There has been a strongly perverse response of fertility to income increase; far from increasing, the rate has declined. Fertility rates have a relationship with income per head, which becomes negative at higher levels of income per capita, and often even at lower levels of income for late starters in economic development. For example, after the acceleration in economic growth, fertility decline has been much quicker in East and South Asia than in Europe. The relationship between the rate of population change and the level of income, resulting from changing mortality and fertility rates, is an inverted u-shaped one. After an initial acceleration, reflecting mainly a fall in mortality rates, the rate of growth of population in developed economies has slowed as fertility rates fall with rising income levels.

The reasons for the fall in fertility are complex, although there is a clear association with rising income. Mason (1997: 443–4) puts forward six arguments, ranging from modern economic development itself to the diffusion of birth control information. All are deemed incomplete. Economists put forward a model consistent with the assumptions of neoclassical economics (Easterlin 2004: chapters 6 and 7). It is assumed that deliberate choices are made by the key decision makers in the relevant households. There are three relevant variables. The first is the natural rate of fertility – the number of children which an average woman has in any given society, a number less than the maximum biologically possible. There are various relevant factors: the health of the mother, affecting the possibility of conception and of coming to a full term; social practices such as lactation, influencing the possibility of pregnancy; and the survival rate of children. A second variable is the desired level of fertility or target number of children. In the conventional economic analysis, this is influenced by income, prices (costs) and tastes. It is assumed that higher income means a greater demand for children – in the parlance of the economist, they are a normal good – and lower income a desire to reduce the desired number of children.

In modern times, there is an obvious increase in the cost of children, as they have become dependent on their parents for a longer period, and with economic development, a diminishing real price of other consumer goods. Children have become a relatively expensive consumer good, since they do not work for most of their childhood and are increasingly involved in tertiary education. The opportunity cost of the time spent in child bearing and rearing has increased with the changing nature of employment and

the rising opportunities for women (Lee 2003: 174).There is a clear preference for other consumer goods, particularly those which have appeared or
become much cheaper with economic development and for which there is a
high income elasticity of demand. One theory points to a shift in emphasis
in the investment of time and resources from the quantity of children to
their quality (Becker 1968). Parents are more prepared to invest in the children they have, particularly as they are much more likely to survive. This is
represented as a significant change in tastes. Tastes may involve preferences
which differ from society to society and over time, for example a desire
for a higher quality of children rather than a greater quantity. The final
variable is the cost of fertility control, whether psychological or economic.
Contraceptive methods are much more developed and acceptable today
than used to be the case, but most commentators believe this is not a causative factor – it is only an instrument which allows much more control if that
control is desired. However, there is a cost in using the methods of fertility
control. Since for most pre-modern societies the actual number of children
often fell short of the desired number, there was no incentive to control
fertility. As mortality and morbidity declined, this ceased to be true, since
the natural rate of fertility rose and infant mortality declined significantly.
Even if there was no decline in the desired number of children, the increase
in surviving children created an incentive to reduce fertility. The costs of fertility control mean that actual and desired rates were not equal. The second
factor is linked and relates to the role of women. The emancipation of
women has highlighted the tensions between making a career and caring for
children. The extension of education, particularly of women, seems to have
speeded up the decline in fertility. Countries which put an emphasis on the
education of women tend to see their fertility rates declining more quickly,
notably communist countries. Women are less likely to get married, they
are more likely to remain childless, they start having children later and they
have fewer children. The desired number of children has fallen.

Mason argues that the regulation of fertility is similar in pre-transitional
and post-transitional populations (Mason 1997: 447). There are small
pre-modern societies in which social controls successfully limit fertility.
In some large societies which have modernised, as far apart as Britain or
Japan, fertility has always adjusted to economic circumstances. There is
significant evidence of the ability of such societies to adjust their fertility
levels to suit economic circumstances and to take an increase in output in
the form of an improvement in output per head (Wrigley 2004). The main
feedback effect in England acts through the crude rate of first marriage,
which moves with real wage rates (Wrigley 2004: 77–9), a relationship
dating back to the sixteenth century and the beginning of parish registra-
tion of marriages, prompting Wrigley to comment that subsistence crises

in England, even in the sixteenth century, had a greater impact on nuptiality and fertility than on mortality (Wrigley 2004; 79). Wrigley (2004: 94–5) argued that the preventive check was much more influential than the positive check in early modern England and suggested that the mechanism through which this occurred involved the need for resources for newly weds to create separate households and the flexibility of an increasingly capitalist agriculture in expelling labour which did not produce a return above its marginal cost. There is a tendency to see demographic behaviour as differing across Europe (Hajnal 1982). The dominance of a structure of preventive or positive checks and of different family types reflects different attitudes to, and the prevalence of, different environments of risk, in the different regions of Europe. The general argument is that the West was much more likely to control fertility than the East. A study done by Galloway (1988: 297), excluding the east and south of Europe, shows fertility to be highly sensitive to grain price fluctuations in most of pre-industrial Europe, with a similar responsiveness across all countries and all periods, whereas the responsiveness of mortality rates varies according to the level of economic development, with England hardly affected at all.

Macfarlane classifies control through three sets of variables – intercourse, conception and gestation variables. The first refers to when sexual relations occur, notably whether a woman marries and when that marriage 'ends'. The second relates to the conditions of work and nutrition and other relevant factors which affect the possibility of conception, such as the use of contraception and the period of lactation. Gestation raises the possibility of abortion or infanticide. The control of fertility operates through the influence of social attitudes and arrangements in each of these three areas, the mix varying from one society to another.

When was the Malthusian constraint eased? This means asking when and where the relevant productivity increase in the rural sector of a particular society occurred, and when and in what conditions societies became able to limit their population expansion. The demographic history of each society, even of different socio-economic groups, is unique and combines relevant factors in a kaleidoscopic mix which requires individual narratives to take account of the particularities of time and place. The explanations of fertility decline are particularly difficult to pin down without careful study of the relevant society. As one commentator has written, 'Low fertility has multiple causes, and convincing explanations may read like country-specific social histories' (Morgan 2003: 598), or another, 'In my opinion, the way out of this unhappy situation is to assume from the start that different fertility declines will have different causes. The goal is then to understand the circumstances under which different causes are likely to operate' (Mason 1997: 446).

The economic model, expanded to take account of factors which demographers and sociologists have drawn attention to, assists in the telling of analytic narratives, by indicating what variables are relevant and how the relevant variables might interact. One of the difficulties in identifying general demographic tendencies is that major events, such as climate change, war and economic depression, which are not directly related to the key relationships discussed above, distort and hide the long-term tendencies to demographic change. It is possible, and important, to take different time perspectives in studying demography, to stand back and to distinguish once more ultimate and proximate causation. There was a release from Malthusian constraints which may have its origins earlier than we think, but became dramatic in the late nineteenth century after a critical period of transition.

THE DEMOGRAPHIC TRANSITION TO THE MODERN REGIME

Sometimes called a theory, the demographic transition is in reality a description of demographic behaviour during the transition to modern economic development (Lee 2003). A theory explores the nature of causation, which is not achieved in most of the work on the demographic transition, but the demographic transition has remained a popular way of expressing a number of robust empirical tendencies in demographic behaviour, both before and after the inception of modern economic development. It claims to have a descriptive universality, although there are deviations from the simple model. For example, the birth rate in France began its descent much earlier than in other European countries, early during the transition phase itself, in the process much reducing the proportion of European population which was French. There was the same decline in the rural sector in the USA.

There are three main stages in the transition – the traditional regime, the transition itself and the modern regime. The traditional regime is a catch-all construct which hides more than it reveals. It is characterised as Malthusian, that is, by a slow rate of population growth approaching zero. Both birth rates and death rates are typically high, usually well above 30 per 1000, but not very far apart. Even a very slow rate of increase, sustained over a long period of time, yielded large absolute increases in population. The relevant expansion concealed periodic reversals, varying in scope, during which population contracted suddenly and sometimes dramatically. Demographic crises punctuated the history of pre-modern societies, sometimes initiated by exogenous shocks such as climate change

(Fagan 2008). Because of high child mortality, the fertility rates needed to reproduce the population had to exceed by a significant amount the gross reproduction rate of about 2.1 needed today.

During the transition, the periodic mortality crises cease. Typically, the average death rate begins to decline significantly, whereas after a temporary rise the birth rate remains steady at about its traditional level and only starts to decline much later. The two rates increasingly diverge, with birth rates of 30 per 1000 and above, and death rates declining to half that rate and the rate of population growth accelerating to an unprecedented level, usually at least 2 per cent, but in some cases as high as 3 per cent per year, representing an ability of a society to double its numbers in a period as short as 20 or so years. The modern regime sees the birth rate follow the death rate down so that eventually both are at or below 10 per 1000. The difference between mortality and fertility rates narrows and the rate of population slows to what it had been under the traditional regime, beginning a contraction in an increasing number of societies.

The dating of the phases and the speed with which a society moves through the three stages vary enormously. The process of transition appears to have accelerated over time. Asian societies are moving much more quickly through the transition and into the modern regime than did Europe. This may be linked with high levels of population density and rapidly rising income levels, but societies which lack both also appear to be beginning the transition. Some theorists see a two phase reduction in fertility (van de Kaa 2002). The first, affecting developed economies, started as early as the nineteenth century, allegedly reflecting mainly a response to falling mortality. The second phase is more recent, but more rapid – it began in the 1960s on most accounts. It is seen as closely associated with changes occurring in the nature of the family and of the household – with rising divorce rates and co-partnership outside marriage, and with a highly individual desire for self-fulfilment. The emancipation of women has speeded up the transition.

Some theorists include migration in the theory, since the rate of population growth in a particular country is determined by net migration as well as fertility and mortality rates. Population movements have been stimulated by climatic change, notably drought, and by a high ratio of population to land, particularly when agriculture was being commercialised and its productivity rising. During the transitional phase, many societies experiencing a rapid acceleration in population growth find themselves with a 'surplus' population. Much of Europe fits this profile. A rise in net emigration was a consequence. As many as 50 million migrants left Europe between 1846 and 1932 (van de Kaa 2002: 3), which helped keep income per head rising. By contrast, the modern regime can be characterised by emerging labour shortages, depending on the level of demand for labour and its growth, and net emigration becomes net immigration. Again many European countries illustrate the point, with an increasing number of both legal and illegal immigrants, difficult to stop within an extended European Union.

The changes in rates during these stages imply significant changes in the age structure of the relevant populations, including shifts in dependency ratios which are important economically. The most dramatic feature of the modern regime is the decline in birth rates. Although it is possible biologically for a woman to have as many as 15–17 children, typically in undeveloped economies the total fertility rate has reached 6 or a little above. In some countries, for example Ethiopia or Saudi Arabia, the rate is still 4 or 5, although the rate has declined significantly during the period of modern economic development. For the most developed, the decline is very large. For as many as 60 countries today, with 43 per cent of the world's population, fertility rates are below the 2.1 replacement level (Lee 2003: 175). In some cases, the replacement level was reached as early as the 1960s (Japan, Hungary and Latvia). The rate is as low as 1.1 (Bulgaria), but is commonly below 1.5. The average for Europe is 1.4 and for East Asia 1.8, and has been at this level for some time (Lee 2003: 168), with the median individual now living in a country with a rate of 2.3 (Lee 2003: 178). Even in countries with high rates of immigration, which tends to keep down the average age of population as well as bringing migrants with attitudes established in their source society, the native-born population have rates which have slipped below 2 (Australia at 1.8). For countries which are not immigrant friendly, such a reduction implies a contraction of population, if it persists.

It takes time for these changes to have an effect on the total size of population, that is, to work through all the different age cohorts in that population. At first, there is after any reduction a significant but temporary change in the age structure of the population. With a one-off change in demographic behaviour, it takes a generation before the impact of these changes works itself out in a change in the age structure and the population regains a stability of structure. When fertility rates decline, there is an initial effect which is beneficial to the growth of GDP, even per capita GDP, since the proportion of the population which is dependent falls and the proportion of the working population rises. This is often described as a demographic gift or bonus (Lee 2003: 182). Such an effect has contributed significantly to the rapid growth of a number of Asian countries where the fall in fertility has been rapid. In some countries, the fall in child dependency has more than countered the rise in dependency resulting from the ageing of the population. However, the beneficial effect is reversed when the smaller cohorts reach working age. This effect is reflected in changes in the participation rate of the relevant populations, that is, the proportion of the population engaged in paid work. Equally, with no change in retirement age, an increase in longevity resulting from a decline in mortality rates has the effect of increasing the dependency ratio, with a negative impact on economic growth rates.

Malthus was definitely right in one respect. The relationship between modern economic development and demographic change is two-way; economic development affects population change, but population change influences economic development. Unhappily neither influence is simple – both are complex and probably specific to particular societies. The general impact of modern economic development on demography is non-linear, with an initially stimulatory influence followed by a clearly negative one. During the process of modern economic development, initially there may be a positive feedback from income growth, with fertility rates rising and mortality rates falling. There is eventually a negative feedback from output and income growth to population growth through the fall in fertility rates. Economic development solves the population problem in some countries by significantly reducing fertility rates, although the implied increase in demand for resources means that the relationship may continue as important. If we assume continuing economic development and a continuing negative relationship with population growth, the pressure of increased population on resources is going to ease. The consequence of falling fertility has been to lead to predictions of maximum world population which are both significantly lower and earlier than formerly predicted. The influence of declining fertility on age structure is magnified by increasing longevity, which on one account indicates an increase in female longevity of 2.4 years per decade, or 3 months per year, from 1840 to 2000 (Oeppen and Vaupel 2002: 1029), 'the most remarkable regularity of mass endeavour ever observed' (ibid.).[8]

The reverse relationship, the longer-term influence of demography on economic development, is controversial. In the early stages of economic development, the growth of population stimulates that development through a number of positive influences – the growth of the market for most products, the stimulus given to investment, particularly through the rate of new household formation, and the expansion in labour supply, which keeps down the cost of labour but also increases its mobility. The stress today is on the negative influences – on the pressure exerted on resources and the damage done to the environment. However, there has never been a case of successful economic development which has occurred in the context of a contracting population. Some of the countries experiencing a fall in fertility represent experiments in the ability of a society to adjust to a declining labour force and to the impact of contracting population on demand. Japan is a pioneer case.

NEO-MALTHUSIANISM

Neoclassical economists have ignored the resources input into economic development, largely because of the resource-saving nature of modern technology. One view, a popular one, is that a slow but persistent accumulation of capital enabled Europeans to win the contest and to ultimately emancipate themselves from the Malthusian threat (Komlos 1989: 204). It can be put another way: the strategy of family multiplication is now replaced by a strategy of technological improvement (Snooks 1996). Resource-saving technical progress has the same effect as expanding the supply of natural resources – in the terminology of neoclassical economics, it is resource-augmenting technical progress. Boserupian episodes are superimposed on the Malthusian model, and eventually dominate. This argument has prompted Komlos to write, 'The industrial revolution . . . can be conceptualized as a breakout of the Malthusian demographic regime' (Komlos 1989: 203) – now a popular point of view. The more sophisticated Malthusian models focus on an incessant contest between population growth and society's resource base, which now includes reproducible as well as natural capital (Komlos 1989: 193). It is argued that natural capital can be substituted by reproducible capital. Such capital comprises human capital and knowledge, in addition to the usual physical capital (Komlos 1997: 200).

But has the day of reckoning simply been postponed? Recent work has brought the Malthusian trap back into the narrative of economic development. The modern environmental movement holds views similar to those of Malthus, and as pessimistic. Malthusian models of the interaction between population and resources are as popular today as they were at the time of Malthus. The volume *The Limits to Growth* (Meadows et al. 1972) and its update *Beyond the Limits* (1992) forecast a Malthusian crisis in the near future, although the latter was much less specific about the dating than the former. Current concerns about global warming and the impact of economic development on the environment of the world emphasise the possible hubris of statements such as those made above, stressing release from the Malthusian trap. Has the negative contribution of the using up of natural capital begun to outpace the positive one of the accumulation of reproducible capital? There are those who argue that Malthus was right about the constraint on population imposed by limited resources, although not necessarily in the form of a limited supply of food. Increased productivity has only postponed the assertion of the resource constraint. Diminishing returns will reassert themselves at some point in the not very distant future. Modern economic development has simply delayed the imposition of the constraint.

It is possible to include land in the production function as a fixed factor of production, one displaying the usual diminishing returns (Jones 2008: chapter 9), and to add a term for the consumption of exhaustible natural resources, notably oil, gas or coal, but also other minerals such as copper, bauxite, iron ore, coal. The rate of depletion of non-renewable resources lowers growth in proportion to the share of these resources in production. It is possible to estimate a drag on growth caused by resource problems. In the words of Jones, '. . . there is a fundamental race between technological progress on the one hand and the growth drag associated with fixed and non-renewable resources on the other' (Jones 2002: 189). And it appears that up to today technological progress is winning the race. Surprisingly, both the factor income share of natural resources and the ratio of the price of most resources to the average hourly wage have declined significantly, suggesting that resources are not becoming scarce relative to labour, but relatively more plentiful. This is probably the result of resource-augmenting technological change. The market valuation of resources indicates that the finite supply of resources is not seen as a major impediment to economic growth. The perception may be wrong.

Nordhaus (1992: 12) has explored the nature of four potentially damaging conditions, which are types of Malthusian crisis, using neoclassical assumptions to articulate the problems. The first is the pure Malthusian model in which the rate of growth of population changes with the level of income and the equilibrium income is at subsistence level – this is the main focus of this chapter. The second is the exhaustion of an essential resource like oil or gas, with an assumption of a lack of substitutability. There has been significant concern that the natural capital of the world is being used up. Deposits of energy or raw material are finite, as are aquifers. Modern farming techniques may be dissipating the top soil, with the thick black soil of the prairies of the USA thinning and, in dry areas, desertification occurring as soil is blown or washed away. The share of total income absorbed by expenditure on a depleting resource rises to one as its price goes up and the rate of growth of the economy converges on the rate at which the essential resource is used up, whatever it is. The third condition is the classical case of diminishing returns to land, in which land is essential to survival, again assumed as having no substitute, and eventually takes all income. The resulting rate of growth in the extreme case is minus the rate of population growth. The best that can be achieved is a zero rate of economic growth achieved in conditions of zero population growth.

The fourth introduces an externality such as global warming, neglected in the previous three cases. The case is similar to the latter two if there is a pollution flow linked with increased output. A variant of this argument points to the building up of a stock of pollutant, for example, carbon dioxide, and the existence of a threshold beyond which the effects become irreversible and catastrophic.

Nordhaus (1992: 16) emphasises that the reassertion of the Malthusian constraint is an empirical matter, not a theoretical one. It depends on a set of actual figures for the level of reserves of scarce resources, the contribution of resources to GDP, the rate of substitutability between the factors, notably capital and land, and the rate and nature of technical change. Using a Cobb-Douglas production function and realistic data yields an annual growth drag of about 0.3 per cent, that is, a permanent reduction of about 7 per cent in annual income, although with other production functions, the figure is lower. This led Nordhaus to conclude, '. . . for the past two centuries, technology has been the clear victor in the race with depletion and diminishing returns' (Nordhaus 1992: 38). Weitzman (1999: 706) has produced a similarly small figure for the drag from the finiteness of resources, about 1 per cent of consumption, but recognises that this reflects the market valuation of the resource and therefore the ability of market participants to recognise a growing scarcity.

This account ignores possible externalities which might result, for example, from global warming. Humans are seen as indirectly damaging the natural environment through their economic activities. The process of using up particular carbon fuels is creating a cost which is not captured by private cost, although the size of the cost is uncertain, both in aggregate and for particular organisations and individuals. The costs of such activity are seen as rising dramatically and as offsetting any productivity gains. The continuing increase in the size of world population and the rise in consumption by that population puts pressure on the environment, notably by the impact of carbon emissions on global warming. The divergence of social costs from private costs may be significant, but it is likely to vary across the world and is very difficult to measure. The complexity of the chains of cause and effect is large. The impact of both broad changes, for example, sea level rises, and narrow changes, such as variations in microclimates, is very uncertain. There are particular adjustment problems which may or may not be large – it is not one new to humankind (see the impact of a previous global warming, between 700 and 1300, and a subsequent cooling, on the distribution of human economic activity – Fagan 2008).

There are two approaches to this problem. One assumes no action is taken and attention is directed at handling the impact of warming on economic activities. There is an increased cost to be borne and distributed. The second assumes counter-action is taken, which in an extreme case prevents any warming due to human activity and estimates the cost of the counter-action. Such a cost is distributed in some way among countries. In practice, it is highly likely that the two will be combined, with some adjustment costs associated with both warming and action taken to avoid the more extreme possibilities of warming.

If the decline in birth rates is as robust as it presently appears, the increase in world population will be much more modest than previously thought and the date of peaking much earlier, both of which elements will reduce the pressure on resources and potential carbon emissions. If the relationship with income levels is as strong as appears, faster economic growth will accelerate the decline in the rate of population increase, paradoxically easing the pressure on resources. There is evidence that the decline in fertility is accelerating. From these arguments, it is likely that preventive checks will allow the world to avoid the positive checks which Limits 1 predicted (Nordhaus 1992: 6). There are multiple equilibria conforming to different mixes of economic output growth and population increase. As the strategy of family multiplication is exhausted, the strategy of technological improvement can help keep the Malthusian trap open. Exhaustion is reached when pursuit of that strategy imposes an excessive stress on resource availability. A crisis in any society can result from the pushing of a strategy to a point at which the return does not cover the cost.[9]

12. Continuity and discontinuity: the meaning of the Industrial Revolution

> A revolution in men's access to the means of life, in control of their ecological environment, in their capacity to escape from the tyranny and niggardliness of nature . . . it opened the road for men to complete mastery of their physical environment, without the inescapable need to exploit each other. (Perkin 1969: 3–5, quoted by Mokyr 1999: 6)

The main focus of this book is the process by which modern economic development has been initiated. It is therefore illuminating to consider the nature of an analytic narrative of the pioneer experience, the British Industrial Revolution.[1] The first transition is unique, if only because the existence of a prior inception colours all later experiences, notably through demonstration effects and competitive pressures. In the absence of an industrial revolution in Britain, the inception would probably have occurred elsewhere, in France, the USA or Japan, for example. It is necessary to explore the ways in which that inception occurs, to see what is shared with others, and to consider how far the pioneer model, or models, were diffused to other economies. Are there patterns of development, and different narratives, which would support the notion of convergence clubs? One issue of particular interest is the differing mix of revolutionary and evolutionary elements of change.

The first section considers the nature of a grand narrative for a general account of modern economic development. It explores a number of statements of the main empirical tendencies associated with modern economic development, often referred to as stylised facts. The second section focuses on the British Industrial Revolution and the currently held interpretation of the pioneer experience. The next section considers the elements of continuity and discontinuity in modern economic development in the context of a distinction between proximate and ultimate causation. The final section analyses the way in which economic development diffused, judging the degree to which the process developed independently in different countries, and the possible patterns of economic development which can be identified in the historical record.

THEORY, HISTORY AND THE STYLIZED FACTS

A grand narrative seeks to embrace the total experience of all economies which have successfully developed, putting in context the role of the leading economy, particularly in so far as it represents an exemplar for others. There is often an assumption that the followers will in some way repeat that experience. Such big history places the inception of modern economic development in a long-term and global perspective. It is often dominated by a meta-narrative reflecting a particular aspect of economic development – ecological, demographic, technological, or institutional/cultural – and interprets the experience of economic history in that light.[2] Of its nature it is bound to be incomplete, but often theory-rich and a critical part of a grand narrative. In its simplest form, neoclassical theory lends itself to a grand narrative in that it concentrates on an aggregative perspective relevant to the lead economy. It assumes a single long-term steady-state equilibrium growth path. The economic histories of Britain, and then the USA, represent that path, the latter growing out of that of the former, but with critical differences. This is the actual path only for the leader economy; for others, it is the counterfactual alternative to which they are converging. The neoclassical grand narrative has at its centre a long-term equilibrium growth path which is approached in an infinite variety of ways – some revolutionary, some evolutionary. The grand narrative is a global one, but not one in which a single experience is endlessly repeated. For the narrator, a grand narrative emerges from an iteration between what has been christened big history and particular narratives at lower levels. The most appropriate narrative to tell is at the level of the nation state, although narratives are also told at the level of a region, an enterprise and even an entrepreneur. The economic history of individual countries is still being told, and in some cases in a most instructive manner (Feinstein 2005), stressing the uniqueness of the experience.

The grand narrative must include an explanation of the inception of modern economic development.[3] There are two contrasting interpretations of the beginning of modern economic development, which highlight two highly critical issues – the degree of discontinuity and the independence of relevant experiences. One sees the transition as rapid and dramatic, in a historical perspective almost instantaneous, and certainly discontinuous. This is summarised in the notion of a 'take-off' (Rostow 1965), an industrialising spurt (Gerschenkron 1962) or simply the inception of modern economic development (Kuznets 1965); we can call this the revolutionary interpretation. The second places the transition in a different time perspective. The transition takes centuries rather than decades, certainly significantly longer than implied in any notional 'take-off'. The movement from the traditional into the modern stage is almost imperceptible and difficult to date. We can call this the evolutionary interpretation. It is almost impossible in such a narrative to date precisely the transition. Typically, in both narratives there is acceptance of the notion of a three-stage transition to modern economic development – pre-modern, the transition and modern – sometimes explicitly (Voth 2003) and sometimes implicitly (Jones 1987 and 1988, Mokyr 1999 and 2004)). Sometimes the transition is divided into different phases, determined by the relationship between output growth and population increase (Galor 2004).

There are good reasons to believe that the same model does not fit everybody. The first transition creates an impulse for others to make later transitions, but also makes necessary an adjustment in the original pattern of development and policy to accommodate the previous success of the pioneer(s). Diffusion models stress the transfer of ideas, technologies, institutions, commodities, capital and even labour from the early starters; the pressures to respond resulting from increased competition in key markets, if they exist; and the demonstration effects resulting from the evidence of prior development, which range from military defeats to the envy of conspicuous consumption elsewhere. Late starters are in a position to benefit from the pool of knowledge already available, and from other inputs such as investment funds and intermediate products. There are definite advantages in being second, third or even the twenty-third mover, in the sense of achieving more rapid economic growth. The Asian Economic Miracle has certainly involved rates of economic growth way above those achieved in the European miracle, and in most cases a distinct acceleration in the rate of economic growth in individual countries.[4] The scale of the modern economic development in Asia is much larger than anything experienced in the West, including the USA and the neo-Europes. Populations in Asia are numbered in billions rather than millions.

As a consequence, the relevant narratives change in a patterned way (O'Brien and Keyder 1978, Gerschenkron 1962 and 1968). There are two ways in which the petty narratives can diverge from the grand narrative. First, there is the variation occurring on the transition path to the long-term equilibrium path. Each path is unique. Once one economy has made the transition to modern economic development, it changes the context for all who follow. The pioneer is a model, but a model with variants which might diverge increasingly from the original model. Secondly, the unique nature of the transition affects the long-term growth rate to which the transitional rate is converging. These narratives can be grouped into those which share similarities, that is, the economies belonging to convergence clubs.

The process of modern economic development is a two-phase process in which there is an initial shift from a concentration on the agricultural sector of the economy to the manufacturing sector – the real industrial revolution, and later a shift from manufacturing to services, which we can call the service revolution. There is also a robust U-shaped relationship between the level of concentration of economic activity and the level of income per head (Imbs and Wacziarg 2003). Economies grow through two stages. First, sectoral diversification increases, until annual income per head, measured in 1985 purchasing power parity (PPP) exchange rates, reaches a relatively high level of about $9000, a medium level of economic development. At this point, the degree of concentration begins to rise, but not yet reaching the starting levels of concentration, which reflected the influence of the initial resource endowments. Such an empirical tendency has all sorts of implications for the role of trade in growth and for the control of risk, assuming that a more diverse economy is less vulnerable to external shocks.

It is possible to generalise about the overall experience of modern economic development. Such a generalisation helps place the pioneer experience in a broader context and assists our understanding of the process of modern economic development. The term stylised facts is used to describe the main empirical tendencies in modern economic development. This is very much a generalisation influenced by the presuppositions of neoclassical growth theory. There are two issues which need to be raised. First, there is the authenticity of those tendencies – are they, in the words of Bairoch (1993), simply myths, incorrect knowledge of history shared by economists and others?[5] Secondly, even if they are true, why are they significant? Their articulation says that modern economic development has occurred in a certain way, with certain regularities of economic behaviour which must be explained in any theory of how economic development itself unfolds. They are important both in showing the way economists interpret the world and in indicating how the relevant theory might be tested. They are identified with the aid of theory, but also provide the basic framework with which any theory must be consistent. These facts reflect the state of relevant data. They most often refer to the period of modern economic development. They sometimes refer to all of history and to aggregates and take a world perspective. They are thereby supportive of the notion of a grand narrative, providing possible core elements.

Lipsey, Carlaw and Bekar (2005: 296) make the following generalisations about the broad sweep of economic history, which represent a general consensus. Since the Neolithic Revolution, there has been an enormous amount of extensive growth, albeit at a slow pace. Most of the extensive growth has gone to support an increase in population, and only to a much smaller extent to a rise in living standards. This is shown by the very significant growth in world population over the long term. There are reversals, sometimes lasting as long as several centuries, for example around the end of the Bronze Age or at the dissolution of the Western Roman Empire. There have been long periods of intensive growth, some lasting several hundred years, but the evidence for this is indirect. The introduction of major new technologies was invariably followed by bursts of population increase. The development of the civilisations of Mesopotamia and of the classical civilisations of Greece and Rome fit the bill. It appears that there have been both a number of long waves of growth, ultimately reversed, and many short episodes, both extensive and intensive.

Without quantitative support, these generalisations scarcely qualify as stylised facts. Maddison (2003), the doyen of the collectors of the statistics of economic development,[6] has tried to give statistical flesh to the main contours of world development over the last two millennia, for the earlier period on the basis of patchy statistics and controlled conjectures. Such an exercise highlights an obvious acceleration in the last two centuries. Over the past millennium, world population has risen by 22 times, with the rate of increase accelerating in the recent past – between 1000 and 1820 it rises by four times, and between 1820 and the present more dramatically by five times. World GDP has risen nearly 300 times, so that per capita income has risen 13 times, with a mere 50 per cent increase before 1820, 'a slow crawl' in Maddison's words, and an eight times increase since. Other accelerations have been as dramatic. During the first millennium of the Christian era, population grew by only a sixth and there was no advance in per capita income. Life expectation at birth in 1000 was about 24 years, with a third of babies dying in their first year, and at present it is 66.

There has been a widening divergence between the group of rapidly growing countries, the Triad of West Europe, North America and Japan plus Australasia, and the rest – in 1820, it was 2:1, and in 1998, 7:1, which qualifies as the Great Divergence, even on these bald statistics. However, the starting divergence has been the focus of some disagreement, both in its putative timing and in its extent at the beginning of the Industrial Revolution, say 1750. Bairoch (1993: chapter 9) has narrowed the gap at that time, to 1 to 1.1–1.3, using the statistics of Maddison and to 1 to 1.1 according to his own. This accords with a growing literature which stresses the similarities in levels of economic development in the pre-modern period, if not a higher level of economic development for Asian economies (Frank 1998). It also accords with the continuing influence of Malthusian mechanisms in constraining the emergence of such a gap until the modern period.

The strongest 'stylised facts' apply to the modern economic regime. Early economic theory often grappled with the facts set out by Kaldor

(1963), and still returns to them (Barro and Sala-i-Martin 2004). These stylised facts were taken from rather primitive statistics. They refer to the experience in the developed economies, notably the USA, and to a period of about one century from the middle of the nineteenth to the middle of the twentieth centuries. They include constant, or rising, aggregate growth rates of output and labour productivity over time, but significant differences between different economies; a significant increase in the capital/labour ratio; a constant rate of profit; a constant aggregate capital/output ratio; nearly constant shares in national income of the rewards going to labour and physical capital; and a savings/investment ratio correlated with the share of profits in income. The last is rather controversial, as already indicated. Later empirical data have tended to confirm all except the third of these, which might be replaced by some tendency to a fall in profitability (Barro and Sala-i-Martin 2004: 13), although nothing comparable with the Marxist prediction of a significant fall.

Charles Jones, an economic theorist, talks about 'broad empirical regularities associated with growth and development' (Jones 2002: 3), or 'the facts of economic growth' (Jones 2002: 1). He is referring to the period of modern economic development, for which there are reasonable statistics, a period of a century in the case of the USA, to which much of his work relates. Writing later than Kaldor, to whom he makes obvious reference, he uses a rather stronger statistical base. Jones reaches broadly the same conclusions as Kaldor, but adds two new areas of interest, the role of trade and of migration in modern economic development. Fact 1: There is enormous variation in per capita income across economies. The poorest countries have per capita incomes that are less than 5 per cent of the per capita incomes in the richest countries. Fact 2: Rates of economic growth vary substantially across countries. Fact 3: Growth rates are not generally constant over time. For the world as a whole, growth rates were close to zero over most of history, but increased sharply in the twentieth century. For individual countries, growth rates also change over time. Fact 4: A country's relative position in the world distribution of per capita income is not immutable. Countries can move from being 'poor' to being 'rich', and vice versa. Fact 5: In the United States over the last century, first, the real rate of return to capital, r, shows no trend upwards or downwards; secondly, the shares of income devoted to capital, rK/Y, and labour, wL/Y, show no trend; and thirdly, the average growth rate of output per person has been positive and relatively constant over time – that is, the United States exhibits steady, sustained per capita income growth. Fact 6: Growth in output and growth in the volume of international trade are closely related. Fact 7: Both skilled and unskilled workers tend to migrate from poor to rich countries or regions.

The focus of the next three accounts is on the period, 1960 to the present, for which the statistics are very much stronger owing to the work of Summers and Heston (1991). Parente and Prescott (n.d.), concentrating on the last 50 years, stress four development facts which any theory of economic development must accommodate. During the last 50 years there has been a large disparity in GDP per head – in 1985 it was of the order of 29 times the average GDP in countries in the top 5 per cent than in the bottom 5 per cent of the country sample (covering all those countries with good enough statistics to use). The range of disparity did not change much between 1960 and 1985. All countries moved up in GDP per head: there is no absolute poverty trap. There have been development miracles and development disasters – about an equal number of countries that have moved up by a factor of 2 or more or down by the same amount between 1960 and 1985: there is no relative poverty trap.

Durlauf, Johnson and Temple (2004) have also summarised the stylised facts for the period 1960–2000. They come up with three stylised facts which confirm many of the facts indicated before, but which raise one or two new issues. Over the 40-year period, most countries have grown richer, but vast income disparities remain. 'For all but the richest group, growth rates have differed to an unprecedented extent, regardless of the initial level of development' (Durlauf, Johnson and Temple 2004: 26). Past performance is a surprisingly weak predictor of future growth, but it is slowly becoming more accurate over time, so that distinct winners and losers are beginning to emerge. Regionally, there are large differences; the strongest performers are in East and South East Asia, which have sustained growth rates at an unprecedented level; the weakest performers are predominantly in sub-Saharan Africa, where some have actually contracted; the record of South and Central America is distinctly mixed. Generally, there is considerable output volatility and dramatic collapses are not uncommon. An optimistic note is the rapid take-off in China and India. For most countries, growth for 1980–2000 was slower than for 1960–80, and this was true throughout most of the income distribution. The dispersion of growth rates has also increased. The slowing after the 1970s is interesting, but in view of recent experience, does not appear to represent a major change of trend.

Easterly and Levine's stylised facts (2001) refer to a similar period: they represent an up-to-date understanding produced by two development practitioners. It's not factor accumulation that matters, it's total factor productivity: that is, differences in growth rates are accounted for, not by increased factor inputs, including capital accumulation, but by the famous residual which is assumed to measure productivity increase due to technical change. Divergence, not convergence, is the big story: the gap between the poorest and the richest has increased massively, suggesting that there is absolute divergence. Growth is not persistent, but capital accumulation is; there is almost no relationship between growth rates for the same country considered over periods of time which are as short as decades. When it rains, it pours: all factors of production flow in the same direction – factors concentrate where they are already abundant, whether it is capital or labour: the consequence is that economic activity is highly concentrated in a geographical sense. Policy matters: what the government does affects the rate of economic growth.

It is useful to bear in mind these stylised facts. They can be supplemented by broader qualitative features of a global history. For the most part, they apply to a developed market-based capitalist economy, in particular the USA. In constructing a grand narrative, they are not particularly helpful. Such a grand narrative would be a story of the movement of broad aggregates, but would link in country scenarios with the worldwide experience. They do point in the direction of lesser narratives which take into account the divergence experiences of different countries and regions. An interesting growth scenario is that of the pioneer, one which has its own set of stylised facts. However, that narrative must be placed in the context of the whole process of economic development and of the interconnections which underpinned the pioneer experience.[7]

THE PIONEER INCEPTION – THE INDUSTRIAL REVOLUTION IN BRITAIN

How does the British experience fit the global experience? What is the profile of the pioneer experience, what we continue to call the British Industrial Revolution?[8] It is possible to repeat the exercise above by indicating key stylised factors, focusing on the Industrial Revolution itself, the British experience during the century from 1760 to 1860, but this is not enough.[9] The analysis starts with proximate factors, but builds up a picture of ultimate factors. The following exposition takes as its starting point Voth (2003), adding additional stylised facts, deemed of significance. The stress in this analysis is on the supply side – on output, labour supply and technology – implicitly playing down the demand side (Mokyr 1999: 58–66). Some commentators such as Snooks have put much more emphasis on the demand side.

The notion of the Industrial Revolution rests on two main factors, an accelerating rate of growth of GDP per head and a significant shift in the structure of the economy towards industrialisation, that is, the rising importance of the manufacturing sector, particularly that part located in factories. First, during the period of the classic Industrial Revolution, at least up to 1830, growth, in both absolute and per capita terms, was any-thing but revolutionary, indeed surprisingly slow. It represented a small acceleration on previous rates. Total factor productivity, estimated in growth accounting exercises, was minuscule. In the words of Crafts and Harley, 'Growth had probably begun to accelerate by the early eighteenth century but modern economic growth only became fully established in Britain in the railway age' (Crafts and Harley 1992: 705), from the 1830s onwards. By modern standards, economic growth in Britain was never fast. On Clark's estimate, the growth of efficiency of production of goods within England moved from zero to about 0.5 per cent; the break occurs in 1790; the rise to 1 per cent occurs later. If we modify this to consider the efficiency of producing income, whether the goods originated at home or abroad, there appears to be a trend rate of 0.2 per cent between 1600 and 1760 and 0.33 per cent between 1760 and 1869 (Clark 2007: 240). The dramatic acceleration comes late in the nineteenth century. For developed countries, in general, the crude rate of growth of GDP per head during the nineteenth century is only about 0.9–1.0 per cent (Bairoch 1993: 7, 141–2).

On another account, there was plenty of growth before the so-called Industrial Revolution, and the waves occurred with some ratchet effect; the level of GDP per capita was on the rise for a long period before the Industrial Revolution. The strongest proponent of this point of view is Snooks (1993), who argues that the last thousand years of English economic history has seen three long waves of economic growth, with growth rates at peak periods during the twelfth and the sixteenth centuries exceeding those during the early Industrial Revolution. There were revers-als, notably from about 1300 to 1500, but after 1500 there is continuing growth in per capita GDP, with only a marked slowing after 1600, rather than an actual contraction. There is a clear sense in which Snooks sees a rising growth trajectory interrupted by exogenous shocks. His estimate of the rate of economic growth shows a positive rate of intensive growth between the end of the eleventh century and the start of the Industrial Revolution, which is not insubstantial, at about 0.3 per cent per annum (Snooks 1993: 20–23). There is criticism of Snooks' conclusions, that they exaggerate the long-term rate of economic growth. It is largely based on the data in the Domesday Book (produced in 1086), and premised on the quality of the data contained there. Only small adjustments remove most of the growth.[10]

Mokyr (1999: 12–14) has made the obvious point, one usually ignored, that a country undergoing the kind of structural change which occurred during the Industrial Revolution is bound to display a slow rate of growth. Over-simplifying the position, we can divide the economy into a modern and a traditional economy – in practice, there were sectors which shared some characteristics of both and several positive interactions between the two economies. The traditional economy can be defined by its mode of production and level of productivity. It consisted largely of the agricultural sector, construction and many services. Before the revolution, the traditional sector is large and the modern sector small, in terms of both contribution to GDP and employment shares. The traditional sector grows only slowly and any acceleration in growth is slight. Even with relatively rapid growth in the modern sector, the weight of the traditional sector is such as to yield a slow overall rate of growth for aggregate GDP and to prevent any significant acceleration until many years down the track, when the modern sector becomes large enough to influence the overall rate. Earlier Mokyr (1985: 5) provided arithmetic to back this up. If the traditional sector is growing at a slow rate of 1 per cent per annum and at the start accounts for 90 per cent of the economy, while the modern sector, which accounts for the other 10 per cent, is growing at an impressive 4 per cent, it will take three-quarters of a century for the modern sector to account for as much as half of output. McCloskey (1991a: 100) calls this the weighting theorem, or more facetiously, the waiting theorem.

Gerschenkron (1968: 34–5 – quoted by McCloskey 1991a: 99) has made the same point, in a rather more punchy manner: 'If the seat of the great spurt lies in the area of manufacturing, it would be inept to try to locate the discontinuity by scrutinizing data on large aggregate magnitudes such as national income . . . By the time industry has become bulky enough to affect the larger aggregate, the exciting period of the great spurt may well be over'. This prompted McCloskey to say: 'Small (and exciting) beginnings will be hidden by the mass until well after they have become routine'. Clark (2007: 249–56) has pointed out other implications of choice of weights for the different sectors of the economy which accord with the market choices of the average consumer, with the emphasis on the basics such as food, clothing and shelter. Sectors which may be regarded as important from other perspectives, including their long-run importance, may be already revealing a rapid rate of efficiency advance much earlier in the day. Clark gives evidence of rapidly improving efficiency well before the Industrial Revolution for two very different cases – books and nails. He indicates that the same holds for a wide range of products. The fact that innovativeness was directed to such products suggests to Clark that profit was not the main motive (Clark 2007: 256). Another piece of evidence for the need to disaggregate is the divergence in the movement of wages in Britain over the period 1700–1850, up 50 per cent in the north and down in the traditional centre of population in the south (Goldstone 2008: 126).

Secondly, there was significant structural change, with the share of employment in agriculture falling from about half in the mid-eighteenth century to a quarter a century later, but it is likely that the process had begun as early as the sixteenth century. This structural change is central to the notion of an industrial revolution. Industrialisation was certainly occurring. The shift is significant, since labour productivity was higher in the manufacturing sector than in agriculture, but it was also relatively high in the agricultural sector and rising. Britain became the first urban industrial society (Crafts and Harley 1992: 705); however, even in 1760, it was not a traditional agrarian society, which is one of the reasons why many commentators began to look back in time to see the origins of the inception of modern economic development. An agricultural revolution has been dated rather earlier than the traditional dating of the Industrial Revolution, by one or two to the sixteenth century, but more persuasively to the late seventeenth and early eighteenth centuries (E.L. Jones 1974). The rise in productivity in agriculture, both by units of land and of labour, not revolutionary in its rapidity, but continuing over a long period, allowed the movement of labour out of agriculture into the industrial sector, as well as an increase in demand for manufactured goods from the agricultural sector and a movement of savings out of the agricultural sector.

How far was there a shift in the structure of industry, with certain sectors taking the lead, cotton textiles, the iron industry and engineering, even transportation, being prominent? Was it a case of mushroom economic development rather than yeast development (Harberger 1998)? There is growing sense that it was. For example the contribution of textiles to the acceleration in the national efficiency rate is large. Between the 1760s and the 1860s this sector contributed 24 per cent of the national efficiency growth rate (Clark 2007: 233). Efficiency in this sector rose at a rate of 2.4 per cent per annum. This reflected a series of well-known technical innovations. Because of competition and the limitations of patent law, the rewards for innovation were small, as shown by the relevant rates of profit and the wealth of the textile entrepreneurs. The benefits went to wage earners and customers, mainly abroad (Clark 2007: 236). As a consequence, there has been some return to the notion of a leading sector or sectors (Rostow 1965). This argument, while consistent with the picture presented by the other facts, is not without its critics (Temin 1997 and Cuenca Esteban 1999).

A third issue relates to the standard of living. The debate over the standard of living during the Industrial Revolution goes back a long way (Hobsbawm 1957 and Hartwell 1961).[11] There are superficially startling differences of view, but on closer inspection they are less clear-cut than appears at first glance. On the pessimistic side, stands Voth (2003), supported by Allen (2005) and Fogel (2004). Living standards were stagnant. Wages did not increase during the Industrial Revolution. Data on height and weight suggest a real breakthrough from hunger and improvement in longevity only at the end of the nineteenth century and only a slight improvement in these critical indicators right through to the late nineteenth century (Fogel 2004: chapter 1). During the early revolution, notably during the first four decades of the nineteenth century, there is a story of dramatically rising inequality, in every aspect of well-being, with the rate of profit rising and the share of profits in national income significantly increased (Allen 2005). This does not pre-empt an argument that the level of well-being in Britain was already, at the beginning of the traditional period of revolution, high relative to other countries (Macfarlane 1997). It certainly argues against revolutionary change in this area. On the optimistic side, stands Clark, who argues strongly for the surprisingly poor benefit received by land and capital owners from the Industrial Revolution and the tendency of the wages of the unskilled to rise faster than those of the skilled. Even he concedes that the improvement was initially slow. All the relevant indicators show that the improvement came later and that during the traditional period of the Industrial Revolution, Voth is probably right. For example, real rents per acre rise well into the second half of the nineteenth century, then begin a dramatic fall. Clark is analysing long-run trends rather than the period of the inception of modern economic growth.

The rewards going to the different factors, particularly to labour, reflect the growth in inputs of those factors. The most dramatic change was rapid demographic growth, with a doubling of population between 1750 and 1830 and a rise in population, from 5.5 million at the beginning of the eighteenth century to over 20 million in the 1860s. This is mainly centred on an unprecedented rise in fertility rates, which is difficult to explain by economic factors given the stickiness of wages (Wrigley et al. 1997); fertility rose by about 40 per cent between 1650 and 1800 (Clark 2007: 243). Fertility was not responding to a non-existent improvement in living standards. The increase had dramatic results. It accounts for most of the large increase in total output. Given the limited growth in agriculture and the declining availability of land per head of population, it led to a dramatic increase in dependence on imports of raw materials and foodstuffs, from almost nothing to 22 per cent of GDP (Clark 2007: 248). The products of the Industrial Revolution – cotton textiles, coal, steel and engineering products – were exported to pay for these imports. Since mortality rates did not change much, the rise in fertility also indicates an increase in the dependency ratio during the revolution, which in itself acts as a drag on the rate of economic growth. The achievement was to maintain income levels despite the dramatic rise in population – this is a real achievement. The so-called mortality revolution (Easterlin 2004: chapter 6) occurred later, during the second half of the nineteenth century, and is not necessarily directly connected with the previous Industrial Revolution.

There was a marked rise in labour input, accounted for by both rising population and an increase in hours worked by workers, which at their peak in the early nineteenth century were about 50 per cent higher than those prevalent in developing countries today. There was clearly a shift from household production and consumption of a broad range of products to reliance on the market for both purchase of substitute products and for the sale of labour time to generate the necessary income to support such purchases: part of the so-called 'industrious revolution' of de Vries (Mokyr 1999: 64–6). To some degree, this increase in labour input countered the rise in the dependency ratio indicated below. Clark (2007: 63–5) has argued that this increase in hours occurred rather earlier than Voth believes and therefore is more drawn out, but it is unclear exactly when it happened.

What about the contribution of capital? The investment ratio rose steadily from about 6 per cent in 1760 to about 12 per cent in 1840, a much slower doubling than originally envisaged in Rostow's takeoff. Savings rates were surprising low. There was no net savings from wages and the ratio of savings from rents and profits was less than 20 per cent and rising only slowly (Allen 2005). Allen (2005: 12) contrasts a rate of 17 per cent out of property income in the Britain of the Napoleonic Wars and a rate as high as 61 per cent for nineteenth-century America.

Britain at the beginning of the Industrial Revolution was already a sophisticated market economy, in relative terms. There are two sides to this sophistication. The commercialisation of the economy was well advanced. Smithian growth, involving the trade and specialisation associated with an increasing division of labour, was already well under way. In this, it did not necessarily differ from China and other Asian economies. Britain was in 1760 a highly commercial economy and a relatively urbanised society. Smithian growth is not the same as industrialisation. A key issue is how far Smithian growth prepared the way for industrialisation. Proto-industrialisation did not necessarily encourage factory industrialisation.[12] Some commentators have seen the Industrial Revolution as a result of export-propelled growth, adding an external commercialisation to the internal one, emphasising the long-drawn-out nature of the expansion of foreign demand (Guha 1981: chapter 7). However, an increasing number of commentators have argued that Britain was not exceptional in this, its sophistication and scale being matched by developments in many parts of Asia.

Secondly, there appeared in Britain a broad social milieu which developed a culture of innovation. There is an increasing tendency to view the Industrial Revolution in a 'global-historical-cumulative' perspective (Hobson 2004: 218). It stresses Britain's 'problem-solving tenacity to work and refine the inventions of others' (ibid.: 217), notably, but not only, those of the Chinese. The British gift lies 'in assimilating and refining earlier Chinese inventions and technical ideas' (ibid.: 194). It is as much imitation as invention, but a remarkably exuberant type of imitation, doing what the Chinese did, but on a scale never seen before. We have already introduced Mokyr's industrial enlightenment. In the words of Goldstone (2008: 134): '. . . what transformed production was a generalized belief in the possibility, even the inevitability, of progress and the conviction that such progress was in reach of anyone who pursued a systematic program of careful observation and experiment and drew on the last scientific knowledge'. This did not emerge overnight. Social barriers between upper-class philosophers, market-driven entrepreneurs, large-scale industrialists, and skilled craftspeople and technicians had largely dissolved, if steadily. Initially, from 1700–1850, the lead in innovation lay squarely with Britain, although the roots of the knowledge relevant to the Industrial Revolution were global. Goldstone isolates six factors which explain Europe's particular path to modern economic development and its primacy in innovation in general, and British leadership in particular (Goldstone 2008: 167–9). The realisation of these conditions was, in his view, contingent and cumulative (Goldstone 2008: 170). The relevant factors were a rejection of the authority and sacrosanct truth of religious texts; a stress on the experimental method backing up the use of reasoned mathematical logic; the popularity of public demonstration of the new knowledge and its practical relevance; the application of an instrument-driven approach to the extension of knowledge by experiment and observation; the emergence of a climate of tolerance and pluralism; and finally, the provision of much scope for entrepreneurship and entrepreneurs.

The two arguments – a limited downplaying of economic growth during the Industrial Revolution, although there is still a break of trend, but a playing up of an interconnected series of cultural and institutional changes over a long period – gives a role to both evolution and revolution. A long period of slow growth in the modern sector saw all the main indicators of economic development showing improvement and a lead over other economies – the level of urbanisation, the commercialisation of the economy, the size of the non-agricultural sector of the economy, the relative prices of foodstuffs and other goods, even the level of wage rates. Despite the protestations of the Californian School, Britain had a clear lead by the traditional date of the beginning of the Industrial Revolution, not only over other European countries, but over Asian economies as well (Allen 2006, Broadberry and Gupta 2006).[13] But they are right that the gap widened significantly as a result of industrialisation during the nineteenth century. The general drift of evidence and interpretation is towards an evolutionary rather than a revolutionary approach. Clark (2007: 9–10) summarises the current position: 'The conventional picture of the Industrial Revolution as a sudden fissure in economic life is not sustainable'. He continues, 'In crucial ways the classic Industrial Revolution in England in 1760–1860 was a blip, an accident superimposed on a longer-running upward sweep in the rate of knowledge accumulation that had its origins in the Middle Ages or even earlier'. However, this upward sweep is much broader than often thought, although concealed to a significant degree. 'An evolutionary account of gradual change is a much more plausible explanation than has previously been appreciated.' There is clear evidence of attitudinal and behavioural change and an increased understanding of how this might have occured (Clark 2007). One way of viewing this picture is that there is a long period of preparation before the industrial revolution proper.[14]

Yet there is a significant sense in which there was indeed an industrial revolution, but that there was both revolution and evolution. The major achievement of the Industrial Revolution is summarised by a graph of the relationship in England between population increase and the real wage index (Wrigley 1988: 65). The relationship was a strongly inverse one until the nineteenth century. Wages moved closely with population growth but in the opposite direction, as a Malthusian analysis would anticipate. The relationship was finally broken in the nineteenth century: the Industrial Revolution was the key process in releasing the Malthusian trap. The Malthusian constraints, although to some degree weakened, were operative before then and prevented too much divergence in per capita income levels in the pre-modern world, in some ways suppressing evidence of the very real divergence between Britain and other societies. The dramatic surge in the economic performance which built up over a quarter of a millennium is largely hidden, if the focus is on the growth rate, in particular of output per head. By the standards of historical experience, what was happening in Britain during the classic period of the Industrial Revolution was unprecedented, but it had solid historical roots. Improvements in productivity occurring before the nineteenth supported a dramatic increase in population, which in itself stimulated economic growth. The muted influence of the small but dramatic beginnings which occurred in many areas of economic and social behaviour – muted at least as expressed in terms of income increases – reflected the suppression of income increase by population expansion.

A narrative told in terms of proximate causes is inadequate to explain

the first inception of modern economic development. Economic development in Britain is not just a matter of an increase in capital or labour
inputs – significant as either might be – or even an acceleration in the
growth of total factor productivity. It is a matter of how these were
achieved, particularly how resources were used and risk controlled, of how
human capital developed and decisions were taken in a favourable cultural
and institutional context, of how market, government and civil society
interacted positively and how technical innovation came to dominate
sector after sector of the economy. It certainly reflected to some degree
the favourable institutional evolution of market and government; it also
reflected an abundance of an inorganic source of energy, coal, but there is
no one simple explanation.

CONTINUITY AND DISCONTINUITY

The inception into modern economic development of late starters, as
Gerschenkron (1962) has stressed, was characterised by much faster rates
of change than in the forward economies, and by much more dramatic tensions. Economic growth is telescoped into a much shorter period of time
than was necessary for the pioneer. In some cases, political change was
also accelerated, sometimes with dire consequences. Russia is an exemplar. In the words of Malia (1994: 65), 'The political formula produced
by Russian backwardness . . . is the compression or telescoping – and
thus the chronic radicalisation – of the stages of the modern movement
towards democracy'. As Malia continues, the formula produced 'a veritable cult of Revolution as the highest form of the modern political process'.
Moreover, political thought tended to be maximalist since it too was com-
pressed and telescoped, political parties existing before they had a political
role and before the groups which they were said to represent existed in any
real sense, such as an industrial proletariat (Malia 1994: 71). But this is an
extreme case.

The attractiveness of the work of Gerschenkron follows from his ability
to generalise about the experience of modern economic development, while
at the same time taking full account of the particularities of individual
experiences (Sylla and Toniolo 1991, particularly chapter 1). He combined
in an almost ideal way theory, narrative and data, always recognising that
quantification was a necessary precondition for the testing of his 'model'.
He was a pioneer for many countries in establishing the basis for estimating rates of economic growth. According to Gerschenkron, the rate of
economic growth at the inception of modern economic growth, that is,
during the great industrialisation spurt, is positively related to the level of

economic backwardness at that time. Gerschenkron's definition of relative backwardness is much broader than often suggested (Sylla and Toniolo 1991: 6). It included savings ratios, literacy rates, some technology-related indicators such as the rate of issue of patents, the level of per capita social overhead capital, and even the nature of ideology. Nevertheless a simple Gerschenkronian definition of relative backwardness would see it measured by the relationship between GDP per head in the relevant economy relative to that in the most advanced economy of the time. A ranking by GDP per head accords reasonably well with Gerschenkron's qualitative judgement as an historian, as might be expected.

Gerschenkron is in broad agreement with neoclassical theory in that it predicts convergence, since the rate of economic growth correlates inversely with the relative level of GDP in the relevant economies. A characteristic of economic growth in such conditions is that its speed is positively related to the level of backwardness, a relationship which agrees with the neoclassical notion of convergence; the lower the relative level of GDP per head, the faster the rate of economic growth, notably, the faster the rate of growth of industrial output. A careful reading of Gerschenkron's work sees a convergence of institutions, as well as of output per head (Harley 1991). The leading countries have a more developed market structure and the more backward hierarchical systems of planning – substitutes, working either through universal banks or through the state for the missing market institutions. As they advance, they converge on the institutional structure of the leaders. Gerschenkron's work can be seen as an early application of the argument for convergence. It led to considerable debate and many attempts to test its main propositions.

Yet there is a proviso: Gerschenkron argues this is only valid for a limited group of European economies in the period before 1914, however much it may seem to be generalisable to all developing economies. Gerschenkron limited the validity of the model to pre-1914 Europe and it is dangerous to extend it beyond these limits. It might be assumed that Europe shared characteristics which other regions did not.

There does appear to be an apparent acceleration in the rate of economic growth as countries enter their periods of 'miracle' at a later and later date. This reflects the fact that these economies are operating well within the frontier of best practice, whether considered from a technical or an organisational/institutional perspective. There is a pool of unexploited knowledge accessible to them. Catching up allows the temporary achievement of faster and faster rates of growth by those who succeed in making the transition. In the context of neoclassical theory, it is argued that the underlying rate to which all are converging is unchanged and surprisingly low. Eventually, any successful economy will have a growth rate which converges on this rate. What we are observing are transitional rates which can only be sustained for a period whose length reflects the initial lag in GDP per head. It is possible to give a misleading narrative of accelerating world economic growth if we consider the dramatic stepping up of the rates of growth in the fastest-growing areas, first, during the British Industrial Revolution, secondly, in the rise of the USA to industrial ascendancy and thirdly, during the Asian Economic Miracle. The underlying rate of growth in GDP per head of population, defined as the long-run steady-state rate, is on most evidence strikingly stable, unsurprisingly, if it simply reflects the steady accretion of technical knowledge at a world level. Any acceleration has been slight.[15]

Gerschenkron talked in terms of levels of medium or extreme backwardness. In other words, we could, within the European context, group countries according to their level of relative backwardness. He saw a gradient of backwardness which sloped upwards in an easterly direction across Europe, with the most extreme examples being in Russia and the Balkans. To some degree, the dating of the first acceleration was later, the more backward the economies, so backwardness corresponded to lateness. Russia displayed an acceleration which qualified as the inception of modern economic development in the 1890s. Gerschenkron broadly agreed with the dating of the take-offs which Rostow had already proposed for various countries.

Gerschenkron made a number of other predictions concerning the pattern of economic development on the basis of the degree of relative economic backwardness of the relevant economy (Sylla and Toniolo 1991: 5). It is interesting that he inverts the usual regression analysis by using relative output levels to predict various characteristics of the relevant economies, rather than using it to predict rates of growth or levels of that output. The characteristics of economic development in the backward economies could be anticipated from their level of backwardness.[16]

The predictions were: that economic growth during the period of inception of modern economic growth would be faster, the greater the level of economic backwardness; that the role of the government would increase in the more backward economies – that is, an active policy was important; that there would be an increased reliance on technology and capital from outside and the adoption of best-practice foreign technology; that agriculture would tend to play a more passive role where backwardness was greater; that the typical size of plant and enterprise would be greater; that there would be in the first industrialising spurt a greater emphasis on capital goods rather than consumer goods production; that there would be downward pressure on the level of consumption in order to release the savings for investment; that there would be patterns of substitution for missing prerequisites absent in the more backward economies, in such areas as capital supply; and that there would be an emphasis on a validating ideology of industrialisation.

The penultimate point is an interesting one, since it indicates institutionalised patterns of substitution for what could be regarded as necessary prerequisites in the early industrialising countries, but which were absent in the more backward. Gerschenkron appeared at certain times to suggest a convergence on the pioneer patterns as incomes rose, but he does suggest some of the substitutions may in the end have proved superior to the original patterns. Considerable effort was put into testing these predictions, with mixed results, partly because the predictions, were not precisely specified or because the relevant data were not adequate to the task.[17]

The political and social context of modern economic development becomes much more significant for late starters. Rapid rates of growth create tensions, both internally and externally. There are rapid shifts in the distribution of status and wealth within the industrialising societies and shifts in the distribution of wealth and military strength between countries. It is not accidental that fascism and communism had their strength in countries where the process of modern economic development occurred in conditions of medium or extreme backwardness and rapid economic change (Gerschenkron). Assimilating rates of growth around the 1–2 per cent mark is much easier than assimilating rates which are above 3 per cent or even as high as 5 per cent. It is scarcely surprising to note that the social and political tensions in the pioneer were much less threatening than in the late starters. The greatest tension develops when a rapid rate of advance is interrupted by a negative shock or shocks.

DIFFUSION, PATTERNS OF ECONOMIC DEVELOPMENT AND CONVERGENCE CLUBS

There are two main interpretations of how the process of economic development occurs. The first argues that its inception occurs in one or, at most, a limited number of separate centres, and is then imitated: it is diffused. The first mover is the prime mover. In the past, there was a tendency to view the Neolithic or the Industrial Revolution as originating in one place and then diffusing outwards. For example, Guha (1981: 64) has divided the cycle of modern economic development into three phases – 'first, the concentration of growth impulses in a nuclear area, resulting in its intensive development; secondly, the rise of a new pattern of international specialisation, as resource scarcities in the nuclear area compel it to rely increasingly on natural resource-rich regions, resulting in the transmission of growth to the latter; and, finally, catching up – through the advantage of cheap labour as well as through politically forced development – of the regions left out of this pattern of specialization'. The pattern can repeat itself as countries in the latter two regions emerge as the new foci of the world economy, initially the USA. More recently, there has been persuasive criticism of such a position, although a recognition that there are today important and unavoidable interactions resulting from the processes of globalisation (Fernandez-Armesto 2001: 184–5). It is not simply a matter of imitation, rather one of responding to significant change caused by modern economic development elsewhere. The second interpretation argues that innovations are introduced separately and independently, almost impossible today, but not so in the past. It is typical for similar processes of change to occur without any connection, provided the challenge is the same and the context similar. Moreover, it is clear that conditions differ sufficiently to prevent a mechanical imitation. 'Diffusion models which, in effect, elevated the status of Britain's precocious transition to a paradigm case are no longer regarded as an illuminating way to comprehend the industrialization of mainland Europe, the United States and East Asia let alone as a basis for policy recommendations to countries still struggling to industrialize' (O'Brien 2006: 6).

The neoclassical model spells out the mechanisms by which a diffusion of modern economic development could occur. It is a market-based one, in which the role of government is to provide an underpinning for efficient market operation. There is direct imitation, the main motivating factors being profit and competition. The removal of barriers to the free flow of ideas, commodities and factors of production integrates world markets and encourages free movement through the market, which by placing resources where they make the highest return, accelerates the convergence of economies. First, there are opportunities for profit made available by the pool of existing technical and organisational knowledge. Secondly, comparative advantage and factor price equalisation underpin the role of trade in spreading economic development. Thirdly, the movement of people supplements the labour forces and management teams in different countries. Those moving carry with them the ideas that support the model. Fourthly, both savers and investors put their money where it produces the highest return, raising the level of capital accumulation in countries where there is little capital and high returns. Direct investment carries with it a package of technological and entrepreneurial know-how, and the whole panoply of tacit knowledge of the successful model of economic development, as well as finance. In an integrated world, there is a natural tendency for diffusion, since there is every incentive and opportunity for laggards to catch up with the leaders.

There are some empirical difficulties with this theory, however attractive it is theoretically. First, there is the influence of the network of the world wide web, to use the McNeills' term (2003), and the nature of each attachment to that network. Individual connections differ. The second relates to the direction of international flows. On the neoclassical account, capital and labour should flow to where they are scarce. There is some truth in this – labour certainly moves to where wages are at their highest, although often prevented by barriers created by government. For capital, the reverse flow occurs: capital tends to flow to the developed economies in which capital has already accumulated. The weakness is with the assumption of diminishing returns to capital. Economies of scale and agglomeration favour existing centres of economic activity (Krugman 1998). Thirdly, the neoclassical theory should hold best in periods of 'globalisation', when barriers to the various movements are reduced. This is not necessarily true. Governments of the leading nation always tend to encourage free trade and work to reduce the barriers to market integration, since their own economy is highly competitive. The period up to 1914 is as much a period of globalisation as the period since 1945. At the core of convergence in the first period was an exchange of manufactured goods for commodities, between the core and the periphery, with capital flows which supported this trade, and an enormous flow of migrants out of Europe to areas of new settlement, particularly the USA. There was a striking reversal of globalisation in the period between 1914 and 1945, when the shocks of two world wars and the Great Depression prompted a massive contraction of international investment and trade, and interrupted the flows of migrants. Nevertheless, there was a marked convergence in income levels among the developed economies, despite the reversal of globalisation.

Increasingly, empirical studies have shown the strength of the peculiarities of each experience of modern economic development. Some commentators have for this reason stressed the lack of pattern. There are two reasons for individuality. The first stresses the lock-in to separate paths, or path dependence. Contextual differences have a resonance which echoes down the centuries. The second stresses contingency. Macfarlane, in referring to the release from the Malthusian trap, achieved almost simultaneously in two islands at the extreme points of the Eurasian land mass, Britain and Japan, comments: 'What happened was not only a gigantic accident, but also an enormous exception. It was a strange occurrence that ought not to have happened, nearly did not happen, yet by a set of coincidences and chances, did happen – twice' (Macfarlane 1997: 389).

Yet there are patterns, groups of countries sharing common circumstances which influence the nature of the growth experience. The notion of convergence clubs can be extended to include groups of countries with similar patterns of economic development, where the similarities can arise from the origin of its population, cultural and historical affinities, common institutional structures, geographical congruencies of locality or ecology or simply common policies, including the initial conditions of neoclassical theory, represented by the degree of relative backwardness. For each group, there may or may not be a model economy from which individual experience diverges in a systematic manner.

When successful economic development seemed limited to the European world, the British model was taken as the starting point and other experiences were seen as repeating the British experience, with patterned variations reflecting different contextual elements, such as resource endowment or the influence of previous development. The model was exported, just like commodities or capital. Any grand narrative of the inception of modern economic development started with the British experience, which then merged into the American experience, as by the end of the nineteenth century the American economy overtook the British in output per head and its technical and organisational level. Any narrative which stressed technical and organisational change recognised the continuity between these two economies. This encouraged a Eurocentric view and the focus on an Anglo-European convergence club. The Anglo model reflects a common origin for institutions and attitudes. There is a similar emphasis on representative democracy, common law, the operation of the market and defence of both property rights and contract. There is a real continuity between British and American leaderships, arising from direct as well as indirect contact. There is a sense in which the American economy carries the inception of modern economic development in Britain to its logical conclusion. The American system of manufacturing is one outcome. In the USA, resource abundance has had a strong influence on the way in which technology has developed (Rosenberg 1972), with resource-intensive technologies being chosen.

This pattern also affected Canada, Australia and New Zealand, and to a lesser extent South Africa (Denoon 1983). Yet the resource and risk environments differ markedly between these neo-Europes and Britain. The relative abundance of land and natural resources has a powerful influence on the pattern of economic development, and the interaction between political and economic arrangements. The relevant narratives reflect these features. The differing factor endowments of the neo-Europes influenced their pattern of modern economic development The greater abundance of land and resources and the associated role of immigration are relevant. There was a much greater potential for self-sufficiency. However, export staples, often resource intensive, acted as leading sectors and influenced the structure of the economy and the distribution of population – cotton, wool, wheat, and gold.

The market mechanism reached its peak of development in the USA. The forces of competition and profit opportunities spread the new technologies.[18] The existence of large, dispersed and even markets encouraged this process, but at the same time the new technologies were associated with the birth of the modern business enterprise (Chandler 1990). As the scale of production and of capital needs rose, competition gave way to oligopoly. The visible hand appeared alongside the invisible hand.

The relative resource position of Britain and the USA is linked with their respective roles in the world. The British economy has been much more enmeshed in the world economy. Its trade ratio has been much higher than that of America – today around the 20 per cent level against 10 per cent. The British economy was before 1914 much more involved in investment flows, particularly in its involvement with the neo-Europes. The flows of investment were linked with trade flows and supported those flows. Britain was the major source of FDI in the pre-1914 world. Most of the investment flowed to areas of new settlement. The American economy has been potentially self-sufficient for most of its history and has had governments which have oscillated between isolationism and leadership in the world economy. The two dominant economies have had a very powerful influence in stimulating economic development elsewhere, in the British case because of its significant involvement in the international economy and in the American case because of its sheer size and the demonstration effects of mass consumption. However, the two economies differ in the nature of their influence on the rest of the world, largely because of differences of scale and of factor endowment. The American economy, always rich, became much bigger, not only than the British, but than any other economy – today being twice the size of the next economy, China, on PPP exchange rates and Japan on current exchange rates. Even today the USA is among the largest countries in population or production, but one of the most sparsely populated.

The colonies of other European countries did not succeed in initiating modern economic development in the same way as British colonies of settlement in the temperate areas, partly because they inherited the institutional patterns of the home country, which represented an obstacle to modern economic development even at home – overcentralisation and an emphasis on extractive institutions. Latin America is a good example (Acemoglu et al. 2001, Engerman and Sokoloff 1994). This was true even where there appeared to be strong similarities in the environments and histories, as with Argentina, Uruguay or Chile (White 1992b).[19] Superficially, these countries appeared similar to the English-speaking countries. However, there was a stress on rent-extracting institutions in most cases and at various times a 'winner-takes-all' politics.

A second factor, the existence of previously developed economies, influenced what happened elsewhere, sometimes through demonstration effects, sometimes through military success, sometimes in meeting the problem of competition from outside enterprises, and sometimes resulting from the movement of factors of production such as capital, with resentment and resistance against inward movements, especially acquisitions. Economic development is sometimes a response to the challenge of development elsewhere, but not all challenges elicit a positive response.

It is interesting to compare the experience in the forward economies of Europe, notably Britain and France. There has in the past been a debate on how Britain led France in initiating industrialisation (Crouzet 1966). Some see the British primacy as purely accidental given marked similarities between the two societies. Crafts (1995) has argued that the British lead was the result of good fortune – it was in some sense random. This suggests that in France the preconditions for the Industrial Revolution were already evolving when the Industrial Revolution was initiated in Britain. The two countries were close in terms of their level of economic development in the period before the Industrial Revolution, France as much a source of technical innovations as Britain. France responded to British priority in industrialisation. O'Brien and Keyder (1978) stressed the degree to which the early starters, Britain and France, differed in their pattern of development, reflecting the fact that a late-comer had to adjust to the previous developments in Britain; it had to create its own path in a competitive world. There were two paths to the twentieth century. There was, for example, a greater emphasis on the final consumer goods rather than on the production of standard intermediate products – on haute couture or fashion rather than textile fabrics, on confectionery rather than milling, on finished ironware rather than mass-produced iron or later steel.

Gerschenkron went further, showing how late starters in Europe developed patterns of substitution to cover what was missing in the relevant economies compared with the pioneer Britain. Institutional patterns in different countries reflected economic conditions, in the words of Sylla and Toniolo (1991: 16): 'To Gerschenkron differences in economic conditions were essentially varying degrees of backwardness'. The nature and role of the state, and also the ideology underpinning that role, was one such institutional difference. Sylla and Toniolo (1991: 17) also comment that, the more efficiently markets functioned, the less was the net impact of state intervention: 'If markets were absent or inefficient in situation of backwardness, as Gerschenkron suggested, the net economic impact of state intervention was likely to be greater than where markets were well-developed'. The role of banks and of government differed in continental economies. Gerschenkron showed how the mechanisms for generating the savings required to finance capital accumulation and for transferring these funds to those making the appropriate investments in physical facilities reflected the degree of backwardness in the relevant economy. Those countries developing in conditions of medium relative backwardness (Germany or the western parts of the Austro-Hungarian Empire) saw an important role for the investment bank, rather than the commercial banks of Britain, and for the directors of those banks, who also provided scarce entrepreneurial inputs to the enterprises in which they invested. Such banks invested directly in the railways and related manufacturing sectors, such as iron and steel or engineering, and in coal mines. In conditions of extreme backwardness (Russia), where even banking was poorly developed, foreign and government capital was significant.

The European economies share enough in common in culture and institutions to make it a reasonable assumption that they would recognise the relevance of a significant model of economic development from outside, modify it and initiate modern economic development. The removal of obstacles to economic development gave the relevant narratives their special character – the unification of Germany, the ending of serfdom, the vagaries of remoteness and climate. It was not only capital which was scarce, entrepreneurial talents were also in short supply. The pattern of development in these economies differs markedly from the British model. There were also independent sources of economic development which made these societies responsive to the new opportunities.

Like the stoppers at the end of a bookshelf, Britain and Japan mark the extremes in the Euro-Asian land mass, but also represent the pioneers in economic development within the respective areas. It is possible to see the Japanese experience as a precursor to other Asian experience. In the Asian Economic Miracle, Japan is the model, which other Asian economies are seen as deliberately or unconsciously imitating. It is interesting to speculate how far the Japanese experience parallels that of Britain and whether it is possible that the Industrial Revolution would eventually have occurred in Japan had something prevented the occurrence in Europe. In the release from the Malthusian trap, Britain and Japan share much in common but the mechanisms for release were very different. It is also true that, despite its economic leadership in Asia, Japan lagged significantly behind Britain. It shared its high levels of commercialisation, its advanced urbanisation, and its relatively productive agriculture, but lagged in the application of new technology in industry.

Highly specific conditions influenced the nature of the Japanese model – resource limitations, outside influence, backwardness, military pretensions. If only in the sense of the diffusion of institutions, the four little tigers all received influence from either Britain or Japan, the respective pioneers in Europe and Asia. In the case of Taiwan (1895–1945) and Korea (1906–45), there was direct colonisation and a direct Japanese influence on the development of the economy. The influence of guidance planning and a more direct intervention by governments in encouraging economic development are examples. In the case of Singapore and Hong Kong, these entrepôt ports were for a longer period British colonies. Later developers in Asia, including China, were greatly influenced by the model of economic development followed in Japan, despite the political hostilities which followed World War II.

There is no doubt that there was in the Japanese case both a preparatory evolution, similar to that in Britain, but also a dramatic reaction to relative backwardness and deliberate imitation of the European model, but not the British model. Institutions were borrowed on an eclectic basis to suit the particular aims of the modernisers. The closure of the Japanese economy before the arrival of Commander Perry's gunboats in 1853 did not assist in promoting economic development. However, the Unequal Treaties and their influence were offset by the declining value of the silver-based currency, encouraging competitiveness, but giving some protection for what were in most instances infant industries. The Meiji restoration in 1868 represented the coming to power of a group of leaders strongly committed to the desire to develop Japan economically and prevent it falling into the same dependence as China. The Japanese government played a very significant role in the economic development of Japan. The Japanese imitation of Europe's imperial expansion gave it a direct influence in Asia, notably in Taiwan, Korea and Manchuria. The political influence can be malign, while the economic influence is benign. It is possible to see Japan as playing a leading role in the spread of modern economic development within Asia, although there is a significant delay, with rates of economic growth in the Asian tigers only accelerating markedly in the 1960s. It is also possible to refer to a larger area, a Sinitic block, which includes China and areas of Chinese influence. Much of the economic development since the 1960s, but particularly since the inception of reform in China in 1978, has had a Chinese input. Curiously, before 1978 the Chinese appeared to be much more successful economically outside China than within China itself.

There has been much speculation about the nature of the Asian miracle and now a general recognition that the pattern of economic development differed in key respects from that in Europe and its offshoots. For example, the role of government has been much more important, taking the form of guidance planning, an interaction between politicians holding power for long periods of time, public officials in key ministries such as

MITI and the managers of large conglomerates, for example the keiretsu or chaebol. Institutional structures have differed, with much less emphasis on the market and a greater role for family business. However, since the 1960s, there has been a tendency to open the economies, if in a rather targeted manner. It is possible to see a distinctive Asian pattern.

Another possible grouping is that of countries which became communist. Communism gave birth to an economic system which for a time rivalled the market system responsible for the initial inception of modern economic development. The Russian Revolution in 1917, followed closely by a major collapse of the market system during the Great Depression, highlighted the existence of a rival pattern of economic development. The Stalinist system, based on centralised physical planning and a deliberate policy of accelerating industrialisation through a high level of investment, appeared initially to be successful – it carried the Soviet Union to great power status. It is possible to underestimate the role of a communist industrialisation strategy in propelling forward what were relatively undeveloped economies in both the Soviet Union and China (Allen 2003) and to ignore the degree to which the Asian economies were protected economies before 1960.

The remarkable economic performance of China throws a spotlight on the divergent pattern for transitional economies, notably between three groups – the Central European economies, the former members of the USSR, including Mongolia but excluding the Baltic Republics, and Asian transitional economies, notably China and Vietnam. In the first, there has been a political revolution which was strongly supported by the population as a whole and economic reform, introduced at a varying pace, from rapid in Poland to much slower in Bulgaria, has been supported by most of the population. These are societies where communism was in control for less than half a century. Entry into the European Union has reinforced both the pace of reform and the positive outcome of reform. In the old USSR, both political and economic reforms have been more restrained, particularly the latter, although political collapse made inevitable a privatisation which encouraged corruption. Resource richness has encouraged this corruption, but underpinned a reversal of the contraction of GDP that followed the collapse of the USSR. The resource position of these countries has rescued them from the contraction which characterised their early years of reform, notably during the 1990s. Whether the gains in income can be used to make market reform more effective is debatable. Political reform has been rolled back to some degree. In Asia, there has been little political reform, more an inevitable decentralisation of decision making, and economic reform has been gradual, sequential and experimental, with a major success from the beginning in accelerating the rate of economic growth. It has also been associated with a steady deregulation of markets and opening of the economy, but both directed and qualified. Reform with its initial gains has been successful in keeping open the window of opportunity. The regimes find their legitimacy in the economic success which has followed reform.

13.   The rise and fall of the Soviet Union: the failed experiment

... the Soviet 'experiment' loomed as the great Other in terms of which the world was obliged to define itself. To the hopeful, it represented the socialist antithesis to capitalism, and the future as against the past. To the fearful, it became the totalitarian menace to the free world of the West, and the enemy of civilisation. (Malia 1999: 3)

One of the most interesting analytic narratives of the recent past involves the failed experiment with communism, as it was played out in the USSR, an analytical narrative not yet properly unravelled, let alone written. In the words of Gregory, 'The Soviet administrative-command economy was the most important social and economic experiment of the twentieth century' (Gregory 2004: 1). As Hobsbawm (1994: 55) asserts in his history of the twentieth century, it is no accident that his dating of that century virtually coincides with the lifetime of the state born of the October Revolution in 1917 and dead by 1991: that revolution has dominated interpretations of the twentieth century. The experiment was an exercise in social engineering, intended to achieve a fair society, but adopting, as one of its preparatory aims, a decisive inception of modern economic development. It is surprising that communism became a mechanism for promoting modern economic development, since, according to Marxist theory, the relevant revolution was supposed to happen in an economy where the problems of development had already been resolved.

A momentous debate occurred during the 1920s concerning the strategy of economic development and the implementation of this strategy. The debate over how to stimulate economic development has raged every since. The Soviet Union aspired to a rapid rate of industrialisation, much faster than anything previously achieved.[1] Implementation of this strategy involved the suspension of the market, with results which were dramatic. This aspiration was to be realised by a highly centralised system of planning, making use of administrative instruction to an extreme degree, justifying the use of the term command economy. For a brief time, there was a rival strategy of modern economic development, distinguished from, and competitive with, the capitalist market system in critical ways – in means rather than ends, although the ends were much more ambitious than anything previously attempted. During the 1930s, this system offered an alternative to a capitalist market system seemingly on the brink of collapse.

There are a number of questions relevant to the communist experiment. The first asks, why in Russia? The Marxist historical dialectic had suggested otherwise.[2] The attempt to create socialism in a backward economy was fraught with all sorts of problems. It is necessary to identify the factors which made the revolutionary events of early twentieth-century Russia likely: this involves analysing factors of both proximate and ultimate causation, elements of continuity and discontinuity and of contingency or inevitability in Russian history. A second question asks, why did the communist experiment fail? Some believe it was doomed from the start (Malia 1994). The failure is obvious, since the communist political system dissolved and with it the economic system: planning was replaced by a market system. Paradoxically, communism assisted in both making Russia a superpower and seriously weakening its capacity to play that role over a protracted period of time.

There are four sections in this chapter. The first section confronts the difficulties of selecting an appropriate analytic narrative for Russia. The second section considers what was unique and what unexceptional about the Russian experience before the Revolution. It focuses on the changing nature of the tsarist economy and on the level of economic development achieved, explaining the 1917 Revolution. The third section focuses on the 1920s debate about the strategy of industrialisation and the policy outcome of the debate. It evaluates the successes of the strategy adopted, which rested on collectivisation of agriculture and the introduction of a planning system. The fourth section turns attention to the failures of the strategy, failures which contributed to the dissolution of the Soviet Union and the ending of the communist experiment. It considers the difficulties of making a transition from a planning to a market system.

CHOOSING AN APPROPRIATE ANALYTIC NARRATIVE

A key issue in Russian history is a perception of persistent economic underperformance. This is usually associated with the divergence of Russia from a normal European pattern, both in income levels and their growth and in institutions and their development. Russia is seen as persistently lagging behind the rest of Europe. Some see this lag as not just economic, but political, social, even cultural. In so far as the latter conditions the former, there is a self-reinforcing negative feedback loop which makes economic underperformance persistent.

There are two perspectives on Russian economic history which serve as bases for different narratives. Throughout Russian history there were two streams of economic development – an induced and a spontaneous stream (Crisp 1976), two rival strategies alternating in importance – economic development imposed from above by the government and a more spontaneous form of economic development based on the operation of relatively free markets. The first perspective stresses the differences of Russia from the European pattern of economic development. It tends to see political economy as critical to the narrative and to the attempted transitions which occurred in Russian history. In this interpretation, the communist interlude was a natural progression along a Russian historical path distinguished in critical ways from the European experience. There was a Russian path dependence, a highly distinctive pathway (Hedlund 2005, Coe 2003). The other stream stresses the degree to which Russia conformed to the usual European pattern of economic development. It regards government intervention as at best superfluous to the prospects of modern economic development and at worst harmful, and elevates the significance of those periods when the government played a comparatively passive role. It sees underperformance as reflecting the suppression of the spontaneous stream by intermittent government interventions. The Soviet failure is interpreted as confirming this interpretation, being an extreme manifestation of the top-down stream.

Russian history involved a series of transitions characterised by institutional upheavals, unusual in their radical nature. No other country has experienced such dramatic institutional transformations. These transitions involved major shifts in the relative importance of government and market in the process of economic development and significant changes of government policy, switches from one stream of economic development to another and back again. There were four such transitions, which can be readily identified, periods of significant institutional discontinuity – first, the imposition of the service state during the sixteenth century, involving the imposition of a universal compulsion to service, linked with the second serfdom and the later extension by Peter the Great to the gentry and the industrial sector of the economy (so-called possessional serfs); secondly, a series of reforms of the semi-feudal institutional structure begun by Alexander II and his ministers – what some have called a quasi-bourgeois revolution; next the Bolshevik Revolution in 1917, most notably its second phase in the Great Turn of 1929, which instituted a central planning system; and finally, the end of the communist system and the transition from a planned to a market system.

The definitive analytic narrative has yet to be written – it probably requires a greater distance from recent events. Some interpret Russia as

European, others as Asian, and others as sui generis – in one expression, Eurasian.[3] Such viewpoints highlight the problem of referent, with whom it is appropriate to compare Russia and its economic experience. Without a relevant comparison, the assertion of underperformance is meaningless. Whereas Gregory (2004) takes the referent as the group of developed countries – the reference is Europe and its offshoots – Allen (2003) has defined Russia as a developing country and compared its performance with other developing countries, moving the comparison outside Europe. The former provides the referent for underperformance, but the latter the referent for a significant degree of economic success.

Viewing Russia in a European mirror tells us as much about Europe as about Russia. Malia (1999) gives four relevant images – Russia as an Oriental despotism, more Asian than European; Russia as an enlightened despotism, much like Old Regime Europe; Russia seen through the prism of convergence on the European pattern; or finally Russia as a 'barbaric yet vital soul' (Malia 1999: 293), Russia as cultural or even ideocratic leader. During different periods of Russian history, different images prevail, but in the Soviet period all the images become important, which explains confusion in the interpretation of the Soviet experiment. Russian history is a touchstone for political attitudes and values. The perspective determines the judgement, or as Abu-Lughod (1989: 30) comments, 'History is inevitably "distorted" by the vantage point of the historian'. Most interpretations reflect the conditions of the time at which they were made, since events have often led to a reinterpretation of previous history.[4] Political preconceptions colour much of the analysis done, both in favour and against the actions of the communist government. The nature of the ideocratic state during the communist period makes this inevitable. '. . . there is more than one way of conceiving the "problems" of Russian economic development' (Gatrell 1986: xiv). There are three interpretations of the direction which Russian history has taken – the liberal, the Marxist and the populist (Gatrell 1986: chapter 1). Two see the Russian experience largely from a European perspective, the other from a Eurasian perspective. The liberal viewpoint sees Russia headed for both a constitutional political arrangement and a spontaneous market system. The Marxist viewpoint sees the need to follow the same path, but with a continuation to revolution inspired by the proletariat. The populist viewpoint believed Russia could skip steps in the European development, notably the capitalist stage, moving straight to a socialist society. Unsurprisingly, the Marxist had a strong run during the Soviet period, and the liberal after the dissolution of the Soviet Union. Because of the continuing resonance of the revolution as an epoch-defining event and the polarisation caused by Cold War conflict, the interpretation of the Russian experience in the twentieth century has been central to an understanding of the role of modern economic development in the co-evolution of world economy, polity and society.

The downfall of the Soviet Union initially generated revisionist attempts to rewrite accounts deemed too favourable to the successes of the Soviet Union in stimulating modern economic development (Gregory 1982). The Soviet experiment was a totally unnecessary and meaningless one, which achieved nothing. Such a revision even extended to rewriting the history of the tsarist period in the direction of emphasising its successes and to downplaying the previously exaggerated role of the government. Some believe that Russia would have been a fully developed economy by now, were it not for the communist interlude. There are both theoretical and empirical problems with the data used to interpret Russian history. Wheatcroft (2005), in a point of view he put strongly at his inaugural lecture as professor, has argued that beneath the statistical distortions imposed by their masters, the collectors of data in Russia continued to do a first-world job in what were third-world circumstances. Once the archives were opened, much more could be said about the Soviet experience. Yet some of the problems are deeper than just discovering relevant data. As Gregory points out, even the calculation of growth rates reflects a choice of price weights for output, with a stark contrast between the results from using prices expressive of planning preferences and prices which exist in a market in which consumers operate free of government intervention and express consumer preferences[5] (Gregory 1993: 136). Gerschenkron (1970) and Bergson (1964) long ago pointed out the inherent ambiguity in estimating growth rates, and the real possibility of interpreting the growth process in a very different way. The Soviet growth experience of the 1930s looks very different using late 1920s prices or late 1930s prices, a striking success as against a much more modest achievement.

The framework of an analytic narrative put together here is directed at answering the following questions: how far has Russia gone in the process of modern economic development? If there is persistent underperformance, what were the main causative factors? There has been fierce debate about how to interpret what was happening in Russia. The use of theory is central to the interpretation of the Russian experience. There are significant variations in the world view of commentators. At a superficial level, these reflect different views of what constitutes the cause of economic backwardness in Russia. At a deeper level, they reflect different views about the motivation of decision makers and the role of market behaviour in general. There is agreement on one thing – the theme giving unity to the Russian narrative which highlights the tension between the pretensions of Russia as a great power and its economic backwardness (Gerschenkron

1970). This is reflected in the work of just about every commentator working on Russia. As one has written: 'The Russian economy during its industrialisation era is a case study of economic growth under conditions of relative backwardness' (Gregory 1982: 4). Such a theme requires a treatment of both the internal and external political economy of Russia – who influenced government policy, how and why, Russia's interaction with the outside world, especially the European world, the nature of its political alliances, and the difficulty of accessing technology from outside. The transitions in Russian history followed dramatic manifestations of the tension between relative backwardness and its aspirations as a great power, usually in a military defeat which revealed the weakness as well as the political pretensions, a defeat sometimes reversed after the full mobilisation of the one resource which Russian had in abundance, people. There has been an obsession with the possibility of invasion, such invasions frequent enough to keep reinforcing such a concern – the Poles during the Times of Trouble, Napoleon's invasion in 1812, the Crimean War (1954–6), even the removal of the fruits of victory at the Congress of Berlin (1978), World War I and the Treaty of Brest-Litovsk in 1917, and Hitler's attack in 1941, and finally the worries of the Cold War. The emphasis on great power pretensions inevitably implies a strategy in which government seeks to realise those pretensions.

An explanation of economic underperformance requires a focus on ultimate causation in the economic history of Russia, notably the influence on economic development of its resource endowment, the threats from its risk environments, the quality of its human capital, and the nature of its institutional structures. The commitment of government and the ability to assimilate foreign technology have also been significant factors in understanding the attempts to initiate modern economic development.

There is fundamental disagreement over the quality of the resource endowment of Russia. Today Russia is a largely commodity-driven economy, in which exports of resource-intensive commodities drive the trading account and the rate of economic growth. It is common to see references to resource abundance, notably, but not only, to its endowment with oil and gas. This tells only part of the story. The resources are certainly there. The thick *chernozem* of the steppes is highly fertile and potentially, with appropriate methods, can give good yields of grain. Before 1914, Russia was one of the largest exporters of grain in the world, and this was not achieved solely by squeezing the peasant producers. The availability of cultivable land per head of population is relatively good. Extension of Russian control into the area of the Stans gave access to land which produced, with irrigation, good yields of cotton, to complement the flax produced elsewhere. The availability of iron ore and coal in Ukraine was favourable. Siberia is rich in a variety of raw materials, not just forest and furs. Yet there are two problems with the resource endowment[6] – the accessibility of the resources and threats from the risk environment.

There are two aspects to the transport problem. The first relates to access to the outside world. Hooson has claimed, 'No country on earth is as crippled by its coastlines or shut in by its own seas as is the Soviet Union' (Hooson 1970: 7). There has been considerable recent discussion of the disadvantage of being landlocked and the effect it has on a country's level of trade and its rate of economic growth. For much of its history, Russia shared most of the characteristics of a landlocked economy. Russia's 'quest for the sea' only opened 'windows' on the world at comparatively late dates. Outlets were found through the Arctic Ocean in the sixteenth century and through the Pacific in the seventeenth, the usefulness of the former being limited by harsh weather conditions and its remoteness from main trade routes, and the latter by inaccessibility to the main centres of population. Control over more useful coastline came in the eighteenth century for the Baltic Sea and in the nineteenth for the Black Sea. The proportion of usable coastline is still very limited, if account is taken of closure by ice and accessibility.

The second aspect of the transport problem is domestic. A country can only be judged rich in resources in the context of the accessibility of these resources. By this criterion, Russia was not resource-rich, especially in the early period of its development. Transport improvement was crucial to its economic development. This argument was advanced strongly by Baykov (1954), who argued, 'In order to utilize Russia's natural resources, the Russian people had to overcome more handicaps than the populations of most of the leading West European nations' (ibid. 140). The old core, the Muscovite centre, was not well-endowed with resources, since it had a limited agricultural capacity and lacked most of the industrial raw materials critical to industrial advance. The movement of grain within the country depended first, on Peter the Great's improvement to the river network during the early eighteenth century, through a series of canals which linked the Volga system and the centre with the north, and secondly, on the construction of the railways, from the 1860s on, which linked the south with the centre and the north, and also with the main export outlets on both the Baltic and the Black Seas (White 1975). The Urals iron industry developed by Peter also depended on good water transport and was not easily connected with sources of coal. It remained wedded to a charcoal-burning technology. Even more critically, the iron and steel industry in Ukraine which underpinned Witte's strategy of industrialisation during the 1890s depended on the linking by railway of the iron ore of Krivoy Rog and the coal of the Donbas. The construction of the 500 kilometre plus Catherine railway in the 1880s provided the necessary link (Portal 1965, Baykov 1954). There is plenty of evidence that the railways in Russia had a bigger impact than in the USA or elsewhere (White 1976). They were critical to the Smithian element in economic development, to the regional specialisation which accompanies the spread of the market and commercialisation.

There are various assessments of the agricultural potential of Russia (Parker 1972, Field 1968, Allen 2003), which compare the position of Russia with that of the USA (discussed in White 1987: 49 and 50–52). These show the almost complete absence of the climatic type most conducive to dense human settlement, called on the Koppen classification the 'humid temperate' zone, characterised by rain all the year with hot summers and mild winters. Only 0.5 per cent of the USSR, according to Parker, falls in this zone, a belt along the Black Sea well outside the core area of Russia (in the USA it is 34 per cent, if we ignore Alaska). Only 1.4 per cent of Russian cropland has adequate moisture and thermal conditions, whereas 80 per cent is thermally deficient and 59 per cent requires irrigation. The old core area is worse off. According to Field, the productivity of Soviet cropland has been less than 60 per cent of that of the USA, a disparity accounted for by geographical problems which limit what can be grown and the yields of crops which can be grown. Allen (2003: chapter 4) has also shown how climate limited yields in Russian agriculture and made appropriate comparisons with less advantaged areas in North America. Consequently, the core area of Russia was vulnerable to ecological pressure as population increased.

It is possible to explain the failure of Russia to fully develop, at least at a date comparable with the economies of Western Europe and North America, through a persistent high risk environment combined with particular resource deficiencies. A comparison with the USA is unfavourable (White 1987). Both were frontier societies in the sense of expansion in territory and in settlement, although in neither society did the frontier fully dominate. As the American settlers moved west across the plains, the Russian were moving south into the steppe and east across the vast expanses of Siberia. Surprisingly, at its peak the movement in Russia was much larger, in terms of territory and population movement, than in the USA. The frontier movement justifies a comparison of the two economies. The Turner thesis sees the frontier as having significantly favourable effects on polity, society and economy. The Russian frontier did not play such a favourable role. Its existence may even have reduced the pressure to improve agriculture in the old core. The natural environment determined the pace of movement and the way in which the new areas interacted with the existing economy. In the American case, the frontier was more benign, conditions in the core area more favourable. In the USA, risk and resources combined to favour economic development; in Russia, they combined to constrain that development. One irony is that the peopling of the frontier depended on a paradox, in that enserfment tied the peasants to the land, whereas the settlement of the frontier required movement. In many cases, serf owners moved whole villages.

The risk environment in Russia has reflected a mix of factors including climatic fluctuations, outbreaks of epidemic disease, civil wars and peasant jacqueries, and outside invasions. Throughout Russian history, the incidence of shocks appears high and their impact significant. The harsh risk environment encouraged an overcentralisation of political and economic activity. There was often a failure of governments in Russia to respond positively to the relevant shocks, or the response, often institutional, was such as to create impediments to the process of economic development. Climatic conditions in Russia are severe. The growing season is everywhere very short. Siberia represents in many ways the most intimidating environment on earth, permafrost being one of the problems. Even in the most fertile areas there was a tendency to dramatic fluctuations in temperature and precipitation and a tendency to drought and other climatic fluctuations which threatened the harvest. Harvest failure was a regular visitor through to the nineteenth century and later. This was particularly true in the most favourable agricultural area, the black earth belt in the Ukraine and western Siberia. Famine was not uncommon in Russia, a danger made more threatening by poor transport conditions in bad years. Nowhere in Russia has a really good combination of soils and climate. The core has reasonable moisture but poor soils, the steppe has deficiencies in rainfall in combination with a fertile soil. Crop yields were low by European standards, which meant that only small downward fluctuations could cause disaster. The level of income was much closer to subsistence, so that fluctuations could easily take a significant proportion of the population below that level. In a normal year, there were the times of suffering when reserves of grain had run out for a significant, but variable, proportion of the population. The response of the grain growers was in normal years to deliberately overproduce grain, which was usually turned into alcohol and to some extent stored to cover the deficits of bad years. The three field system and strip farming was retained much later than elsewhere, partly because of a risk control function. The demand for other products fluctuated directly with the harvest and favoured household production, the so-called *kustars*, over factory production. The *kustars* were much more adept at handling the associated risk. There is a sense in which proto-industrialisation in Russia acted as an obstacle to factory industrialisation and served to reinforce a dual economy. Risk was much more diffuse than these examples show. 'All lands (as well as all property, for that matter) were subject to arbitrary state confiscation' (Hellie 1999: 636). 'The consequences of the absence of contract right among the Muscovites themselves were that risk aversion and enforcement costs were high and certainty and private capita accumulation were low' (Ibid.: 637–8).

Malnourished populations are also subject to epidemic disease. Russia was vulnerable to major epidemic outbreaks. For example, plague was a problem much later than in the rest of Europe, the outbreak of 1780 being well documented (Alexander 1980). Other diseases were also the cause of intermittent *crises démographiques*. The danger of invasion was ever present and war to protect the western border a common experience, at different times with Poles, Swedes, Turks, the Austrians, the Germans, even the British and French. This required heavy expenditures on up-to-date military preparedness, access to Western technology and institutional adaptations in Russia which allowed it to use fully its main resource of people. The existence of a threat was not limited to conventional warfare. In the south, there was for a long period the threat of slave raiding from the Crimean Tartars. For something like four centuries, slave raiding was a major threat to the factor of production scarcest on the frontier, labour (Hellie 1979, McNeill 1964). As McNeill has argued, a long series of annual raids, directed against the bordering agricultural population to the north and west, pushed the fringes of agricultural settlement back within the tree lines and, helped by pestilence, produced something approaching a desert across the Pontic steppe. The steppe region was exposed and dangerous. Over the long term, losses averaged at a minimum 2000 a year, and increased when the Ottomans took over the Black Sea slave trade from the Genoese after 1475, and slave trading became the main economic activity of the Crimean Tartars. At its peak, in the period 1600–50, probably between 150000 and 200000 Muscovites were taken by Tartar slavers, a high proportion of the steppe population (Davies 2007: 25). Between 1468 and 1694 there were 65 major raids (Davies 2007: 24). The danger did not disappear in the eighteenth century. Fortified lines were built, including the famous Belgorod line, at considerable cost. A series of fortified lines marked the southern movement of the frontier. A continuing threat of incursion on the frontier, even within the core area, reinforced the centralisation of the Russian polity. The steppe area was dangerous for a long period of time, acting as a brake on the cultivation of the *chernozem*.

In every respect, the human capital required for modern economic development was lacking. Literacy levels were low, at levels characteristic of undeveloped economies. Schooling was an unusual occurrence. In both respects, the small urban sector was much better off than the rural areas which dominated Russian life. As late as 1914, 75 per cent of the population remained rural – this had changed little by the Great Turn of 1929. The Malthusian balance of high birth and death rates, with periodic demographic crises, kept subsistence close to survival levels. During the second half of the nineteenth-century, population was growing rapidly and putting pressure on resources. Life expectation was comparatively short. Malnourishment was common, making the population vulnerable to both epidemic and endemic diseases, and making it likely that much of the population lacked both energy and the capacity to operate a commercial economy.

The transitions through which Russia has passed involve radical institutional restructuring. There is more continuity than appears on the surface, as those who stress path dependency argue. Most interpretations of Russian history focus on the inflated role of government and the minor role of the market. Such interpretations note the absence of civil society and the weaknesses of the market system. The argument stresses the ineffectiveness of the institutional changes which promoted decentralisation. There has been a tendency to autocracy in Russia – a stream of strong leaders from Ivan the Terrible, through Peter the Great to Stalin, to Vladimir Putin, and considerable continuity of authoritarian government. The Mongol invasion of the thirteenth century had a profound, if controversial, effect on the political organisation of Russia, reinforcing the tendency to autocracy. In order to assert its independence of the Tartar Horde, Moscow became like the Mongols. This was reinforced by the influence of Byzantium, the eastern Roman empire, exercised through the Orthodox Church and its notion of Moscow as the third Rome. Orthodoxy, nationality and autocracy became the slogan of the conservatives.

There are various reasons for the persistence of autocracy, including size of territory, and the difficulty of transportation; the harsh risk environments, even in the more benign areas; the periodic risk of external invasion; the imperial profile of Russia – the only European empire which was a landed rather than a maritime empire; and its particular historical experience, its path-dependent development. There is nothing inevitable about this path, but what happened in the past often closed off other options in relevant periods.

While autocracy was perceived as critical to the survival of Russia, highly centralised government did not penetrate the society in a way which gave the autocrats strong infrastructural power. Russian governmental and social structures were in practice often weak and fragile (Malia 1994: 69). There was systematic instability – greater than elsewhere in Europe, because of the combination of a crude military-bureaucratic autocracy and a primitive two-class lord-peasant society which generated both the political oppressiveness of the state and the social oppressiveness of serfdom. Times of trouble occurred when direction from the centre was weak. Through the period from the sixteenth to the eighteenth centuries there were huge peasant revolts, during which government structures quickly and easily collapsed. The best known are those of Stenka Razin and Emilian Pugachev in the eighteenth century (Alexander 1969).

One corollary of the stress on autocracy is the lack of civil society. While the peasant village has its own forms of organisation and decision making and interacted with the government largely through recruitment for the army and the payment of taxes, any form of civil society was seen as potentially subversive of the prerogatives of the autocracy. A vestige of civil society only appeared after the reforms of Alexander II. The autocracy developed administrative organisations whose main responsibility was to suppress such activities where possible, such as the third section. The irony is that it was the autocrat who usually pushed through reforms during the key transitions, supported by a small group of bureaucratic reformers. As Mosse (1996: 273) wrote: 'the Tsarist reforming groups in the bureaucracy and their helpers as planners and executors formed the essential infrastructure of perestroika [reform]'. Without support from autocrat and enlightened bureaucrats, reform was impossible.

The somewhat rigid social structure of Russia reflected the nature of the service state and the low level of urbanisation in Russia. The social orders in Russia (*sosloviya*) were clearly defined and relatively stable. With the exception of the nobility and the peasants, they were few and weak. Supporting the tsar and his/her family were the nobility. The nobility was a relatively small group, highly differentiated in status. There were many nobles with little income and few serfs. The emphasis for the nobility was on service in the army or bureaucracy. The life of most of the nobility was urban based and the cities of Russia largely administrative centres. Land was a source of either status or subsistence and, despite its relative abundance, highly valued. Both society and economy were dominated by the peasants. Before the emancipation in 1861, the serfs were tied to either private or state land, in roughly equal numbers, in theory unable to move, although in practice many moved to the frontier.

Other groups in Russian society were weak. The lack of industrial development and the limited nature of commercial expansion made the level of urbanisation relatively low, by the standards of the more developed European economies, and the number of resident merchants or professionals small. There was little space for a display of entrepreneurship since poor status attached to commercial activity. Other groups who might have moderated autocracy were absent or uninterested. After Peter, the church was firmly under state control. In Russia, there was no equivalent to a theology adjusting over time to changing circumstance and compatible with individualism and progress, no equivalent of the Reformation or the Renaissance, no genuine scientific revolution or industrial enlightenment.

Hellie stressed the three service revolutions creating the service state, which, he argues, persisted right through Russian history, until undone with the dissolution of the Soviet Union. The imposition of the service obligation on the whole population represented the first major institutional transition. This transition is seen as having roots in the nomadic tendency for all to be at the immediate service of the Khan. Hellie's first service revolution was the so-called *oprichnina* of Ivan the Terrible during the late sixteenth century, whereby a service gentry was tied to the land in return for service to the government, and the *votchina*, or land held in the equivalent of fee simple, largely disappeared. Enservicement of the gentry implied enserfment of the peasants. This service revolution was extended by the creation of serfdom – the introduction of the 'forbidden years' in the 1580s, when the peasants could not move, and the law code of 1649, which finally tied the peasant to both lord and the land. Eastern Europe, notably Russia, saw the imposition of serfdom at the very time at which it disappeared, or was disappearing, in the west, where its disappearance freed the rural economy commercially and allowed a Smithian specialisation to occur (North and Thomas 1973).

In the interpretation of the second serfdom there developed two theories.[7] One sees it as imposed from above, either with strong leadership from the nobility, as in Poland where they dominated the state, or from the autocracy, as in Russia. In the latter, it was linked to a service revolution since the service gentry required the labour input of their serfs in order to be able to provide obligatory service (Hellie 1971). The whole system has a rationale which was removed when the nobility was emancipated from the obligation of service in 1762. The second theory sees it as coming from below because of the increasing immiseration of the peasantry and their rising level of indebtedness. The onerous conditions of the late sixteenth and early seventeenth centuries in Russia and the continuing importance of war caused problems for the peasants, who reacted by depopulating the old centre of Russia. Many fled, increasing the pressure on those who remained. Peasants even sold themselves into slavery to escape worsening conditions (Hellie 1979). The combination of poor natural conditions and negative shocks of various kinds, such as war or civil disturbance, put the peasantry in distress. They often sought the protection of lords by tying themselves to land and lord. In this theory, the changes of law simply validated a process occurring independently. Both forces were at work, but the initiative came from above.

The second phase of the service revolution occurred under Peter, when a table of ranks reflecting service to the state defined nobility and when serfdom was extended to the manufacturing sector of the economy. The gentry were only freed from compulsory service in 1762, but by then had internalised the compulsion to serve, so the apparent liberation made little difference. Most of the nobility continued to serve in various ways. Despite the removal of the main rationale for serfdom, with the freeing of the nobility, the serfs were only emancipated in 1861, but remained tied to the commune, only freed briefly after 1910 by Stolypin's reforms which encouraged the creation of an owner-occupier farming sector.[8] The third service revolution occurred under Stalin, when the obverse of the guarantee of full employment was the universal compulsion to work, if often in the gulags. Stalin is seen as having brought the service state to a dramatic climax.

The second transition was an attempt to undo the service obligation and to modernise the institutional structure of the society, first under Alexander II, and later under his two successors and their chief ministers Witte and Stolypin, a transition which proved a failure, terminated by World War I and the Revolution. Its role in the process of modern economic development is controversial, particularly as a dramatic reversal occurred under the Soviets, with the extension of government control right through society and economy by the communist regime. The market operated imperfectly and civil society was practically non-existent, although what happened between 1861 and 1917 is a hint that it might have blossomed in different circumstances. Civil society was incompatible with autocracy, just as a command economy was incompatible with the efficient operation of markets. A final transition occurred as a result of the breakdown of the communist system, both politically and economically, and the revival of the market mechanism.

The service revolutions were linked to two related conceptions. First, they were linked to the notion of a patrimonial state in which the tsar deemed all property to be held at his/her grace and favour and subject to withdrawal, if the tsar wished it (Pipes 1974). There was 'a total merger of power and property' (Hedlund 2001: 221). The law was an administrative instrument of the autocracy. Under the Soviet regime, private property rights were again extremely limited. Secondly, there was the Soviet notion of the economy as equivalent to, and run as, one large enterprise, an extreme form of a command economy, linked with a command polity, under what at one stage was described as a totalitarian system. The government sector expanded, swallowing up the whole economy. In the period of War Communism, the budgets of individual enterprises were even merged with the government budget.

THE TSARIST ERA AND REVOLUTION

There are two key questions relating to the pre-Soviet period: did tsarist Russia successfully make the inception into modern economic development, and if so, exactly when? If she had begun the process, how far was government policy and its policies responsible for this? These questions have been given different answers. The answers given here are in the affirmative, with important qualifications. On the eve of World War I Russia had begun the process of modern economic development, but it was precarious, hardly self-sustaining, because the onset of war soon after the inception makes it impossible to identify whether it had and had not. The impact of rapid industrialisation on the level of political and social conflict within Russia had significant but controversial effects. The role of government was critical to this process of rapid industrialisation, but the conflict engendered made impossible the application of consistent policies.

It is unclear when the backwardness of Russia began. There are some, including Blanchard (2000), who argue that it was not true at the time of Peter the Great or even later, and that it was as much to do with the inception of modern economic development elsewhere as with the failings of the Russian economy; Russia simply failed to develop with the rest of Europe. One reason for this backwardness is the overwhelming predominance of a low-productivity rural sector. On any account, the modern sector of the economy was small, the industrial sector, at least factory industry, poorly developed. Certainly there is an irony in the emergence of Russia as a great power at a time when it was beginning to lag seriously behind the forward economies of Europe (Malia 1999). Political and military strength reflected the size of Russia and its large population, and the ability to mobilise labour, not the productivity or diversity of the economic system. The emergence of the service state coloured everything which was done in Russia. Attempts at its dismantling were usually half-hearted and only temporarily freed up the system. Mobilisation of resources could be sustained for short periods of time, but had lasting effects on the nature of the system, reinforcing the service state. They were often followed by attempts to reform the system, often superficial tinkerings at the margins of the existing system, easily reversed.

Peter the Great is seen as responsible for turning Russia into a European power and a Europe-oriented economy. The creation in 1703 of the new capital at St Petersburg symbolised this reorientation. The expansion of Russia's borders to the west and the creation of empire made possible, even necessary, Russia's entry into the concert of European powers. It fought recurring wars with Sweden, Poland-Lithuania, Turkey and the remnants of the Tartar Horde to establish control over key areas in the west and south. The partition of Poland late in the eighteenth and the acquisition of Finland early in the nineteenth centuries marked Russia's decisive entry onto the European stage. Such a political orientation reflected a growing dependence on Europe for export markets and as a source of imports, for capital and for technology and organisational know-how. The Russian economy became increasingly integrated into the European economy. It exported resource-intensive commodities, such as grain, in return for manufactured goods, including machinery. It had an ambivalent attitude to borrowing from outside and to the intrusion of foreign direct investment, but by the end of the nineteenth century fully accepted encouragement of both as a part of a policy of rapid industrialisation.

The main focus of attention in the Tsarist era is on the period between 1885 and 1913, during part of which the Minister of Finance, Witte, developed policies which successfully accelerated the process of industrialisation. Growth during this period, at 3.3 per cent per annum, 1.75 per cent per head, looks impressive. Witte stabilized the value of the rouble and placed Russia on the gold standard in 1897. Foreign investment financed something like half the total investment of the 1890s, with most coming from France, reflecting the political alliances of Russia. Witte's policy used public works, notably railway building, to stimulate the development of heavy industry behind a protective tariff wall and to encourage an inflow of foreign investment into Russia, in order to raise the investment ratio and to stimulate a simultaneous inflow of entrepreneurial and technical inputs. Access to foreign technology depended on the activity of foreign enterprises (McKay 1970).

Russia in 1913 was a dual economy, the rural peasant-dominated sector with considerable disguised underemployment, and a small modern sector, largely dominated by foreign capital and government utilities. The agricultural sector still accounted for over 50 per cent of total output (Gregory 1982) and the level of urbanisation was only 14 per cent (Bairoch 1993). The success of a Witte-type policy depended on the pursuit of a cautious foreign policy in order to keep the budget in order. Despite a world recession in 1900 and a defeat in the war with Japan (1904–5), followed by revolution, there was a significant economic advance, but one which did not greatly raise living standards in towns or countryside. The overall growth rate reflected largely what happened in the agricultural sector. Agricultural output, productivity and exports were rising in the period 1860–1914 (Gregory 1982). The frontier kept agriculture expanding, because the area opened up in the fertile black earth area was much more productive than the core areas of Russia. Within the core area, there was enormous pressure from population on the carrying capacity of the land. Before the start of World War I there is an agrarian crisis in the older settled parts of Russia. A disparity in regional performance explains the opposed views of commentators.

It is realistic to describe the acceleration in economic growth as '. . . a one-off resource boom with a veneer of some tariff-induced industrialisation' (Allen 2003: 26). The momentum of modern economic development seems to be lacking (Allen 2003: chapter 2). Mosse (1992: 283) rightly noted that, unlike in the West, Russia's progress was never self-sustaining. Some impressive productivity increases in agriculture, seemingly at 0.8 per cent per annum, seem to have run their course, bringing yields to levels equal to comparable areas in Canada and the northern United States and leaving little scope for further improvement. The world boom in agricultural prices, which propelled this sector forward, came to an end in 1913. Railway expansion, with its stimulating impact on the economy, especially heavy industry, had also reached its peak. The reliance of the textile industry on tariffs suggests that a textile-led export boom was unlikely.

The question to ask is – if the rate of economic growth was impressive why did the revolutions of 1905 and 1917 occur? Did the enormous social and political tensions generated by accelerated growth within an autocratic state cause revolution, or were the revolutions the result of contingent factors related to the impact of war, in particular World War I's dire consequences for the supply of food to the towns, and the obvious deficiencies of the Russian government in fighting both wars? The true situation is that the shock of war seems to have hit a vulnerable polity, society and economy, one ripe for change. The industrialisation effort brought increased stress on the population, notably within the countryside, mainly to finance the investment effort which underpinned the industrialisation drive. The government imposed heavy indirect taxation on the peasantry in an effort to finance its own efforts and to push exports of grain. Such measures were essential to the maintenance of a positive current account, a stable rouble and the encouragement of foreign investment. Economic acceleration was associated with an acceleration in the political demands for a voice in decision making. The absence of civil society did not help.

The Bolsheviks, although a small group, were strongly led and motivated. It was a party of professional revolutionaries, the vanguard of the working class, as Lenin conceived it. The Revolution occurred supported by two elemental movements which the Bolsheviks were unable to control – the seizure of enterprises by their workers and the seizure of the land by the peasants. The peasant army disintegrated and the peasant soldiers returned to the villages to share in the redistribution of land. As Hobsbawm (1994: 61) has noted, the only real asset the Bolsheviks had was 'the ability to recognize what the masses wanted: to, as it were, lead by knowing how to follow'. In the absence of control, the government institutionalised the two movements. It used them to secure its own position as the government, giving it time to organise the Communist Party. There was a dramatic change in the nature of both government and economy during the period of civil war which followed the Revolution (1918–21), known as War Communism. These features accorded with Bolshevik notions of what a communist economy would look like, although the initial view was that control of the banks might be adequate for planning the economy, but could also be interpreted as an expedient response to the requirements of a civil war. Any government, whatever its political persuasion, might have been forced to make them key parts of policy. As a consequence of the confiscation of foreign assets, the economy became largely a closed economy. Because of civil war, the degree of participation in the international economy would have declined massively in any event. The key features involved the emergence of a barter economy, as hyperinflation removed the rationale for market operation. Public goods were made available free. The Russian economy became a moneyless economy, as money became worthless as a result of the hyperinflation which followed the government's printing of money to finance its expenditures. Nationalisation of the means of production meant that most enterprises, whether large or small, had their financial affairs conducted through the government's budget. Enterprises of all sizes were socialised. Grain was requisitioned by force from the peasants, who had seized the estates. Armed groups of workers used force to extract the food needed to win the civil war. The threat of the return of the landlords was enough to make this policy palatable while it was a real threat.

The end of the civil war exposed the potential vulnerability of the regime to economic disaster. The economy had been de-industrialised and de-urbanised by the devastation and demands of war, revolution and civil war. The proletariat on which the success of the revolution notionally depended had disappeared, leaving the Bolshevik government without support. Total output had fallen to a fraction of its pre-war level. The peasants were on the verge of revolt as a consequence of forced requisitions. The distributional system had broken down, particularly between town and country. Disorganisation was universal. The revolution was not about to spread to the more developed economies, so the Bolsheviks could not depend upon communist control of developed economies. The New Economic Policy (NEP) was an effort to ensure recovery. Its introduction represented a compromise with the peasants and other elements of the old regime. It restored the market mechanism, and was based eventually on the restoration of a conventional financial system, including banking operations and a stable currency. Requisitions from the peasants were replaced by a tax in kind and later a tax in money. The peasants were allowed to retain their holdings and free to produce and sell on a free market. Industrial enterprises outside the commanding heights of the economy were returned to private ownership. The state sector was placed on an independent accounting basis. Nepmen were everywhere organising petty trade. NEP represented, in Lenin's memorable phrase, one step back in order to make two steps forward, although it was seen by some as a strategy which might be adopted on a more long-term basis. Recovery was largely achieved by 1926–7. There were problems, not the least the movements in the terms of trade between town and country, which were sometimes dramatic as in the scissors crisis of 1923 and the procurement crisis of 1927–8.

THE GREAT DEBATE, THE GREAT TURN AND THE EMERGENCE OF A COMMAND ECONOMY

Russia in 1917 was a developing country, with some striking periods of acceleration in the rate of economic growth in its previous history, notably during the 1890s, which left the level of GDP low by international, notably European or North American, standards. During the 1920s, there was an illuminating debate about the strategy of industrialisation, which focused on government policy and how to accelerate the rate of economic growth decisively above the long-term equilibrium rate. The growth model used by Feldman (1928) in this debate has been referred to many times in interpreting what happened during the Soviet period (most recently by Allen 2003): it represented a precursor of the early growth theory of Harrod (1939) and Domar (1946).[9] The economic debate was linked with a political struggle within the Communist Party and different views on the prospects of the survival and success of the revolution in Russia. Successful economic development was seen as critical to the survival of the regime. Trotsky's notion of permanent revolution saw the Russian Revolution as only sustainable with the emergence of communist regimes in developed economies (Deutscher 1954). Despite Marx's comments about the possibility of an early revolution in Russia, in the words of Hobsbawm (1994: 57), 'detonating' a chain of revolutions in the developed world, and the possibility of an exceptional departure from the general path of political change encapsulated in the Marxist model, the regime could only survive with outside support. Stalin, with a firm grasp of the reality of the situation, adopted a different view, summarised as 'socialism in one country', an acceptance that for a period of time the revolution in Russia was isolated, that Russia had to fend for itself. Stalin's sense of realism proved to be the only appropriate response to the existing international situation: it gave his position great strength.

The economic debate focused on the rate of industrialisation and the role of investment in that industrialisation. By 1926–7, when recovery to 1913 levels of output was achieved, it became obvious that to maintain continuing high rates of economic growth required a high level of net investment. It was no longer enough to simply restore and maintain existing capital equipment. The first focus of debate was the rate at which Russia could grow economically. This depended on the level of investment: the higher the investment ratio (equivalent to s in our previous analysis), the faster the rate of growth. The crux of the matter was the supply of foodstuffs from country to town, from peasant producers to workers, and the terms of trade between manufactured goods and foodstuffs. The terms of exchange became a critical indicator of the health of the NEP economy and the stress created by the investment effort. It is usually assumed that investment is at the cost of consumption. One extreme view was that the consumption of the present generation could be sacrificed in order to achieve higher consumption in the future. This argument exaggerates the trade-off between consumption now and consumption in the future. Feldman, in his model of economic growth, showed how quickly in a developing country with the right policies consumption could rise alongside a rise in investment (Spulber 1965). For that reason, the first five-year plan (1928–32) which aimed to do exactly that, with rapidly rising consumption, was not necessarily a cynical deception. There was never an intention to hold down consumption for a generation. The novelty of the Feldman approach was to divide the manufacturing sector between a capital good and a consumer goods sector, a division which had a lasting effect on strategic thinking in the Soviet Union, underpinning the so-called law of the primacy of capital goods. The capital goods sector could either direct its output back into expanding that sector or increasing the potential of the consumer goods sector to increase output, so, even if the investment ratio did not increase, a faster rate of economic growth could be achieved by increasing the ratio of capital goods devoted to their reproduction.

Who was to abstain from consumption in order to make the necessary initial savings? The obvious answer in a country dominated by the rural sector was the peasantry. Foodstuffs were to be diverted to feed workers building the infrastructure of an industrial state, but these workers could assist the effort through low wages, although urban incomes were higher than rural incomes. There has been a considerable debate about who provided the savings. During the debate, the issue was how such a transfer was to be achieved if the rural sector was to be the source of savings. Could it be done through a free market mechanism? The problem with using the pricing mechanism was that the peasants, with incentive removed, could engage in a market strike, simply refusing to sell their surplus, which is what happened in 1927. There were several major problems – the reduction in the surplus as a result of the disappearance of the landlords and other large surplus creators; the ability of the NEP system to deliver both the labourers, and the foodstuffs, needed to expand the urban labour force; the response of the peasants to government pricing policy, and the role of collectivisation in both controlling the peasantry politically, largely through the Machine Tractor Stations, and providing the surplus to the towns.

Bukharin and his supporters believed NEP was a viable mechanism for a strategy of industrialisation, but growth might initially be 'at a snail's pace' (Spulber 1965). The return from investing in the countryside was potentially higher than the investment in industry. The argument called for more balanced growth. On the other side, Preobrazhenskii argued for a deliberate exploitation of the peasants through the price mechanism and an unequal exchange in order to achieve primitive socialist accumulation (Spulber 1965). He never spelled out how the government should react to a peasant strike. The clear aim was for the most rapid industrialisation which required a high level of investment in the industrial sector. Initially, Stalin threw his lot in with Bukharin and the left members of the Politburo were defeated. What finally emerged was the Great Turn of 1929, comprising rapid industrialisation supported by a highly centralised physical planning system and the collectivisation of agriculture. It was, in the words of one commentator: '. . . a great social experiment' (Allen 2003: 1). Two defining characteristics of the planning system were a soft budget constraint and optimum tautness. The former meant that enterprises could produce at a loss. This meant that peasants withdrawn from the rural sector could be employed in the industrial sector at wages exceeding their marginal product, provided they had been surplus to labour requirements in agriculture (Lewis 1954). The latter meant that output targets were over-ambitious, but stretched managers and workers to exceed what they would otherwise have achieved with more realistic targets.

Such a system, at great political and human cost, seemed to achieve much during the period from the 1930s to the 1970s, when it began to fail. The main achievement of the industrialisation effort is well summarised by Hobsbawm (1994) and given strong statistical support by Allen (2003). Both believe that Russia should be compared with other developing economies, not with developed economies (Gregory 1982: 160–5). Hobsbawm (1994: 382) argues that for an economy which was at the semi-subsistence level and wished to lay the foundations for modern industry the system worked, even with a degree of crude flexibility. In the words of Hobsbawm

'. . . for a backward and primitive country isolated from foreign help, command industrialisation, with all its waste and inefficiencies, worked impressively. It turned the USSR into a major industrial economy in a few years and once capable, as Tsarist Russia had not been of surviving and winning the war against Germany in spite of the temporary loss of areas containing a third of her population and, in many industries, half the industrial plant'. Allen argues (2003: 4), '. . . when compared to poor, Third World countries, Soviet performance was extremely good even taking account of the post-1970 growth slowdown'. In a world of divergent growth performance, with convergence only among the already developed, Soviet performance is exceptional, save only for the case of Japan (ibid.: 5–7). The Soviet Union performed well as a developing country and outperformed the average OECD country, even allowing for convergence in this group. This justifies Coe's conclusion (2003: 90): 'as a bearer of modernity, albeit not the best form, the Russian path represented a vast improvement over premodern life'.

The performance in raising the level of consumption should not be underestimated. There is general agreement that consumption rose by about 3 per cent per annum between 1950 and 1980, but what happened at the start, during the 1930s? Allen has clearly shown that, contrary to the general belief that living standards fell between 1927 and 1938, there was on average a 20 per cent rise during the first two five-year plans, although he admits that the rise was uneven, both temporally and geographically, and that the relevant population had to work longer hours to gain the increase. The early period saw a fall and the rural population did much worse than the urban population, unless the relevant peasants moved from the country to the towns. A temporary reversal occurred as a consequence of World War ll. Right up to 1970, there was an improvement in all the indicators of health, child mortality, longevity, height and body weight. Such an outcome shows that it was not inevitable that a dramatic rise in investment would be accompanied by a fall in consumption nor that the rise in consumption planned in the first five-year plan was simply a cynical exercise. It is easy to overlook the achievements of the Soviet system. Paradoxically, some of those achievements hastened the end of the regime, for example, the emancipation of women and extension of universal education.

In a backward economy, in which the infrastructure of market operation is weak and there is almost no civil society, state-induced economic development can reach extremes. The alternative to having private capital and entrepreneurs as the drivers of economic development is to have the government do the job. In some societies, a tradition of economic development imposed from above is strong. This is the case for Russia, although there has been significant disagreement about how successful it has been in achieving its goals (compare Crisp 1976 with Kahan 1985 or Spulber 1964 and Allen 2003 with Gregory 1982). Peter the Great initiated the drive to modernisation in Russia, and in the tsarist period there was an alternation of centralised and decentralised periods of more rapid economic development. The drive to modernise is not simply a matter of strategy, it is also a matter of public ownership and control. In a command economy, the economy is run like one large enterprise, with a highly centralised control system. The Soviet Union after the Great Turn, between 1929 and 1991, is the model of a command economy. It was a structure later imposed on a number of Eastern and Central European countries and imitated under Asian communism, notably by China, North Korea and Vietnam. The nature of government is autocratic – there is both command polity and command economy. The government uses the planning system to instruct. Some aspects of the system justify the use of the term totalitarian, although the term has become unfashionable, with the realisation that no government can control everything, since there are significant areas, even in the Soviet Union, where the government lacked control.

There is a twofold paradox in the case of the communist government which took over in Russia after the revolution in 1917. First, the Soviet Union was the last European empire to survive, dissolving eventually in 1991, and then not fully (Hobsbawm 1994: 372). After an early assertion of self-rule, most of the old tsarist empire was brought back into the fold. With the dissolution, 15 separate units emerged, but there are many more autonomous regions or areas with populations which might have reason to opt out, as the recent experience of Chechnya shows. The communist regime was in many ways the inheritor of the political traditions of the tsarist regime. The Great Patriotic War (1941–5) reinforced those traditions. There was, after 1917 and again after 1991, much more continuity than often thought, autocracy and the imperial role the most pronounced.

Secondly, the Soviet Union had as one of its main aims the rapid economic development of the areas which it controlled. The regime equated economic development with industrialisation. It adopted a policy of the most rapid industrialisation possible. It believed that it could short-circuit the long and painful process of modern economic development within a market system, by using administrative fiat within a planning system. The short-cut involved bypassing the stage in which labour-intensive economic production is emphasised, a route the Asia of the economic miracle pursued.[10]

The Soviet Union offered a political and economic system alternative to the representative democracies and capitalist market systems of the already developed world. The ends – ambitious industrial targets – and the means – planning – adopted in the Soviet Union, were imitated in many developing countries, from India to China. A rival economic and political system emerged at a time, during the 1930s, when the capitalist market system appeared to be in imminent danger of collapse. As Hobsbawm (1994: 465) has noted, the chief contribution of Lenin's Bolshevism to changing the world was organisation, rather than doctrine, and this is being borne out in China and Vietnam. In the words of another authority: 'The prime objective of Soviet-type economies . . . was the political control of a national economy – in isolation from, and in defiance of, the world market' (Lockwood 2000: 1).

THE FAILURE OF THE SOVIET EXPERIMENT AND THE PROBLEM OF THE 'LAST' TRANSITION

Economic difficulties underpinned the political collapse of the Soviet Union after the regime lost the validation of economic success. The performance of the Soviet economy began to deteriorate during the 1960s, and particularly the 1970s, as the rate of economic growth slowed. By the 1980s it had slowed to a crawl. Whereas between 1928 and 1970 GNP had grown at a rate in excess of 5 per cent, the annual rate then fell steadily: to 3.7 per cent during 1970–5, 2.6 per cent during 1975–80 and 2 per cent during 1980–85 (Allen 2003: 189). The similarity of the original pattern of growth to that of the East Asian tigers has been noted – major contributions from the growth of the capital stock and labour force and a comparable rate of productivity increase (ibid.: 190). TFP change went negative during the 1980s and it is this deterioration which requires an explanation.

Some commentators have argued that the Soviet system did not encourage technological change, which was of particular importance as the initial deficiency of capital was corrected and all surplus labour mopped up. It was good at imitating and at moving labour from the traditional to the modern sector. What the Soviet economy could not do was to make the transition from extensive to intensive development, or find sources of growth in innovation when the relatively easy production gains from employing underemployed labour were exhausted. There was a pronounced deterioration in the output produced by an additional unit of investment; incremental capital-output ratios rose dramatically. But this proximate cause requires a satisfactory ultimate explanation. There are various explanations of why the slowing in growth and deterioration in the effective use of capital was happening, some based on the deficiencies of a planning system, others on the particularities of the growth performance during the 1970s and 1980s.[11]

Allen offers an argument based on poor decisions of strategy, some on mistakes which could have been avoided, others resulting from external conditions relating to Star Wars and the Cold War in general. The first rested on a poor use of investment, reflecting policy decisions wasteful of capital (Allen 2003: 198–206). The desire to be self-sufficient and to develop Russia's own resources partly accounts for the difficulties. Allen notes a variable performance in different sectors of the economy. First, there was a new stress on expanding existing, rather than building new, capacity, which was a particular problem in the steel industry. Secondly, there were diminishing returns to investment in the extraction of raw materials, notably for iron ore and both coal and oil. New projects were undertaken in Siberia, where costs were much higher. Allen also supports the argument, put by a number of commentators, that the Cold War increased the share of GDP devoted to the military, from 12 per cent 1966–70, to 16 per cent in 1981–5, and even more significantly diverted research resources and innovational capacity from civilian to military purposes. He argues that this accounts for most of the decline in productivity increase between the 1960s and the first half of the 1980s, as much as 2 per cent of the decline in annual growth – not the whole of the decline but a good part of it (ibid.: 210–11).

The failures of the system are often argued to be institutional failures – the neglect of the market, the over-extension of government, the continuing atrophy of civil society. The outcome was said to be a removal of incentives to innovate, an unresponsiveness to consumer demand and a growing inefficiency of the economy. Hobsbawm (1994: 382–5) has argued that there were three particular shortcomings which meant the Soviet system was unsuitable for a more developed and complex economy. The first is the failure of collectivised and state agriculture; the second the over-bureaucratisation of the planning system; and the third the inflexibility of the economic system. The performance of the agricultural sector was always poor. The Soviet Union became reliant on imports of grain. There were a number of reasons for such a poor performance. The first has been discussed before: natural constraints, including the deficiencies of soil and climate. The second is the organisational structure of agriculture, which removes any incentive to an improvement in productivity. It is significant that the private plots of the collective and state farmers produced a disproportionate amount of certain key products. Thirdly, the low priority given to agriculture deprived it of the investment it required.

Some problems were inherent in a planning system, and in particular in the system actually adopted by the Soviet Union. There is plenty of analysis of these problems (Gregory 2004). One prediction in the 1960s held that, extrapolating past trends, everyone in the Soviet Union would be employed in the planning apparatus by the end of the century: the *nomenklatura* would include every citizen. As the priorities in planning became plural and as the number of ministries multiplied to deal with an increasingly sophisticated economy (Malia 1994: 332), it became difficult to use the planning system to meet the differing objectives – planning works best when objectives are simple and priorities clear. Over-bureaucratisation is inherent in the kind of planning system adopted, one which eschewed the use of the market almost completely. Even modern fast-speed computers would be incapable of transferring the information required to make planning work. In reality, the planning system was kept going by the taking of short-cuts – the limit of one iteration in the movement of information up and down the economic system, and by corruption – the activity of *tolkachi*, who papered over the cracks.

There were grave weaknesses with the particular kind of economic system adopted. The system was overly rigid and proved difficult to reform. The system was lacking in the incentives to make the appropriate decisions, whether at the macro or the micro levels. It put an undue emphasis on output rather than sales or costs, ignoring the wishes of the consumer and neglecting the efficiency with which inputs were used. There was a failure to take account of profitability and to react to changes in world prices. The economic system failed to encourage innovation since it put the emphasis on production, not costs. There was a tendency to gigantomania – everything was done on a large scale. It did not pay proper attention to the price of scarce capital. The law of the primacy of capital goods kept reasserting itself, despite many attempts to redirect attention and resources to the consumer goods sector and to agriculture. The economy was isolated from world markets, with prices out of line with internationally competitive prices and a failure to benefit from trade or foreign investment. Isolation of the communist camp did not help.

There are some who believe that political and economic systems were inherently unworkable. Malia has argued that the Leninist means were the only way to realise the Marxist programme and socialism could only be reached by Stalinist methods. Creating a just or socialist society meant abolishing private property, prices and the market. It is worth quoting Malia at length, 'Russia's role was to provide to the experiment [of making socialism] with a social tabula rasa in the form of a civil society pulverized by modern war, thereby creating a void of countervailing power that permitted the party to realise its fantasy . . . Russian chaos alone could have produced a national authoritarianism of purely regional significance; but it was ideological socialism that proved to be the sufficient condition for precipitating the world-historical tragedy' (Malia 1994: 504). It is deemed wrong to see the unfolding events as a working out of Russia's path-dependent fate or the communism regime as a mechanism for generating significant economic development. It is tempting to interpret all behaviour within the Soviet Union in a cynical manner as self-interested and potentially rent-seeking. Some concession is made by commentators to the influence of ideology, or ideas in general, but only in the early years before the dominance of Stalin. There is a growing literature which argues that the mature Soviet system, and other communist systems, were dominated by rent-seeking, and that this is what made them unworkable and caused their eventual breakdown (Gregory 2004). '. . . by the time of Stalin, the economic system began to function like a mercantilist state. The Soviet Union had become a rent-seeking society by the time it entered its "mature" stage' (Boettke and Anderson 1997: 49–50). The system is described as 'a modern example of a mercantilist economy' (Boettke and Anderson 1997: 39). The strongest parallel between sixteenth and seventeenth century mercantilist economies and the Soviet Union lay in the heavy restriction of the market by state-granted monopolies. Even in a highly regulated economic system, the market reasserts itself in the corrupt relationships which emerge and begin to dominate. If some activity is potentially profitable in a free market context, it is likely to be worth paying a bribe to subvert a regulation preventing that activity. In this sense government regulation encourages corruption, an extreme form of rent-seeking. The Soviet Union was seen as ripe for this, once the initial élan of ideology was lost.

The period since the dissolution of the Soviet Union in 1991 can be divided into two – a period of dislocation and massive contraction in output and incomes, and a period of boom in the demand for commodities and rising prices, which led to a reversal of the contraction in Russia. During the first period, GDP fell to something approaching half its pre-dissolution level, a contraction not dissimilar to that which occurred after the Revolution and following civil war, although it is difficult to know exactly how large was the grey economy. The latter expansion conceals two major problems. Much of the difficulty during the 1990s resulted from the speed and comprehensiveness of reform and the lack of an infrastructure to support the new market-based system. Both political and economic reforms were carried out in a hurry, as the political system collapsed. Markets were deregulated, enterprises privatised, the economy opened up, in what has been called the big bang or, more callously, shock therapy. There is a real problem in operating a market system without an appropriate infrastructure. It was soon realised that the principal task of the new regime was to establish appropriate institutions. The second problem is that Russia, partly because of its institutional deficiencies, is exposed to the worst effects of the resources curse. As the networks provided by the Communist Party disappeared, rent-seeking behaviour became rampant. Privatisation dissipated the resources which Russia possessed. The absence of the institutional structure which supports market activity in developed economies makes slow and careful institutional reform more likely to be successful, but this was not really an option in the conditions of Russia during the 1990s. The Chinese model of gradual and experimental reform in a context of the retention of a strong measure of central political control has proved much better at generating modern economic development. There is also a retention of a strong element of planning and administrative control. The Soviet way is not the only one.

PART V

Conclusions

14. Causes and complexity

> 'There are such things as historical and theoretical temperaments. That is to say, there are types of minds that take delight in all the colours of historical processes and of individual cultural patterns. There are other types that prefer a neat theorem to everything else. We have use for both. But they were not made to appreciate one another. (Schumpeter 1954: 815, quoted in Broadberry 2007: 4)

There are two implications of the argument put in this book. The first stresses the importance of the analytical narrative. The second emphasises the purpose of producing an analytic narrative. It seeks to find continuities while recognizing the influence of contingencies. Understanding the way in which modern economic development was initiated is a step towards identifying policies and institutional structures which both ignite and sustain that development. What historians do '. . . is to interpret the past for the purposes of the present with a view to managing the future, but to do so without suspending the capacity to assess the particular circumstances in which one might have to act, or the relevance of past acts to this . . .' (Gaddis 2002: 10).

The final chapter includes three sections. The first briefly highlights the two different approaches to explaining the inception of modern economic development. It indicates how the different players regard each other and the reasons for at best a persistent mutual neglect and at worst an overt antagonism between the two relevant groups. It emphasises the need for an operational reconciliation of the two approaches. In the next section, there is a review of what is required in order to write a good analytic narrative. The final section summarises the answers to the questions put in the first chapter, and reviews the nature of the grand narrative to be written in the future.

CONVENTIONAL WISDOMS

It is disappointing that, given all the ink spilled, there is still no persuasive general explanation of the inception of modern economic development. Often the problem is presented as if there are only two explanatory possibilities: either modern economic development is the result of the contingencies of history – it was an amazing accident – or it was inevitable, its unfolding a matter of specific timing and location. The first explanation sees the discontinuity as the result of a chance series of random events, which might not have happened. Played again, the result might be different, although such a replaying is technically a-historical; there is, and can only be, one scenario. The second explanation is that there is no mystery. The inception is inevitable after the gradual build-up of advantageous conditions. The important movement is the crossing of a threshold beyond which the inception becomes inevitable, although there are clearly both evolutionary and revolutionary elements.

Historians tend to embrace the first approach, economists the second; the first approach requires a narrative, the second a general theory. The World History School embraces a contingent interpretation (Goldstone 2008, Hobson 2004). An increasing body of economic literature inclines towards inevitability, usually based on scale effects following from population increase and the expansion of various informational networks, including commercial networks (Christian 2005, Wright 2000). Wright emphasises the recurrence of the multiple steps taken by various societies towards increasing complexity, with the independent innovations at the heart of such increasing complexity, such as the transition to agriculture in at least five separate centres in the world (Wright 2000; Chapter 6), the discovery of writing at least twice (Wright 2000: 95), and even the repetition of technical inventions at the heart of the Industrial Revolution (Wright 2000: 191). A failure in one place simply meant that it would occur elsewhere, if a little later. Since the world became truly global in its communications network several centuries ago, it is no longer possible to observe independent industrial revolutions.

Both approaches have inherent weaknesses which make the attempted explanation an inevitable failure. The inception of modern economic development is not a random event – it has causes difficult to identify but not a matter of chance, nor is it an inevitable outcome – it could easily have been aborted in all successful cases. In each case, it is easy to imagine obstacles which might have prevented the inception, negative feedback effects which could reverse the gains by counteracting positive ones. This is true at each stage of the economic ascent of human beings; at one stage, humans were possibly in danger of extinction. Could such constraints have postponed the inception indefinitely? There is no way of answering such a question.

Guha (1981: 18) has summarised the main reason for the inadequacies. An acceptable theory of economic development, like the theory of evolution, has no predictive power, being unable to generate predictions refutable in the normal Popperian manner: 'its value is entirely explanatory'.

This reflects the unpredictability of any path of development 'because it is not a matter of unique necessity but of recurrent change'. Every stage in the sequence follows from the last as one of a set of probabilities rather than an inevitable consequence. 'Development is a stochastic process, not a royal road down which the world economy is propelled by some inexorable Newtonian law of motion.' There is a different scenario for each successful inception, and possibly a considerable degree of path dependence. Only an analytical narrative can deal with this.

There is a tendency to portray the two positions as caricatures of what they should be. It is easy to set up straw men to criticise. Allegedly, the problem with neoclassical economics, and by implication with its theory of economic growth, is that it is proximate, aggregative and a-historical. Because it deals only with the immediate or proximate, it is superficial, never really telling us why certain events occur. It does not move beyond the obvious. It excludes ultimate causation and focuses on proximate causes. In the words of North (2005: Chapter 6), it is frictionless, that is, it assumes institutions are infinitely malleable and transaction costs zero. It takes a macro approach, using the production function to simplify and to represent the overall economy, but does little to see what is going on in the famous 'black box' of the production function.[1] It misses the way in which change occurs in the real world, for example artificially separating technical change and capital accumulation. It stresses outcomes rather than processes; it often views change as a matter of comparative statics, overplaying the notion of equilibrium. It ignores intentionality. It neglects the long links of cause and effect in the real dynamics of historical change. It believes every country shares the same experience; we are all motivated in the same way and engage in the same behaviours. It exaggerates the degree to which the real world experience is amenable to model building, seen by Colander (2000: 138) as the main characteristic of modern economics. Simplification of experience makes possible rigorous models of behaviour and the testing of significance. Over-simplification makes the real world amenable to this kind of understanding. This viewpoint often sees modern economic development as inevitable, the result of spontaneous individual behaviour; maximising agents operate unhindered in the context of strongly efficient markets. It is supremely optimistic in its view of the potential universality of economic development.

By contrast, the problem with narrative history is that it is ultimate, particular, and a-theoretical. In always seeking the ultimate explanation, it often becomes lost in the mists of time, in a fool's infinity of never-ending links in the chain of causation. There is always another cause behind the one in focus. It stresses historical specificity, the uniqueness of the sequence of events and the contextual circumstances which make up the narratives and fails to recognize the need for theory in selecting what is relevant among a multitude of potentially relevant events and a veritable kalei-doscope of general circumstances. Often the approach seems anecdotal. It ignores the need for selection. It believes everyone, and every country, has a different experience, that every culture is different, even theoretical concepts differing from society to society. It believes in cultural and other forms of fixity; motivation is embedded in culture. All the experiences are exceptional, the result of accident. Economic development is a rare event, the chance result of a series of specific events and circumstances. Instead of inevitability, we have accident.[2]

Commentators have often taken positions which deliberately exclude a consideration of the alternative approach. There are many reasons for this – the deadweight of the human capital acquired in education, the need to simplify in order to understand, the tyranny of 'groupthink', and the influence of unconscious political assumptions. The criticisms are unfair as a description of individual contributions since there is validity in both approaches; they both contribute to an understanding of modern eco-nomic development and its inception. It is a fatal handicap to be either a-historical or a-theoretical. Any good approach to an explanation of the inception of modern economic development must take into account both the general and the unique. There is a need for balance and for someone to successfully reconcile and integrate the two approaches. This is what the analytic narrative can achieve.

There is therefore a third interpretation, sharing features of the two approaches. The exact identity of the pioneer and timing of success can be seen as accidental but the inception of modern economic development somewhere in the world at some point of time can be regarded as highly likely. What requires explanation is the occurrence of the inception at par-ticular moments and in particular places, say Britain in the late eighteenth century or Japan in the late nineteenth. A valid approach requires both proximate and ultimate causation; deals with both aggregates and specif-ics; comprises both theory and history. It sees something to be explained, not by chance or inevitability, but by complex processes of causation. There is a uniqueness of experience, an experience repeated in different circumstances by follower economies, circumstances including the previ-ous successes. The experiment of modern economic development has been tried a limited number of times. In the absence of the British pioneering experience, France or Japan, or even the USA, might have independently initiated the inception. The inception is like other social phenomena in its complexity, any explanation itself complex. It is desirable to aim at an economy of explanation, avoiding redundancy, but not incurring a significant loss of comprehension. Rigorous mathematical and statistical methods have been used, with limited results. There are no mono-causal explanations, no simple relationships. There are many non-linearities, critical thresholds and feedback effects, and many enabling and hindering conditions. There is a need to express the complexity in a narrative account of the particular experience. In the words of Bairoch (1993: 164): 'there is no "law" or rule in economics that is valid for every period of history or for every economic structure'. We must note the inevitable over-simplification in any generalising theory, but not reject the theory. The narrative account should be analytical, its features governed by existing theory, but also dynamic, with a proper account taken of the nature of historical change. It is not just any story, rather a story told with a clear aim in mind – explaining a particular sequence of events. Such a narrative teases out the long, convoluted and particular chains of causation which lie behind the process of modern economic development, their identification assisted by a subtle application of theory.

THE NATURE OF THE ANALYTIC NARRATIVE

The writing of appropriate analytic narratives can solve the mystery of the causation of modern economic development. There may be puzzles already solved with the aid of the judicious use of theory but the solutions do not answer the big question, providing an explanation of the inception of modern economic development. An analytical narrative, incorporating the lessons of this book, has not yet been written. The writing of such a narrative is best started by indicating its general requirements.

First, the purpose of the narrative must be clearly understood, the problem requiring a solution adequately specified. Specifying the purpose makes possible the selection of material relevant to the narrative. In the context of this book, the relevant purpose is to provide an explanation of the inception of modern economic development. The purpose fixes the valued endpoint, or a goal state, which the narrative must show as the outcome of a series of events and developing circumstances. The task is to choose an outcome at a relevant moment in time. The outcome in this case is the modern economy, one characterised by self-sustained economic development. Such an approach requires a clear definition of economic development, with an explicit distinction between causes, context, characteristics (defining features) and consequences (outcomes).The purpose and endpoint together define the scope of the narrative, which is to identify the processes resulting in the developed state, thereby giving it coherence.

The danger is to slip into determinism. Changing the purpose, or the endpoint, changes the nature of the narrative. Different outcomes lead to different explicanda and interpretations of the previous sequence of events. The methodological problem of history is that 'the outcome determines the narrative constructed to "lead inexorably" to it' (Abu-Lughod 1989: 12). If the outcome implies a current European economic dominance, such history inevitably appears Euro-centric. Trying to explain the causes of modern economic development means taking that development for granted and reading back in time, an exercise much disliked by 'purist' historians. However, pretending that the story is told without preconceptions about the outcome is dishonest: we know the relevant outcomes. The specific outcome and its timing determines the degree of development of the relevant economy. Such an approach can close off the experience of economies which have not developed or developed in a different way. A revisionist view, taking a different vantage point, has pointed out the similarities of experience in a number of economies which did not develop, especially similarities with those that did (Abu-Lughod 1989, Blaut 1993, Frank 1998, Pomeranz 2000). Identifying such similarities helps identify the causes of modern economic development, whether ultimate or proximate, and to exclude invalid arguments.

Secondly, the level of analysis must be clearly indicated. Of relevance are different narratives: a history of the world economy or grand narrative, an economic history of an industry, a country or the region of a country, even a business history or the biography of an important businessman. The grand narrative is the ultimate aim of all economic history, the starting point for any other narrative at a lower level. The writing of country narratives is done in the context of a grand narrative, which explains why levels of economic development differ across the world. What a grand narrative is not is a master narrative, such as a Euro-centric narrative of the rise of the West, which assumes some kind of European exceptionalism and persistent advantage (Marks 2007: 14); recent work has shown the deficiencies of such an approach.

Having a set of unrelated narratives does not assist in understanding the process of economic development. The narratives should be connected through the use of common concepts and a common theoretical framework. There should be a synergy between different levels: they cannot exist separately or independently. Such commonality underpins a pyramid of explanation, paralleling the pyramid of narratives. It is important to take the narrative down to an appropriate level. Any narrative may require sub-narratives which create the base for more ambitious narratives. A neglect of the lesser narratives may hide the strong elements of localised discontinuity which characterise the inception of modern economic development, thereby concealing the critical processes of change. The level of the narrative may be selected according to the degree of discontinuity which is revealed. There is a process of iteration between the different narrative levels. A satisfactory grand narrative requires the support of country narratives, and successful country narratives require the support of a persuasive grand narrative.

Thirdly, the narrative must be more than descriptive; it is analytic in that explanation requires a supporting theory. A narrative does not consist of a random set of anecdotes relating to a broad theme, unless the purpose is simply entertainment rather than information. The more ambitious the narrative, the more important is theory in justifying the arguments advanced and selecting an appropriate narrative. The use of theory must take account of the nature of the problem. The obvious candidate as a starting theory is the body of economics, which is why most of the book is an extended analysis of the role of neoclassical growth theory in explaining the inception of modern economic development. The puzzles arising from the telling of the narrative and their solution indicate the possible nature of the relevant theory. Such theory is not necessarily limited to one disciplinary area. Not all theory is helpful, nor is an excessively eclectic approach. There should be no inconsistencies in the use of theory. It must be clear how different theories link together.[3]

Fourthly, the narrative must focus on the key mechanisms of change which take an economy from a state of undevelopment to one of development. The writing of separate narratives allows the investigation of these mechanisms and an indication of their possible generality. There is a need to identify key decision points in the process of economic development and the possibilities which arise at such points. The narrative is concerned with links between a sequence of events in real time and the way in which circumstances and behaviour interact in shaping those events. It involves real dynamics, not comparative statics. Because it is analytic, the narrative addresses the issue of causation, in the context of a definition of the phenomenon under analysis, which is a complex process.

The narrative seeks to identify the important steps in the chain of causation, including any feedback loops, whether positive or negative. A key aspect of the chains of causation is the existence of positive and negative feedback loops. During the pre-modern regime negative loops prevail; during the modern regime the loops are positive. In the words of Mokyr (2003: 31), 'Before the Industrial Revolution, the economy was subject to negative feedback: each episode of growth ran into some obstruction or resistance that put an end to it'. Most negative feedback mechanisms rest on diminishing returns of some kind – such an assumption has been a dominant influence in the evolution of economic theory. The diminishing returns, even from macro-inventions, explain why in the pre-1750 environment technological progress failed to generate sustained economic growth.

An obvious answer to diminishing returns are the effects of increasing scale, which ensure economies of scale, scope and of agglomeration. There may also be network effects and key tipping points at which the size of key variables attain critical mass. Mokyr (2002: 21, footnote 26) adds that small changes can move the system from being homeostatic and relatively controlled to a 'supercritical regime' in which the rate of change keeps accelerating. And further (2002: 33), 'Eventually positive feedback becomes so powerful that it becomes self-sustaining'. One reason for these transitions is scale and the intensifying communication and commercial networks, but it is not the only enabling factor.

There are three key areas in which negative feedback loops became positive ones – demography (dealt with in Chapter 11), institutions (Chapters 8 and 10) and technology (Chapter 9). The first involves the positive interaction between natural and cultural selection, in particular as it secures a release from the Malthusian trap. The second highlights the emergence of a positive interdependence between government and market, resting on the emergence of strong government mediated by the development of civil society. The third links the dynamism of advances in knowledge and in technology. All these mechanisms work differently in different societies.

Fifthly, it is useful to set up a narrative in such a way that it can be repeated for other cases at the same level. There should be a reusable template. It is desirable to construct a set of country studies, and critical to write narratives which offer insights because they confront the same issues and ask the same questions. It is possible to identify the generalities and the peculiarities in each narrative. The narratives should build on natural comparisons, with a sparing but timely use of the counterfactual. Explanation requires comparison for two reasons: it assists in identifying how far we can generalise and allows the narrative to be used to test theories in a world where statistical testing is scarcely feasible. Such natural comparisons can be carried out in a particular sequence, if that assists in finding a persuasive explanation. It is also possible to group experiences. Because of path dependence every experience is exceptional, but in certain circumstances groups of individual cases represent 'clubs'.

A counterfactual narrative can be constructed which represents different hypothetical possibilities. Thought experiments are valid preliminaries to writing analytic narratives. The usefulness of such models is limited, but it makes possible a first exploration of the possible influence of individual variables. This assists in exercises in comparative statics, where formal models are used and the value of exogenous variables can be changed. It assists in understanding the mechanisms at work and their possible impact. Counterfactual comparisons are at one remove from a real narrative and no substitute for real comparisons.

Sixthly, the telling of an appropriate narrative should be structured in a way that can test the usefulness of the relevant theory. The extension of the analytic narrative to a number of cases and their comparison can be used to test the validity of the analytic narrative. This is important since laboratory testing is impossible, and statistical testing seriously flawed. The test is the reasoned adequacy of the narrative as an explanation of the inception of modern economic development. Each persuasive narrative increases confidence that other narratives are valid explanations of economic development. At the moment, the accounts of economic development are fragmentary and largely unconnected.

Seventhly, a good analytic narrative uses history, theory and data in a balanced way. Most studies have inadequacies in one of these areas – a failure to take full account of the uniqueness of experience, an overly rigid or simplified use of theory, or a carelessness in the selection and use of relevant data. The nature of the narrative assists in determining what theory and what data are relevant, just as the theory shapes the narrative. The survival of relevant data may limit the way in which a narrative is developed, but a good narrative is consistent with whatever relevant data are available. There is a process of iteration between theory and history, and between analysis and narrative. Narratives offer insights into theory just as theory, offers insights into narratives. Such an iteration is at the heart of the analytic narrative. Each opposing element is tested against the other in a continuing process of refining both.

A persuasive explanation of the inception requires the application of good theory and of a narrative approach which explore the relevant chains of causation. Any attempt by one approach to exclude the other is bound to produce a limited understanding of the process. Neither the economist nor the economic historian can go it alone; each needs the other to complement its advantages and to offset its disadvantages.[4] There is therefore no one all-purpose explanation for the inception, no one model which fits all experiences. Explanation requires attention to the complexities of individual experiences. Only through individual narratives can the full complexity of the relevant experiences be captured. The extent to which we can generalise is limited, but it is important to discover the nature of these limits, of which there are two main ones. First, there are many individual determinants and many ways in which these determinants interact. There is value in a general analysis which identifies possibly important determinants. Often this analysis tells what appears obvious, for example that the investment ratio is important. The exact way in which these determinants interact in different countries is unique to the time period or to the country. Secondly, there are different explanations for different success stories; there are many paths to modern economic development.[5]

In the future, there are bound to be more, and these paths are likely to be unanticipated, as in the past.

Examination of the work already completed shows how far we have to go, despite the quality of researchers and their work. Reading even the best work shows work in progress rather than anything approaching the achievement of a fully developed analytical narrative. It reveals many unresolved puzzles and often a tentative probing for conclusions. One difficulty is the disproportionate effort devoted to theoretical models, an effort which is producing diminishing returns.

THE WAY FORWARD

Tackling the mystery of economic development is a difficult task. It requires the asking of many relevant questions, as we saw in Chapter 1. The book has indicated how far we have gone in answering them. Such answers will be at the core of an appropriate analytical narrative, indicating which analytic narratives have particular interest. It is appropriate to change the order in which the questions are asked, beginning with the 'what' question.

The phases of economic history have been presented in this book as a pre-modern regime which lasted for most of human history, a modern regime, largely the topic of economics textbooks, and a transition between the two. The nature of the transition, referred to as the inception of modern economic development, has been the focus of interest. Before we can discuss causation, we need to indicate the characteristics of the transition, distinguishing them from the context and the consequences. To explain the characteristics of the transition, we need to briefly consider the pre-modern and modern regimes.

The pre-modern regime is by no means a stationary state, since there is continuous change in all societies and at all times, but the underlying pace of change before the inception of modern economic development is glacial. The pre-modern regime is one in which there are many growth episodes of varying length, even long cycles of growth and contraction associated with climatic change and the rise and fall of various civilisations all over the world. Pre-modern economic growth differs from modern growth in key respects. There are negative feedback effects which prevent improvement becoming sustained, so that over the long term technology changes slowly and irregularly, population expands at a snail's pace, in bursts with long reversals, and output per head scarcely rises. The Malthusian trap is just one of these. By contrast, modern economic development is a process of sustained economic growth at an historically unprecedented rate.

Technology changes dramatically, populations rise to undreamed of levels and income per head soars. There are all sorts of positive feedback effects which ensure the curtailment of any reversal; a recession is usually short-lived. Christian (2003) illustrates the sheer scale of the increase in energy use by humankind and the environmental change resulting from the increased complexity of human organisation over the period of modern economic development.

The transition from old to new regime involves the transition from a trap which prevents a permanent escape from poverty to a path of long-term equilibrium growth. The acceleration in the rate of growth of output per head is both obvious and significant, although it occurs more gradually and later than often thought. The transition involves an inverse U-shaped behaviour of growth rates, an acceleration followed by a deceleration, with the U-shape becoming more pronounced, the later the transition begins for a particular country. There is more discontinuity for late starters than pioneers. At the core of such a transition is the act of innovation; in the transition, technical change ceases to be unusual and isolated and becomes systematic and cumulative. Usually this requires embodiment in investment, but the act of investment is subsidiary to the introduction of new products, new production processes, new institutional arrangements and even new business models. It also involves a restructuring of the economy, away from the primary, first to the secondary and then to the tertiary sector, largely based on innovation in the latter two sectors, with a fall in costs and a diversification of product encouraging a large increase in demand. Since both tendencies – the acceleration in rates of growth per capita and the structural change – are initially likely to be hidden by the weight of traditional sectors of the economy, some disaggregation is necessary to identify both the timing and location of change.

The 'why' of any reasonable explanation has two main features. The ability and willingness to innovate is the key. First, this requires a consideration of motivation and how it is moulded. We can assume all individuals aim first for survival and then to improve their standard of living; more is preferred to less. How this motivation is realised is socially conditioned. In some societies, it gives rise to activities which discourage economic development: it pushes individuals into rent-seeking activity. Institutional structures which encourage the creation of new income and discourage rent-seeking are important to the inception of modern economic development – they create a powerful positive feedback loop. The appearance of a culture of innovation is a critical factor in the transition.

Secondly, much of the initiation of economic development involves the assimilation of existing technology and the organisational structures which embody it, but there is no easy access to such technology. This is particularly but not only true for followers. There is no automatic and costless access to the existing pool of knowledge. Many societies find the process of imitation difficult.

The 'how' question is the most interesting of all. The book focuses on how the process of modern economic development begins. Positive feedback loops came to dominate negative feedback loops. Economies pass a threshold at which the positive feedback effects become predominant. Some of the positive feedback effects appear over a long period of time – centuries even – others after a short period. Some come and go. It is the mutual reinforcement of different mechanisms which ensures no falling away. While for most of history there has been a slight advantage to the positive over the negative, in recent times the positive has been massively reinforced and the negative weakened. At a key moment, the interaction of such effects leads to an 'explosion' in growth – even a 1 per cent per capita growth rate is explosive in its consequences. The biggest positive loops relate to population, technology and the increasing complexity of society. Increasing population stimulates increased complexity in two ways. It increases the pressure for higher productivity in the Boserupian way. It also increases the scale of informational and commercial networks. Institutions and attitudes become more favourable to the process of modern economic development. Government, civil society and market contribute.

It is relatively easy to answer the 'who' questions. The 'where' question is also related to the 'who' question. There appear to have been at least two possible separate starting points for modern economic development, at the far extremities of Euro-Asia: Britain and Japan. Location and geographical configuration are important. This largely determines which are the critical sub-narratives. Britain initiated the process of modern economic development and was followed by two groups of economies, a group of countries which were part of the European miracle and at a rather later date, another group which was part of the Asian miracle. An interesting issue is how far the inceptions within these groups was independently achieved and how far they represented an imitation of the pioneers. Since the latter group achieved their inception after the former, there was an influence from the former to the latter. The Japanese inception is clearly a response to the earlier inception in Europe and North America, at least in the effort to catch up quickly, but its success reflects a context already favourable to that inception. Over a long period of time, positive feedback effects accumulated in both societies to offset the negative ones. It appears that the British model is very much sui generis and that other parts of Europe could have initiated the process independently, and this would probably eventually have been true of Japan. It is also interesting to consider economies which evolved in a similar way to the pioneers, but failed to make the transition, such as in Asia Sung China or Mughal India, or within Europe the Italian city states or the Netherlands.

Within these economies, the main individual agents of economic development were merchants, industrialists, farmers and government officials, but also inventors, the consumers of the new products and those who worked in the new industries. The main organisational players were the family, the modern business enterprise and its precursors, and the various arms of government.

Recent work has shown persuasively that a European lead in levels of output or trade was achieved later than thought, although there is a tendency to exaggerate the performance of Asian economies in order to rectify a previous neglect. The Great Divergence must have occurred in significant ways before the intrusion of Europe into other parts of the world, if only because this was made possible by a clear military superiority, which reflected critical economic advantages. There also came into existence in some parts of Europe a culture of innovation absent in Asia (Goldstone 2008). What is clearly established is that Asian economies shared many of the characteristics of European economies and sustained a high level of economic activity comparable with that in Europe, whether in industrial output, the level of urbanisation or the extension of trade. Moreover, globalisation within the Eurasian context has a long history. In this sense, most of Asia was ripe for development and had gone through its own evolution.

The timing is a critical issue, but differs from developed economy to developed economy. The critical 'when' question concerns the degree of discontinuity and the period over which the key changes occur – are there key changes which are revolutionary, concentrated into a short period of time, or are the relevant changes evolutionary, stretched over a long period? The answer is an unequivocal yes to the use of the term revolution, given the dramatic change over what has been by historical standards a relatively short period of time. However, conventional datings imply far too fast a transition. The transition occurred, not within two or three decades, rather in one to two centuries, which prompted Goldstone (2008: 94) to describe it as 'something of a slow-motion revolution, rather than a sudden change'. Moreover, there was also evolution leading up to this transition. There are two critical issues – how far income per head was rising before the transition and how far Europe and Asia shared the same experience. Maddison (2001) sees a doubling in income per head over the period between 1000 and 1800, but other data on wages or on height (Koepke and Baten 2005) do not support this. There is a growing consensus that there was at best a small improvement, an emphasis on cyclical movements rather than a long-term upward trend. Moreover, the experiences of Europe and Asia appear similar. Both experienced the same general changes, but in highly specific and critical ways. There certainly was change in both regions – population grew over the long term and the level of urbanisation rose. The nature of the changes in institutions, technology and attitudes is important, since it made highly likely the revolution. There is both evolution and revolution for the pioneer economies, although the mix varies from country to country. For late starters there is more discontinuity, but only societies in an advantageous state could access the appropriate technology and organisation; even in those countries, there had to be favourable evolutionary changes.

Does a grand narrative exist, which shows how modern economic development has been achieved? A number of commentators have written economic histories of the world, focusing on particular themes, most notably changes in technology and organisation. Some attempt what Christian (2003: 1) calls World History, 'the history of human beings as a single, coherent story, rather than as a collection of the particular stories of different communities'. The main lesson of the World History School is that it is difficult to write sub-narratives for individual countries without having such a grand narrative in mind. However, what demands an answer is the failure of most of the world to make a successful transition to modern economic growth, so the grand narrative must explain both success and failure. From the beginning, the pool of knowledge drawn on by those making a successful transition has been a global one. During the period of modern economic development, collective learning became predominant, supplementing natural selection and individual learning as adaptive mechanism of the human species. The pool of knowledge expanded and is drawn on by late starters to assist their inception of modern economic development. Such a narrative puts a strong emphasis on the internationalisation of the world economy, the connecting of all humans in vast and intricate, but open, networks, with the transmission of ideas a major driver of innovation. It is in this context that the maximum sustainable long-term steady-state growth path marks out the path of modern economic development which innovation makes possible. This pool is not as accessible to all as is often assumed: there are significant and persistent barriers to imitation of best-practice technology. The neoclassical emphasis on convergence of technology, and the supplementary notion of positive access costs, is a reasonable one.

The argument can be simplified. The most prominent barrier is the lack of particular kinds of capital. Rising income generates rising savings and the accumulation of capital, in some senses the core positive feedback loop. However, output and the resulting income are flows resulting from the services of various capital stocks. Economic development is therefore the result of a build-up of the positive interaction of various capital stocks to a threshold level. The most visible form of capital is physical capital, a manifestation of technology, so that the vintage, or dating, of the capital suggests its productivity. There are three other types of relevant capital – natural, human and social. Natural capital has been dealt with in the chapter on resources (Chapter 5) and in the chapter on release from the Malthusian trap (Chapter 12). Most important inputs into production originate in natural capital – agricultural products, aquifers and deposits of raw materials or of fossil fuel. There is also human capital, discussed in Chapter 6, without which both physical and natural capital are of little use. Economic development makes certain demands on the exercise of skill and imagination of entrepreneurs, managers and workers. In the pre-modern regime, the typical peasant producer is all three and this requires a productivity unaffected by poor nutrition and health problems, including stunted mental growth (Collier 2008: 2). Such factors influence the aptitudes of the whole workforce. Education further increases the productivity of labour, improving trainability and access to the pool of best-practice knowledge. There is also social capital, the focus of interest in the chapters on human capital (Chapter 7) and on institutions (Chapter 8), really a particular kind of human capital, but developed outside the process of production itself within the networks which characterise human society. Social capital allows the unlocking of the full potential to increase productivity implicit in technology. The access to social capital determines the capacity of any society to self-organise and to solve problems relevant to the process of modern economic development. It is built up over time, particularly as a result of the operation of civil society. Societies have different amounts of social capital, or in common terminology different densities of civil society or levels of social capability. It is difficult to incorporate social capital into the causation of modern economic development since it is not linked to particular investments and therefore is difficult to measure.

All attempts to explain modern economic development have as their justification a choice of policies which promote an accelerated rate of development, through the creation of a culture of innovation. Understanding gives the possibility of forecasting future performance and influencing outcomes. The usefulness of relevant research is not just to understand causation but also to make policy recommendations. The former is a prerequisite for the latter. There are no general prescriptions valid for all economies. In certain circumstances, it is advantageous to have an open economy, in others not. In certain circumstances, it is critical to have government intervention, in others not. In certain circumstances, it is necessary to extend the scope of the market, in others not. Policy must fit the particular context. It is dangerous to attempt to take from simple models policy prescriptions seen as valid for all economies (witness the lack of success of the Washington Consensus). The context in which a particular policy is introduced does matter. This explains why the absence of economic development is commonplace. If asked to advise on a policy for economic development in a particular country, my response would be – give me time to study the particular circumstances and specific historical path of development, then it will be possible to make sensible recommendations, but I would be making the recommendations as both a trained but open-minded economist and an experienced but theoretically sensitive historian. We can conclude with the comment, 'There is a trade-off between generality and content in all theories. The more general a theory, the more detail that distinguishes one situation from another it must omit. Hence the less detail it can explain' (Lipsey, Carlaw and Bekar 2005: 107) and '. . . there is no one correct way to make the trade-off between generality and context-specific, explanatory power. Each choice must depend on the problem at hand' (ibid.: 108).

Notes

PART I

1. The term 'modern economic growth', first used systematically by Kuznets (1965), implies a distinction between economic growth in general and modern economic growth. There are characteristics which are specific to the latter, notably its sustained and systematic nature. The term also implies that at some moment in history the modern era commenced and modern economic growth began; conventionally that moment occurs in Britain at the end of the eighteenth and the beginning of the nineteenth century. Despite the frequent critiques of both positions there is good reason to use them as a starting point. The book considers the sense in which both are valid interpretations of the modern economic experience. The book deliberately avoids getting bogged down in discussions of what constitutes modernity.

CHAPTER 1

1. It is highly desirable to aim for an elegant economy of explanation; this is described as the principle of Ockham's razor. It is desirable to avoid redundancy in explanations, the inclusion of variables which contribute nothing to the explanation. Simplicity and elegance in themselves are not a guarantee that an explanation is adequate. This is true even in science, where it is not difficult to find examples where the simplest explanation proved to be markedly inferior to explanations which were much more complex.
2. In the relevant literature, there is often a distinction made between economic development and economic growth. Cameron (1997: 9) defines the former as '. . . economic growth accompanied by a substantial structural or organizational change in the economy, such as a shift from a local subsistence economy to markets and trade, or the growth of manufacturing and service outputs relative to agriculture'. As Cameron points out, neither necessarily represents economic progress, which involves ethical judgements about what is good and bad. For example, the distribution of the associated income may be uneven and considered bad. Or there may be environmental externalities significant enough to offset the positive effects of economic development.

    We might add 'potential' to the word increase since a relevant population could in theory take out the benefits of economic development in increased leisure, meeting their subsistence needs with a diminishing input of labour. In practice, until recently this was done on a significant scale – in other words, over most of the period of modern economic development the number of hours worked each week by an average worker diminished significantly.
3. Rostow (1965) popularised the notion of self-sustaining growth. Despite the many criticisms to which the notion was subjected, it still identifies a central element of the experience of modern economic development.
4. This transition occurred after a period of increased work effort, a period aptly described by de Vries (1994) as the 'industrious revolution'. A significant part of the increased output which was achieved during the early stages of the Industrial Revolution was a result of an increased labour input.

341

5.   The potential of developed economies to support a significant and sustained increase in welfare is greatly increased, but it is still possible for that potential to be unrealised for short periods of time, such as during a major downturn in the business cycle, like the Great Depression of the 1930s, or for some countries during war, as in World War II. The key issue at such times is the ability of affected societies to recover from such set-backs. The destructive impact of modern war is illustrated by the devastation wreaked on the defeated economies of Germany and Japan by World War II. Their capacity to bounce back is a nice illustration of the way in which modern economic development is self-sustaining.

6.   The prejudice can be extreme. In communist societies, the measure of output excluded services. There is also currently considerable concern in developed economies about outsourcing manufacturing abroad and the resulting loss of manufacturing jobs, even if they are replaced by positions in the services sector.

7.   This is sometimes called the index number problem. There is no unambiguous measure of the rate of economic growth, nor of any other economic magnitude. There are arguments in favour of using various weights to assess the contribution of particular individual elements to the aggregate. The ambiguity is inherent in measurement itself and compounds the problem that the statistics themselves contain a margin of error and are always out of date.

8.   There is a warm tribute given by modern practitioners to this pioneer work (Harley 2001). National income accounting was stimulated by Keynesian economics and is applied retrospectively to the historical experience of countries for which there are adequate data.

9.   The placement of the apostrophe in 'economist's history' suggests that it was written for economists, rather than by economists.

10. The existence of such thresholds or critical masses involves relationships which are non-linear and therefore difficult to model or study mathematically. For example, if the investment ratio rises beyond a certain level, then there may be a disproportionate impact on the growth of income – the incremental capital output ratio may decline.

11. This theory is analysed because of its claim to be rigorous (probably justified), its persisting role in the teaching of economics, notably the interpretation of modern economic development (unlikely to diminish), and the sheer weight of the relevant literature devoted to its development, notably over the last 15 to 20 years (unlikely to lessen).

CHAPTER 2

1.   The theory is concisely set out in Helpman (2004: 10–13)). Most empirical growth work is based on this theory (Durlauf, Johnson and Temple 2004: 28).

The main characteristic of neoclassical theory is generally an attachment to efficiently operating markets (Romer 1986, 1987 and 1990: 10). A simple neoclassical world is one of constant returns and therefore of perfect competition and strongly efficient markets. Despite this, the work of Romer on increasing returns to ideas has made necessary an acceptance of some degree of imperfect competition, often associated with the monopoly element arising from the existence of a patent. Neoclassical economics has managed to absorb the main implications of the new growth theory into the existing model, without changing it to a significant degree. The way in which Dixit and Stiglitz introduced imperfect competition into the story retains many of the assumptions of neoclassical economics (Lipsey, Carlaw and Bekar 2005: 34). This issue is dealt with in more detail in Chapter 10.

Colander (2003: 1135–6) has reduced the defining attributes of neoclassical economics to six: a focus on allocation of resources at a given moment of time; acceptance of utilitarianism: a focus on marginal trade-offs; an assumption of far-sighted rationality;

methodological individualism; and an emphasis on equilibrium, usually one which is unique and stable. Despite some departures from these attributes, a quick glance at a graduate-level textbook on economic growth, such as Barro and Sala-i-Martin (2004; see, for example, chapters 2 and 3, which are pure utilitarianism), shows that they are all there in strength. Colander has exaggerated the degree to which economics as an institutionalised discipline has disappeared; individual economists may have departed in dealing with particular problems which cry out for such a departure, but this is still rare, particularly in the area of growth theory. The stress on models and maximising behaviour continues to hold.

There is still dispute as to what constitutes the defining core. At a minimum, a neo-classical model is one which engages in a 'systematic exploration of the implications of rational behaviour in economics' (Hoff 2000: footnote 4). Such behaviour is that of individuals. Rodrik (2007: 3) sees the following methodological predisposition as at the core of neoclassical economics: 'social phenomena can best be understood by consider-ing them to be an aggregation of purposeful behaviour by individuals – in their roles as consumer, producer, investor, politician, and so on – interacting with each other and acting under the constraints that their environment imposes'. Neoclassical economics therefore stresses deliberate choices made by individual decision makers with a clear objective function. He goes further and defines neoclassical economics as a set of first-order principles which follow from neoclassical economic reasoning – property rights, sound money, fiscal solvency and market-oriented incentives.

Neoclassical economics is usually seen as rather more than an emphasis on individual rational behaviour – it is 'a short-hand for models that postulate maximizing behaviour plus interactions through a complete set of perfectly competitive markets' (Hoff 2000). There is still a tendency to emphasise competition and competitive markets, but slowly the ubiquity of imperfect competition is being accepted, as the assumptions required by perfect competition are re-examined.

Rational choice models have much to offer in advancing our understanding, par-ticularly where they are now used to show that individual decisions can frequently lead to equilibrium positions decidedly inferior to other equilibrium positions. Choices are not always, perhaps not even frequently, efficient in the sense that they yield a social optimum (David 1985). Economies become locked into inefficient technical, and by extension, institutional, choices.

2. Some have called this the Golden Age path. It assumes that the upper bound is always achieved, an optimistic growth scenario. In such a scenario, the implementation of the relevant technology is 'frictionless'. Because in the simple model institutions are assumed to be infinitely malleable, transaction costs are close to zero, which is why in a formal sense institutions are irrelevant.

3. Because of the force of compounding, such a rate of growth, although superficially low, still results in levels of GDP per head at huge multiples of the base income, whether we make comparison over time in the same country or between countries at the same moment of time. Within a generation, income levels in the relevant country would have doubled and the level of income in that country would exceed that of economically stagnant countries by 2:1, if they had started at the same level.

4. It is an unfortunate weakness of the English language that the term investment covers both investment in financial assets and investment in productive capacity – in practice, the former is a savings decision and the latter an investment decision, but in economic theory the two are usually fused despite the fact that, although they may be linked, they are separate decisions. Since much investment is financed by the internal funds of an enterprise – depreciation allowances and retained profits – savings decisions are often made simultaneously with investment decisions. Neoclassical economics talks of savings decisions as if they were automatically investment decisions, which they are not – neither Harrod nor Domar did so (see Helpman 2004, chapter 2 for an example of this, or C.I. Jones in any of his work). Capital accumulation is in practice both – savings put into shares and bonds and investment in physical assets.

5. Harrod (1939) assumed that the actual rate of growth could diverge from the warranted rate, that is, the rate s/v, since ex ante savings could diverge from ex ante investment.

6. In practice, the rate of growth of population and the labour force tend to fall with economic development.

7. Neoclassical models often also include a term for depreciation of capital, d, which is added to the sum, $n + m$, but to keep the analysis simple, we ignore this. Some theorists therefore use the rate $n + m + d$ to indicate the growth in capital needed to keep the ratio of capital to labour (measured in efficient units) constant. It is further possible to fuse the two, labour growth and technical change, by assuming that technical change is labour augmenting, that is, equivalent in its effect to a growth of the labour force. Then we simply measure labour in effective or efficient units. If the productivity of labour doubled, the number of units of labour would double.

8. If there is a large pool of underemployed labour in the rural or traditional sector, the growth rate of employment could be increased above $s/v - m$, that is, above the rate of population growth for a lengthy period of time, and the easiest mechanism for doing this was thought to be an increase in savings and investment (Lewis 1954). Underemployed or unemployed labour from the traditional sector could be drawn into the modern sector until there is none left.

9. We assume away any valuation problems which occur in the world of markets and prices (Harcourt 1972), which might mean that there are perverse effects. In other words, if the price of labour rises, a more labour-intensive technology emerges as the equilibrium technology rather than a more capital-intensive one. There is a considerable literature on so-called Wicksell effects, which is largely ignored today.

10. Actually, this is a reasonable assumption for developed economies since fertility rates typically fall below 2 as income rises.

11. The proper approach is to improve the measurement of the inputs of capital and labour, in such a way as to reduce total factor productivity to zero. There are three ways of doing this. The first involves following the work of Arrow and allowing for learning by doing, which means lower costs in the future, both for the enterprise and for the economy at large. Choosing a technology means choosing a future trajectory of falling costs. The reduction in overall costs can be related to the level of total output or, as with Romer's (1986, 1987 and 1990) first endogenous model, to the stock of capital already accumulated. The term learning by doing, using and watching captures better the increase in productivity which results from experience. Some of the learning effects can be captured by an enterprise, but there are social benefits gained by all. Added up, the small benefits are significant. Learning is, in the words of van der Klundert and Smulders (1992: 181), a public good. The accumulation of knowledge is an accidental by-product – an externality – of some activity in the economy, such as production or capital accumulation. In this case, a simple increase in the exponent of the capital term in the production function leads to increasing returns rather than constant returns to scale and to capital no long displaying diminishing returns, but this is not inevitable. As van der Klundert and Smulders (1992: 184) assert, 'There is no a priori reason to believe that externalities from learning-by-doing are large enough to compensate for internal diminishing returns to capital'. Another kind of externality is government investment in infrastructure, which raises the return to private investment, and does so continuously as government expenditures on infrastructure rise with total output.

    A second approach includes technical improvement in the capital input itself, through what used to be called a vintage approach, allowing that different vintages of capital embody different levels of productivity. This would expand the number of units of capital represented by recent investment. The third technique for removing the residual involves the use of a definition of broad capital which includes human capital. The level of skills and experience of the labour force itself raises productivity levels. Human capital is often used in fixed proportions with physical capital and raw labour does not enter the production function at all. There are constant returns to broad capital. Alternatively, it is possible to augment the production function by including human capital in one of two other ways. The first is as a separate term, included in a production function in the same way as physical capital (Mankiw, Romer and Weil 1992). The alternative is to include it in the labour input, making the labour input reflect time of input as labour improves its skills. The term can make allowances for the level of education and the return from that education (C.I. Jones 2002: 54–63). Increasingly, there is a term for education, which can be added to the term for capital or for labour; the former is more popular among neoclassical theorists and the latter is more popular among development economists (Soludo and Kim 2003: 37).

12.   The capital term FkK/Y is usually written as α, and with constant returns to scale the labour term is $1 - \alpha$. It is not uncommon for a conventional value to be given to α, but there are attempts to estimate it directly. The usual method is to estimate the share of capital in the income distribution. An alternative approach is to estimate α from the production function equation either for levels or for first-order differences. Theory favours the former since it takes better account of long-term changes. Changes in α do not necessarily affect the ranking of countries by dA/A, but do affect the relative contributions of the different elements to economic growth in one country (Soludo and Kim 2003: 38–9). The size of the residual reflects the size of the capital and labour terms. Since capital usually grows significantly faster than labour, the size of α is critical to the size of dA/A – the greater is α, the smaller is dA/A.

13.   There is an excellent review of the theoretical strengths and weaknesses of some of the empirical findings of growth accounting in Barro and Sala-i-Martin (2004: chapter 10).

14.   While there is a significant imprecision in the estimates, the general trend and relative importance are indicated by the analysis.

15.   Lipsey, Carlaw and Bekar (2005: 121–30) argue that the residual is really the return for undertaking uncertainty (risk).

16.   The results of their study show, for example, about half of the productivity growth in the USA is derived from foreign technology.

17.   It might also be asked whether an uneven income distribution, however defined, or an increase in the unevenness, is bad for economic development. Kuznets (1956–64) found that income inequality increased initially as incomes rose and then fell. There are several arguments why this has happened. It is argued that higher income earners saved more and that the higher level of investment associated with economic development required a rise in savings to finance it. This might occur through a redistribution of income by source. The influence of the Kuznets effect appears to have declined in recent times. The Asian experience seems to have contradicted it. In developed economies, consumption has increasingly become a driver of economic growth, particularly, with savings mobile from country to country. However the continuing tendency to equality of savings and investment ratios in individual countries, and their movement in the same direction, also confirms a continuing home country bias in both savings and investment (Feldstein and Horioka 1980). Certainly, in the fast-growing Asian economies, high savings rates are associated with high investment rates, but neither is necessarily associated with a growing unevenness of income distribution.

18.   Joan Robinson (1974) discussed this difficulty of the concept of equilibrium many years ago. It is difficult to see how any analysis can avoid at least an implicit use of the concept of equilibrium.

CHAPTER 3

1.   There are two arguments which can be used to controvert this. The first rejects the likelihood, even desirability, of rational choices (Simon 1955). This critique has been made from many different angles. The second points out that apparently efficient choices can lead to inefficient outcomes and for rational reasons a system becomes locked into these choices (David 1985).

2. My tutor in economic history at Pembroke College, David Joslin, was fond of criticising Rostow's notion of the take-off by pointing out that many Latin American countries appear to have taken off many times, a logical impossibility. In other words, the relevant growth was not sustained.

3. The communications revolution has made information much more quickly and easily accessible. It also makes more frequent and more dramatic demonstration effects which show new products and new processes at work. It also means that the law of one price is much more likely to hold. Processes of arbitrage are unhampered by ignorance or time delays in getting information. However, in the new world, information is not costless, or rather knowledge is not costless, since there is so much information that there is an expensive process of selection which must be undertaken before information becomes knowledge which is potentially valuable.

4. The Solow factors can be broadly described as proximate factors. The other factors are largely those which explain differences in the proximate factors. They can be called ultimate or fundamental factors. The distinction is developed in the next chapter (Chapter 4).

5. On the basis of the initial level of income per head and of levels of education, Durlauf and Johnson (1995) distinguished four groups, each with significant geographical homogeneity.

6. In technical jargon, they converge to one another if their initial conditions are in the basin of attraction of the same steady-state equilibrium (Galor 1996: 1056, footnote 4).

7. Adopting criteria for identifying membership of the upper group which are too wide can lead to exit as well as entry into the group (Földvári and van Zanden n.d.). The recent use of Markov chain transition matrices shows in the experience of recent transitions between relevant national income groups some evidence for an outcome in which economic development becomes universal.

8. The key questions for Pritchett are then, what initiates an acceleration or a deceleration in the actual rate of economic growth? What is the role of episodes of reform or of shocks in this? (Pritchett 2000: 247). How likely is the change of pace to persist?

9. It is easy to indicate the nature of the fallacy. Imagine that there are ten mothers. Their heights range from 5 foot 1 inch upwards by the inch. Make a random selection of their heights and then do the same for ten imaginary daughters using the same heights. Does there seem to be a convergence, despite the fact that there clearly is not? This is analogous to an exercise which relates growth rates to initial output per head – the illustration comes from C.I. Jones (2002: 76).

10. Some analysts make membership far too broad. For example, a paper by Földvári and van Zanden (n.d.) uses as criteria a faster rate of economic growth than the leading nation and a threshold level of GDP per capita relative to the leader, which for an unexplained reason comes down from 80 per cent to 60 per cent in the most recent period. Such criteria place as much as 65 per cent of countries within the upper convergence club, and also mean that countries exit as well as enter, which contradicts the self-sustaining nature of modern economic development. With such loose criteria, most inequality is now between countries within the club, rather than between member and non-member countries. Tightening the criteria makes membership much more uncommon and also makes more tendentious the eventual entry of all countries.

11. Extreme poverty is defined as one dollar a day income, poverty as two dollars. Allowance has to be made for price movements over time, so the year must be speficied.

CHAPTER 4

1. Somehow the Keynesian case became reabsorbed into neoclassical economics as a special case. Neoclassical economics tends to fuse savings and investment decisions,

seeing the latter as automatically following from the former, whereas they are conceptually, and usually in practice, separate decisions. It is unacceptable to assume Say's law, that, at least ex ante, investment is not automatically equal to savings. In the timeless world of neoclassical economics, this is not even seen as a problem.

2. There is an excellent body of theory which is growing, which sees the investment decision as the exercise of a real option.

3. One implication of the neoclassical model, in its simplest form, is that government policy appears irrelevant to the rate of growth (C.I. Jones 2002: chapter 8). A significant implication of endogenous theories of growth was to draw a very different conclusion.

4. See appendix 2 in Durlauf, Johnson and Temple (2004) for a full list of the variables, amounting to nearly 150. Even much more targeted studies, such as those of Levine and Renelt (1992) and Sala-i-Martin (1997), have large numbers of variables, 40 variables and 64 variables respectively.

5. Kremer et al. (2001) also argue that beliefs about the long-run evolution of the world income distribution must rely heavily on what they call priors, that is, starting assumptions, since in this case empirical estimates of the ergodic distribution (that is, the future distribution implicit in the tendencies for change in such distributions in recent times) are noisy, that is, subject to multiple uncertain influences. The same argument might be made for all regression analysis.

6. The classic recent example is Acemoglu et al. (2001).

7. Ignoring something does not make it go away.

8. The key to explaining the inception of modern economic development is not to discover necessary conditions, but to identify sufficient conditions. However, the problem is that the sufficient conditions appear to differ from successful experience to successful experience.

   The neoclassical model of modern economic growth rests on the assumption that the world is ergodic; it tends to move towards an identifiable equilibrium position. In reality, the world is non-ergodic. We can ask whether it is useful, even necessary, to make the assumption that the world is ergodic, in order to understand the processes which characterise it, including modern economic growth. The neoclassical model is useful in identifying economic motivation and economic tendencies, but it stops well short of explaining how these motivations or these tendencies appeared in the first place. There is a grave danger in the neoclassical approach of what Tilly (1992: 33) calls the 'crevasse of teleology', in which historical outcomes are used to explain causes. The narrative is read backwards. The past is read solely in the context of the present or rather a putative future based on the present of the most developed economy. There is a worse trap, if we assume that all decisions made in history are rational ones, which is what choice theory does. It is assumed that decisions are deliberate, based on the best information available, not repetitive decisions based on tradition or convention, nor the result of constraints on behaviour nor the influence of ideas with little overt economic relevance. The neglect of process is a major weakness in economic theory. Fortunately, the literature on path dependency has shown that even in a world where decision makers try to be rational, we can be locked into decisions which prove to be inefficient, producing outcomes inferior in some sense to the alternatives which might have been made. Decisions made are constrained, even in a rational word. The alternative approach is a 'blank wall of randomness'. In this understanding, uniqueness means a lack of any pattern and a lack of well-worn pathways. This also abuses reality. At whatever early date we like to start, there was never an infinite range of possible futures. There were always several distinct possibilities. Identifying those futures requires both theory and narrative.

9. Extending the neoclassical theory, some theories try to incorporate the main engines of historical change in a model as endogenous elements. There are three main candidates for this process of endogenization – savings behaviour, population change and technical change. It is much more difficult within the neoclassical model to make other elements endogenous, such as culture, institutions or even geography, unless you assume

they adjust automatically to economic requirements. The high level of complexity resulting from making these important elements endogenous makes it difficult to model the key relationships in such a model. The difficulty of producing a model in which, if possible, all relevant variables are made endogenous immediately imposes a limit on the explanatory power of the neoclassical theory.

There is a number of models of savings behaviour. Three stand out, the first two concerned with how an individual should optimise savings levels. The first two are consistent with neoclassical theory and rational individual choice. The first is the notion of a single, infinitely lived consumer. There has been much work in applying the original Ramsey model on savings decisions to the more general growth model (Barro and Sala-i-Martin 2004, chapters 2 and 3). A simple rule has been put forward for the optimum rate of savings, which is seen as reflecting an equalisation of the marginal rate of substitution of production across time and the rate of time preference, also taking into account the declining marginal utility of income. A second model sees the economy as composed of a series of overlapping generations, each with a finite lifetime. The discounting of time is rather different in such a model. Both these models yield a steady growth state with a constant savings rate. In these first two models, the savings of enterprises is seen as the saving of its shareholders. No allowance is made for institutional savings, since all income is individual income. An alternative approach is neo-Keynesian, seeing savings as coming principally from profits and not from personal income, and reflecting the distribution as well as the level of income. A high rate of investment generates a high rate of savings through the growth of the share of income claimed by profits. Savings do not drive investment, investment drives savings. This reversal of the usual causation accords much more with the empirical fact that most investment is financed by funds internal to the enterprise – depreciation allowance and retained profits. If the enterprise is regarded as a coalition of various stakeholders, not just an expression of one privileged group, the shareholders, then optimum savings theories seem irrelevant. Furthermore, the integration of international capital markets has not broken the link between national investment and savings ratios (Feldstein and Horioka 1980). They tend to move together as would be expected if most savings to finance investment comes from the internal funds of the investing enterprise.

The rate of population change reflects the level of income per head, but not in a simple manner. There is no simple chronological relationship between income and population. There is an enormous amount of noise, as shocks influence the movement of both mortality and fertility rates. The timing of changes differs from society to society. It is possible to postulate a robust long-term relationship between the rate of population growth and income per head. Initially, the theory of the demographic transition sees reduced mortality having a larger influence than reduced fertility. Population growth accelerates before it decelerates. Reduced fertility eventually kicks in at a later stage. Income reaches a certain threshold level, at which fertility rates begin to turn down, but the level depends on a number of factors, such as the level of educational expenditures or the degree of emancipation of women. The decline in the rate of population growth is closely associated with the emancipation of women, including their increased access to education, the introduction of labour-saving devices within households and improved career prospects. It is also true that, as income rises, the relative price of children as a consumer good rises relative to other consumer goods. Tastes also change, as with respect to children, parents desire quality as much as quantity. Eventually, reduced fertility can decrease the size of n to zero, although an allowance for migration is an important qualifier.

Much of the work on economic growth theory in the recent past has been devoted to a better understanding of technical change and how to make it endogenous. Much of the new or endogenous growth theory is concerned with this issue. Clearly determination of the size of two of our original variables, m and v, reflects an understanding of technical change. The former reflects the impact of such growth on the rate of rise of productivity and the latter its articulation in an aggregate measure of the efficiency of the basic technology, the capacity of capital to produce output. The level of technical change is itself related to the level of economic development, for example the level of investment in R&D which is made possible by the relevant income level. Both can be the result of economic processes which are market based and profit driven. The issue of patents and the exploitation of a monopoly position mean that the model must incorporate imperfect competition. It assumes the innovation itself, even invention, is the result of profit-oriented activity, although the profit may be won at some distant time in the future. The capacity to absorb technical knowledge is a complex issue. The rate of technical advance reflects the development of pure research and the link between pure and applied research in developed economies with infrastructures favourable to technical progress. Patents provide the monopoly element which promotes the relevant investment in applied research. There is a self-sustaining element and a major issue of externalities or spillovers if some of the knowledge generated becomes public, which is very difficult to avoid.

10. There was in this area a debate among historical sociologists and political theorists highlighted by a book published in 1998 by a group of practitioners, who provided examples of analytical narratives (Bates et al. 1998) and by the systematic critique sparked off by this publication. Some of this work overlaps economic history. The theory used in this work was rational choice theory applied in the context of game theory. Game theory is limited in its relevance to the mystery to be resolved here. As a number of commentators have pointed out, it is applicable to a range of puzzles narrow in scope, usually characterised by stability rather than change. Where change is the focus of attention, it is not an appropriate method to use. The main supporters of the analytic narrative accept that there is a broad range of theories which can be used. The relevance of the theory has to be shown, since ready-made off-the-shelf theories are not always appropriate.

CHAPTER 5

1. What is clear is that climate changes over time. At least up to now natural fluctuations have dwarfed those caused by humans. Most people forget that the last ice age occurred as recently as between 28,000 and 10,000 BC.

2. Temperate latitudes are defined as those above the tropics of cancer and capricorn and below somewhere about 25 degrees. If we focus on temperate latitudes, it is clear from the historical record that there have been significant long-term fluctuations in climate, having a significant impact on economic life, and that these fluctuations have been synchronous across the world (Galloway 1986). During the last thousand years, there have been two relatively cold periods during which conditions changed rapidly – with minima reached around the mid-fifteenth and the late seventeenth centuries. It appears that the carrying capacity of the land was reduced and population growth slowed during the little ice ages or was reversed as a result of the impact on fertility and mortality rates. However, the current period has been a notably warm one in the history of the earth, at least since the last ice age, 13,000 years ago.

   A further argument is that the evolution of intelligence was faster in colder, more challenging areas, exerting more cognitive demands on humans, where, for example, it was necessary to catch game and store meat rather than rely on relatively abundant vegetable sources (Lynn 2006: chapter 16).

3. It is impossible to write an analytic narrative of a particular country without taking proper account of its specific geographical conditions and how they interact with other causative elements. The importance of these geographical element may differ but they are never without importance. For example, Japan has developed economically despite its resource deficiencies, not because of them.

4. Just three civilisations – Europe, China and India – accounted for 70 per cent of the population in 1400 and even more at 80 per cent today.

5. Resources are defined by market demand, they therefore have market value, which makes possible some sort of measurement. However, in the absence of well-developed markets it is difficult to compare oranges and apples.
6. Even in this case, there are some who argue that the resource constraint was irrelevant to Japanese economic development until the militarisation of the 1930s (Yasuba 1996).
7. It is interesting to consider the West Indies or the South in the USA in this context. They both had disease environments which were threatening to whites. The different immunities of native, white and black populations in these regions have influenced their historical development.
8. There is much material on the decimation of the native population of the Americas. On one extreme account, it declined to a tenth its pre-Colombus figure. A similar decline has been suggested for Australia. The extent of the decline in Siberia is unclear.
9. The terms come from Price (1987).
10. There is a growing literature discussing the causes of a failure to develop economically in Africa.

CHAPTER 6

1. Bowman (1980) initiated a great debate when he showed that, viewed dynamically, enterprises can simultaneously increase their returns and reduce risk. There is a good discussion of these issues in chapter 2 of North (2005).

   It is not difficult to find examples of distributions where the expected mean return is close to zero. Venture capital funds operate on the basis that one good success compensates for a number of failures. Wheat farmers subject to drought know that one good year compensates for the bad years. Failure in a more general sense, at both macro and micro levels, can also result from an excess of caution, too many type two errors, failures to take a risk.

   Strictly speaking, shocks are events occurring outside the model of the economic system. Some of the shocks discussed here are in their origin endogenous to most relevant economic models. A shock is simply defined as a large unanticipated event with negative consequences – it might include a significant change of behaviour, say a change in the pattern of demand.
2. There is a problem of terminology, which is discussed below – in the interim, the term risk is used interchangeably with uncertainty.
3. The real options approach indicates a much more sensible approach to ignorance, uncertainty and risk.
4. Bernstein (1996) has written an excellent historical review of the treatment of risk.
5. Tversky and Kahneman won a Nobel Prize for their work on 'framing'.
6. At one time, it was fashionable to set out a general equilibrium model for the allocation of resources, including an expanding pool of resources, which applies not only to the present but to all future years, and embodies a set of prices which incorporates all such risk and clears the relevant markets. The greater is the risk, the higher are the relevant prices since they incorporate relevant risk premia. The market reflects the risk situation. The approach rests on a set of unacceptable assumptions, so that such a model, while still taught, is not regarded as a valid description of the real world.
7. Moss (2002) has set out all the difficulties of a market system taking into account risk.
8. The concept of value at risk has been developed by Dowd (1998).
9. There are two kinds of error made at the micro level by relevant decision makers. Type two errors are those involving a failure to initiate projects which would have brought a reasonable return – as compared with a type one error, which is to implement bad projects. A lack of economic development is a result of a myriad of type two errors. At the micro level, the failure of an enterprise may reflect an excess of caution.

10. Despite the attention devoted to it in the financial literature, risk mitigation is far more important than risk management – from the overall societal perspective, it is far more important to reduce the risk exposure, by installing sprinkler systems for example, than to redistribute the risk, by taking out an insurance policy, although both are significant.

11. It is intriguing to consider the influence of risk on the transition from a hunter-gatherer society to an agricultural one. Hunter-gatherer societies were typically organised to spread risk. A whole literature on reciprocal altruism emphasises the way in which sharing over time eased risks, but such arrangements could act as an obstacle to the introduction of agriculture, which exposes the relevant societies to a different kind of risk. Initially, agriculture reduces the level of diversification. For that reason, there was a slow addition of domesticated crops and animals to the range of resources available. For undeveloped economies, those at the hunter-gatherer or agricultural stages, including settler societies, the level of natural risk is typically high and influential, with a pioneer risk environment characteristic of particular places.

CHAPTER 7

1. The way in which neoclassical theorists treat human capital is illustrated by C.I. Jones (2002).
2. The nature of the base level of literacy or intelligence is a contentious issue.
3. Learning by doing and observing involves no obvious investment.
4. Work on height became the focus of much interest.
5. It is uncertain whether proto-industrialisation acted as a preparation for full industrialisation, or whether it acted as a barrier. The situation varied from country to country. In Britain the former appeared to be true, in Russia, the latter (White 1987).
6. There is a sense in which this is untrue. Large areas planted to a single crop, such as grains, are more vulnerable to disease. Fortunately, science has managed to keep about ten years ahead of the mutation of fungi and prevent major destruction by plant diseases.
7. There is a good literature on famine in Russia.
8. There is considerable work on the Irish famine and its causes.
9. The policy of the Chinese government both in building and filling storage granaries and in improving the transport system to move grain in bad times is well documented.
10. Intelligence tests have Asian countries consistently outperforming European countries, and European countries outperforming African countries. As the text shows, the implications are not racial; indeed it is difficult to select homogeneous racial groups. The units used here, as elsewhere in the book, is the state.
11. It is clear that some human groups, such as the Aborigines in Australia or the Inuit in Canada and the inhabitants of Siberia, have highly developed visualisation skills, which help them survive in environments which have few distinguishing marks. Diamond would not find the specificity of intelligence factors surprising and Lynn has accepted this.
12. Moreover, it appears to be rising significantly faster in developing countries such as Kenya, where some interesting studies have been carried out. An improvement in various environmental factors which influence IQ suggests a real possibility of an improvement over time as successful economic development occurs. There is therefore some evidence of convergence in national intelligence levels.
13. Neoclassical economists argue that, even if the deliberate and self-conscious intention were not to maximise profits, competition forces decision makers to do this or have their enterprise go bankrupt. Competition is seen as acting rather like natural selection: only maximisers survive.
14. It is only necessary to read the satires of Juvenal to realise that this was true in imperial Rome.

15. The influence of religion has been a major focus of interest. How far does religion allow a rational attitude to the world, to understanding it and controlling, maybe understanding in order to control? Placing human beings at the centre of being and encouraging control over nature is probably good for economic development, although not always for the environment. This is linked with the attitude to science and to religion. There are those who argue that even in medieval Europe, Catholic as it was, there was an interpretation of science as revealing the laws by which God's world was regulated (Stark 2005). One historian refers to the 'celestial lawgiver', a god who prescribes the laws of nature and asserts, 'In Europe, belief in such a providential figure, and the quest for "his" purposes and grand design, had been a (perhaps the) central motive for scientific inquiry' (Darwin 2008: 200) This was not true of other religions. There were lapses, some of them famous, such as the persecution of Galileo. In this sense, there was from the beginning a favourable disposition among Christians towards economic development and certainly no incompatibility between religion and science, and certainly none between religion and economic development.

The eschatology of a religion is a key factor. Does the religion accommodate an improvement in the position of the individual here on earth? Certainly the eschatology of some religions has seen scope for improvement in the here and now. Some make plenty of allowance for this, seeing worldly success as a sign of grace. Others have also argued that individuality emerged as a direct, or personal, relationship to God. The key issue is whether individuals embrace a religion because of what they are doing already or whether a pre-existing religious position encourages them to do what they doing. It is not just the Protestant ethic, which has often been seen as extremely helpful in promoting the impulse to economic development. It is also argued that the monasteries anticipated the institutional arrangements of a capitalist economy. The accounting requirements of profit and loss were explored by such institutions. These organisations developed the capacity to develop economically. The link between Protestant attitudes and religion has been investigated at length and this kind of analysis extended to include the main tenets of Confucianism and their link with the Asian Economic Miracle. There is a danger here, since Confucianism was once seen as a barrier to economic development. It is hard to see the same set of attitudes and values as at one time an obstruction to economic development and at another time a stimulus.

Some religions can play an obstructive role. The tendency of Islamic countries to have become relatively poor (they were not always so) is seen as incontrovertible (Kuran 2004: 122–5). Some argue that religion has nothing to do with the poor performance, that the Islamic culture is irrelevant since it is malleable. Certainly Islam is not fixed in its effects but variable. However, it has clearly come to impede innovation and significant change.

CHAPTER 8

1. The interpretation of institutions as rules can incline to a top-down approach, putting the spotlight on the politics of rule making. It ignores the problem of motivation for rule makers, rule enforcers and rule followers, which reflects different belief systems. It also implies wrongly that private order is possible without such rules, or that private order is not necessary to supplement the operation of the rules. The rules approach puts the emphasis on the politics of rule making and sees changes in institutions as resulting from a change in the interests or knowledge of key political decision makers.

2. Economists are prone to over-simplify the role of institutions and to engage in a kind of casual empiricism in finding proxies for complex institutional structures (Szostak 2006: 9). The growing emphasis on institutions is to some degree an admission of the failure of conventional analysis, but it also reflects the growth of a body of institutional economics following from the work of Coase (1937) and Williamson (1985), and from

the influence of Douglass North (1981, 1990 and 2005), particularly since he won the Nobel Prize for Economics.

A much-quoted argument in favour of institutions as a very significant ultimate cause of economic development has been put by Acemoglu and his collaborators (2001). The paper has distinguished the economic performance of former colonies, noting persistent differences. It emphasises the divergence between colonies of settlement and colonies of temporary sojourn, not a new distinction. The paper takes geography as a starting point. Differences of mortality rates, obviously linked with the temperate/tropical dichotomy, encouraged European settlers to choose to settle in certain regions of the world – the USA, Canada, Australia and New Zealand are prominent, rather than other areas such as India and Asian societies or most of Latin America and Africa.

In another paper, Acemoglu et al. (2002) points out that at the time of settlement the neo-Europes were not the most prosperous areas, but emphasises a significant later reversal of fortune, with a successful economic development of the colonies of settlement. In other words, geography, specifically their resource endowment, did not favour the colonies of settlement, yet they succeeded in developing more successfully. On this argument, institutions, rather than geography, determined the relative performance. However, the interpretation of geography is narrow and the specifics of the interaction between geography and institutions insufficiently analysed.

Obviously ignored is the influence of the density of previous settlement, as the experience of South Africa has shown. The neo-Europes were characterised by pre-settlement populations who were decimated by disease because of a lack of immunity to European diseases and therefore by empty lands available for settlement. Many other areas, not settled by Europeans, had large existing populations which acted as a discouragement to European settlement. The two areas therefore inherited two different institutional models.

The first, in colonies of temporary sojourn, has been labelled a model of extraction. Where valuable natural resources existed, this encouraged the application of an extraction model. The political systems were authoritarian and usually highly centralised. A thin upper group from outside imposed itself on the native population and used their position to skew the income and wealth distribution in their favour. They used the tax system and both the control of labour and the ownership of land to set up a system of plantations and mines for which the labour was locally recruited, often forced in some way and from which handsome returns were derived. Slaves or indentured labour might be brought in from outside. The market was heavily regulated and civil society not allowed to flourish. Such a model allowed any ruling group to extract rents from the economy, even after independence. Often decolonisation, whenever it occurred, left in place the extraction model. There was considerable continuity in the institutional arrangements. The nature of the model was reinforced by the identity of the colonising power.

The second model was a model which combined the operation of markets and the emergence of democracy. The political system was largely decentralised, particularly in comparison with colonies of temporary sojourn. There was considerable local autonomy, and increasingly a dense civil society. The emergence of the model was linked to the establishment of small-scale owner occupier agriculture, which reflected relatively easy access to land, and the early movement to democratic systems. Income and wealth were relatively evenly distributed. Some commentators focus on the role of the frontier in democratising such societies. The institutional structure favoured the operation of the market, backed by legal systems which protected both property rights and contract. Representative government, dense markets, and a strong civil society are the foundations of a strong economic performance, particularly in the Anglo world. These ex-colonies displayed significant economic development at an early date, attaining a high level of income per head while still agricultural societies.

In the example above, a clear distinction in institutions appears linked with economic performance. What determines the evolution of the appropriate institutions? Even in the example it is necessary to consider the way in which the institutions developed in the source societies. It was not a matter of the source society in arrested development, as one authority has described it (Hartz 1964). The influence of the colonising power is crucial to the later institutional development of these societies, but the later institutional development is constrained by important geographical factors, such as climate and vulnerability to disease, the endowment with fertile land, and the density of existing populations.

3. In a society which is democratically organised and market based, it is often argued that transaction costs are lower than in one which is centralised and in which government regulation is the norm.

4. This means that the disruptions arising from wars or revolutions may have positive effects, by breaking up these coalitions.

5. The key issue is not only the evolution of appropriate institutions but the interaction of such institutions with other advantageous elements.

6. There is a growing literature on the implications of the Cold War and its outcome. Fortunately, this literature is becoming more subtle and more balanced. For a good initial judgment see Hobsbawm (1994).

7. The causes of the dissolution of the Soviet Union include economic failure. The legitimacy of surviving communist regimes depends on continuing economic success.

8. This was not initially recognised, but the significant contraction in GDP in Russia and other successors of the Soviet Union focused attention on the institutional problems of the area. One reaction is to continuously deny either the present actuality or the future possibility of continuing economic growth in the transitional economies.

9. Stark (2005: 56) has given a definition of capitalism which is helpful: 'Capitalism is an economic system wherein privately owned, relatively well organized and stable firms pursue complex commercial activities within a relative free (unregulated) market, taking a systematic, long-term approach to investing and reinvesting wealth (directly or indirectly) in productive activities involving a hired workforce, and guided by anticipated and actual returns'. This rather begs the question, since it generalises without specifying what exactly is meant by each term.

10. It is interesting to speculate when the patrimonial state disappeared in different parts of Europe. In England, the Tudors established the trappings of the modern state. In Russia, significant aspects of patrimonialism survived through to the Revolution.

11. However, they are not directly linked with the tendency to innovate, but rather reflect a desire for a rational understanding of God's creation and validation of the desire to control nature.

12. Maybe the economy within the state is a more appropriate description, but that describes much better the polity and economy of the old Soviet Union of the twentieth century than the Britain of the eighteenth century. There the government ran the economy as one large enterprise. At different times, control over this apparatus may still rest with a small group of insiders, as it did in the Soviet Union, although it is easy to exaggerate the degree to which any government can control the detailed operations of a complex economic system.

13. Infrastructural power is the ability to pursue policies which promote economic development by providing the supports needed for such development. Despotic power is the ability to intervene in an intermittent way, usually to maintain a modicum of central authority and/or to satisfy some whim.

14. The difference is that a cluster comprises enterprises in close geographical proximity, a network does not necessarily involve such closeness. Porter (1998) sees the existence of clusters as critical to national competitive advantage.

15. It is no accident that the market and the nation state emerged together in Western and Central Europe.

16. For example, Britain, an isolated and backward region within Europe at the time, was a colony of Rome, conquered in 55 AD and subject to Roman control for several centuries. Again, in 1066, Britain was conquered, this time by the Normans, part of the penetration of Europe by the Vikings, who became the new ruling class.

17. A trade deficit might be a natural development, not signifying any exploitation. For example, in the second half of the nineteenth century during its heyday, Britain ran a significant deficit on its current merchandise account, which was more than covered first by the export of services linked to the trade that it dominated and second by a stream of dividend and interest payments which were the return on previous investment. So large were the latter that they financed not just the deficit but a significant and continuing outward flow of FDI. Britain was in the process of transition from being the workshop of the world to becoming a rentier economy. However, this does not imply exploitation.

18. Some commentators assert that it is by exploiting another country that a country develops the capacity to cross the relevant threshold. The failure of the inception of modern economic development in the rest of the world is put down to the success of the already developed world. Previous successes make later successes more difficult to achieve, rather than vice versa. Such a view sees international business transactions as in some way zero-sum games in which the partners are either winners or losers, and the division of the spoils depends on political or military strength, a mercantilist view of the world. Government policy is designed to achieve the winner's position. Such policy was at one stage universal.

  On one account, the world is divided into three zones – the centre, which comprises the small group of developed economies, the periphery, those economies as yet not developed but already integrated into the world economy, and finally the outside, those societies still outside the world economy, which are difficult to find today (Wallerstein 1974). According to Wallerstein, the relationship between centre and periphery is one of dependence, the latter becoming increasingly dependent on the former. The centre exports manufactured goods in return for agricultural goods and raw materials, and allegedly does it at exchange rates and prices which are unfavourable to the periphery. The centre invests in activities advantageous and profitable to the centre and repatriates the relevant profits when this is convenient. The centre also sends out its surplus people in waves of migration. The relationship is an exploitative one, in which the developed countries grow at the expense of the peripheral countries. This has been called by one commentator the development of undevelopment (Frank 1998).

CHAPTER 9

1. As one commentator has noted, 'A surprising feature of the literature on technology and industrialisation is that there are very few systematic studies of the impact of specific technologies' (Bruland 2004: 143).

2. Another distinction is between a technology and a technique. The former is a set of principles concerned with a broad range of activities, their application and development. The latter is a particular way of doing a particular thing, often represented by a blueprint. A technology consists of a set of related techniques.

  A good example of this is to be found in the work of Lipsey, Carlaw and Bekar (2005: 55–6), which expands the analysis to include all inputs, including natural endowments as well as physical capital, and all structures as well, including what they call facilitating and policy structures, the latter being the medium for public policy. These structures are interpreted very broadly. Such an opening up allows for all sorts of feedback effects and all sorts of influences on technology.

3. In any successful economic system there are two important kinds of economic decision – innovation and imitation: both are necessary to economic success, but require differing cultural characteristics – creativity and rationality. Goldstone argues persuasively that '. . . The West leapt ahead not by relentlessly pursuing the path of calculable efficiency, but by taking unknown risks on novelty' (Goldstone 1987: 119), in other words, by being creative and innovating. By contrast, Stark (2005) puts the emphasis on a

pattern of successful imitation as important as the initial leap, one which leans more on rationality.

Once the process of modern economic development has started, the process of promoting innovation becomes institutionalised and rationalised (Baumol 2002). There is therefore need for an institutional system which both gives scope to the entrepreneur to innovate and also encourages a rapid process of imitation. The two activities require differing institutional arrangements. This chapter explores the nature of these arrangements.

4. A nice illustration is the communications revolution. During the 1970s and 1980s, the rate of TFP growth halved in the USA and the capitalisation of enterprises relative to GDP on the stock market also fell significantly.

5. The positive feedback is obvious today. Developed economies dominate both R&D expenditures and the generation of patents.

6. The argument is often circular, in that the constructed world yields outcomes built in through the assumptions made.

7. There is some evidence, both theoretical and empirical, that the realised rate of technical advance in recent times is stable. Research and development involves expenditures, often themselves stable relative to both total revenue and to gross investment (Baumol 2002). Even if new discoveries are unevenly spread, large companies operating in imperfect markets tend to release that technology in a planned way, dictated by significant constraints – the level of initial expenditures required, the reluctance of all enterprises to undermine the value of existing physical and human capital, and the limited organisational capacity of the enterprise, so that it can only innovate within the constraints of its own organisational capacity.

The literature throws up many cases of a theory which rests on historical patterns of behaviour – price theory for oligopoly or the determination of the level of research and development expenditures in a particular sector of the economy. The issue moves beyond the mere establishment of a context. Any realistic view of the determination of such important economic variables as price or level of expenditure on research and development recognised the absence of an economic theory relevant to common market structures such as oligopoly and the need for an historical explanation.

8. Technologies and the associated techniques put into place in different economies as a result of the process of imitation described above are not sufficiently different to regard them as new, and to qualify for patent protection.

9. Country risk is the risk generated by the existence of national boundaries. Its main components are political and economic. See White and Fan (2006).

CHAPTER 10

1. Pritchett describes this as political economy with neither mistakes nor ideas (2004: 226–228).

2. This is summarised by the propositions, that planning solves the problems which planning creates or that the market solves the problems that the market creates. In other words, there is a hard-to-resist momentum in movement towards extreme positions in the role of government or of the market. Russian history illustrates the former, and the recent emphasis on what Australians call economic rationalism illustrates the latter. Those who run government and who take leadership positions in government are not always, perhaps not even often, motivated by a narrow self-interest. Ideological issues supersede narrow economic self-interest, at least for limited periods of time, as for example during the early period after the Bolshevik Revolution in Russia. Any consideration of the pervasive influence of religion in the past shows that religion is not always a mask for economic interests.

3. The experience of many Latin American countries fits this pattern all too well.

4. The internal dynamics of a group are usually ignored. There is no interdependence of satisfaction, no shared goals and no group activities.
5. Such groups are the stuff of civil society, as discussed in Chapter 8.
6. For example, it is common to study voting behaviour in neoclassical political economy from the perspective of economic self-interest, but this is usually limited to single issues, an unrealistic perspective. Such behaviour in other studies is analysed with a mixture of motives in mind.
7. The role of institutions in a socially optimum system is to give the opportunity for individuals to do this, whether in the political or the economic area. A failure of institutions to do this results in a significant level of transactions costs associated with the decision-making process involved in any transaction. The aim of institution building, or for that matter any reform of such institutions, is to minimise the frictions constraining the exercise of individual decision making, so that the key decisions are not distorted.
8. Conquest has a long history and, as Snooks has argued, was a major strategy of leaders of strong countries well before economic development become an important goal. The motive is often seen as strategic, the extension of military power and political influence.
9. This also applies to others who enter into an economic relationship with the investing enterprise. Any asymmetry of investment can have the same result whoever the decision makers are – it makes those who have made the greater investment vulnerable to opportunistic behaviour. If the commitment by any important stakeholder in a transaction, including government, is not seen as credible, the investment is unlikely to be made in the first place.
10. In the existing economic literature, there is often a confusion between institutions and policies, a confusion which reflects the tendency to discuss institutions in terms of their outcomes instead of their defining characteristics and to take a loose definition of what constitutes an institution. The two notions are fudged, hence the separation of the issues in Chapters 8 and 10.
11. As we have indicated in Chapter 4, a policy is 'a conditional rule, a mapping from states of the world to actions' (Pritchett 2004: 231). According to Pritchett, there are three steps in the making of policy: the setting of an institutional 'rules of the game', the making of 'policy' (an announcement of mapping from state of the world to policy actions), and 'policy implementation', in which some agent has to decide on the policy action to take, depending on their claim about which state of the world has been realized. There is a strong bias in favour of the status quo (Castanheira and Esfahani 2003: 171-2), explaining the difficulty of effecting a reform of institutions.
12. Indeed, one school of strategy making is the planning school.
13. See Allen (2003).
14. The response to this weakness in the Soviet Union was to have a planning system which lacked many of the necessary features of planning. In practice, there was little that could be genuinely described as planning in the USSR.
15. The case of Airbus is a good one.
16. Where this is not the case, there may be other protective factors which assist the development of the relevant industries. In the late nineteenth century, the unequal treaties prevented Japan from imposing protective duties, but a currency on the silver standard depreciated in a way which provided the equivalent of such protection.
17. Multinational enterprises which invest abroad appear in the developing country relatively late in the process of development (Dunning and Narula 1996).
18. Rather irrationally, many commentators add together exports and imports in a ratio of trade to output, in order to indicate the relative importance of trade; this is a form of double counting.
19. In certain circumstances, even trade can be immiserating, leading to a loss of income. This is unusual. Trade is usually not a zero-sum game, although this depends on the structure of the international economy and the nature of the payments system. It is possible, and often done, to study trade and investment flows at the international level

free of any influence from the political context in which such flows occur. The usual textbook treatment assumes away the government and the influence of political factors. Attention is focused on the most desirable policy with respect to trade and investment, where all economic decisions are made on the basis of economic optimality.

Openness means the absence of barriers to the entry of the relevant economic flows. Some barriers arise from the additional costs associated with international rather than domestic transactions. There are still transport and communication costs which are significant. A significant barrier is simply ignorance, both of opportunities and of risk. It is no accident that there are pronounced clusters of trading and investment partners. Individuals are more familiar with certain parts of the world. Other barriers arise from the additional risk to which the relevant players are exposed in engaging in international transactions. The danger of expropriation varies over time, but it is a real danger in many parts of the world. This is particularly relevant where significant resources are committed abroad or tangible assets are exposed to opportunist exploitation by foreign governments or other players. Others arise from actions taken by governments, which in some way regulate and restrict inward flows, through tariffs and quotas on trade, or exchange controls on the movement of currencies. Such barriers include all sorts of non-tariff restrictions, such as inspection and quality control, and anti-dumping laws, or restrictions on the repatriations of profits from foreign investments.

20. Trade is explained by gravity models much better than by economic models, or more exactly the proportions of developed and undeveloped economies in its trading pattern, and even where a country located and its distance from advanced economies, and the relative size of the partner economies. Patterns of investment are best explained by investment clusters.

CHAPTER 11

1. There are many good analyses of the Malthusian trap (one example is Macfarlane 1997: chapter 1 'The Malthusian Trap').
2. Boserup (1965 and 1981) has seen technical change as caused by ecological pressures.
3. Income is used here, but the Malthusian analysis can be played out in terms of material consumption per person (Clark 2007: 310) or in terms of the wages of unskilled workers.
4. However, even a very slow rate produces a large population over a sufficiently long period of time.
5. The degree to which the world is regarded as Malthusian differs enormously from commentator to commentator. Goldstone (2008) appears to hold this view but the pre-modern world is seen as Malthusian by Clark (2007) – a world of universally low incomes.
6. Because death was so concentrated in the early part of life, life expectation for those who survived childhood was much better than appeared from simple averages.
7. It is interesting that the same applies to the USA during its settlement (Easterlin 2004: chapter 10).
8. They note the conservatism of official forecasts, which indicate a lack of belief that this trend can continue into the future (there seems to be a widespread belief that the fall in fertility will soon be reversed: see the assumption of UN forecasts of world population).

   Even during the modern era, the demographic experience is continuously disturbed by shocks, some of which are large in their effects. It is difficult to disentangle long-term trends from short-term shock and fluctuations. The two world wars and the Great Depression had a powerful influence on the short-term movement of the relevant demographic rates. It is very difficult to identify, let alone establish, the causation of the long-term trends.
9. The key strategy of technology improvement can keep the Malthusian trap open. Its

potential is by no means exhausted. This is relevant to strategies of conquest – all empires fall at some stage and not often for environmental reasons, as sometimes claimed, or strategies of trade, which are limited in their impact.

CHAPTER 12

1. There are two sources – one statistical, the other resulting from qualitative histories.
2. Big history is often selective, focusing on a particular theme.
3. In a comprehensive review of the British Industrial Revolution, Mokyr (1999: 7–8) identified four schools of thinking concerning causation: first, the social change school, emphasising most often the emergence of markets; secondly, the industrial organisation school, stressing the appearance of the factory and the modern business enterprise; thirdly, the macroeconomic school, concerned with aggregate performance indicators such as rates of growth and investment ratios; and fourthly, the technological school, focusing on the stream of technical innovations. There are various identifications of the determinants of economic growth similar in their coverage. Bin Wong (1997: 58–9) lists five determinants: Smithian growth reflecting the extension of the market, with the resulting specialisation and benefits of an increasing division of labour; investment or capital accumulation; scale effects; technical change; and organisational change. Stern (1991: 128) has six which include capital accumulation; research, development and innovation; management and organisation; and allocation of output across directly productive sectors, which comprises both Smithian and scale effects. He also adds the contributions of human capital and infrastructure. Most of the causes indicated by Mokyr, Wong or Stern move beyond proximate causes and are at least medium term in their influence: they require a narrative approach. Such an approach could pick up different themes, to be the focus of any narrative – for example, the way in which institutions such as the market evolved, the changing nature of industrial organisation, the growing accumulation of both physical and human capital, and the emergence of a context favourable to both invention and innovation.
4. There is a parallel between the process of economic development in nineteenth-century Europe and twenty-first-century Asia, but the scale is very different, and hopefully the outcome, when economic competition became military competition, will not be repeated.
5. Bairoch identifies 20 such myths – Bairoch (1993: xiv).
6. The early pioneer was Kuznets and his main contemporary rival is Bairoch.
7. It is even possible to go one step further and talk about growth scenarios which are characterised by particular stylised facts (McMahon and Squire 2003: chapter 4). Such scenarios might be developed to describe the growth experience of the so-called convergence clubs.
8. Capital letters are used when the term Industrial Revolution is used to describe the pioneer experience in Britain in the late eighteenth and early nineteenth centuries.
9. The traditional narrative of the British Industrial Revolution told a story of heroic innovators and entrepreneurs.
10. There is an obvious limit to the time over which the higher growth rates of the Industrial Revolution could have been possible, since the early levels of GDP per head before 1000 implied by backward extrapolation would be below subsistence levels.
11. The previous debate was inconclusive, largely because of lack of data and a focus on different aspects of the standard of living.
12. In some cases, proto-industrialisation may have assisted the introduction of factory industry, but in most cases it did not, resulting in an economic involution, that is, a perpetuation of low incomes.
13. The Californian School has done much to rectify a previous lack of balance, but there

is a danger of introducing another. There is something to explain and an explanation based on chance is inadequate.

14. This is insufficient reason to drop the use of the term revolution. As de Vries has pointed out with respect to the notion of an industrial revolution, the revisionists '. . . were interested in cleaning the temple of the "false god of the take off," not in pulling down the pillars' (de Vries 1994: 251).

15. Japan is an interesting illustration, with growth rates of total output of 10 per cent in the 1950s and 1960s, 4 per cent in the 1970s and 1980s and a little above zero in the 1990s, although the early rates represent some element of recovery from the destruction of World War II. There is clearly convergence on the long-term equilibrium path.

16. This highlights the problem of causality. For example, does a high level of investment cause more rapid economic growth or does more rapid economic growth cause a high level of investment?

    There is considerable debate concerning the element of continuity in culture, policies or structures. The usual assumption is that institutional change is both incremental and path dependent: '. . . it is simply a fact that the overwhelming majority of change is incremental, gradual, and constrained by the historical past' (North 2005: 64). Institutional elements are often seen as amenable to government action: they can on occasion be radically reformed or undergo revolutionary change during revolutionary times, but this is unusual.

17. Only those which have some quantitative aspect could be tested and even then it is not always clear how the relevant indicator might be constructed. The debate over the role of the investment bank is a typical case.

18. There is a strong argument that the market initially promoted technical change, but by the end of the nineteenth century this was less true.

19. There is a chapter which compares the economic performance of Australia and Argentina, and the reasons for a significant difference.

CHAPTER 13

1. Recent experience has shown how surprisingly rapid growth rates can be sustained over significant periods of time.

2. Marx himself came to realise that the commune left to its own spontaneous development might offer an alternative path to socialism than the development of an industrial development. Engels added the need for the spread of the revolution among the developed countries as a support (Gatrell 1986: 21–2).

3. There is an extremely interesting discussion of where the frontier between Europe and Asia is located and how far Russia is European or Asian.

4. History is often rewritten to suit the victors – the current situation is no exception.

5. As Kaldor (1939) pointed out, prices, even with free markets, reflect the distribution of income. There used to be courses on welfare economics and compensation tests in an effort to make a judgement concerning whether one situation was better than another.

6. Just as the good resource endowment of the USA still required creative exploitation in order to generate rapid economic growth, so the resource constraints of Russia could also has provoked a positive response. However, unlike Japan, there was no good transport access to compensate for resource deficiencies and no creative response.

    The role of natural resources in the economic development of Russia has changed dramatically. As old constraints have been eased, new ones have emerged. Many of the arguments which relate to the negative aspects of a good resources endowment are now seen as relevant to Russia. The resources curse is seen as a real threat, although natural resources have been instrumental in rescuing Russia from slow growth and poor implementation of the transition from a planned to a market economy.

7. Domar (1970: 20–21) set out the basic conditions for the emergence of forced labour,

whether slavery or serfdom. There are three elements of agricultural structure relevant to the status of labour – the existence of free land, of free peasants and of non-working landowners: all three cannot exist simultaneously. He argued that the exact combination which comes into being depends on political behaviour, notably the influence of government measures. If there is free land and non-working landowners, such as a service gentry, the existence of a free peasantry ceases, particularly if the government takes action to safeguard the position of the non-working landowners, for example to ensure that there are servitors to meet its military needs. In Russia, this was a dominating factor (Hellie 1971). There was a scarcity of labour relative to land and a determination on the part of government to protect the country's military strength. This could be ensured by binding the peasants to the military servitors. Domar advanced other arguments why serfdom emerged – the decline in the power of magnates who were free to attract scarce labour – as had happened in Western Europe when labour became scarce after the Black Death – the fiscal interests of the government in keeping the peasants immobile, and the collective responsibility of the peasant commune and their interest in retaining members. Taxation was shifted from the land to the person (poll tax) and the status of the nobility was reflected in the number of souls, rather than the hectares of land that they owned.

8. Stolypin's policies were described as 'the wager on the strong', because they sought to create a group of prosperous peasants who would be the main support of the regime in the countryside.
9. The Feldman model has been much discussed and is still an interesting attempt to consider the dynamics of a developing economy.
10. The Soviet path bypassed the development of those sectors in which it had a relative factor abundance, labour-intensive sectors, and emphasised those in which it did not, capital-intensive sectors.
11. One explanation focuses on the nature of technology, emphasising a much more restricted substitutability between capital and labour than was the case elsewhere, notably in developed economies. Rather than a Cobb-Douglas elasticity of substitution of one between capital and labour, it was much closer to zero, about 0.4 (Weitzman 1970, Easterly and Fischer 1995). This meant that, when there was no additional labour with which to combine it further, capital investment produced little return. There is no good reason why this might be the case – the evidence on substitutability elsewhere does not support this argument.

CHAPTER 14

1. It is necessary to look closely into the black box to understand how inputs are turned into outputs. This requires a consideration of ultimate causation.
2. It is also unlikely that the successful accident will be repeated, because first, development creates undevelopment, and secondly, development creates ecological problems.
3. The historical sociology literature on the subject uses rational choice and game theory, both inappropriate for this kind of problem, since they produce their best results in relatively stable short-term conditions and at the micro level. Their usefulness is limited.
4. The best exponent of this argument is Snooks (1993); he appears rather like a prophet crying in the wilderness,
5. The Asian Economic Miracle is the best example.

Bibliography

Abramovitz, M., 'Catching up, forging ahead, and falling behind', *Journal of Economic History*, 46 (2), June 1986: 385–406.

Abramovitz, M. and David, P.A., 'Reinterpreting economic growth: parables and realities', *American Economic Review*, 63 (2), Papers and Proceedings of the 85th Annual Meeting of the American Economic Association, May 1973: 428–39.

Abu-Lughod, J.L., *Before European Hegemony: the world system A. D. 1250–1350* (Oxford University Press, Oxford and New York: 1989).

Acemoglu, D., 'Introduction to Economic Growth', unpublished text, 2006.

Acemoglu, D., Johnson, S. and Robinson, J.A., 'The colonial origins of comparative development: an empirical investigation', *American Economic Review*, 91 (5), 2001: 1369–401.

Acemoglu, D., Johnson, S. and Robinson, J.A., 'The rise of Europe: Atlantic trade, institutional change and economic growth', Memo, MIT: 2002.

Aghion, P. and Durlauf, S.N. (eds), *Handbook of Economic Growth* (Elsevier, Amsterdam: 2005).

Aghion, P. and Howitt, P., *Endogenous Growth Theory* (MIT Press, Cambridge, MA: 1998).

Aiello, A.E., Lanon, E.L and Sedlak, R., *Against disease: the import of hygiene and cleanliness on health* (The Soap and Detergent Association, Washington, 2007).

Akerlof, G.A., 'The market for "lemons": quality uncertainty and the market mechanism', *Quarterly Journal of Economics*, 84 (3), August 1970: 488–500.

Akerlof, G. and Yellen, J., 'The fair wage-effort hypothesis and unemployment', *Quarterly Journal of Economics*, 105 (2), May 1990.

Alesina, A. and Drazen. A., 'Why are stabilizations delayed?', *American Economic Review*, 91 (5), December 1991: 1170–88.

Alexander, J.T., *Autocratic Politics in a National Crisis: the imperial government and Pugachev's Rising 1773–5* (Indiana University Press, Bloomington, Ind. and London: 1969).

Alexander, J. T., *Bubonic Plague in Early Modern Russia: public health and urban disaster* (Johns Hopkins Press, Baltimore, MD: 1980).

Allen, R.C., *Farm to Factory: a reinterpretation of the Soviet industrial revolution* (Princeton University Press, Princeton, NJ and Oxford: 2003).

Allen, R.C., 'A pessimist's model of growth and inequality during the British Industrial Revolution', Unpublished paper, Department of Economics, Oxford University, 2005.

Allen, R.C., 'Collective invention', *Journal of Economic Behaviour and Organisation*', 4, 1983: 1–24.

Allen, R.C., 'The British Industrial Revolution in global perspective: how commerce created the Industrial Revolution and modern economic growth', Unpublished Paper, 2006.

Allik, J. and Realo, A., 'Individualism-collectivism and social capital', *Journal of Cross-Cultural Psychology*, 35 (1), January 2004: 29–49.

Altman, M., 'Staple theory and export-led growth: constructing differential growth', *Australian Economic History Review*, 43 (3), 2003: 230–55.

Anderson, J.L., *Explaining Long-term Economic Change* (Macmillan, London: 1991).

Artadi, E.V. and Sala-i-Martin, X., 'The economic tragedy of the XXth century: growth in Africa', NBER Working Paper no. 9865, 2003.

Arthur, W.B., 'On learning and adaptation in the economy', Sante Fe Working Paper no. 92–07–038, 1992.

Arthur, W.B., 'Inductive reasoning and bounded rationality', *American Economic Review (Papers and Proceedings)*, 84, 1994: 406–11.

Ashton, T.S., *The Industrial Revolution* (Oxford University Press, London: 1948).

Azariadis, C. and Stachurski, J., 'Poverty traps', Research paper no. 913, Department of Economics, Melbourne University, August 2004.

Bairoch, P., 'Main trends in national economic disparities since the Industrial Revolution', in Bairoch, P. and Levy-Leboyer, M., eds., *Disparities since the Industrial Revolution* (Macmillan, London: 1981).

Bairoch, P., *Economics and World History: myths and paradoxes* (The University of Chicago Press, Chicago: 1993).

Barro, R.J., 'Determinants of economic growth: a cross-country empirical study', NBER Working Paper no. 5698, National Bureau of Economic Research, August 1996.

Barro, R.J., 'Notes on growth accounting', Working Paper no. 6654, National Bureau of Economic Research, July 1998.

Barro, R.J., 'Growth accounting', chapter 10 of Barro, R.J. and Sala-i-Martin, X., *Economic Growth*, 2nd edition (The MIT Press, Cambridge, MA and London: 2004).

Barro, R.J. and Sala-i-Martin, X., 'Convergence', *Journal of Political Economy*, 100, 1992: 223–58.

Barro, R.J. and Sala-i-Martin, X., *Economic Growth*, 2nd edition (MIT Press, Cambridge, MA and London: 2004).

Bates, R.H., Greif, A., Levi, M., Rosenthal, J.-I., and Weingast, B.R., *Analytic Narratives* (Princeton University Press, Princeton, NJ: 1998).

Baumol, W.J., 'Productivity growth, convergence, and welfare: what the long-run data show', *American Economic Review*, 76 (5) 1986: 1072–85.

Baumol, W.J., *The Free Market Innovation Machine* (Princeton University Press, Princeton, NJ: 2002).

Baumol, W.J., Litan, R.E., and Schramm, C.J., *Good Capitalism, Bad Capitalism and the Economics of Growth and Prosperity* (Yale University Press, New Haven, Conn. and London: 2007).

Baykov, A., 'The economic development of Russia', *Economic History Review*, New Series, 7 (2), 1954: 137–49.

Beck, T. and Laeven, L., 'Institution building and growth in transition economies', World Bank Policy Research Working Paper 3657, July 2005.

Becker, G. and Barro, R.J., 'A reformulation of the economic theory of fertility', *The Quarterly Journal of Economics*, 103 (1), Feb. 1968: 1–25.

Bergson, A., *The Economics of Soviet Planning* (Yale University Press, New Haven, Conn. and London: 1964).

Bernard, A.B., 'Trends and transitions in the long run growth of nations', Unpublished paper, 2001.

Bernstein. P.L., *Against the Gods: the remarkable story of risk* (John Wiley and Sons, New York: 1996).

Bernstein, W.J., *A Splendid Exchange: how trade shaped the world* (Atlantic Monthly Press, New York: 2008).

Berry, S., 'On the problem of laws in nature and history: a comparison', *History and Theory*, 38 (4), December 1999: 121–37.

Bhalla, S.S., *Imagine there is No Country: poverty, inequality, and growth in the era of globalisation* (Institute for International Economics, Washington, DC: 2002).

Bin Wong, R., *China Transformed: historical change and the limits of European experience* (Cornell University Press, Ithaca, NY and London: 1997).

Blainey, G.N., *The Tyranny of Distance: how distance shaped Australia's history* (Sun Books, Melbourne: 1966).

Blanchard, I., 'Russian and Soviet economic development in historical perspective, c. 1700–1998', in Elspeth Reid et al. (eds), *Edinburgh Essays: Russia on the edge of the millennium* (Nottingham: 2000).

Blaut, J.M., *The Colonizer's Model of the World: geographical diffusionism and Eurocentric history* (Guilford Press, NY: 1993).

Blaut, J.M., *Eight Eurocentric Historians* (Guilford Press, NY: 2000).

Bloch, H. and Tang, S.H.K., 'Deep determinants of economic growth: institutions, geography and openness to trade', *Progress in Development Studies*, 4 (3), 2004: 245–55.

Bloom, D.E., Canning, D. and Sevilla, J., 'Geography and poverty traps', *Journal of Economic Growth* 8, 2003: 355–78.

Bloom, D.E., Sachs, J.D., Collier, P. and Udry, C., 'Geography, demography, and economic growth in Africa', *Brookings Papers on Economic Activity*, 1998 (2), 1998: 207–95.

Boettke, P.J. and Anderson. G., 'Soviet venality: a rent-seeking model of the communist state', *Public Choice*, 93 (1–2), October 1997: 37–53.

Boserup, E., *The Conditions of Agricultural Progress* (Aldine Publishing Co., Chicago: 1965).

Boserup, E., *Population and Technological Change: a study of long-term trends* (University of Chicago Press, Chicago: 1981).

Bourguignon, F. and Morrisson, C., 'Inequality among world citizens: 1820–1992', *American Economic Review*, 92 (4), September 2002: 727–44.

Bowman E.H., 'A risk/return paradox for strategic management', *Sloan Management Review*, spring 1980: 17–31.

Braudel, F., *A History of Civilizations* (Penguin Books, London: 1993).

Bray, F., *The Rice Economies: technology and development in Asian Societies* (University of California Press, Berkeley, Los Angeles and London: 1986).

Brenner, R., *Merchants and Revolution: commercial change, political conflict, and London's overseas traders, 1550–1653* (Verso, London and New York: 2003).

Broadberry, S., 'Recent developments in the theory of very long run growth: a historical appraisal', The Warwick Economics Research Paper Series, 818, Department of Economics, University of Warwick, 2007.

Broadberry, S. and Gupta, B., 'The early modern great divergence: wages, prices and economic development in Europe and Asia, 1500–1800', *Economic History Review*, 59 (1), 2006: 2–31.

Brock, W.A. and Durlauf, S.N., 'Growth empirics and reality', *World Bank Economic Review*, 15, 2001: 229–72.

Brooks, P., *Reading for the Plot: design and intention in narrative* (Vintage, New York: 1985).

Bruland, K., 'Industrialisation and technological change', chapter 5 in Floud, R. and Johnson, P., eds., *The Cambridge Economic History of Modern Britain, Vol. 1 Industrialisation, 1700–1860* (Cambridge University Press, Cambridge: 2004), pp. 116–46.

Cameron, R., *A Concise Economic History of the World: from paleolithic times to the present*, 3rd edition (Oxford University Press, New York and Oxford: 1997, 2003).

Carpenter, D., 'What is the marginal value of analytic narratives?', *Social Science History*, 24 (4), winter 2000: 653–67.

Caselli, F., Esquivel, G. and Lefort, F., 'Reopening the convergence debate: a new look at cross-country growth empirics', *Journal of Economic Growth*, 1(3), 1996: 363–89.

Castanheira, M. and Esfahani, H.S., 'The political economy of growth: lessons learned and challenges ahead', in McMahon, G. and Squire, L. eds., *Explaining Growth: a global research project*, IEA Conference Volume 137 (Palgrave Macmillan, Houndsmill, Basingstoke: 2003), pp. 159–212.

Cavalli-Sforza, L.L., *Genes, Peoples, and Languages* (North Point Press, New York: 2000).

Chandler, A.D., *Scale and Scope: the dynamics of industrial capitalism* (The Belknap Press of Harvard University Press, Cambridge, MA and London: 1990).

Christian, D., 'World history in context', *Journal of World History*, 14 (4), 2003: 1–15.

Christian, D., *Maps of Time: an introduction to big history* (University of California Press, Berkeley, Los Angeles and London: 2005).

Cipolla, C.M., ed., *The Fontana Economic History of Europe* (Fontana/ Collins, Glasgow: 1973).

Clark, G., 'The great escape: the Industrial Revolution in theory and in history', Working Paper University of California, Davis, 2003: 1–77.

Clark, G., *A Farewell to Alms: a brief economic history of the world* (Princeton University Press, Princeton, NJ and Oxford: 2007).

Coase, R., 'The nature of the firm', *Economica*, 4, 1937: 386–405.

Cochran, G. and Harpending, H., *The 10,000 Year Explosion: how civilisation accelerated human evolution* (Basic Books, New York: 2009).

Coe, M.T., *The Russian Moment in World History* (Princeton University Press, Princeton, NJ: 2003).

Colander, D., 'The death of neoclassical economics', *Journal of the History of Economic Thought*, 22 (2), 2000: 127–43.

Colander, D., 'Are institutionalists an endangered species?', Middlebury College Economic Discussion Paper no. 03–03, February 2003.

Cole, A.H. (ed.), *Industrial and commercial correspondence of Alexander Hamilton anticipating his report on manufactures* (A.M. Kelley, New York: 1968).

Collier, P., *The Bottom Billion: why the poor countries are failing and what can be done about it* (Oxford University Press, Oxford and New York: 2007).

Collier, P., 'The hunger myth', *Australian Financial Review*, 14 November 2008.

Collins, S. and Bosworth, B.P., 'Economic growth in East Asia: accumulation versus assimilation', *Brookings Papers on Economic Activity* no. 2, fall 1996: 135–203.

Corden, W.M., 'Booming sector and Dutch disease economies: a survey', *Oxford Economic Papers*, 35, 1984: 359–80.

Crafts, N.F.R., 'Macro-inventions, economic growth and "industrial revolution" in Britain and France', *Economic History Review*, 48, 1995: 591–8.

Crafts, N.F.R. and Harley, C.K., 'Output growth and the Industrial Revolution: a restatement of the Crafts-Harley view', *Economic History Review*, 45 (4), November 1992: 703–30.

Crafts, N.F.R., 'Social Savings as a measure of the contribution of a new technology to economic growth', Working Paper no. 06/04, Department of Economic History, London School of Economics, July 2004.

Crisp, O., *Studies in the Russian Economy before 1914* (Macmillan, London: 1976).

Crosby, A.W., *Biological Imperialism: the biological expansion of Europe 900–1900* (Cambridge University Press, Cambridge: 1986).

Crouzet, F., 'Angleterre et France au XVIIIe. siecle: essai d'analyse compariée de deux croissances économiques', *Annales – Economies-sociétés-civilisations*, 21 (2), mars–avril 1966.

Cuenca Esteban, J., 'Factory costs, market prices, and Indian calicos: cotton textile prices revisited, 1779–1831', *Economic History Review*, 52 (4), 1999: 749–55.

Cuenca Esteban, J., 'The rising share of British industrial exports in industrial output, 1700–1851', *Journal of Economic History* 57, 1997: 879–906.

Darwin, J., *After Tamerlane: the global history of empire since 1405* (Bloomsbury Press, New York: 2008).

David, P.A., 'Clio and the economic of QWERTY', *American Economic Review*, May 1985: 332–7.

David, P., 'Transportation innovations and economic growth: Professor Fogel on and off the rails', *Economic History Review*, 22, 1969: 506–525.

Davies, B.L., *Warfare, State and Society on the Black Sea Steppe, 1500–1700* (Routledge, London and New York: 2007).

Davis, L.E., et al., *American Economic Growth: an economist's history of the United States* (Harper and Row, New York, Evanston, Ill., San Francisco and London: 1972).

Dawson, D., 'The marriage of Marx and Darwin', *History and Theory*, 41, February 2002: 43–59.

Dawson, D., 'The assault on Eurocentric History', *Journal of the Historical Society*, 3 (3–4), summer/fall 2003: 403–27.

Deane, P., *The First Industrial Revolution* (Cambridge University Press, Cambridge: 1965).

Deane, P. and Cole, W.A., *British Economic Growth 1688–1959: trends and structure* (Cambridge University Press, Cambridge, England: 1964).

de Long, J.B., 'Productivity growth, convergence, and welfare: comment', *American Economic Review*, 78 (5), 1988: 1138–54.

de Long, B. and Shleifer, A., 'Princes and merchants: European city growth before the Industrial Revolution', NBER Working Paper no. 4274, 1992.

Dennison, E.F., *The Sources of Economic Growth in the United States* (Committee for Economic Development, New York: 1962).

Denoon, D., *Settler Capitalism: the dynamics of dependent development in the southern hemisphere* (Clarendon Press, Oxford: 1983).

de Soto, H., *The Other Path: the invisible revolution in the third world* (Harper and Row, New York: 1989).

de Soto, H., *The Mystery of Capital: why capitalism triumphs in the West and fails everywhere else* (Basic Books, New York: 2000).

Deutscher, I., *The Prophet Armed: Trotsky 1879–1921* (Oxford University Press, New York and London: 1954).

de Vries, P.H.H., 'The Industrial Revolution and the industrious revolution', *Journal of Economic History*, 54, 1994: 249–70.

de Vries, P.H.H., 'Are coal and colonies really crucial? Kenneth Pomeranz and the Great Divergence', *Journal of World History*, 12 (2), 2001: 407–46.

de Vries, P.H.H., 'Governing growth: a comparative analysis of the role of the state in the rise of the West', *Journal of World History*, 13 (1), 2002: 67–137.

Diamond, J., *Guns, Germs, and Steel: the fates of human societies* (W.W. Norton and Co., New York: 1997).

Diamond, J., *Collapse; how societies choose to fail or succeed* (Viking Penguin, London: 2005).

Djankov, S., Glaeser, E., La Porta, R., Lopez-de-Silanes, F. and Shleifer, A., 'The new comparative economics', Unpublished paper, World Bank and Harvard and Yale Universities, 2003.

Domar, E.D., 'Capital expansion, rate of growth, and employment', *Econometrica*, 14, April 1946: 137–47.

Domar, E.D., 'The causes of slavery or serfdom: a hypothesis', *Journal of Economic History*, 30 (1), March 1970: 18–32.

Dowd, K., *Beyond Value at Risk: the new science of risk management* (John Wiley, London: 1998).

Dugger, W.M., 'Instituted process and enabling myth: the two faces of the market', *Journal of Economic Issues*, 23 (2), June 1989: 607–15.

Dunning, J.H. and Narula, R., eds., *Foreign Direct Investment and Governments* (Routledge, London and New York: 1996).

Durlauf, S.N. and Johnson, P., 'Multiple regimes and cross-country growth behaviour', *Journal of Applied Econometrics*, 10 (4), October–December 1995: 365–84.

Durlauf, S.N., Johnson, P.A. and Temple, J.R.W., 'Growth econometrics', chap.8 in Aghion, P. and Durlauf, S.N. (eds.) *Handbook of Economic Growth* (Elsevier, Amsterdam: 2005).

Easterlin, R.A., *The Reluctant Economist: perspectives on economics, economic history, and demography* (Cambridge University Press, Cambridge: 2004).

Easterly, W., *The Elusive Quest for Growth* (MIT Press, Cambridge, MA and London: 2002).

Easterly, W., *The White Man's Burden: why the West's efforts to aid the rest have done so much ill and so little good* (Penguin Books, London: 2006).

Easterly, W. and Fischer, S., 'The Soviet economic decline', *World Bank Economic Review*, 9: 1995: 341–71.

Easterly, W. and Levine, R., 'It's not factor accumulation: stylised facts and growth models', *World Bank Economic Review*, 15 (2), 2001: 177–219.

Eaton, J. and Kortum, S., 'International patenting and technology diffusion', NBER Working Papers no. 4931, November 1994.

Elster, J., 'Rational choice history: a case of excessive ambition', *American Political Science Review*, 94 (3), Sept. 2000: 685–95.

Elvin, M., *The Pattern of the Chinese Past: a social and economic interpretation* (Stanford University Press, Stanford, CA: 1973).

Engerman, S. and Sokoloff, K.L., 'Factor endowments, institutions, and differential paths of growth among new world economies: a view from economic historians of the United States', NBER Working Paper no. H0066, December 1994.

Fagan, B., *The Great Warming: climate change and the rise and fall of civilizations* (Bloomsbury Press, New York: 2008).

Feinstein, C.H., *An Economic History of South Africa: conquest, discrimination, and development* (Cambridge University Press, Cambridge and New York: 2005).

Feldman, G.A., 'On the theory of the rates of growth of the national income', Gosplan 1928, reprinted in Spulber, N. (ed.) *Foundations of Soviet Strategy for Economic Growth: selected Soviet essays, 1924–1930* (Indiana University Press, Bloomington, Ind.: 1965).

Feldstein, M. and Horioka, C., 'Domestic saving and international capital flows', *Economic Journal*, 90, June 1980: 314–29.

Ferguson, N., ed., *Virtual History: alternatives and counterfactuals* (Pan Books, London: 1997), especially the Introduction: 1–90.

Fernandez, R. and Rodrik, D., 'Resistance to reform: status-quo bias in the presence of individual-specific uncertainty', *American Economic Review*, 91 (5), December 1991: 1146–55.

Fernandez-Armesto, F., *Civilisations: culture, ambition, and the transformation of nature* (Touchstone, Simon Schuster, New York: 2001).

Feyrer, J., 'Convergence by parts', Draft of paper, February 2003.

Fforde, A., 'Persuasion: reflections on economics, data and the "homogeneity assumption"', *Journal of Economic Methodology*, 12 (1), March 2005: 63–91.

Field, N.C., 'Environmental quality and land productivity: a comparison of the agricultural land base of the USSR and North America', *Canadian Geographer*, 12, 1968: 1–14.

Findlay, R. and O'Rourke, K.H., *Power and Plenty: trade, war and the world economy in the second millennium* (Princeton University Press, Princeton and Oxford: 2007).

Fischer, D.H., *Price Revolutions and the Rhythm of History* (Oxford University Press, Oxford: 1996).

Fishlow, A., *American Railroads and the Transformation of the Ante-Bellum Economy* (Harvard University Press, Cambridge, MA: 1965).

Fishlow, A., 'Internal transportation in the nineteenth and early twentieth centuries', in Engerman, S.L. and Gallman, R.E. (eds), *Cambridge Economic History of the United States*, vol. 2 (Cambridge University Press, Cambridge: 2000): 543–642.

Floud, R. and Johnson, P., eds., *The Cambridge Economic History of Modern Britain, Vol. 1 Industrialisation, 1700–1860* (Cambridge University Press, Cambridge: 2004).

Fogel, R.W., *Railroads and American Economic Growth: essays in econometric history* (Johns Hopkins University, Baltimore: 1964).

Fogel, R., *The Escape from Hunger and Premature Death, 1700–2100* (Cambridge University Press, Cambridge: 2004).

Fogel, R.W. and Engerman, S.L., *Time on the Cross: the economics of American negro slavery* (Little, Brown and Co., Boston: 1974).

Földvári, P. and van Zanden, J.L., 'Global income distribution and convergence 1800–2000', Unpublished paper, n.d.

Foreman-Peck, J., *New Perspectives in the late Victorian Economy: essay in quantitative economic history 1860–1914* (Cambridge University Press, New York: 1991), especially chapter 3, 'Railways and Late Victorian economic growth': 73–96.

Frank, A.G., *ReOrient: global economy in the Asian age* (University of California Press, Berkeley, CA: 1998).

Frayn, M., *The Human Touch: our part in the creation of the universe* (Faber and Faber, London: 2006).

Friedman, M., 'Do old fallacies ever die?', *Journal of Economic Literature*, 30, December 1992: 2129–32.

Friedman, M. and Schwartz, A.J., *A Monetary History of the United States 1867–1960* (Princeton University Press, Princeton, NJ: 1963).

Fukuyama, F., *The End of History and the Last Man* (Avon Books, New York: 1992).

Fukuyama, F., *Trust: the social virtues and the creation of prosperity* (Hamish Hamilton, London: 1995).

Gaddis, J.L., *The Landscape of History: how historians map the past* (Oxford University Press, Oxford and New York: 2002).

Galbraith, J.K., *The New Industrial State* (H. Hamilton, London: 1967).

Galloway, P.R., 'Long-term fluctuations in climate and population in the pre-industrial era', *Population and Development Review*, 12 (1), March, 1986: 1–24.

Galloway, P.R., 'Basic patterns in annual variations in fertility, nuptiality, mortality, and prices in pre-industrial Europe', *Population Studies*, 42 (2), July 1988: 275–302.

Gallup, J.L., Sachs, J. and Mellinger, A.D., 'Geography and economic development', *International Regional Science Review*, 22 (2), 1999: 179–232.

Galor, O., 'Convergence? Inferences from theoretical models', *Economic Journal*, 106 (432), July 1996: 1056–69.

Galor, O., 'From stagnation to growth: unified growth theory', in P. Aghion and S. Durlauf, eds., *Handbook of Economic Growth* (North Holland), 2005.

Galor, O. and Moav, O., 'Natural selection and the origin of economic growth', *The Quarterly Journal of Economics*, 117(4), 2002: 1133–179.

Gatrell, P., *The Tsarist Economy 1850–1917* (B.T. Batsford Ltd., London: 1986).

Gerschenkron, A., *Economic Backwardness in Historical Perspective* (Harvard University Press, Cambridge, MA: 1962).

Gerschenkron, A., *Continuity in History and Other Essays* (Harvard University Press, Cambridge, MA: 1968).

Gerschenkron, A., *Europe in the Russian Mirror: four lectures in economic history* (Cambridge University Press, New York: 1970).

Ghemawat, P., *Redefining Global Strategy: crossing borders in a world where differences still matter* (Harvard Business School Press, Boston, Mass.: 2007).

Ghosh, A., and Wolf, H., 'Context and threshold dependence in growth', NBER Working Paper no. 6480, Cambridge, MA, 1998.

Goldstone, J.A., 'Cultural orthodoxy, risk, and innovation: the divergence of East and West in the early modern world', *Sociological Theory*, 5 (2), autumn 1987: 119–35.

Goldstone, J.A., *Revolution and Rebellion in the Early Modern World* (University of California Press, Berkeley: 1991).

Goldstone, J.A., 'Whose measure of reality?' *American Historical Review*, 105 (2), April 2000: 1–8.

Goldstone, J.A., 'Efflorescences and economic growth in world history: rethinking the "rise of the West" and the Industrial Revolution', *Journal of World History*, 13 (2), 2002: 323–89.

Goldstone, J.A., *Why Europe? The rise of the West in world history, 1500–1850* (McGraw Hill Higher Education, New York: 2008).

Gottfredson, L.S., 'Of what value is intelligence?', in Prifitera, A., Salkofse, D.H. and Weiss, L.G. (eds), *WISC-IV Clinical assessment and Intervention*, 2nd ed. (Elsevier, Amsterdam: 2008).

Gottfredson, L.S., 'Pretending that intelligence doesn't matter', *Cerebrum*, 2 (3), 2000: 75–96.

Gottfredson, L.S., 'Why g matters: the complexity of everyday life', *Intelligence*, 24 (1), 1997: 79–132.

Goudsblom, J., *Fire and Civilisation* (Allen Lane Penguin, London: 1992).

Gregory, P.R., *Russian National Income 1885–1913* (Cambridge University Press, New York: 1982).

Gregory, P.R., *Before Command: an economic history of Russia from emancipation to the first five – year plan* (Princeton University Press, Princeton: 1994).

Gregory, P.R., *The Political Economy of Stalinism: evidence from the Soviet Archives* (Cambridge University Press, Cambridge: 2004).

Greif, A., *Institutions and the Path to the Modern Economy: lessons from medieval trade* (Cambridge University Press, Cambridge: 2006).

Guha, A.S., *An Evolutionary View of Economic Growth* (Clarendon Press, Oxford: 1981).

Gurr, T., 'Historical trends in violent crime: a critical review of the evidence', *Crime and Justice: an annual review of research*, 3, 1981: 295–353.

Habbakuk, H.J., *American and British Technology in the Nineteenth Century* (Cambridge University Press, Cambridge: 1962).

Hajnal, J., 'Two kinds of preindustrial household formation system', *Population and Development Review*, 8, 1982: 449–94.

Haley, G.T., Tan, C-T., 'The black hole of Southeast Asia: strategic decision making in an informational void', *Management Decision*, 34 (9), 1996: 43–55.

Hanushek, E.A. and Kimko, D.D., 'Schooling, labour-force quality, and the growth of nations', *American Economic Review*, 90, 2000: 1184–208.

Harberger, A., 'A vision of the growth process', Presidential Address, Annual Meeting of the American Economic Association, 1998.

Harcourt, G.C., *Some Cambridge Controversies in the Theory of Capital* (Cambridge University Press, Cambridge: 1972).

Harley, C.K., 'British Economic Growth, 1688–1959: trends and structure', Project 2001; Significant works in Twentieth-Century Economic History.

Harley, C.K., 'Growth theory and industrial revolutions in Britain and America', *Canadian Journal of Economics*, 36 (4), November 2003: 809–31.

Harley, C.K., 'Reassessing the Industrial Revolution: a macro view', in Mokyr, J. (ed.) *The British Industrial Revolution: an economic perspective* (Westview Press, Oxford: 1999). 756–65.

Harley, C.K., 'Substitution for prerequisites: endogenous institutions and comparative economic history', Chap. 2 of Sylla, R. and Toniolo, G. (eds), *Patterns of European Industrialisation: the nineteenth century* (Routledge, London and New York: 1991): 29–44.

Harris, R., 'Government and the Economy', Chap. 8 of Floud, R. and Johnson, P. (eds), *The Cambridge Economic History of Modern Britain, Vol. 1, Industrialisation, 1700–1860* (Cambridge University Press, Cambridge: 2004).

Harrison, L.E., *Who Prospers? how cultural values shape economic and political success* (Basic Books, New York: 1992).

Harrod, R.F., 'An essay in dynamic theory', *Economic Journal*, 49, March 1939: 14–33.

Hartwell, R.M., 'The rising standard of living 1800–1850', *Economic History Review*, xiii, 1961.

Hartz, L., *The Founding of New Societies* (Harcourt, Brace and World, New York: 1964).

Hausmann, R., Pritchett, L. and Rodrik, D., 'Growth accelerations', NBER Working Papers no. 10566, 2004.

Hawke, G.R., *Railways and Economic Growth in England Wales, 1840–1870* (Clarendon Press, Oxford: 1970).

Hedlund, S., 'Property without rights: dimensions of Russian privatisation', *Europe-Asia-Studies*, 53 (2), March 2001: 213–37.

Hedlund, S., *Russian Path Dependence* (Routledge, London and New York: 2005).

Hellie, R., *Enserfment and Military Change in Muscovy* (University of Chicago Press, Chicago: 1971).

Hellie, R., 'Muscovite slavery in comparative perspective', *Russian History*, 6, 1979: 133–209.

Hellie, R., *The Economy and Material Culture of Russia 1600–1725* (The University of Chicago Press, Chicago and London: 1999).

Hellie, R., 'The structure of Russian imperial history', *History and Theory: theme issue*, 44, December 2005: 88–112.

Helliwell, J., *How Much do National Borders Matter?* (Brookings Institution Press, Washington, DC: 1998).

Helpman, E., *The Mystery of Economic Growth* (The Belknap Press of Harvard University Press, Cambridge, MA and London: 2004).

Hibbs, D.A. and Olsson, O., 'Geography, biogeography, and why some countries are rich and others are poor', Proceedings of the National Academy of Science (PNAS), 101 (10), 9 March 2004: 3715–20.

Hicks, J.A., *Theory of Economic History* (Clarendon Press, Oxford: 1969).

Hill, A. 'The environment and disease: association and causation', Proceedings of the Royal Society of Medicine, 58 (1965): 295–300.

Hirschman, C., 'Population and development: what do we really know?', Unpublished paper, September 2004.

Hobsbawm, E., *Age of Extremes: the short twentieth century 1914–1991* (Michael Joseph, London: 1994).

Hobsbawm, E.J., 'The British standard of living 1790–1850', *Economic History Review*, x, 1957.

Hobson, J.A., *Imperialism, A Study* (Allen and Unwin, London: 1938).

Hobson, J.M., *The Eastern Origins of Western Civilization* (Cambridge University Press, Cambridge: 2004).

Hodgson, G.M., *How Economic Forgot History: the problem of historical specificity in social science* (Routledge, New York: 2001).

Hoff, K., 'Beyond Rosenstein-Rodan: the modern theory of coordination problems in development', *Proceedings of the Annual World Bank Conference on Development Economics*, 2000, supplement to the *World Bank Economic Review*.

Hofstede, G., *Cultures and Organisations* (McGraw Hill, London: 1991).

Hooson, D.J.M., 'The geographical setting', in Autry, R. and Obolensky, D. (eds), *An Introduction to Russian History* (Cambridge University Press, Cambridge: 1970).

Hooson, D.J.M., 'The geographical setting', in Auty, R. and Obolensky, D., eds., *An Introduction to Russian History* (Harvard University Press, Cambridge, MA: 1977).

Homer, S. and Sylla, R., *A History of Interest Rates*, 3rd edition (Rutgers University Press, New Brunswick, NJ: 1996).

Hoover, K.D. and Perez, S.J., 'Truth and robustness in cross-country growth regressions', *Oxford Bulletin of Economics and Statistics*, 66 (5), December 2004: 765–98.

Hsieh, C.-T., 'What explains the industrial revolution in East Asia? Evidence from the factor markets', *American Economic Review*, 92, June 2002: 502–26.

Huntington, S.P., *The Clash of Civilizations and the Remaking of the World Order* (Simon Schuster, New York: 1966).

Iberall, A., 'Human sociogeophysics – Phase 11 the diffusion of human ethnicity by remixing', *GeoJournal*, 9 (4), Dec. 1984: 387–391.

Iberall, A. and Wilkinson, D., 'Human sociogeophysics – Phase 1: explaining the macroscopic patterns of man on earth' *GeoJournal*, 8 (2), June 1984: 171–179.

Imbs, J. and Wacziarg, R., 'Stages of diversification', *American Economic Review*, 93 (1), March 2003: 63–86.

Imlah, A.H., *Economic Elements in the Pax Britanica* (Harvard University Press, Cambridge, Mass.: 1958).

Islam, N., 'Growth empirics: a panel data approach', *The Quarterly Journal of Economics*, 110 (4), 1995: 1127–70.

Islam, N., 'What have we learnt from the convergence debate?', *Journal of Economic Surveys*, 17 (3), 2003: 309–62.

Jones, C.I., 'On the evolution of the world income distribution', paper prepared for the *Journal of Economic Perspectives*, 1997.

Jones, C.I., *Introduction to Economic Growth*, 2nd edition (W.W. Norton and Co., New York and London: 2002).

Jones, E.L., *Agriculture and the Industrial Revolution* (Oxford University Press, Oxford: 1974).

Jones, E.L., *The European Miracle: economies, environments and geopolitics in the history of Europe and Asia*, 2nd edition (Cambridge University Press, Cambridge, 1987).

Jones, E.L., *Growth Recurring: economic change in world history* (Clarendon Press, Oxford: 1988).

Jones, E.L., 'The real question about China: why was the Song economic achievement not repeated?', *Australian Economic History Review*, 30, 1990: 5–22.

Jones, E.L., *Cultures Merging: a historical and economic critique of culture* (Princeton University Press, Princeton, NJ and Oxford: 2006).

Jones, E.L., Porter, S. and Turner, M., 'A gazetteer of English urban fire disasters', *Historical Geography Series*: 13 (Geo Books, Norwich: 1984).

Jones, G. and Schneider, W.J., 'Intelligence, human capital, and economic growth: a Bayesian averaging of classical estimates (BACE) approach', *Journal of Economic Growth*, 1, 2006: 71–93.

Jorgenson, D.W. and Griliches, Z., 'The explanation of productivity change', *Review of Economic Studies*, 34, July 1967: 249–80.

Kahan, A., *The Plough, the Hammer, and the Knout: an economic history of eighteenth century Russia* (University of Chicago Press, Chicago: 1985).

Kaldor, N., 'A model of economic growth', chapter 13 in *Essays on Economic Stability and Growth* (Gerald Duckworth and Co., London: 1960), pp. 259–300.

Kaldor, N., 'Capital accumulation and economic growth', in Lutz, F.A. and Hague, D., eds., *Proceedings of a Conference held by the International Economic Association* (Macmillan, London: 1963).

Kaldor, N., 'Welfare proposition in economics and interpersonal comparisons of utility', *Economic Journal*, 49 (195), 1939: 549–52.

Kemp, T., *Economic Forces in French History* (Dennis Dobson, London: 1971).

Kemp, T., *Historical Patterns of Industrialisation* (Longman, London and New York: 1978).

Kennedy, P., *The Rise and Fall of the Great Powers: economic change and military conflict from 1500 to 2000* (Random House, New York: 1987).

Kenny, C. and Williams, D., 'What do we know about economic growth? Or, why don't we know very much?', *World Development*, 29 (1), 2001: 1–22.

Kindleberger, C.P., *The World in Depression, 1929–1939* (University of California Press, Berkeley, CA: 1973).

King, R.G. and Rebelo, S.T., 'Transitional dynamics and economic growth in the neoclassical model', *American Economic Review*, 83 (4), September 1993: 908–31.

Knack, S. and Keefer, P., 'Does social capital have an economic payoff? A cross-country investigation', *The Quarterly Journal of Economics*, 112 (4), Nov. 1997: 1251–1288.

Knight, F.H., *Risk, Uncertainty and Profit* (Augustus M. Kelley, New York: 1964).

Koepke, N. and Baten, J., 'The biological standard of living in Europe during the last two millennia', *European Review of Economic History*, 9, 2005: 61–95.

Kohli, R., 'The transition from official aid to private capital flow: implications for a developing country', UNU-WIDER Research Paper, World Institute for Development of Economic Research, 2004.

Kolchin, P., *Unfree Labour: American slavery and Russian serfdom* (The Belknap Press of Harvard University, Cambridge, MA and London: 1987).

Komlos, J., 'Thinking about the industrial revolution', *Journal of European Economic History*, 18 (1), spring 1989: 191–206.

Komlos, J., 'The Industrial Revolution as the escape from the Malthusian trap', Discussion Paper in Economics, 57, Department of Economics, University of Munich.

Kremer, M., Onatski, A. and Stock, J., 'Searching for prosperity', NBER Working Paper no. 8250, April 2001.

Krugman, P., 'The myth of Asia's miracle', *Foreign Affairs*, 73 (6), 1994: 62–78.

Krugman, P., 'The role of geography in development', Unpublished paper prepared for the Annual World Bank Conference on Development Economics, April 1998.

Kuran, T., *Islam and Mammon: the economic predicaments of Islamism* (Princeton University Press, Princeton, NJ and Oxford: 2004).

Kuznets, S., 'Quantitative aspects of the economic growth of nations', *Economic Development and Cultural Change, 1956–1964.*

Kuznets, S., *Economic Growth and Structure: selected essays* (Heinemann Educational Books Ltd., London: 1965).

Landes, D.S., *The Unbound Prometheus: technological change and industrial development in Western Europe from 1750 to the present* (Cambridge University Press, Cambridge: 1969).

Landes, D.S., *The Wealth and Poverty of Nations: why some are so rich and some so poor* (W.W. Norton, New York: 1998).

Large, E.C., *The Advance of the Fungi* (H. Holt and Co., New York: 1940).

Lee, J.Z. and Wang Feng, *One Quarter of Humanity: Malthusian mythology and Chinese realities* (Harvard University Press, Cambridge, MA and London: 1999).

Lee, R., 'Population dynamics of humans and other animals', *Demography*, 24 (4), November 1987: 443–65.

Lee, R., 'The demographic transition: three centuries of fundamental change', *Journal of Economic Perspectives*, 17 (4), fall 2003: 167–90.

Lenin, V.I., *Imperialism, the highest stage of capitalism: a popular outline* (Moscow Progress Publishers: n.d. – taken from the Collected Works Volume 22).

Levathes, L., *When China ruled the Seas: the treasure fleet of the dragon throne, 1405–1433* (Oxford University Press, New York and Oxford: 1994).

Levi, M., 'An analytic narrative approach to puzzles and problems', in Shapiro, I., Smith, R. and Masoud, T., eds., *Problems and Methods in the Study of Politics* (Cambridge University Press, Cambridge: 2004), pp. 201–26.

Levine, R. and Renelt, D., 'A sensitivity analysis of cross-country growth regressions', *American Economic Review*, 82 (4), September 1992: 942–63.

Lewis, W.A., 'Economic development with unlimited supplies of labour', *The Manchester School of Economic Social Studies*, vol. 22, May 1954: 139–92.

Li, H., Squire, L. and Zou, H-F., 'Explaining international and intertemporal variation in income inequality', *Economic Journal*, 108(446), 1998: 26–43.

Lindauaer, D.L. and Pritchett, L., 'What's the big idea? The third generation of policies for economic growth', *Economia*, Fall 2002: 1–37.

Lipsey, R.G., Carlaw, K.I. and Bekar, C.T., *Economic Transformations: general purpose technologies and long term economic growth* (Oxford University Press, Oxford and New York: 2005).

List, F., *The National System of Political Economy* (Cosimo Inc., New York: 2005).

Lockwood, D., *The Destruction of the Soviet Union: a study in globalisation* (Macmillan, London: 2000).

Lucas, R.E., 'On the mechanics of economic development', *Journal of Monetary Economics*, 22, July 1988: 3–42.

Lucas, R.E., 'Some macroeconomics for the 21st century', *Journal of Economic Perspectives*, 14, 2000: 159–68.

Lynn, R., *Race Differences in Intelligence: an evolutionary analysis* (Washington Summit Publishers, Augusta, GA: 2006).

Lynn, R. and Vanhanen, T., *IQ and Global Inequality* (Washington Summit Publishers, Augusta, GA: 2006).

Macfarlane, A., *The Savage Wars of Peace: England, Japan and the Malthusian trap* (Blackwell Publishers, Oxford and Malden, MA: 1997).

Maddison, A., *Dynamic Forces in Capitalist Development: a long-run comparative view* (Oxford University Press, Oxford and New York: 1991).

Maddison, A., 'Ultimate and proximate growth causation: a critique of Mancur Olson on the rise and decline of nations', *Scandinavian Economic History Review*, (36), 1988: 25–9.

Maddison, A., 'Dutch income in and from Indonesia', *Modern Asian Studies*, 23 (4), 1989: 645–70.

Maddison, A., *The World Economy: a millennial perspective* (Development Centre of the Organisation for Economic Cooperation and Development Paris: 2001).

Maddison, A., *The World Economy: historical statistics* (Development Centre OECD: Paris).

Malia, M., *The Soviet Tragedy: a history of socialism in Russia, 1917–1991* (The Free Press, New York: 1994).

Malia, M., *Russia under Western Eyes: from the bronze horseman to the Lenin mausoleum* (The Belknap Press of Harvard University, Cambridge, MA and London: 1999).

Malthus, T.R., *An Essay on Population* (Cambridge University Press, Cambridge: 1803).

Mankiw, N.G., 'The growth of nations', *Brookings Papers on Economic Activity*, 1995 (1), 1995: 275–326.

Mankiw, N.G., Romer, D. and Weil, D.N., 'A contribution to the empirics of economic growth', *Quarterly Journal of Economics*, 107 (2), May 1992: 407–37.

Marks, R.B., *The Origins of the Modern World: fate and fortune in the rise of the West* (Rowman and Littlefield Publishers, Inc., Lanham, MD: 2007).

Mathias, P., *The First Industrial Nation: an economic history of Britain 1700–1914* (Methuen and Co., London: 1969).

Mason, K.O., 'Explaining fertility transitions', *Demography*, 34 (4), November 1997: 443–54.

Masters, W.A. and McMillan, M.S., 'Climate and scale in economic growth', *Journal of Economic Growth*, 6, 2001: 167–86.

McCloskey, D.N., 'The open fields of England: rent, risk, and the rate of interest, 1300–1815', in Galenson, D.W., ed., *Market in History: economic studies of the past* (Cambridge University Press, Cambridge: 1989): 5–51.

McCloskey, D.N., 'Kinks, tools, spurts, and substitutes: Gerschenkron's rhetoric of relative backwardness', in Sylla, R. and Toniolo, G. eds., *Patterns of European Industrialisation: the nineteenth century* (Routledge, London and New York: 1991), 92–105.

McCloskey, D.N., 'The prudent peasant: new findings on open fields', *Journal of Economic History*, 51 (2), June 1991b: 343–55.

McGuire, M.C. and Olson, M., Jr., 'The economics of autocracy and majority rule: the invisible hand and the use of force', *Journal of Economic Literature*, 34 (1), 1996: 72 96.

McKay, J.P., *Pioneers for Profit* (University of Chicago Press, Chicago: 1970).

McMahon, G. and Squire, L., eds., *Explaining Growth: a global research project*, IEA Conference Volume No. 137 (Palgrave Macmillan, Houndsmill, Basingstoke: 2003).

McNeill, J.R. and McNeill, W.H., *The Human Web: a bird's eye view of world history* (W.W. Norton and Co., New York and London: 2003).

McNeill, W.H., *Europe's Steppe Frontier, 1500–1800* (University of Chicago Press, Chicago: 1964).

McNeill, W.H., 'Passing strange: the convergence of evolutionary science with scientific history', *History and Theory*, 40, February 2001: 1–15.

Meadows, D.H. et al., *The Limits to Growth* (Universe Books, New York: 1972).

Metzer, J., 'Railroads, in Tsarist Russia: direct gains and implications', *Explorations in Economic History*, 13, 1976: 85–111.

Milanovic, B., 'Income convergence during the disintegration of the world economy, 1919–39', Policy Research Working Paper 2941, The World Bank, January 2003.

Milanovic, B., *Worlds Apart: global and international inequality 1950–2000* (Princeton University Press, Princeton, NJ: 2005), especially chapter 1: 'The three concepts of inequality defined': 7–11.

Milward, A.S. and Saul, S.B., *The Economic Development of Continental Europe* (George Allen and Unwin, London: 1973).

Mitch, D., 'Education and skill of the British labour force', Chap. 12 of Floud, R. and Johnson, P. (eds), *The Cambridge Economic History of Modern Britain, Vol. 1 Industrialisation, 1700–1860* (Cambridge University Press, Cambridge: 2004).

Mokyr, J., ed., *The Economics of the Industrial Revolution* (Rowman and Allanheld, Totwa, NJ: 1985).

Mokyr, J., *The Lever of Riches: technological creativity and economic progress* (Oxford University Press, New York: 1990).

Mokyr, J., 'Editor's introduction; the new economic history and the industrial revolution', in Mokyr, J., ed., *The British Industrial Revolution: an economic perspective*, 2nd edition (Westview Press, Boulder, CO and Oxford: 1999), pp. 1–127.

Mokyr, J., *The Gifts of Athena: historical origins of the knowledge economy* (Princeton University Press, Princeton, NJ: 2002).

Mokyr, J., 'Long-term economic growth and the history of technology', in Aghion, P. and Durlauf, S., eds., *Handbook of Economic Growth*.

Mokyr, J., 'Accounting for the Industrial Revolution', chapter 1 of Floud, R. and Johnson, P. eds., *The Cambridge Economic History of Britain, Vol.1 Industrialsation, 1700–1860* (Cambridge University Press, Cambridge: 2004), pp. 1–27.

Mokyr, J. and Voth, H.-J., 'Understanding growth in Europe, 1700–1870: theory and evidence', Unpublished paper, 2006.

Morgan, S.P., 'Is low fertility a twenty-first-century demographic crisis?', *Demography*, 40 (4), November 2003: 589–603.

Moss, D.A., *When All Else Fails: government as the ultimate risk manager* (Harvard University Press, Cambridge, MA and London, England: 2002).

Mosse, W.E., *An Economic History of Russia 185–1914* (I.B.Tauris, New York: 1996).

Murrell, P., 'Institutions and transition', Paper prepared for the *New Palgrave Dictionary of Economics*, 2nd edition, Palgrave Macmillan, Houndsmill, Basingstoke, 2005.

Navolari, A., 'Collective inventions during the British Industrial

Revolution: the case of the Cornish pumping engine,' *Cambridge Journal of Economics* 28: 347–63.

Nef, J.U., *The Rise of the British Coal Industry* (George Routledge and Sons, London: 1932).

Nelson, R.R. and Wright, G., 'The rise and fall of American technological leadership: the postwar era in historical perspective', *Journal of Economic Literature*, 30 (4), December, 1992: 1931–64.

Nolan, P., *China's Rise, Russia's Fall: politics, economics and planning in the transition from Stalinism* (Macmillan Press, Houndsmill, Basingstoke: 1995).

Nordhaus, W.D., 'Geography and macroeconomics: new data and new findings', Proceedings of the National Academy of Sciences (US), 103 (10), March 7, 2006, 3510–17.

Nordhaus, W.D., 'Lethal model 2: the limits to growth revisited', *Brookings Papers on Economic Activity*, 1992 (2), 1992: 1–59.

Nordhaus, W.D., 'Do real-output and real-wage measures capture reality? The history of lighting suggests not', Cowles Foundation Paper no. 957, Yale University, 1998.

North, D.C., *Structure and Change in Economic History* (Norton, New York: 1981).

North, D.C., *Institutions, Institutional Change and Economic Performance* (Cambridge University Press, Cambridge: 1990).

North, D.C., *Understanding the Process of Economic Change* (Princeton University Press, Princeton, NJ and Oxford: 2005).

North, D.C., Summerhill, W. and Weingast, B.R., 'Order, disorder and economic change: Latin America vs. North America', in Bueno de Mesquita, B. and Root, H., eds., *Governing for Prosperity* (Yale University Press, New Haven, Conn.: 2000).

North, D.C. and Thomas, R.P., *The Rise of the Western World: a new economic history* (Cambridge University Press, Cambridge: 1973).

O'Brien, P.K., 'European economic development: the contribution of the periphery', *Economic History Review*, 35, 1980: 1–18.

O'Brien, P.K. ed., *Railways and the Economic Development of Western Europe*, 1830–1940 (St Martin's Press, New York: 1983).

O'Brien, P.K., 'Intercontinental trade and the development of the third world since the Industrial Revolution', *Journal of World History*, 8 (1), 1997: 75–133.

O'Brien, P.K., 'Provincializing the first industrial revolution', Working Papers, Department of Economic History, London School of Economics, 2006.

O'Brien P.K. and Keyder, C., *Economic Growth in France and Britain, 1780–1914* (Allen and Unwin, London: 1978).

Ocampo, J.A., 'Structural dynamics and economic growth in developing countries', United Nations Economic Commission for Latin America and the Caribbean (ECLAC), Santiago, Chile, 2003.

Oeppen, J. and Vaupel, J.W., 'Broken limits to life expectancy', *Science*, 296, 10 May 2002: 1029–30.

Olson, M., *The Rise and Decline of Nations* (Yale University Press, London: 1982).

Oshima, H.T., *Economic Growth in Monsoon Asia: a comparative survey* (University of Tokyo Press, Tokyo: 1987).

Overton, M., *Agricultural Revolution in England: the transformation of the agrarian economy 1500–1850* (Cambridge University Press, Cambridge: 1996).

Parente, S.L. and Prescott, E.C., 'Changes in the wealth of nations', *Quarterly Review, Federal Reserve Bank of Minneapolis*, Spring, 1993, 3–16.

Parker, W.H., *The Superpowers: the US and the Soviet Union compared* (Macmillan, London: 1972).

Peacock, A.J. and Wisemen, J., *The Growth in Public Expenditures in the United Kingdom* (Princeton University, Princeton, NJ: 1961).

Perkin, H.J., *The Origins of Modern English Society, 1780–1880* (Routledge and Kegan Paul, London: 1969).

Perkins D., *Agricultural Development in China, 1368–1968* (Edinburgh University Press, Edinburgh: 1969).

Pierson, P., 'Big, slow-moving and . . . invisible: macro-social processes in the study of comparative politics', in Mahoney, J. and Rueschemeyer, D., eds., *Comparative Historical Analysis in the Social Sciences* (Cambridge University Press, New York: 2003).

Pipes, R., *Russian under Old Regime* (Penguin Books, London: 1974).

Poe, M.T., *The Russian Moment in World History* (Princeton University Press, Princeton, NJ and Oxford: 2003).

Pomeranz, K., *The Great Divergence: China, Europe and the making of the modern world economy* (Princeton University Press, Princeton, NJ: 2000).

Portal, R., 'The industrialisation of Russia', in Postan, M.M. and Habakkuk, H.J., eds., *The Cambridge Economic History of Europe*, 6 (2), (Cambridge University Press, Cambridge: 1965), pp. 801–74.

Porter, M., 'Clusters and the new economics of competition', *Harvard Business Review*, 6 (6), 1998: 77–90.

Prebisch, R., *The Economic Development of Latin America and its Principal Problems* (UN Department of Economic Affairs, Lake Success, New York: 1950).

Price, C.A., 'Immigrants and ethnic origins', chapter 1 of Vamplew,

W., ed., *Australian Historical Statistics* (Fairfax, Syme and Weldon Associates, Melbourne: 1987).

Pritchett, L., 'Understanding patterns of economic growth: searching for hills among plateaus, mountains, and plains', *World Bank Review*, 14 (2), 2000: 221–50.

Pritchett, L., 'A conclusion to cross-national growth research: a forward "to the countries themselves"', in McMahon, G. and Squire, L. eds., *Explaining Growth: a global research project*, IEA Conference Volume 137 (Palgrave Macmillan, Houndmill, Basingstoke: 2004), 213–43.

Putnam, R.D., *Making Democracy Work: civic tradition in modern Italy* (Princeton University Press, Princeton, NJ: 1993).

Quah, D., 'Convergence empirics across countries with (some) capital mobility', *Journal of Economic Growth*, 1, 1996: 65–124.

Quah, D., 'Cross-country growth comparisons: theory to empirics', Working Paper, London School of Economics, 2000.

Raby, G.W., 'Equipping an Agricultural Economy: perspectives on technical and institutional change in south-eastern Australian agriculture, 1788–1860', Unpublished Ph.D. thesis, La Trobe University, 1990.

Ramsey, F.P., 'A mathematical theory of savings', *Economic Journal*, 38, 1928: 543–9.

Ridley, M., *The Origins of Virtue: human instincts and the evolution of cooperation* (Viking Press, New York: 1997).

Robinson, J., *The Accumulation of Capital* (Macmillan, London and St Martin's Press, New York: 1965).

Robinson, J.V., 'History versus equilibrium', *Thames Papers in Political Economy*, Thames Polytechnic, London, 1974.

Rodrik, D., ed., *In Search of Prosperity: analytic narratives on economic growth* (Princeton University Press, Princeton, NJ and Oxford: 2003).

Rodrik, D., *One Economics Many Recipes: globalization, institutions, and economic growth* (Princeton University Press, Princeton, NJ and Oxford: 2007).

Romer, P.M., 'Increasing returns and long-run growth', *Journal of Political Economy*, 94, October 1986: 1002–37.

Romer, P.M., 'Growth based on increasing returns due to specialization', *American Economic Review*, 77, May 1987: 56–62.

Romer, P.M., 'Endogenous technological change', *Journal of Political Economy*, 98, October 1990, Part 11: S71-S102.

Rose, A.K., 'One money, one market: estimating the effect of common currencies on trade', Seminar Paper, 678, 1999, Institute for International Economic Studies, Stockholm University.

Rosenberg, N., *Technology and American Economic Growth* (Harper and Row, New York: 1972).

Rosenberg, N. and Birdzell, L.E., *How the West Grew Rich: the economic transformation of the industrial world* (I.B. Tauris and Co. Ltd., London: 1986).

Rosenstein-Rodan, P., 'Problems of industrialization in Eastern and Southeastern Europe', *Economic Journal*, 53, June 1943: 202–11.

Rostow, W.W., *The Stages of Economic Growth: a non-communist manifesto* (Cambridge University Press, Cambridge: 1965).

Sachs, J., *The End of Poverty: how we can make it happen in our lifetime* (Penguin Books, London: 2005).

Sahlins, M., *Stone Age Economics* (Aldine-Alderton, Chicago: 1972).

Sala-i-Martin, X., 'I just ran four million regressions', NBER Working Paper no. 6252, 1997.

Sala-i-Martin, X., '15 years of new growth economics: what have we learnt?', Columbia University, Department of Economics Discussion Paper Series 0102–47, April 2002.

Sala-i-Martin, X. and Subramanian, A., 'Addressing the natural resource curse: an illustration from Nigeria', Unpublished paper, Columbia University, May 2003.

Schumpeter, J.A., *History of Economic Analysis* (Oxford University Press, New York: 1954).

Sen, A., 'Starvation and exchange entitlements: a general approach and its application to the Great Bengal famine', *Cambridge Journal of Economics*, 1, 1977: 33–59.

Senhadji. A., 'Sources of economic growth: an extensive growth accounting exercise', *IMF Staff Papers*, 47 (1), 2000, 129–57.

Sewell, W.H., 'Marc Bloch and the logic of comparative history', *History and Theory*, 6, 1967: 208–18.

Shattuck, L., *Report of a general plan for the promotion of public and personal health* (Harvard University Press, Boston, 1850 reprinted by Amo Press, 1977).

Simon, H.A., 'A behavioural model of rational choice', *Quarterly Journal of Economics*, 6 (4), 1955: 99–111.

Snooks, G., 'Does the longrun in economics matter? A timely approach to the present and future', The 1993 Shann Memorial Lecture, Discussion Paper no. 93, 16 July 1993, Department of Economics, The University of Western Australia.

Snooks, G.D., *Economics without Time: a science blind to the forces of historical change* (Macmillan, Basingstoke: 1993).

Snooks, G.D., *The Dynamic Society: exploiting the sources of global change* (Routledge, London and New York: 1996).

Snowdon, B., *Conversations on Growth, Stability and Trade: a historical perspective* (Edward Elgar, Cheltenham, UK and Northampton, MA: 2002).

Soludo, C.C. and Kim, J., 'Sources of aggregate growth in developing regions', chapter 2 in McMahon G. and Squire L. eds., *Explaining Growth: a global research project*, IER Conference Volume 137 (Palgrave Macmillan, Houndmill, Basingstoke: 2003), pp. 32–76.

Solow, R.M., 'A contribution to the theory of economic growth', *Quarterly Journal of Economics*, 70, February 1956: 65–94.

Solow, R.M., 'Technical change and the aggregate production function', *Review of Economics and Statistics*, 39, August 1957: 312–20.

Spulber, N., ed., *Foundations of Soviet Strategy for Economic Growth: selected Soviet essays, 1924–1930* (Indiana University Press, Bloomington, Ind.: 1965).

Spulber, N., *Soviet Strategy for Economic Growth* (Indiana University Press, Bloomington, Ind.: 1964).

Stark, R., *The Victory of Reason: how Christianity led to freedom, capitalism, and western success* (Random House, New York: 2005).

Stern, N., 'The determinants of growth', *Economic Journal*, 101 (404), January 1991: 122–33.

Stuart-Fox, M., 'Evolutionary theory of history', *History and Theory*, 38, December 1999: 33–51.

Summers, R. and Heston, A., 'The Penn World Table (Mark 5); an expanded set of international comparisons, 1950–1988', *Quarterly Journal of Economics*, 106, May 1991: 327–68.

Swan, T.W., 'Economic growth and capital accumulation', *Economic Record*, 32, November 1956: 334–61.

Swan, T.W., 'Golden ages and production functions', in Sen, A. (ed.), *Growth Economics* (Penguin, Harmondsworth: 1970).

Sylla, R. and Toniolo, G., eds., *Patterns of European Industrialisation: the nineteenth century* (Routledge, London and New York: 1991).

Szostak, R., 'Classifying natural and social scientific theories', *Current Sociology*, 51 (1), January 2003: 27–49.

Szostak, R., 'A growth agenda for economic history', Unpublished paper, 2006.

Szostak, R., 'An interdisciplinary analysis of economic growth', *International Journal of Interdisciplinary Social Science*, 2 (3), 2007: 305–16.

Szostak, R., *The cases of economic growth: Interdisciplinary reflections* (Spring, Berlin: 2009).

Tawney, R.H., *Religion and the Rise of Capitalism: a historical study* (Harcourt, Brace and World, New York: 1962).

Temin, P., 'Two views of the British Industrial Revolution', *Journal of Economic History*, 57 (1), March 1997: 63–82.

Temple, J., 'The new growth evidence', *Journal of Economic Literature*, 37, March 1999: 112–56.

Tilly, C., *Coercion, Capital, and European States* (Blackwell, Cambridge, MA and Oxford: 1992).

Tversky, A., and Kahneman, D., 'Judgment under uncertainty: heuristics and biases', *Science*, 185, 1974: 1124–31.

Van de Kaa, D., 'Second demographic transition', in Demeny, P. and McNicoll, G. (eds), *Encyclopaedia of Population* (Macmillan, New York: 2003).

Van der Eng, P., 'Economic benefits from colonial assets: the case of the Netherlands and Indonesia 1870–1958', *Research Memorandum*, Groningen Growth and Development Centre, GD 39, June 1998.

Van der Klundert, T. and Smulders, S., 'Strategy for growth in a macro-economic setting', Unpublished paper, Tilburg University, 1992.

Ville, S., 'Transport', Chap. 11 of Floud, R. and Johnson, P. (eds), *The Cambridge Economic History of Modern Britain, Vol. 1 Industrialisation, 1700–1860* (Cambridge University Press, Cambridge: 2004).

Von Tunzelmann, G.N., *Steam Power and British Industrialisation to 1860* (Clarendon Press, Oxford and New York: 1978).

Von Tunzelmann, G.N., *Technology and Industrial Progress: the foundations of economic growth* (Edward Elgar, Aldershot, UK and Brookfield, Vt., US: 1995).

Voth, H., 'Living standards during the Industrial Revolution: an economist's guide', *American Economic Review*, 93 (2), January 2003: 221–6.

Wallerstein, I., *The Modern World-system* (Academic Press, New York: 1974–89).

Weber, M., *The Protestant Ethic and the Spirit of Capitalism* (Charles Scribner's Sons, New York: 1958).

Weede, E. and Kampf, S., 'The impact of intelligence and institutional improvements on economic growth', *Kyklos*, 55, 2002: 361–80.

Weitzman, M., 'Soviet postwar growth and capital-labour substitutability', 60, 1970: 676–92.

Weitzman, M.L., 'Pricing the limits to growth from minerals depletion', *Quarterly Journal of Economics*, 114 (2), May 1999: 691–706.

White, C.M., 'The impact of Russian railway construction on the market for grain in the 1860s and 1870s', chapter I in Symons, L. and White, C.M., *Russian Transport: an historical and geographical survey* (G. Bell and Sons, London: 1975): 1–45.

White, C.M. 'The concept of social saving in theory and practice', *Economic History Review*, Second Series, 29 (1), February 1976: 82–100.

White, C.M., *Russia and America: the roots of economic divergence* (Croom Helm, London, New York and Sydney: 1987).

White, C.M., 'Government structures and economic development: eighteenth-century Russia and America in a long-term perspective', *Australian Slavonic and East European Studies*, 4 (1–2), 1990: 153–76.

White, C.M., 'The proper concerns of economic history – ultimate and proximate growth causation', *Scandinavian Economic History Review*, 40 (2), 1992: 47–50.

White, C.M., *Mastering Risk: environment, market and politics in Australian economic history* (Oxford University Press, Oxford: 1992b).

White, C.M., and Fan, M., *Risk and Foreign Direct Investment* (Palgrave Macmillan, London: 2006).

Wilkinson, R.G., *Poverty and Progress: an ecological model of economic development* (Methuen and Co Ltd., London: 1973).

Williams, E.E., *Capitalism and Slavery* (Capricorn, New York: 1966).

Williams, R., *Lies, Deep Fries and Statistics* (ABC Books, Sydney: 2007).

Williamson, O.E., *The Economic Institutions of Capitalism: firms, markets and relational contracting* (The Free Press, New York: 1985).

Wittfogel, K., *Oriental Despotism: a comparative study of total power* (Vintage, New York: 1981).

World Bank, *The East Asian Miracle: economic growth and public policies* (Oxford University Press, New York: 1993).

Wright, G., 'Towards a more historical approach to technological change', *Economic Journal*, 107 (444), September 1997: 1560–6.

Wright, G., 'Can a nation learn? American technology as a network phenomenon', Unpublished paper, 1997.

Wright, G. and Kunreuther, H., 'Cotton, corn and risk in the nineteenth century', *Journal of Economic History*, 35, 197: 526–51.

Wright, R., *Nonzero: the logic of human destiny* (Pantheon Books, New York: 2000).

Wrigley, E.A., *Continuity, Chance and Change: The character of the industrial revolution in England* (Cambridge University Press, Cambridge: 1990).

Wrigley, E.A., 'British population during the long eighteenth century, 1680–1840', Chapter 3 in Floud, R. and Johnson, P. (eds) *The Cambridge Economic History of Modern Britain, Vol. 1 Industrialisation, 1700–1860* (Cambridge University Press, Cambridge: 2004): 57–95.

Wrigley, E.A., Davies, R.S., Oeppen, J.E. and Schofield, R.S., *English Population History from Family Reconstitution: 1580–1837* (Cambridge University Press, Cambridge: 1997).

Yasuba, Y., 'Did Japan ever suffer from a shortage of natural resources before World War II?', *Journal of Economic History*, 56 (3), September, 1996: 543–60.

Young, A., 'The tyranny of numbers: confronting the statistical realities of the East Asian growth experience', *Quarterly Journal of Economics*, 110 (3), August 1995: 641–80.

Index